Portraits of
Our Past

The Jewish Publication Society
gratefully acknowledges a gift from
The Lucius N. Littauer Foundation
in support of the publication of this title.

Portraits of Our Past

JEWS OF THE GERMAN COUNTRYSIDE

Emily C. Rose

THE JEWISH PUBLICATION SOCIETY
Philadelphia
2001 • 5761

The Jewish Publication Society
2100 Arch Street, 2nd Floor
Philadelphia, PA 19103
www.jewishpub.org

Design and Composition by Book Design Studio

A note on transliterations: The transliteration of Hebrew, Jewish-German, and Yiddish words is not an exact science. In some instances, the author adopted spellings that reflect local dialects. Note also that the Hebrew letter ח is transliterated as "ḥ."

Library of Congress Cataloging-in-Publication Data

Rose, Emily C.
 Portraits of our past : Jews of the German countryside / Emily C. Rose
     p. cm.
Includes bibliographical references (p.) and index.
  ISBN 0-8276-0706-7
  1. Jews—Germany—History—1800-1933. 2. Germany—Rural conditions. 3. Germany—Ethnic relations. 4. Jews, German—Illinois—Chicago—History—19th century. 5. Rose, Emily C.—Family. I. Title.
  DS135.G33 R55 2001
  305.892'4043—dc21

2001029137

09 08 07 06 05 04 03 02 01   10 9 8 7 6 5 4 3 2 1

...I remember how the Jewish men of the village community would gather before the synagogue on a Saturday evening, watching the sky for the appearance of the first stars, whereupon they would enter the house of worship and conclude the day of rest with the offering of the traditional prayers. This act seemed to me symbolic, the countrymen lifting up their eyes to the heaven to draw strength for the work of the week to come.

—Rabbi Emil Schorsch

"The Rural Jew: Observations on the Paper of Werner Cahnman"
Year Book Leo Baeck Institute

Table of Contents

Illustrations

Maps and Price Guide

Family Trees

Plates

Illustrations

Illustrations

The Discovery:
Two Portraits

Two large, old oil portraits hung above the fireplace mantel in the living room of my grandparents' spacious New York City apartment. In one painting a portly, well-dressed gentleman held a silver snuffbox and looked out from the canvas with authority. In the other, an elderly woman wore a lace bonnet with red bows. Three strands of luminous pearls adorned her dress. She did not look at me; in fact, her eyes did not focus at all. For some reason I had never inquired about the portraits, and no one in the family had ever told me anything about them. I had no inkling of how meaningful they would become to me.

In 1992 I began to research my family's history. Among the papers I collected were several pages of a handwritten, German-language Jewish family register. I was told that a relative had copied down the information before he fled Germany. With help I could read "Berlizheimer," a name I knew, and "Gundelfinger," a name I had never heard before. I could decipher the name of the village, "Mühringen," written at the top of the page. No one had ever mentioned Mühringen to me, nor had any stories about the village or the people been handed down. I only knew that my ancestors had come to America "early" from Germany.

Before my husband and I went on a trip to Germany in 1994, I tossed the pages of the family registers into my suitcase. I had assumed that due to the destruction wrought during the Second World War, I would not be able to locate any information about my family. Nevertheless, finding myself with a lot of time on my hands while my husband attended a language school, I decided to drive several hours south from Frankfurt am Main to find Mühringen, the village of my forefathers.

JOSEPH DAVID BERLIZHEIMER (1761–1855)   The portraits on these facing pages were probably painted between 1835 and 1855. Each measures 18″ x 24″. (Private collection, Dr. Bruce Levi.)

GUSTEL BERLIZHEIMER (B. KAZ) (1779–1861)   Gustel's peculiar gaze is explained by a notation in an 1835 document. A Mühringen village official wrote that she was blind and therefore could not sign her name to her son's marriage contract.

My reaction to Mühringen was not at all what I had expected. It was not a place lined with narrow, dark streets, but a typical German village. Window boxes overflowing with bright red flowers gave color to the substantial houses that lined the lanes. As I walked through this small village, I felt an instantaneous emotional connection to my Berlizheimer great-great-great-grandfather. I was moved when I came upon some of the Berlizheimer graves in the secluded hillside cemetery set in the Mühringen woods. Huge leafy trees shaded the more than 850 headstones, many of which had sunk into the earth over the centuries. The cemetery, hidden from view in the woods, had escaped desecration during the decades of National Socialism. Just below the village hall and nursery school, a memorial plaque marked the site of the former synagogue. It had been damaged during the Kristallnacht pogroms of November 9, 1938; was used as a gun factory during the war, and was later torn down to make room for a new school. A few old photographs captured the synagogue's simple elegance. I found one of the houses where my ancestors had lived and worked. It was next to the Jewish elementary school, where the rabbi and teacher also had their apartments. In the school's basement, I saw the women's ritual bath, or *mikveh*, which continued to fill with water from an underground spring. While walking down the street, I noticed shallow stone chiseling on some of the old buildings' right doorposts, each outlining the traditional shape of a mezuzah. In such a brief time, I had gathered so many traces of my past.

Excited by my discoveries, I reexamined the handwritten family register and found the name of the village of my great-great-grandmother Gundelfinger. I visited Michelbach an der Lücke; it too was a typical German village, although smaller and more rural than Mühringen. Again I felt connected as I found my ancestors' graves, shaded by the trees in the small Jewish cemetery just outside the village. The cemetery had been desecrated during the Nazi period but had been restored after the war. I could walk down the lanes where the Gundelfingers had lived for centuries. The synagogue here also had been pillaged during Kristallnacht, and it had been used as a German munitions warehouse during the war. It had been restored in the 1980s as a memorial museum, earning it the title of the oldest synagogue still extant in Baden-Württemberg. It was easy to imagine my relatives walking on Judengasse, Jews' Lane, to the synagogue for *Shabbos* services.

Immediately I wanted to know everything about these people, but their past was hidden in papers I could not read. I decided to photocopy documents that might give me information about their lives. The archives in

EUROPE, 1990s The geographical boundaries of my research centering around southern Germany. (All maps by Kartographie Michael Hermes, Göttingen, 2000.)

these rural villages and towns had survived World War II intact because they had not been the targets of Allied bombing. The documents in the regional and state archives had been moved during the war to safe locations, and most of those documents had survived as well. I was able to photocopy official family registers, tax and property information, emigration applications, government documents about the Jewish communities, and documents about my family. I could decipher the old German script just well enough to find surnames in the huge stacks of old registers and documents. Each time I found the signature of one of my ancestors, either in German or in Hebrew, on a fragile yellowed page, I felt that my history was coming alive. I was overwhelmed by the sheer quantity of documents I had been able to collect.

In recent years, German historians and archivists have written many local and regional history books about the Jews in Germany. Much to my surprise, several of these studies highlighted my forebears and their families in the eighteenth and nineteenth centuries. I sought out the authors of the ones that included information about "my families," as I now thought of them. These writers and a great number of other experts generously shared their knowledge with me.

Toward the end of my three weeks of research, one of these historians translated some documents for me. He read: "Joseph David Berlizheimer took over the house previously owned by Moises Kaz in Rottweil." The name Moises Kaz leaped from the page! I remembered that wonderful name from my copy of the family register. According to my reckoning, he was my great-great-great-great-grandfather. Rottweil was just forty-five minutes south of Mühringen, so off I went. There the director of the town archive showed me the large houses that Moises Kaz and his descendants had bought in the nineteenth century. I could imagine the very small community worshiping in the synagogue located on the upper floor of his house. It struck me that the lives of the Jews living in the towns must have differed from those of Jews who had lived in villages like Michelbach and Mühringen.

Back in the United States, I just stared at the stacks of documents. My history was in them, but I could not read a word. Luckily, elderly non-Jewish Germans living in my area were able to translate the documents from the difficult-to-read old German script. Little by little, I pieced together my ancestors' lives. A word here, a date there, a name of a spouse or child in a family register—each pushed my research in so many different directions. Through extensive detective work and research, my family's story started to come together.

I came to appreciate that the portraits of my ancestors had historical significance. We do not know how many oil portraits were painted of rural Jews in the early nineteenth century, but surely these visual records were not as commonplace as those depicting Christians. No matter how many portraits continued to adorn Jewish homes in the early twentieth century, the dislocation and destruction caused by the Nazis resulted in the rare survival of those works to this day.

The Discovery: Two Portraits

At first I thought that the information I gathered from the documents was unique to my family since it did not fit with my conception of Jewish life in Germany. As I read historical books about other regions of south Germany, however, I realized that the lives of my family were indeed typical of these rural Jews. Then it struck me: it was *my* view of the Jews in Germany that had been very limited and, in many respects, completely wrong. I had thought of their history in the context of either the lives of the peddlers and talmudic scholars in eastern Europe or the lives of the famous bankers who had lived in the large German city ghettos prior to the nineteenth century. My images had skipped from the horrors the Jews had suffered in the Middle Ages to their middle-class, urban, and acculturated existence in the twentieth century. I shared the common point of view, often heard in the United States, that most of the Jews had been forced to emigrate in the nineteenth century because of intolerable anti-Semitism, disappointment in the failed Revolution of 1848, or a desire to avoid military service. Books and movies had given me the impression that relations between Christians and Jews were either all positive or all negative: either everyone had gotten along well before the time of the Nazis, or relations had been heavily influenced for centuries by overt or hidden, but virulent and pervasive, anti-Semitism. Compared to Jews in eastern Europe, German Jews usually were depicted as not traditionally religious and as eager, if not desperate, for assimilation. Most of these and other stereotypes and generalities about the German Jews just did not mesh with the documents and other sources I was reading.

Before I began my research I had known the names of a few Berlizheimer distant relatives, but now I searched out other descendants of the Berlizheimer, Gundelfinger, and Kaz families through contacts I had learned about while I was in Germany. I was able to interview personally or by telephone twenty distant cousins who had been forced to flee Germany in the 1930s. My new "family" evolved into an important resource as well as a bastion of inspiration and support. Although they did not know about their great-grandparents' lives or of the historical processes that took place in the nineteenth century, these newly found relatives shared with me details about daily life in Mühringen, Michelbach, and Rottweil in the early twentieth century. I realized that although my upbringing by the descendants of German Jews in the United States had been vastly different from my relatives' lives as rural Jews in Germany, we nonetheless shared a common bond and heritage.

My research began in an admittedly haphazard manner, but over the next few years I refined and put into use the research and analytical skills I had learned as a European history major. My husband and I returned to Germany the following summer, and by then I was better equipped to do serious research. Since I could now make out the old German script, I was able to identify additional documents. The result was an accumulation of copies of thousands of pages of primary documents.

My genealogical historical research centered on the Kingdom of Württemberg in the southwestern region of what is now Germany. Up to the last decades of the nineteenth century, Germany was composed of a multitude of independent states. Historical dates, specific laws, and even customs varied in each geographical and political area, but I discovered that the Jews' life experiences were replicated throughout Germany.

Gradually the scope of my research broadened from just my direct ancestors to include their extended families and other members of their communities. From that point this undertaking became more than the story of my family. Rather, my ancestors had begun to tell the story of the rural Jews in south Germany. The documents expanded my research to include the Jews within their communities and the political, economic, and social events that had a direct and momentous impact on their lives. I searched in piles of dusty contracts for information about their dowries and inheritances. In the minute books of the village and town councils, I discovered both the usual and unique events of their lives.

In the summer of 1996, I found an 1827 petition in the Württemberg State Archive in Stuttgart regarding the early stages of Jewish emancipation. I was amazed that my Berlizheimer ancestor was one of the signatories. Naturally I wanted to understand the impact of these larger events as well as his involvement in them. After the hundreds of pages of speeches, parliamentary debates, and pamphlets were translated, my view of the life of the rural Jew changed again. I was forced to examine the documents and the personal remembrances I had gathered up to that time against the broader background of history, and this caused me to expand the scope of my research beyond the boundaries of Mühringen, Michelbach, and Rottweil.

My research continued in 1997, when, having gained even more experience reading old German script, I uncovered additional details. I also extended my research to the lives and descendants of the daughters and wives who, through their arranged marriages, had established connections

DISCOVERING THE PAST Examples of the old documents and volumes where I uncovered information about my family and the lives of the village Jews. (GArchiv Mühringen, Stadtarchiv Horb; photo: Marek Leszczyński.)

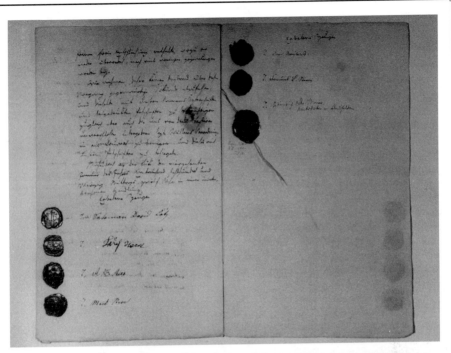

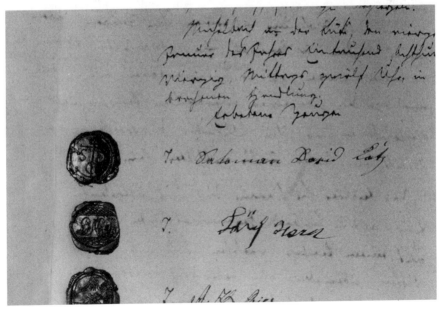

SIGNATURE PAGE OF A FAMILY DOCUMENT, 1840 This will was witnessed by members of the Jewish Community. (GArchiv Wallhausen-Michelbach, [Bernhard] Jacob Gundelfinger, Contract #302; 1843; photo: Marion Reuter, Schwäbisch Hall.)

to other Württemberg communities and to other German states. I could now trace these family and business networks throughout south Germany.

The story of the rural Jews would not be fully realized if I dealt only with documented historical events. I knew that an integral and pervasive part of the story was the daily life of the village Jews. Over the years I read the genre stories about the southern German countryside written by Berthold Auerbach, a very popular mid-nineteenth-century author. I felt a special affinity with his memoirs about his youth in a village near Mühringen because I had found that he was related to my family by marriage. As I read other memoirs and books, I could also imagine my relatives worshiping and performing religious rituals. Since readers of this book have different religious backgrounds and knowledge, an overview of religious life in eighteenth- and nineteenth-century rural Germany can be found in a special section, Traditional Jewish Life in the Villages and Small Towns.

A final discovery was the recent documentation and analysis of a small cache of centuries-old papers relating to Jewish life in the villages. This collection of old and damaged sacred papers and other artifacts had been stored in the attic *genizah* of Michelbach's synagogue until it was discovered by chance during the restoration of the building. Not realizing what they had found, the workmen had thrown the papers in the garbage. Luckily, the village mayor recovered some of them. What a thrill it was to see the fragile prayer books, pages from the Talmud, and almanacs written in Hebrew, in German, or in German written with Hebrew characters. Still intact was a tiny prayer book that had been carried by a pious peddler. I fancied that perhaps a Gundelfinger had used it to recite his daily prayers.

These yellowed fragments of the past brought me full circle, connecting my past with the present. Today no Jews live in Mühringen, Michelbach, Rottweil, or the other rural communities that once dotted the land. Only a few vestiges of the past remain. And so the portraits that hung in my grandparents' living room must be a symbol and remembrance of thousands of German rural Jews. This story of their existence in the eighteenth and nineteenth centuries is my attempt to give voices to those silent memorials.

The Story Begins: Setting Down Roots

Joseph David Berlizheimer and Gustel Kaz stood under the marriage canopy (*ḥuppah*) in the courtyard of the synagogue. He was thirty-six and probably not yet the portly figure portrayed in his later years. She was only seventeen, not yet the blind woman depicted in her portrait. The setting was a tiny village nestled against a wooded hillside along a quiet, meandering river. The year was 1797—almost a new century and the beginning of a new era for the Jews in the German lands. The members of the Mühringen Jewish community joined in the celebration.

How did David and Gustel come to marry in a tiny village in the south German lands? We cannot know for sure. In all probability, in the centuries after the year 70, their ancestors were dispersed from Palestine into southern Europe, thus beginning their lives as Jews in the Diaspora. During the late Roman times, some of these forebears migrated from the regions of modern France and Italy northward into the trading cities along the major rivers. In the few towns and cities where Jews were given permission to settle and live in ghettos, they became traders, moneylenders, and craftsmen, enjoying a flourishing cultural and religious life. Their numbers in the German lands grew to between 20,000 and 25,000 in the early Middle Ages. All those living in the German-speaking lands in central Europe were called Ashkenazim (Hebrew for "Germans"), and were distinguished from the Sephardim—the Jews living in the Orient, Africa, and the Iberian peninsula.

The medieval Jew lived in a precarious world. The all-powerful papacy preached that the Jews had rejected Jesus as the Messiah and then brought about his death on the cross. As their punishment, the Church declared, they were condemned to live on earth in a degraded state. Christians believed that Jews were permitted to exist only as tolerated aliens who served as visible proof of the truth of Christianity. From friezes decorating the walls of important cathedrals in which they were depicted as blind and incapable of seeing the light, to the pronouncements of parish priests, the Jews personified Satan. The word "Jew" came to have diabolical associations in every European language. In the eyes of the "righteous" Christians, Jews were forever the enemy of Christianity—condemned to roam the world until Judgment Day, thus giving rise to the legend of the eternal Wandering Jew.

In 1096 the Crusaders' zeal to fight the infidels turned against the perceived enemy within—the Jews who lived in the cities along the route to the Holy Land. The Crusaders massacred more than twelve thousand Jews; many of those, faced with the choice of baptism or death, chose to die as martyrs. From that time on, Jews were forbidden to join the guilds and could work only as pawnbrokers or moneylenders—professions forbidden to Christians by canonical law. Pope Innocent III at the Fourth Lateran Council in 1215 further stigmatized the Jews when he ruled that they had to wear a yellow badge or pointed "Jew's hat" in order to prevent any mistaken sexual relations between Jewish men and Christian women. Jews were permitted to swear oaths according to the precepts of their religion. In some courts, however, they were forced to swear their oaths while standing barefoot on freshly slaughtered sow skins.

Beginning in the twelfth century, false accusations of ritual murder, or blood libel, found a fertile breeding ground. In well-publicized cases, Jews were accused of murdering Christian children and drinking the blood during Passover, a holiday often called the Easter Festival by Jews and Christians. The Jews were also charged with stealing the Host and ritually molesting it to reenact their murder of Christ. If a Christian child disappeared or died mysteriously, especially during the Passover and Easter season, tensions rose. Sometimes Christians took justice in their own hands and massacred the falsely accused. Difficult political circumstances and an alleged desecration of the Host led to anti-Jewish riots in 1298 in several German cities; more than five thousand Jews were murdered.

Although they continued to live under fear of persecution, restrictions, and exorbitant tax levies, the Jews rebuilt their communities and even founded new ones, some of which prospered by the end of the thirteenth century. A half-century later, economic and political tensions again mounted when famine, poverty, and a great plague ravaged Europe. The Black Death, which decimated as much as a third of the population of Europe—some 25 million people—from 1346 to 1351, did not spare the Jews, as the crowded urban centers along trade routes were especially devastated. It was easy for the masses to accept the libelous accusation that the Jews, incarnations of the devil, had poisoned the wells in a plot to destroy the Christians. With that rallying cry, mobs massacred those Jews who had survived the plague, and at least three hundred Jewish communities were destroyed.

The few surviving Jews were not allowed to return to their towns and cities, but whenever possible they settled in villages close to where they had lived so that they could continue to do business with former customers and clients—until, as was often the case, the local ruler expelled them on a whim. Occasionally a Jewish family or two lived in a town, but laws or arbitrary restrictions always circumscribed their activities. It was in the sixteenth century that Christians took on surnames as a sign of being a part of society, but most Jews still used their Hebrew first name followed by their father's first name.

Life was not so promising for the Jews in central Europe that they could ignore better prospects elsewhere. From the thirteenth to the fifteenth centuries, many Jews immigrated to Poland and Lithuania, where, in order to expand the middle class, the rulers offered better economic opportunities. During those centuries the Jewish population in those lands grew from five thousand to thirty thousand.

In the German-speaking lands, the themes of medieval anti-Jewish literature found a new spokesman in the church reformer Martin Luther. In his early years, Luther sought to convert the Jews to Christianity, but he became frustrated and then enraged when they did not accept his teachings. After 1530 he preached a strong anti-Jewish doctrine and published several vitriolic pamphlets, including *Von den Juden und ihren Lügen* (Concerning the Jews and their lies) and *Vom Schem Hamphoras und vom Geschlecht Christi* (On the ineffable [unknowable] Name). Luther claimed that he no longer had any sympathy for the Jews' wretched plight: their suffering was well deserved because of their failure to embrace Christianity, making Jews "the devil's children damned to hell." He spelled out specific recommendations for his followers:

> What should we Christians do with this contemptible, damned people, the Jews?... I will give my true advice. [They] should throw brimstone and pitch upon them; if one could hurl hell fire at them, so much the better.... Let their synagogues and schools be set afire.... Let their houses be similarly razed and destroyed.... Let all their prayer books and Talmuds be taken from them.... Their rabbis should be forbidden to teach on pain of loss of life and

limb.... Let safe conduct on the highways for them be abolished completely.... Let them be forbidden to practice usury.... And if all this is not enough, let them be driven like mad dogs out of the land.[1]

Luther's treatises caused widespread dismay among both Jews and prominent church leaders, and the circulation of these writings was quite limited. Perhaps due to the severity of his proposed measures and the importance of the Jews to the economy, not one of Luther's recommendations was carried out against the Jews at that time.

The religious movements and territorial wars in the sixteenth and seventeenth centuries resulted in each individual ruler's having the ability to decide the religious affiliation of his subjects. From this time onward, the people in each village would be either Catholic or Protestant, and relations among even neighboring communities were divided along religious lines. Protestants and Catholics did not socialize or intermarry. The final great upheaval was the Thirty Years' War (1618–48), when Catholics and Protestants fought each other, rocking the German lands and destroying much of central Europe. At this time, some Jewish traders and dealers were able to expand their business opportunities. An elite few, the court Jews, were invited to serve the financial needs of the royalty, the high nobility, and the Catholic Church.

The war left many rulers in desperate need of cash to support their armies and their luxurious lifestyles. They needed the services of moneylenders and purveyors. Moreover, under the Holy Roman Empire of the German Nation, the Church and more than three hundred nobles owned small autonomous territories or states. Some of these independent rulers invited Jews into their areas. Thus, little by little, small settlements of Jews were established in the German countryside. No one pretended that the rulers tolerated the Jews for humanitarian reasons. Rather, they served to increase the rulers' tax base and to enlarge their opportunities for trade and business. Jews constituted a financial asset, just like agricultural fields and buildings.

How had Jews maintained their Jewish life in those centuries of disruption when they were not allowed to live in Jewish communities? Perhaps at times they had not been able to form a minyan—the quorum of ten adult men for communal prayers—or bake matzos for Passover or find kosher wine for the sanctification (*Kiddush*) prayer. But Jewish life did survive, and what emerged from those times was a continuity of religious belief, history, and custom.

After centuries of being scattered in small groups, Jewish families once again could join together to worship and build their religious communities. Jews settled in Mühringen, in the southern German region, toward the latter half of the sixteenth century. The first documented Jewish inhabitant was "Jew Baruch" who lived there as early as 1579. Located in the upper Neckar region, Mühringen lay between the Black Forest and the Swabian Alb. It followed the contours of a stony hill; instead of having a street address, each building was described by its location in the upper, middle, or lower village. From the upper village a steep path led to the village of Nordstetten and the market town of Horb am Neckar. The Eyach River in the lower village flowed to the great Neckar River a few miles away.

While the ownership of Mühringen changed hands several times during this period, the feudal lords allowed the Jews to settle there, and by 1677 they were one-quarter of the taxpayers. By 1735 Baron Christian von Münch, a banker from Augsburg, had increased his considerable holdings by becoming the feudal lord of Mühringen and two neighboring villages. His small fortress-castle perched on a hill above the village. By the middle

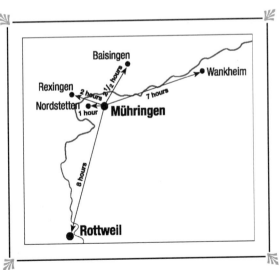

JEWISH VILLAGES IN THE BLACK FOREST DISTRICT   This map shows the actual amount of time it took a person to reach the neighboring villages and towns by foot. (Mühringen Jewish Community Report, StAL E212 Bü 41 [1828].)

SOUTHERN GERMANY IN THE EARLY NINETEENTH CENTURY A geographical guide to the story of the Kaz and Berlizheimer families.

of the eighteenth century, he had increased the number of Jews to forty-four tradesmen, of whom thirty-seven were taxpayers.[2] Some of them probably were descendants of those Jews who had been expelled centuries before from Horb and Rottweil but had remained in the area for economic trade reasons.

Few Jewish family records survived the centuries of upheavals. In all probability, Joseph David Berlizheimer or his parents, David and Nanette, were allowed to settle in Mühringen during the early or middle of the eighteenth century. They most likely came from the village of Markt Berolzheim, where in the early eighteenth century, eighteen taxpaying house owners supported a synagogue and a community ritual bath. The Berlizheimer family traveled 125 miles west to their new home. Gustel's grandfather Leopold (Löw) Kaz and his wife, Karoline, settled in Mühringen before 1766. Their surname gave no clue to their origins because the name "Kaz" signifies only that they were *Kohanim*, the descendants of the tribe of Aaron who were the priests of the Temple in Jerusalem. Leopold and Karoline's son, Moises, married in 1779 when he was twenty-nine. His bride, Sara, was the fourteen-year-old daughter of Mayer Samuel.

As their ancestors had done in earlier times in other places, the settlers established a religious community. These were not voluntary congregations. Rather, just as the Christians were necessarily members of a church, so too the Jews who resided in a location had to be affiliated with its religious community. Every married male was a member of the community (*kehillah*), which was responsible for governing its members and representing them in the secular world. This organizational structure suited the rulers, who taxed their subjects via these corporate organizations. Since the obligation to pay the required taxes fell on the whole community, the richer members often had to guarantee payments and even pay the taxes for the poorer members. The community also paid taxes levied on it by the kaiser of the Holy Roman Empire.

The members of these local communities were organized into a larger rural Jewish corporate organization (*Landjudenschaft*), unique to the German-speaking lands, that administered their affairs autonomously. The communities around Mühringen initially organized themselves into the Black Forest (Schwarzwald) District to deal with the most pressing need of the region—a sanctified burial ground. During the seventeenth century, the organization founded and paid the costs of a fenced cemetery, and each community paid

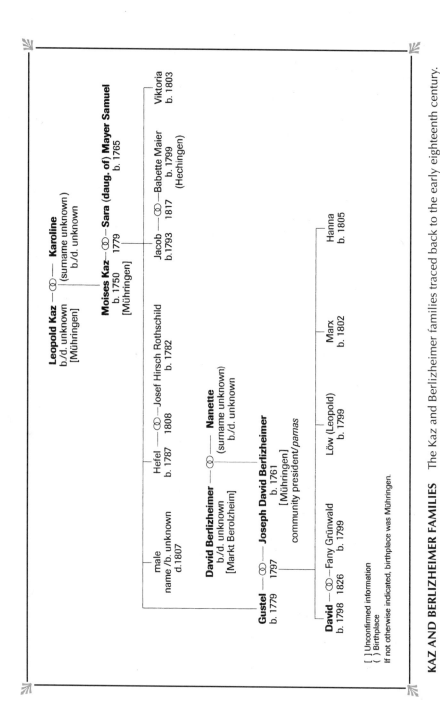

KAZ AND BERLIZHEIMER FAMILIES The Kaz and Berlizheimer families traced back to the early eighteenth century. Names in bold indicate the author's ancestors. (All family trees by Utesch Medienservice, Hamburg, 2000.)

MÜHRINGEN JEWISH CEMETERY   Pictured are some of the oldest graves. By custom all the headstones faced east toward the site of the ancient Temple in Jerusalem. All the early inscriptions were carved in Hebrew characters. (Photo: Emily C. Rose.)

a fee for its upkeep. The Black Forest District was permitted to own a small plot of wooded land on the side of a steep hill in the Mühringen woods, about a quarter of a mile above the village center.

The Jews of Mühringen prayed and studied in private homes until 1728, when the community was allowed to build a synagogue. It was constructed at the highest point of the main village, fulfilling the interpretation of rabbinical literature that says that the synagogue should rise higher than the other houses in the village. Since the Jews were most certainly aware that it was more prudent that the village church should rise above all other buildings, the roof of the synagogue was lower than the steeple of the Catholic church located just down the hill. The community sold the rights to the synagogue seats to its members to raise income, and members with sufficient assets contributed additional funds and ritual objects as well. The cost of the seats was quite high (72 gulden), especially compared to other fixed as-

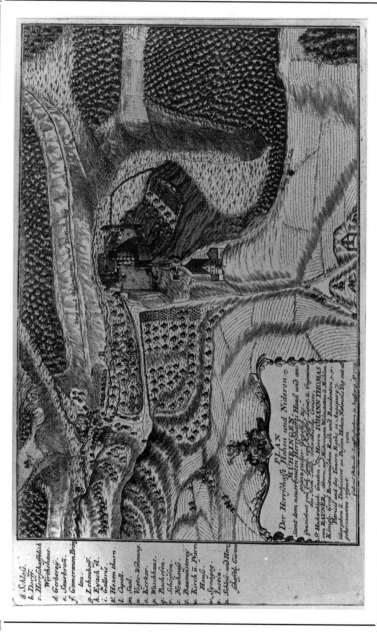

1735 ENGRAVING OF MÜHRINGEN The 1728 synagogue building (w), listed in the legend after the church (u), was situated across from the Catholic church at the curve in the road leading to the castle. This is one of the earliest depictions of a rural synagogue. More significantly, the Jewish house of prayer was listed as one of the important buildings in the village. (Copper engraving by Gabriel Bodenehr, Augsburg. Privat collection, F. H. G. B.)

sets (120 gulden for an apartment). Not surprisingly, some members had to pay for their seats in installments. For example when Joseph Eppstein bought one seat in the men's section "next to David Marx," and one in the women's section "next to Gustel Hirsch," the purchase was inscribed in the village protocol register. He made a down payment (15 gulden) and committed to pay five yearly installments.

The district organization hired its first rabbi, Elias Weil, in 1728. The rabbi moved from Haigerloch, a nearby town with many economic and family connections with the Mühringen community. For his services he received a salary and an apartment. Its second rabbi, Nathanael Weil (no relation), brought into the little community the shadow of the critical events occurring in distant parts of Europe. In 1692, when Nathanael Weil was only five years old, his two half-brothers were murdered, dying as martyrs in Stühlingen; his father died shortly afterward. With his mother he traveled to Fürth, where he studied at its renowned yeshivah, a school of higher Jewish study. He then studied at one of the main yeshivot in Prague, then a famous center of Jewish learning in the Austro-Hungarian Empire. As an outstanding student of the prestigious rabbi Abraham Brod, Weil spent time with him at yeshivot in Metz, France, and in Frankfurt am Main, and married Rabbi Brod's niece. Rabbi Weil returned to Prague in 1717 to serve as head of a yeshivah with thousands of students and as assistant rabbi of the city—positions, however, that brought him only limited remuneration. In November of 1744, when soldiers tried to plunder his and other homes in the Jews' Lane, the

1 gulden = 60 kreuzer	
1 egg	1 kreuzer
1 hen	45 kreuzer
1 cow	125 gulden
1 horse	300 gulden

A GUIDE TO PRICES AND COSTS   This list shows the relative value of goods in the rural southern German region during the nineteenth century. (Adapted from Otto Ströbel, *Michelbach a. d. Lücke, Geschichte einer Dorfgemeinschaft zwischen Christen und Juden* [Crailsheim: Hohenloher, 1993], 53–54; Kartographie Michael Hermes, Göttingen, 2000.)

Jews, under Rabbi Weil's leadership, successfully defended themselves for three days.

The following month, on December 18, Empress Maria Theresa, one of the reputedly enlightened despots, expelled the Jews from Prague, forcing more than a thousand families to leave the city. Nathanael Weil, at age fifty-seven, was appointed the rabbi for the Black Forest District. Many of his students followed him to Mühringen, where he set up a Talmud school. One of his four sons served as his secretary as he continued his scholarly work writing commentaries on the Talmud (a multivolume compilation of the interpretations of the Torah codified in the sixth century). Rabbi Weil remained in Mühringen for only five years and was then called to the city of Karlsruhe to serve as the chief rabbi of the Jews of Baden. He tried unsuccessfully to have one of his sons appointed as his replacement.

Mühringen was located near the border of the Duchy of Württemberg. In 1733 Württemberg's Catholic duke, a foreigner himself, brought in another foreigner, the Jewish financial genius Joseph Süss Oppenheimer from Frankfurt, to supervise Württemberg's finances. Süss filled the duke's coffers and amassed a huge fortune for himself. He enjoyed the luxurious life of the court, including sexual dalliances with Christian noblewomen. Nevertheless Süss remained Jewish. Süss antagonized all the established power structures, which referred to him only as "Jud Süss." The day after the unexpected death of the duke, Süss was imprisoned and charged with numerous crimes. A special commission could not prove any specific charges, so it sentenced him to death for moral corruption and the violation of the country's laws. Priests tried to force him to convert to Christianity, but he died a Jew, proclaiming, "I have lived as a Jew; I will die as a Jew." On the snowy morning of February 4, 1738, thousands of people from the city and the surrounding countryside, and more than six hundred court dignitaries sitting in specially constructed stands, gathered in the Marktplatz in Stuttgart. The Christian masses jeered and cheered as Süss was hanged in a cage. They vented their hostility against the agent of change, the symbol of modern government, the foreigner, the Jew. In stark contrast to the Christians' reactions, a Jewish spectator reported that all the Jews wept. For years afterward these events were the themes of anti-Jewish pamphlets and artwork. Jews, on the other hand, commemorated Süss's unjust death as a martyr with a day of fasting and repentance on the anniversary of his death.

These attitudes undoubtedly had an impact in Mühringen. In 1750, the number of Jewish families almost equaled that of the sixty Christian

RABBI NATHANAEL WEIL (1687–1769) Nethanel ben Naphtali Zevi Weil was rabbi of the Black Forest District (1745–1750) and in Karlsruhe (1750–1769) and author of commentaries on the Talmud, including the 1755 *Korban Netanel*. Rabbi Weil was so honored and revered that when he died, Jews throughout Europe mourned his death, and the government provided a military escort for the cortege. The Hebrew inscription on his headstone read in part: "The genius rabbi, the light to the generation, to all his righteous followers.... How many miracles were attributed to him.... [The Hebrew people] will remember him from generation to generation." (Berolzheimer collection, Courtesy of Leo Baeck Institute, New York.)

THE HANGING OF JOSEPH SÜSS OPPENHEIMER, FEBRUARY 4, 1738, IN STUTTGART "Jud Süss" was depicted at the height of his power (upper left) and on the day of his execution (upper right). Süss Oppenheimer's corpse was left in families, and the Catholic villagers began to voice their concerns. Two years later Christians fought the Jews in the streets, looted their houses, and destroyed the fence around their cemetery. Despite these events the baron continued to allow more Jews to live there, and the village's Jewish population continued to grow. In 1766 the baron collected a large amount of trade and commercial taxes (1,245 gulden) from the members of the Jewish community. The tax records stated that based on income and assets, Emanuel Levi was the richest Jewish man in the community by far. He traded in fabric and goods, dealt in financial instruments, and served as the court agent in Haigerloch. He paid twice as much tax (150 gulden) as Joseph Abraham and Samson Bernheim, who traded in cloth, cotton, and leather. Emanuel Levi and two other families owned houses or apartments and small gardens in the village. Four others paid much less (40 to 80 gulden), and twenty-five paid an even smaller, but still substantial, amount (15 to 25 gulden). Three men and four widows did not pay any trade tax. Less than two decades later twenty families owned apartments clustered in several buildings, one of which was called Jews' Building (Judenbau).

The Black Forest District continued to grow and to attract important rabbis. Rabbi Simon Veis, a scholar from Flehingen, served there from 1751 until 1771, when he was called to Darmstadt. The next rabbi, David Dispeck, was born in the tiny village of Diespeck. After studying at yeshivot in Frankfurt am Main and Fürth, Dispeck supported his family by trading in gold, silver, goods, and jewelry until he lost all his assets in 1767. After repaying all his debts, he received his rabbinical appointment in 1772 in the Black Forest District. Four years later, the community bought a large two-story building next to the synagogue. The cantor (*hazzan*) lived in an apartment on the ground floor, and the rabbi's apartment and a community room occupied the second floor. The community built a ritual bath in the basement, where it was always filled with water from a natural source.

Rabbi Dispeck founded a yeshivah in Mühringen. Problems and internal fights, however, forced him to seek a new position in the bishopric city of Metz in 1779. There he served as rabbi of the burial society, and teacher and head of the yeshivah, and then became the district rabbi in Baiersdorf. He published *Pardes David* (David's garden), an interpretative collection of talmudic themes.

Rabbi Dispeck endeavored to install his son-in-law Jacob Samuel Schwabacher as his successor in Mühringen. Rabbi Schwabacher came from Fürth and was the former rabbi of a large community in Gailingen. Mühringen's community did not accept him, but the other communities did, so he maintained his seat in Nordstetten until Mühringen finally elected him as its rabbi as well. It was then decided that he would spend half the year in Mühringen and half the year in Nordstetten.

When the communities needed to enlarge their cemetery, the village administrator, the mayor, and the Christian community ceded them land (for 24 gulden) adjacent to the cemetery. The leaders of the Mühringen community, Bär Hilb and David Kusel, signed in German on behalf of the local Jewry. Rabbi Abraham Weil, grandson of Rabbi Nathanael Weil and son of the well-known rabbi Tia Weil of Karlsruhe, became the rabbi from 1789 until 1797, when he was called to be chief rabbi in Sulzburg, Baden.

This succession of trained German-born rabbis brought the Mühringen community prestige among the other rural Jewish communities, which could support only untrained or minimally trained rabbis brought in from eastern Europe. Even the poorest peddlers and beggars took pride in belonging to such an important community.

During the last decades of the eighteenth century, Joseph David Berlizheimer and Moises Kaz had both achieved the status of "protected Jew" in Mühringen. Baron von Münch allowed only those who had sufficient assets to reside officially in his feudal estate. He gave them a letter of protection in exchange for an admittance fee and a yearly protection payment. Of course he could increase these payments unilaterally; for instance, in 1773 he raised them considerably (acceptance fee of 75 gulden and the yearly payment of 25 gulden). The protection contract included access to the judicial courts and often an official license to do business. For the duration of the contract, the protected Jew could not be expelled. His children and widow, however, did not continue to receive these rights after his death. Moreover, because the contract was only between the protector and the Jew, it was not necessarily valid if the protector died or sold his feudal estate. In official transactions and registers, protected Jews were always referred to as such because the title showed that they enjoyed a special legal status. ʻSchutzjuden ʻ

By the time he married in 1797, Joseph David had established himself as a fabric dealer and trader. Other Jews specialized in different goods; the most popular were grain, hops, notions, leather, and feathers. Some men who were cattle dealers entered that trade because they were also the kosher butchers; they served both Jewish and Christian customers. Jewish dealers and traders might take on surnames, but often this was not necessary since, for the most part, they dealt one-on-one with their customers and suppliers. Some traveled by horse or by horse and wagon, covering about three miles an hour. In their villages they bought houses or apartments and paid trade taxes. These Jews usually had enough assets to be granted protected status.

The majority of Jews, however, could not afford the high protection payments or admittance fees, nor did they have sufficient assets to warrant acceptance. They were protected only by basic societal norms: they could not be murdered or raped. In all official registers in the German lands, they had "Jew" written before their names. They lived in the village, but they could be expelled at any time for any reason.

Most of these unprotected Jews were peddlers. The peddler traveled on the dirt roads and paths, visiting hamlets along the way. The peddler's week began on Saturday evening. After attending the concluding Sabbath service (*Havdalah*), he would trek all night with a heavy pack on his back to reach a Christian village by Sunday morning. Then each day he would trudge to another place. Until Friday morning he was present in the villages and hamlets—but not part of them. He did not look like a peasant. Even after the Jews were no longer required to wear the Jewish badge or hat, the peddler's distinct clothes, more akin to city clothes, and his bearded face set him apart. His ritual dietary laws made it difficult for him to obtain food at the farmers' tables. Although the farmers did not understand the religious rituals, they knew about these rules. Consequently, they only offered water, black coffee, or a slice of bread. At some Christian inns the owner scratched a special mark on one metal pot (sometimes a "K" for kosher) used by the Jews to cook their food: the Christians knew not to use it. The peddler could then prepare some potatoes or smoked meats he had brought from home. If the peddler could not reach a friendly inn before nightfall and was forced to spend the night in a farmer's barn, the farmer might overhear him reciting the Hebrew evening prayers by heart, or reading from his tiny travel prayer book. In the morning Christian farmers could observe the peddler putting on his phylacteries (tefillin), wrapping his prayer shawl (tallis) around his shoulders, and chanting his prayers. [3]

The peddler loaded his cumbersome pack with fabrics, hides and skins, notions, feathers, bedding, or wool. Many peddlers dealt in used clothes, or in all kinds of used goods, or in anything they could buy or exchange. Even if they could not afford to actually buy, say, a cow and then resell it, they could

TRAVEL PRAYER BOOK These pages in Hebrew from a late-eighteenth-century prayer book contained selections from the Talmud and quotations from ancient rabbis. Pious itinerant peddlers would have carried these tiny books in their packs. Shown at just under its actual size. (Michelbach an der Lücke *genizah,* Kreisarchiv Schwäbisch Hall; photo: F. Gil Hüttenmeister, Tübingen.)

act as the go-between—the schmoozer—and make a little money by arranging deals. Some peddlers sold goods on commission for Jewish merchants. Peddlers changed their wares in response to their customers' needs, economic fluctuations, availability of goods, and seasonal variations.

The Christians who earned their livelihood in the same manner were called peddlers, but many Christians called the Jewish peddlers by the pejorative term *"schacher* Jews." The word *schacher* derived from the Hebrew word for "trade," but popular belief held that the word originated from the Hebrew for "black" or "underhanded dealings." It was incorporated into the vocabulary of the criminal underworld in the seventeenth century. The phrases *"schacher trader"* and *"schacher* Jew" came to have many meanings: petty trader, small-time dealer, old-rag dealer, pawnbroker, secondhand trader, street trader, hawker, huckster, and haggler.

On an even lower economic level the Jewish beggars and wanderers (schnorrers) were not protected by any ruler but cared for by the local Jewish communities. They wandered from community to community, living off charity on the Sabbath. Smaller communities often invited beggars to remain over the Sabbath so that they then had the necessary minyan for religious services. In all the communities, the "guests" received tickets for meals in private homes. The beggars repaid their hosts' hospitality by sharing news gathered from visits in other communities or information about potential marriage partners. Because beggars were an economic burden on the Jewish community, they usually were forced to move on after the Sabbath. On Sunday morning their Sabbath hosts might send them on their way with a little traveling money. These beggars at times could find work peddling in the *schacher* trade or selling on commission prayer books and other small ritual items at the markets. While the municipal governments did not contribute anything to support the beggars, officials often complained about their presence in the villages.

There was also a very small but visible underworld of Jewish petty thieves and crooks who preyed predominately on merchants and travelers. Criminal bands, made up of both Christians and Jews, lived and worked together. Their special thieves' jargon, *Rotwelsch*, was a mixture of German and Hebrew; its very existence supported the public's incorrect belief that all criminals were Jews.

In many ways this stratification mirrored the hierarchical divisions in the Christian community: the noble family, the farmers who owned enough land to use a horse to work their property, the poorer farmers who needed only an ox to serve their needs, the landless village artisans, and the day laborers. However, while the Christians rarely shifted their position in society, the Jews, as we shall see, had greater class mobility (both upward and downward) within short periods of time.

Men such as Moises and Joseph David were always traveling—from Mühringen to the neighboring villages within their weekly business area and to the weekly and seasonal markets. The traders and peddlers visited the cattle and goods markets in nearby Horb and in Rottweil and Schramberg, which were about eight hours away. As well as conducting business, the travelers also exchanged news and made direct contacts with potential marriage partners for their sons and daughters. Jewish traders were an integral part of the markets. If the organizers planned a market on Saturday or a Jewish holiday by mistake, they rescheduled the event.

Jews of all economic levels traveled to the major regional fairs, some of which were international events. The biannual Frankfurt am Main fair took place for several weeks in the spring and fall. More than a thousand Jewish traders attended the Leipzig fairs (although they were not allowed permanent residence there) and carried out important business, primarily in textiles and furs. The significance of these events was reflected in the Jewish calendars and almanacs, which included the dates of markets and fairs taking place all over central and western Europe. The dates of the Christian holidays, also included in the calendars, were important pieces of information since Jews were not allowed to work or do trade on those days. Using this information, the peddlers would set up their routes for the coming weeks.

When crossing the political borders of various states and independent territories, the Jews were treated in a degrading manner. Customs officials collected a customs fee on the goods and livestock of all traders, Christian or Jew. But officials also assessed an additional fee—the body toll—on the Jews, ostensibly as a protection fee. The individual towns and rulers established the exact amount charged in each territory. This toll added to the cost of doing trade and, of course, diminished the meager profits for the poor petty traders. The emotional cost was even more difficult to bear. The Jew was taxed as if he were a cow; in some places custom duties were classified under the following categories: "Honey, Hops, Wood, Jews, Chalk, Cheese, Charcoal...."[4] Even when a funeral party crossed customs borders, the Jewish body toll was assessed on everyone in the cortege—including the corpse!

Occasionally Jews could negotiate the exact amount of the body toll, especially if the local government appreciated their contribution to the economy. In the 1780s, for instance, the president of the Black Forest District asked the mayor of Rottweil in a written memorandum to lower the recently increased Jewish body toll to its previous level. The town council agreed because the Jewish traders and peddlers were needed to ensure the success of the yearly markets.

The Christian peasantry had an ambivalent relationship with the Jews. On the positive side, year after year, generation after generation, they dealt

Schramberg. Weil an dem auf den Samstag als den 6ten Dec. fallenden Nikolai-Kramer- und Viehjahrmarkt die Juden nicht erscheinen können; so wird selber vorher, als am Donnerstag den 4ten December abgehalten werden.

Den 12ten Nov. 1800.

P. Hochgräfl. Bissingis. Oberamt allda.

MARKET ON THE SABBATH CHANGED The notice reads: Public Notice. Announcement, Schramberg. Because the St. Nicholas Day Goods and Cattle Market falls on Saturday, the 6th of December, the Jews cannot participate; this market will be held earlier on Thursday, the 4th of December. 12 November 1800. The county official of Schramberg. (Stadtarchiv Rottweil, *Wochenblatt* [Weekly paper], 21 November 1800, 1.)

צול וארי דניס נ"ס יום

ה יח נ
ו יט כא
ז כ כב ♦
א פ' פרה
א כא וכב אוקלי מורכמי'
ב כב כג כד קלין ווארדיון
ג כג כד כה אשה ♦
ד כד כו
ה כה ו ח
ו כו ז כח מיט פאסטן ♦
שטיניום'הופה'ח ז נז כש
א כח ל' לעטארי ♦
ב כש לא מענץ
סראנ ק"ז בדסלוי הספורט הילסהיים קרוניך
סטול וורמסין בורג עדקוכבערג קאמטו כריז
קאניק ריימס ברוט קולון בך קיניג גרען

צול אא שבת נרי אא כ"ס יום

חמולר נ' י"ג נ"ו ♦
דה מיוט וינטשם ג פריה נמך מיכן ♦

ר"ח ר א ד ר פרכנרו ♦
ח ב א ♦
חנוכא סוכה ו נ ג ניכלוס ♦
טקץ ד ד ז מפאמט סאנ ♦
א ח ח פאריע טעטטנג ♦
ב ו ♦
כ י שנוא
ר יא
מ יב
עשרה בטכה ו י נ לצום
ר יד ווינש
א טו
ב טז
ג יז
סו יח קוומטעטפי
ח יט
ו כ
ווחי ללל ארונ' ז יח כא שנ

צול אא אב אא תניח למ"ב פו

הטולר ח' ט"ו תת"ר ♦
ראם מיוט וונשאג אוטוג פר מיטם ♦

ש"ח יב ב א כח
נ ב נש
ר נ ל
ה ר לא
ו ה א ח אגנסס שטפקן ♦
דכרים וש"מ ב ו רגצת
ג א (כ)
ט באב א ס
ו י
ח יא
וו ח יב
ווחתנן וטנ' יג ו טו
ג"ו (יד)
תשמח עשר ב יד טו

עכשטן ואמי ביו דען ערטטן מגזם
דווהה' (מב) זאן מנחה וקבלת
טכת מוג זיכן ♦
עלסטן מגומטוס ביו דען לוויים זול
ווואנגטטין דו מיט ר"ל מנחם זאן
ומנחה וקב"ס מוק הוכר ויכן ♦
פן פגנטטין מגומטוס ביו דען לעכטן
וטטעעוכר דו מיט ט"ו חלול זאן
ומנחה וקב"ס מוק זעקס מוזערג ♦
פון ויוטר ביו רמה המחה תקל"ה ל פ' קי
זאן מנחה וקב"ס מוק הוכר זעקם ♦

with the same Jews or their descendants. A few times a year, the various peddlers would come to the peasant's farm and in the farmhouse kitchen show the family members what goods were for sale. The farmer would buy a little merchandise or tell the peddler what items he needed the peddler to bring on his next visit. The peddlers would relate news about the villages, the peasant's neighbors, and even about the faraway cities the Jews visited for the yearly fairs. Both farmers and peddlers alike profited from these contacts.

At times, however, the farmers could not pay for the goods they needed. During the winter months before the harvest, they could pay only a little on account. The peddlers and the farmers would then make oral agreements that the farmers would pay for the goods after the harvest. Sometimes both parties signed simple written promissory notes. Often a farmer needed a cow but could not afford to buy one (at a price of more than 100 gulden), so a Jewish dealer would rent a cow to him. The rental contract listed exactly the rights of each party: the owner retained the rights to the cow, while the farmer had the use of the cow's milk and manure and had to care for the animal. The profit from the future sale of the cow and its calves usually went to the owner, but sometimes the farmer shared the profits.

The Christian peasants worked small hereditary tenant farms and paid the feudal rulers rent and taxes usually equal to about one-third of their crops. The territorial lords set the financial obligations, and, by the seventeenth century, most of them demanded at least partial cash payments. The Jewish merchants and dealers served as moneylenders for the peasants. They usually lent small amounts of money and gave short-term advances. In other situations Jews made loans or issued letters of exchange or promissory notes that extended over several months or years. When the peasants needed cash to meet these feudal obligations or to pay for their children's weddings, they often did not have the necessary surety or assets to obtain the money from traditional lenders. Again they would turn to the Jews. Since

---

CALENDAR AND ALMANAC PAGES Calendars and almanacs were printed in Hebrew and in German using Hebrew characters. The columns of the calendar page displayed considerable information: the weekly Torah portion; Jewish holidays and fast days; day of week; day of Jewish month; corresponding day of secular month; secular calendar notations and Christian holidays; and market locations and dates. Sunset times for the Sabbath were also listed. Often zodiac signs illustrated the months. Some almanacs imparted proverbs and folk wisdom. This calendar from 1793–94 (5554 in the Jewish calendar) is shown at just under its actual size. (Michelbach an der Lücke *genizah,* Kreisarchiv Schwäbisch Hall; photo: Marion Reuter, Schwäbisch Hall.)

these loans often were not registered publicly, and the Jews usually kept their personal accounting records in Hebrew or in German in Hebrew characters, the peasants could keep their financial affairs private from their neighbors and business associates.

These business relationships could become difficult and tense if the farmers did not have sufficient money to pay for the goods they needed or the debts they had incurred. Small-scale abuses and unfair trading practices existed on both sides. Christians, for example, sold a sick cow as healthy, an old horse as young, grains by incorrect weights, and old goods as new. Jews asked higher-than-market prices for their goods and bargained for hours. If one party perceived that he had been grievously wronged, both might end up doing business with other people in the future. The Jews did lend money at a higher rate than other lenders, but they took no surety and thus assumed all the risks. Borrowers who could obtain a loan from Christians or conventional lenders did so, but those needing money quickly or in secrecy turned to the Jews. The perception of whether Jews were moneylenders or usurers, peddlers or *schacher* traders, depended on economic times and the Christians' anti-Jewish feelings. When peasants dealt with Jews in times of duress, it was inevitable that the Jews were blamed for all or at least a considerable part of the peasants' woes.

In the eighteenth century almost all Jews spoke a dialect that was a mixture of Hebrew words and their particular local dialect. Because these Jewish-German dialects (*Jüdischdeutsch*) were extremely close linguistically to the various local German dialects, non-Jews could understand and use many of their phrases. In the second half of the century, the introduction of standard German texts written in Hebrew characters began the slow transition from Jewish-German to standard German. Each person's economic, social, religious, and cultural background determined his use of language. Just as the local dialects were considered a manifestation of ignorance and backwardness compared to High German, so too was the Jewish-German dialect seen as a symbol of the Jews' separateness and lack of culture.

Jews were a tiny minority of the total population and played a marginal role in the overall economy. To the Christians, however, they seemed numerous and ubiquitous. In the eyes of the peasants, Jews were not only all identical and interchangeable, but also strange and different. The economic basis of their lives was worlds apart. Christian farmers and craftsmen worked with their hands performing hard physical labor. Jewish peddlers appeared to just talk and deal with money. Christians had no empathy with the arduous lives they actually led.

This, then, was the society and culture surrounding Joseph David Berlizheimer, his bride, Gustel, and the Jews who witnessed their wedding ceremony under the ḥuppah at the close of the eighteenth century in the hilly southern German countryside. The history of the previous centuries had been difficult, but Joseph and Gustel were looking forward to starting a family and deepening their roots in Baron von Münch's Mühringen.

The story of Gustel's father, Moises Kaz, exemplified neither the opulent life of the court Jews nor the onerous existence of the peddlers and traders. His life was not typical of either the Jews who settled in the villages or those who lived in the cities. Rather, as a high-level purveyor and moneylender in a town, he represented the group of Jews who formed the narrow economic and social stratum below the court Jews.

Moises Kaz's father had been one of the taxpayers paying the lowest amount of trade tax (15 gulden) in Mühringen in 1766. Through hard work and by cultivating an efficient network, Moises raised himself from petty trader to merchant status. In 1788 he bought two apartments (for 240 gulden) in the Jews' Building, which was owned by the baron. A few years later he bought a large, expensive house, the "Blue House" (for 1,822 gulden), in a prime location in the middle village. After their wedding Joseph David and Gustel moved into the large house and lived with Moises, Sara, and Gustel's brother and sisters.

Around 1780 Moises expanded his trade area to the town of Rottweil. The town was one of the Jew-restricted cities, towns, and villages that far outnumbered the villages where the Jews could live and work. Even if Jews were permitted to do business in these places, the townspeople limited the Jews' trading transactions to protect and promote the Christians' interests. However, since these places had great economic potential, Jews plied their trade there anyway.

Rottweil was typical of those towns and cities that did not need or want Jewish residents and resisted the encroachment of the Jewish dealers on their internal business. It had been an important imperial town in the Holy Roman Empire; as such, it had its own laws and policies under the ultimate authority of the Hapsburg emperor in Vienna. The guilds held a great deal of economic and political power. Located only forty miles north of the Swiss

MÜHRINGEN, 1780 The large building with the emblem flag was the baron's inn and brewery, Zum Adler (the Eagle Inn). Moises Kaz's house was the next house on the road leading up to the castle. Adjacent to his house was Zum Hirsch (the Deer Inn). Moises' two-story house was built of large stones and had an iron oven in the general store.

ROTTWEIL Strategically perched over a gorge cutting through the Neckar River Valley, the spires of the Gothic Catholic churches rose high above the wall and turrets surrounding the city. (Stadtarchiv Rottweil, postcard, 1850.)

Confederation and fifty miles east of France, Rottweil had been an important trade center and manufacturing town for metals and cloth.

In the thirteenth century Rottweil had a population of three thousand, including about two hundred Jews living interspersed with Christians in the Jews' Lane. The Jewish district, with its school and ritual bath, was located near the town center. Although Rottweil itself was spared during the Black Plague, the Jews living there were either killed or forced to flee into the countryside. The few survivors were not allowed to return.

Rottweil's strong political and economic position was weakened considerably by the ravages of the Thirty Years' War and by its subsequent isolation as a Catholic town surrounded by Protestant areas. It had been able to maintain its economic and political position only because its twenty-five surrounding villages were obliged to sell goods to its townspeople at low prices and to furnish grain and fodder to the town. Many Jewish peddlers and traders traveled to Rottweil, which was a hilly eight hours' journey from the Mühringen area.

As they crossed over the Neckar River via drawbridge and entered the walled medieval town, the Jews entered a very different world. The guilds protected the local craftsmen and shopkeepers from the real or perceived threats posed by any new trader or craftsman. In the same vein, but with even more fervor, they took actions against the Jewish peddlers. In one instance the authorities, alarmed that trade in fabric, leather, and skins had been added to the usual peddling of old clothes and used goods, published restrictive rules titled "The Authoritative Regulations Concerning the Jewish House-to-House Peddlers and Their Claims."

While the citizens and the town government restricted the Jewish peddlers, they often had no alternative but to rely on the Jewish money-lenders and suppliers. These Jews were treated differently because they had cash as well as access to larger amounts of money through their networks in the cities of the German states, France, and the Swiss Confederation. They also had the necessary organization of middlemen and access to available means of transportation. They made commitments, took risks, and discharged their obligations within stringent time constraints.

Moises Kaz fulfilled that need for Rottweil. Although he had been involved in considerable business in the district for years, his actions in 1787 brought his relations with the authorities of the imperial city to another level. Two local men robbed and strangled an elderly widower. When the criminals tried to sell some of the stolen goods to Moises, he immediately recognized the items and identified the perpetrators to the authorities. The murderers were hanged a few months later. The town council acknowledged Moises' great service to the public welfare when it granted him, per his request, an extension of his customs fee agreement. The next year he asked the town council to halve his annual customs fee (from 40 gulden to 20 gulden). He stated that since he no longer employed two workers, he could not do business that winter in the surrounding villages. The town magistrate granted Moises' request.

The Coalition Wars against France from 1792 to 1800 brought very difficult times to Rottweil. Just as in other times of military conflict, such as the Thirty Years' War, Jewish suppliers took on even more important roles in the economy. During these years Moises traveled all over the southern German-speaking regions, procuring goods and making deals. Using the excellent post roads he went to Heidelberg, Freiburg, Donaueschingen, and Augsburg. These cities were several days' to a week's distance from Mühringen. Moises used his own wagon or carriage, or he paid to use the fast carriage transportation service provided by the Thurn und Taxis noble family. If it was too far to return to Mühringen for the Sabbath, he would spend the day in other towns. When he did business in Donaueschingen, he had contact with David Kusel from Mühringen, who was court factor for the Fürstenberg prince. Kusel did some transactions with Rottweil as well, but a few times Moises had to carry out a number of Kusel's contracts on very short notice.

The town of Rottweil was pleased with Moises Kaz's services over the years, and especially with his role as an army procurer and agent during the early war years. The town leaders held him in high esteem—a most unusual status for any Jew. The town council decreed that if it had to pay money to any adversary in the future, it would go to Moises for help. Among his many transactions was a large cash loan (7,000 gulden) to the town. On some occasions when the government was unable to repay him on schedule, it gave the order to "tell the Jew to be patient."

By April 1799 Rottweil was again in a crisis. The French army, under the high command of Napoléon Bonaparte, marched through the town and demanded cash, rather than the usual grain and goods, from the town government. The treasury was empty, and the government was faced with the extortion demands of an army that threatened to sack the town if it did not turn over the money immediately. Rottweil had no choice but to sell the silver owned by its churches and guilds to "Jew Moyses Katz [*sic*] of Mühringen."[5] The town council unanimously decided to sell him the silver because he had been a most honest partner for some time and he offered a good price. The council chose its deputies to make the transaction, including a goldsmith to watch the weighing. Moises Kaz signed the contract "Moises Kaz from Mühringen" in Hebrew. Important leaders of the town signed for Rottweil: the treasurer (representing the town council), the town cashier, and the speaker for all the guilds.

This was such an emergency that in just four days the guilds, the Catholic churches, and the convents collected their treasures to save the town. The churches and convents handed over their religious pieces, including framed pictures, a complete altar, chalices, and altar decorations; the guilds turned in numerous goblets and mugs and pieces of silverware. The pure silver items weighed approximately eleven pounds, and the gilded silver pieces about ten and a half pounds. While the monetary value of the precious metals did not seem so high (3,417 gulden 45 kreuzer), the intangible value was considerable.

Thus, Moises saved Rottweil by acting quickly and by taking the risk that he might actually be unable to sell the silver and gold in those difficult and dangerous wartime years. The town never forgot his efforts.

In another instance, Moises provided very necessary supplies to a cloister in the town. In 1800 the French demanded provisions from the Cloister of the Johanniter, a branch of the Order of the Knights of Malta, which was usually exempt from such threats. When the leader of the order, Baron von Loe, sent Moises a purchase order memo, he closed it with the phrase, "We will for always be yours." Twice Moises responded with letters (written and probably signed by his sons or his employees) with the closing, "Your friend, Moses Katz [sic]."[6] These very personal communications to the German baron showed an unusual closeness between a Jew and a noble. Once again Moises dealt with high-level officials directly, and they seemed to respect him as a well-known and honest goods purveyor and broker. Four years later the cloister still owed him a considerable sum (5,000 gulden), which could have been for the goods or for additional loans.

While the story of Moises Kaz does not represent the general situation of rural Jewry, it does illustrate the rapid rise of a small group of Jewish merchants, traders, and suppliers. The Christians' financial dependency on Jewish merchants and moneylenders would open a new world of opportunity to them.

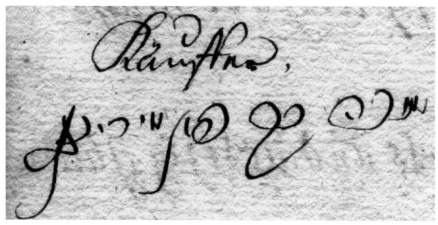

MOISES KAZ'S SIGNATURE Moises Kaz always signed his name in Hebrew on contracts and other official documents. (GArchiv Mühringen, Stadtarchiv Horb; Contracts Protocollum, 16 April 1796, 144B; photo: Marek Leszcyński.)

MOISES KAZ'S SEAL   Its design was a simple garland encircled by a large, thin anchor with the letters "M" and "K" flanking the anchor. Unlike on the seals used by the Jewish communities and rabbis, no Hebrew letters or Jewish symbols decorated this seal. It was the seal of a Jewish businessman in the Christian world in 1801. (Stuttgart, Württembergsisches Hauptstaatsarchiv B352 Bü 82 [1801].)

New Times

Joseph David Berlizheimer and Gustel continued to live with her family in Mühringen as their family grew to include three sons, David, Löw, and Marx. Each son was given his Hebrew name on the day of his circumcision (*berit milah*). The naming custom for girls was somewhat different. A month after their daughter's birth, her parents invited all the Jewish children to their home for a special celebration (*Holegrasch*). When everyone was assembled, they placed their baby in a cradle, and all the children lifted the cradle as high as they could. They shouted in loud, boisterous voices, "What will be the name of the child?" and then "Hanna," her vernacular name, was announced. After the children repeated the ritual three times, the teacher said a prayer. Each child received some sweets, in keeping with the happiness of the event.

The new century and a new government brought fundamental changes to the lives of the Jews in the southwest German region. Until that time Mühringen had been an independent territory ruled by a noble family. By the Peace of Lunéville of 1801 and in subsequent arrangements, Duke Friedrich II of Württemberg lost his small territories west of the Rhine River but gained rights over territories east of the Rhine. Mühringen thus became part of "New Württemberg," which incorporated more than eighty previously independent territories ruled by imperial knights and nobles, ecclesiastical principalities, and free imperial cities. Württemberg's geographical area doubled, as did its population—to 1,340,000 inhabitants. When the duke took over his new territories, about 500,000 Catholics became part of the Protestant duchy. The government structure was similar to other European countries: the duke was advised by his ministers and privy council, and these governmental organs (which we will call "the government") issued edicts to be implemented by the lower levels of government. It was the responsibility of the district governments to carry out the edicts and communicate directly with the central government. Villages and towns came under the authority of county administrations that reported to district governments. Mühringen was one of the villages in the county of Horb in the Black Forest Governmental District.

Until 1801 the duke of Württemberg had allowed only 534 Jews to reside in his duchy. Even the family of Madame Chaile Kaulla, the court bankers and jewelers, met with strong resistance from businessmen and government officials when they requested permission to do business and live in its capital Stuttgart. But power and money prevailed, and Duke Friedrich did allow that family to settle there. After 1801 the number of Jews under his rule suddenly jumped to seven thousand. In real terms, however, their number remained tiny when seen against the new Württemberg population.

Württemberg was one of the thirty-two German states that formed the new Confederation of the Rhine. For a short time it was a satellite state of Napoleonic France and thus subject to the Napoleonic codes and laws. At the beginning of the nineteenth century, the territorial and civil status of the Jews was an issue being faced by governments throughout Europe. French law had given the Jews full citizenship rights in 1791, and when Napoléon annexed the regions west of the Rhine, Jews in these areas were granted citizenship rights as well. This short period of equal rights demonstrated to the Jews how easy the process of obtaining full civil rights could be in the best of situations. Then, in March 1808, Napoléon issued his Infamous Decree (*Décret Infâme*) placing new restrictions on the Jews in regard to freedom of settlement and economic activities, and drastically worsening their situation.

The duke of Württemberg did not make such sweeping or immediate changes regarding the Jews. The Duchy of Württemberg became a kingdom in 1806, and Duke Friedrich assumed the title of king. The king's privy council began to consider matters related to the Jews, examining specific problems and writing long reports. The government did not adopt standardized legislation. Rather, it reacted on an issue-by-issue basis.

In 1806 a court agent and community president in Sontheim petitioned the king to "liberate him and his fellow believers" from the Jewish body toll. The government abolished it two years later, bringing financial relief especially to the poor peddlers, who no longer had to pay those fees out of their meager income.[1] This action brought some emotional solace for all the Jews who had been demeaned by that unjust assessment for centuries.

In the same year, the initiation of military conscription for Jewish males obligated them to serve in the king's army. The military service edict allowed the Jewish soldiers to observe the Sabbath and the dietary laws. Just like Christian draftees, they could pay for substitutes. The substitution fees, to be paid to the general war treasury, were set high enough (250 gulden, and subsequently 450 gulden) that this option was feasible only for the very rich Jews.[2] The Jews were also ordered to do compulsory labor on public works, although they were exempt from doing so on the Sabbath.[3] In short, they now had the same obligations and duties as Christian subjects, but without the same civil or political rights.

When the small independent territories had come under the duchy, the nobles and the church rulers had kept their property rights and considerable power. The government's efforts to tighten its control over these groups led to an edict in 1812 that regulated the previously random amounts protected Jews had paid to their protectors. It specified new fees (6 gulden in villages) that would be paid to the treasuries of the central government rather than to the coffers of the individual rulers. In practice, a stronger sense of stability prevailed; more people received protection, provided they had sufficient assets and certificates of good behavior.[4] Most communities, however, continued to restrict the number of Jews who received protection by contesting the applications and setting high protection standards. Not surprisingly, the wealthy Kaulla family members were among the few who qualified to live in Stuttgart, which required that its protected Jews have a huge amount of assets (20,000 gulden). Moreover, Jews still could only live in a place where a Jewish community already existed.

The government, in its efforts to limit the considerable power of the guilds, issued a decree in 1809 that was especially threatening to Christian craftsmen. In response to a petition from a shoemaker who had been refused admittance to the shoemakers' guild, the government ordered that qualified protected Jews be accepted into the guilds. For more than five hundred years the Jews had been prohibited from joining the guilds; now the guild system would be legally open to them. This decree had the potential to immediately affect the lives of everyone in the towns and the villages, but anti-Jewish feelings and the logistics of implementing the decree slowed its impact. From the outset, guild members were alarmed at the prospect

Den Hoch-Fürstl. Brandenburg-Onolzbachisch-Herrschafftlichen
Zoll / für angezeigte

114.

nemlichen / hat allhie
entrichtet / soll derowegen vor dißmal (außer den gewöhnlichen
Pflaster- Brucken- und Weg-Zöllen / welche zu deren Erhaltung/
nach ein und andern Orts altem Herkommen / entweder denen
Städt- und Märckten gehören / oder andern Personen zu solchem
Ende zu gebrauchen und zu berechnen überlassen) frey fort paßirt
werden. Actum?

1724.

Jude
paßiret den Zoll zu Schlotheim.
den

Rottweil
Juden-Zoll 10. Kreutzer.
den

RECEIPTS FOR THE JEWISH BODY TOLL   Only the Jews had to pay these special tolls when they crossed territorial borders. The printed receipts were filled in by the customs officials.

The first receipt reads: "Jew Pass for the Customs Toll for Schlotheim. The [date] 17..." (Nuremberg, Germanisches Nationalmuseum, Inv. H.B. 7771.)

The second receipt reads: "Rottweil. Jews Toll 10 kreuzer. The [date]." Those Jews who came to do business paid 20 kreuzer. (Stadtarchiv Rottweil.)

The last receipt reads in part: "The Highest Prince Brandenburg. The Toll for Löb from Michelbach. Specifically passage until 7 in the morning. [total] 24 kreuzer. Wallhausen [a few miles from Michelbach]. 7 September 1728." [Signed] Löb. (State Regional Archive Třeboň, Czech Republic, Herrschaft Schwarzenberg A5 AJ 1(a); photo: Dr. Gerhard Taddey.)

PASS FOR A JEW TO ATTEND THE SEASONAL MARKET   The receipt reads: "Highest Prince and Highest Baron Oettingen; Nördlingen Market; For a Walking Jew. 15 kreuzer. The [date]". (Nuremberg, Germanisches Nationalmuseum, Inv. #H.B. 4240.)

of Jewish guild members. They feared competition and were certainly appalled at even the suggestion of having to deal with Jews within their economic and social organizations. They were invested in the status quo and did nothing to carry out the government's edict.

A constant concern at all levels of government was the problem of foreign beggars coming into the kingdom. The central government's police authority regularly issued regulations specifically aimed at thwarting the entry of Jewish beggars. Destitute, without the required passports or financial assets (25 gulden), they had no alternative but to sneak across the border. Without a source of income or official papers, Jewish beggars faced the constant risk of being expelled from the kingdom.

The Jewish community in Mühringen continued to grow, becoming one of the largest in the kingdom. In 1807 the village was composed of 734 inhabitants, including about 342 Jews. Joseph David bought a substantial two-story house on the main street in the lower village in 1810. In those years most of the houses in Mühringen cost between 700 and 850 gulden. Joseph David's fabric trade continued to grow, and he became one of the leaders of the community.

Other Jews were prospering and expanding their spheres of influence far away from Mühringen. David Kusel went from his position as court agent for the Fürstenberg prince in Donaueschingen to court agent in Karlsruhe. In Mühringen, his son-in-law replaced him as the president of the community, while Hirsch Samuel Rothschild took over as the court agent for the Fürstenbergs.

The community underwent important changes as well. Rabbi Abraham Ris became the rabbi of the Black Forest District. His father, Rabbi Raphael Ris, led the important Jewish communities of Lengnau and Endingen in Switzerland. However, because of some difficulties with the leaders of the Mühringen community, Rabbi Abraham Ris was forced to settle in Nordstetten for several years.

The community decided to replace its first synagogue, which was (as its leaders recalled two decades later) small and unattractive. From 1807 to 1810, the community built a modern stone synagogue at a substantial cost (20,000 gulden). To finance the project, it borrowed one-third of that amount from Baron von Münch. Built on the site of the first synagogue and community house, the new synagogue enjoyed a prime location in the village. To accommodate the larger building, the community tore down the old

RABBI ABRAHAM RIS Born in 1763 in Alsace, France, he served as the rabbi of the Black Forest District from 1793 to 1812. In an 1820 lithograph, Rabbi Ris was depicted in his library studying the Talmud and surrounded by Jewish texts—the Hebrew Bible, the Talmud, and commentaries by Jewish sages such as Maimonides. (Private collection, Switzerland.)

MÜHRINGEN SYNAGOGUE   The Mühringen Jewish community built a modern stone synagogue from 1807 to 1810 at a substantial cost (20,000 gulden). (In Paul Rieger, *Jüdische Gotteshäuser und Friedhöfe in Württemberg.* [Stuttgart: Oberrat der Israelitischen Religionsgemeinschaft Württemberg, 1932], 104.)

synagogue and relocated the community house. The community house was lifted onto rollers and moved fifty feet down the hill to its new location adjacent to the new synagogue. A Christian architect designed the building in a style distinct from the rural churches. The new synagogue resembled a house with high, narrow, rounded windows. The new roof still was not higher than the steeple of the Catholic church.

Joseph David and Gustel's son, David, was among the first boys to celebrate his Bar Mitzvah in the new synagogue. The entire community would have witnessed the 1811 ceremony when, at age thirteen, David was called to the Torah for the first time and became an adult member of the community.

When Rabbi Abraham Ris's elderly father needed his son's services in Lengnau in 1812, the Black Forest District appointed Rabbi Gabriel Adler as

MÜHRINGEN SYNAGOGUE, INTERIOR   The sanctuary could hold about five hundred male worshipers; its balcony (called the *Weiberschul* or *Frauenschul*) accommodated about two hundred women. Large candelabras dramatically lit the interior. (In Paul Rieger, *Jüdische Gotteshäuser und Friedhöfe in Württemberg*. [Stuttgart: Oberrat der Israelitischen Religionsgemeinschaft Württemberg, 1932], 105.)

its new rabbi. Rabbi Adler belonged to a family of prestigious rabbis, and his decision to come to Mühringen reflected the importance of that community. His father was Markus Adler, head rabbi in Hanover, and his mother was the daughter of the renowned rabbi Pinchas Katzenellenbogen, who was originally from Poland and had served in Bavaria. The government, just starting to extend its influence into the affairs of the previously autonomous Jewish communities, made certain demands on the candidate before he could be hired. With the authority of the government, a high church official, a school inspector, and a rabbi gave Rabbi Adler an examination covering theology and philosophy. Since Rabbi Adler was a foreigner (from Frankfurt am Main in Hesse), he also needed special permission from the king to become a rabbi in the kingdom. This permission was granted based on his satisfactory examination and his status of protected Jew granted by Baron von Münch.

The five "Israelite" communities and Rabbi Adler drafted the customary rabbi's contract in Hebrew. Five leaders of the Mühringen community, including Joseph David Berlizheimer, and the leaders of the other four communities signed the contract. Since the seat of the rabbinical district would be Mühringen, that community would be responsible for his housing. Rabbi Adler's fixed salary (275 gulden) was divided among the five communities, based on the number of families in each place. Mühringen paid the most, followed by Rexingen, Nordstetten, Baisingen, and Mühlen am Neckar. The contract listed the fees the rabbi would receive for the special services he would perform.[5]

Rabbi Adler served several large communities in which certain members could afford to pay for these special services. His extra income varied, depending for the most part on the number of marriages he performed. In some years he augmented his income by as little as 30 gulden, and in other years by as much as 200 gulden. Since the rabbi lived rent-free and tax-free, his salary and variable income allowed him to live comfortably.

Each of the five communities also employed a cantor. In the smaller communities the cantor also served as the religious school teacher. In Mühringen, Hayum Levi served as the cantor only. His salary was small (111 gulden), but he received fees (some years totaling 200 gulden) for performing special services for individuals. While members of the community turned to the rabbi for the more important life cycle events, they paid the cantor for smaller weekly or monthly rituals and ceremonies.[6]

Fees for Rabbinical Services

Services performed for the entire community

Preach the Great Sermon twice a year	3 gulden each time
Preach at other times	Extra amount
Participate in the community tax and asset evaluations	8 gulden

Services as legal arbiter

Administer oaths	1 gulden 30 kreuzer
Administer special court oaths	2 gulden plus transportation costs
Ritual slaughterer (*shohet*) certification	3 gulden
Widow's dispensation before remarriage	The fee was based on the situation of the widow: if she had only a dowry and trousseau, 3 gulden; if she had other assets and income, 4 gulden 30 kreuzer.
Official school examination	No fee
Training and certifying a member to be called up to the Torah	1 ducat (equal to 5 gulden)

Services for legal process prior to a marriage

Wedding letter	1 gulden
Wedding documents	30 kreuzer per document. If the bride's dowry and the groom's assets amounted to less than 1,000 gulden, he received a set fee (6–8 gulden). If the dowry and assets exceeded that amount, he was given a prorated fee (30 kreuzer per 100 gulden).

Services for the family of a deceased person

Graveside speech	3 gulden
Inheritance process	If the community appraised the inheritance, the heir paid the rabbi a small sum (40 kreuzer per 100 gulden inherited). When the heirs were minors or orphans, then the rabbi, not the community, undertook the division of property. If the rabbi decided the division of assets, he was paid 5 gulden, plus 30 kreuzer per 1,000 gulden inherited. In the case of a dispute, each party paid the rabbi a fee (1 kreuzer per gulden of inheritance in dispute).

Fees for Services Provided by the Cantor

From worshipers receiving honors in the synagogue

For the honor of being called to the Torah on the Sabbath or a holiday	6 kreuzer
For a pregnant woman coming to the synagogue for the first time	10 kreuzer
For the honor of a boy's Bar Mitzvah at age 13	10 kreuzer

Services related to the women's ritual bath*

For a bride's first visit	30 kreuzer
For a bride's second visit	15 kreuzer
For each monthly immersion	6 kreuzer
For the visit of a pregnant woman before childbirth	10 kreuzer
For cleaning the bath	8 kreuzer

Services performed as the ritual slaughterer (*shohet*)

	8 kreuzer
To butcher small livestock	2 kreuzer
To butcher poultry	1 kreuzer

Services performed on family occasions

To write the wedding documents (instead of the rabbi)	30 kreuzer for each party
To witness the signatures in engagement documents and marriage contracts	10 kreuzer
To chant special prayers for the bride: for her first time in the synagogue on the Sabbath before or after her wedding, or after the announcement of her engagement	10 kreuzer
To chant prayers for the groom	15 kreuzer
To chant prayers at weddings	Cumulative sum of individual fees: 25 gulden per year
To chant prayers for a new mother before childbirth	22 kreuzer
To chant prayers at circumcision ceremonies	Cumulative sum of individual fees: 36 gulden per year

*Provided by the cantor or his wife

New Times

In other villages, the cantor was paid 2 gulden for blowing the ram's horn (shofar) at High Holy Days services. This might have been included in Hayum Levi's regular duties, or another member of the community might have had that honor.

Cantor Levi, serving a large community, earned almost double his fixed salary for these very necessary services. The variable income of the cantors in the other communities was proportionately lower, depending on the number of families and their standard of living. Both factors would also affect a cantor's income as the ritual slaughterer.

Those aspects of religious life that required payment for services reflected the communities' social and economic stratification. Poor Jews living in the village and wandering beggars were not able to pay the required fees. They would have foregone all but the most necessary services unless wealthier community members like Joseph David Berlizheimer and Moises Kaz paid on their behalf.

Another community employee was the caller to synagogue (*Schulklopfer*), who usually also worked as the synagogue caretaker (*shammes*). Each weekday morning he banged on the wooden shutter of every Jewish house using a special long-handled mallet to "knock for synagogue." On Saturday mornings the *Schulklopfer* did not use the special knocker because that was considered work. Instead, he rapped with his fist or called loudly for the residents to come to services. He received a smaller salary than the cantor (ranging from 40 to 74 gulden). In one small village the cantor-teacher also served as the *Schulklopfer*.

The story of Moises Kaz continued along a different path than that of most of the Mühringen Jews. At age fifty-three he chose to leave Mühringen permanently and build his future in a very different environment, a place with greater economic potential. The changing situation in Rottweil offered Moises an opportunity that he just could not ignore. After the Peace of Lunéville, the imperial city of Rottweil became part of the Duchy of Württemberg. When the duke's troops came to claim the town, it did not possess the financial or logistic power to resist. Catholic Rottweil thus became part of the Protestant duchy of Württemberg, and its previously autonomous government now had to report to the duke through levels of administrative bureaucracy.

Though Moises was a protected Jew in Mühringen, he wanted the same civil status in Rottweil. He had enjoyed a special status for his service to the town during the earlier Coalition and Napoleonic Wars and had been granted an exemption from the Jewish body toll and customs fees for several years. Moises applied for permission to reside and do business in Rottweil. The town magistrate supported his application, writing that Moises had served the community and the town well. In 1803 Friedrich the Second, the duke of Württemberg, granted Moises special protected status to do business and to live in Rottweil. According to the protection letter, Moises and his son Jacob were required to swear an oath of loyalty to the duke, pay taxes, and pay protection money annually (40 gulden). In case his customers and other tradesman had not learned of his new status, Moises paid for a notice in the local newspaper to announce it.

> I inform my trade friends and acquaintances that on December 15, 1803, the highest government authorities have granted my son and me protection and settlement in Rottweil.
>
> Moses [*sic*] Kaz, Protected Jew

Moises moved his family, including his wife, Sara, two sons, and two daughters, from Mühringen in 1806. He bought his first house, a substantial building, at auction, bidding above the asking price (2,335 gulden). No one complained to the authorities, and the town council ratified the contract.

Other Jews tried to gain protection, but the town officials treated them in a different manner. Abraham Samuel Bernheim of Hechingen, a tradesman in Rottweil, applied for protection for himself, his wife, and their eight children. The mayor reported that Abraham was a good man, but seven years earlier the tradesmen had complained that he sold goods that he was not allowed to sell. The duke granted Abraham limited protection: residence for himself, but not for purposes of commerce, and not for his family. Abraham continued to do business in Rottweil and brought his family to live there anyway, but the local government did not take any action to stop these violations of the duke's orders.

MOISES KAZ'S HOUSE   Seen at the far right side of this view, Moises Kaz's house had a ground floor, three upper stories, a basement, and a stable and pigsty behind the building. The building had thick strong walls and eaves along the front. In the style of sixteenth-century buildings, the front facade was brightly painted. A protruding three-sided bay window rose to the height of three stories. Below each window, artisans had carved and painted picturesque oriels. The designs were guild signs or coats of arms. This house carried with it the prestige and the price that reflected how far he had risen from his beginnings in Mühringen. (Postcard, 1895–98, private collection, Guntram Vater, Rottweil.)

Hirsch Levi was not even that fortunate. During the war years he was a very small purveyor of foodstuff and since then had dealt in old clothes. When Hirsch requested protection, many merchants voiced heated complaints against him. The mayor defended his reputation and went so far as to chastise some tradeswomen who had brought an unfounded accusation that Hirsch had swindled them of a considerable sum of money. The mayor refused, however, to support Hirsch's application, stating that Hirsch was a man without money and had been forced to flee from another place. He was allowed to continue his trade in old clothes but remained an unprotected Jew.

The merchant guild of Rottweil complained directly to the king about both the Jewish traders residing there and those who lived elsewhere but traded and peddled in the town. King Friedrich's minister responded that the guilds should report any violations regarding peddling to the authorities and the police. The guilds pressured the government to restrict the trade concessions given to protected Jews, but the government rejected the petition, stating that the trade concession was a part of the protected status.

Even Moises, whenever he tried to cross real or imaginary barriers, felt the impact of the prevalent negative attitudes toward Jews. When in 1806 he bought at auction (for 4,100 gulden) one of the oldest, most prestigious houses close to the town hall, the council refused to ratify the contract, claiming that Jews up to that time had no right to buy a house there. The council seemed to ignore the fact that Moises already owned a house in Rottweil. The contract's ratification was postponed while the local government sought a decision from the courts. The high court responded immediately that based on his protection status, Moises Kaz had the right to buy property to carry out his business. The court noted that an earlier statute stated that only strangers could not buy houses, but Moises was no longer considered such. It concluded that if a Jew had a protection letter, no law prohibited him from buying a house. Based on that favorable decision, Moises sold his first house and bought the new one. The citizens sent additional complaints to the government, but it refused to change its opinion.

On occasion, Christians lacked sufficient funds or goods to pay off their debts and were forced to sell their land at auction to raise the funds. Since Jews were not permitted to own agricultural land, they could not buy land or take the property in lieu of debt payment. Faced with this situation, Moises presented two petitions to the government in 1806 and 1807. He asked for permission to buy land at auctions or at estate sales, or to take possession of property in lieu of cash for debt payments. When these petitions were denied, he applied again, explaining that his aim was not to hold the properties but to sell or rent them. The local government officials supported Moises' application, acknowledging that he purchased land belonging to people who could not find any other buyer. The officials suggested the king make an exception for Moises since he had helped many people and charged fair interest rates, not usury. The officials' support only went so far to serve Christian interests. Because they did not want any Jew to own land for a long time, Moises would be required to sell any land he bought within a set time period.

The issue of Jewish ownership of land was so politically important that Moises' petition rose to the highest levels of the government. The Ministry of Internal Affairs requested an expert opinion from the high court. Its judicial expert decided that a protected Jew was not a citizen of Württemberg, so he should have the same status as a foreigner. A foreigner was forbidden to own agricultural land for more than two years, even when he had obtained the land through inheritance or bankruptcy. The expert explained that this rule would protect the people from Jewish usurers, in the hypothetical situation that a few rich Jews would come into a poor village and buy all the land or take it all over because of farmers' debts.

Just as the Ministry of Justice and the Ministry of Internal Affairs officials were ready to grant Moises' petition to buy property at auction with the obligation to sell it within two years, the king issued his own decree in response to the petition of "protected and trader Jew Moises Kaz." King Friedrich wrote that he did not share the fearful worries of the councilors and ministers, which he felt were based mainly on "intolerance" and "the limited spirit of the era." The king decreed that any subject who was capable of developing land or having it developed could do so regardless of his faith. The king urged the authorities to use principles in their dealings with future petitions that would be "worthy of the spirit of higher enlightenment."[7]

That special decree issued for Moises Kaz in 1807 was issued as a general decree four years later. The king envisioned the Jews transforming themselves into peasant-farmers like the Christians, but economic, political, and practical realities made this vision virtually impossible to achieve. In Mühringen, for instance, Baron von Münch owned almost all the land; only four farmers owned small plots. Land was passed on within families, and only dire straits would force any farmer to sell his land. Even if agricultural land had been available to the Jews, they had no experience in farming. It

+ But surely Enlightenment ideas made it possible for Moses to be bold enough to appeal to the king's advisors & the king enlightened enough to grant this striking change in ancient policy.

Portraits of Our Past

was not surprising that few men even attempted to become farmers. Instead they transferred their trade, business skills, and contacts into a new economic arena by becoming land brokers and land traders. Moises' initiative and perseverance in a personal matter opened new opportunities for Jews throughout Württemberg.

Moises' new house on the main street of Rottweil's market area offered a prime location for his store. He attended the trade fair in Frankfurt am Main every spring and autumn. Upon his return from those journeys, he took out large advertisements in the Rottweil newspaper to let the public know about the new goods: all qualities and types of imported fabrics, cashmere and silk shawls, women's clothing, neckwear, silk and cotton socks, leather summer and winter gloves, women's shoes, buttons, and many other articles. The advertisements ended with the customary assurances of very good and very inexpensive service. The emporium offered jewelry and dry goods and bought and sold used goods. Moises was also involved in the cattle-rental business, dealing with farmers in and around Rottweil. His business enterprises encompassed many sectors of the economy and utilized progressive marketing techniques. Moises continued doing business with the town, occasionally serving as its financial agent with the important responsibility of collecting and cashing promissory notes.

Moises' accumulated assets (25,000 gulden) grew to be comparable to several of the lesser court Jews. In Rottweil his wealth raised him to the same economic level as members of the very small upper class in the town. This status brought him special privileges that had not yet been offered to the other Jews in the town. Although he was not a citizen of Rottweil, the town council granted Moises the privilege of buying firewood at the special citizen's price. To merit this benefit, he had to quarter soldiers.

The Jews in Rottweil wanted and needed institutions to fulfill their religious obligations. Moises was the organizer and the financial backer of the new community that was established in 1806 as a branch of the Mühringen community. The fledgling community, the first in Rottweil since the Middle Ages, gathered to pray in Moises' house, where he set up a synagogue in a heated room on the third floor. The women's section (*Weiberschul* or *Frauenschul*) was most likely in the same room, separated from the men's section by a screen. Employees, helpers, itinerant peddlers, or beggars would be asked to remain over the Sabbath to help make up a minyan. Also, the married women needed a ritual bath, so Moises built an octagonal *mikveh* next to a clothes washhouse he owned. Upon his request, the town council authorized the necessary supply of water to the *mikveh* from the town's well. Several members shared the expenses, including the water fees and upkeep. The community wanted to have a synagogue building and petitioned the king for permission to buy the church owned by the Johanniter Cloister. The Ministry of Finance refused its request without explanation, but it was probably unimaginable that a church be used as a synagogue. The synagogue remained in Moises' house.

Moises' sons were an integral part of his business. One studied business and helped his father by writing for him. Upon this son's untimely death in 1807, Moises petitioned the government, requesting protection in Rottweil for his future son-in-law, Josef Hirsch Rothschild from Mühringen. Moises explained that he needed someone to replace his deceased son in his business dealings, and the government granted his petition. Josef Hirsch's father served as the court agent of the Fürstenberg princes in Donaueschingen. Josef Hirsch had done business in the area for several years and brought some assets (1,000 gulden) to the marriage. Hefel and Josef Hirsch lived in Moises' house after their marriage.

In 1815 the adjacent house, owned by the police commissioner, came on the market. This time, when Moises purchased it (for 3,400 gulden), there was no complaint by the town council. Moises cut a door on the first floor between the two houses and shared the store and the office with his son-in-law. Josef Hirsch and his young family used the first floor apartments in both houses. Moises and his family lived on the second floor of both houses. On the third floor, a new heated room next to the existing synagogue became the women's section.

The situation of other Jews in the town varied dramatically. Hirsch Levi was again refused protection. The magistrate feared that more than two protected Jews would not be good for the merchants or the public because "the Jews do not contribute to the town in any way." Hirsch finally got protection in 1811 when the mayor attested that he was a good person and gave him a certificate of good behavior. Two years later Hirsch died and, quite surprisingly for a poor peddler, left a moderate estate. His widow and son remained in the town for a few years until she remarried.

On the other hand, quite surprisingly, neither the townspeople nor the authorities resisted Abraham Bernheim's entrance into a new business venture in 1807. Abraham and his wife bought half a house that already had a commercial permit for use as an inn. Abraham opened Zum Goldenen Becher (the Golden Goblet Inn). For centuries Jews had produced and sold kosher wine, so becoming an innkeeper was a natural extension of that trade. Serving kosher food and offering overnight accommodations for the growing number of Jewish tradesmen and peddlers who spent weekdays in the town were sound business opportunities for Jews. Often the established innkeepers, threatened by potential competition, would prevent Jews from opening new, or buying already established inns. In this instance no one officially contested Abraham's new venture. Unlike Christian innkeepers, who limited themselves to the hospitality business, Abraham managed the inn as the foundation for his ancillary businesses: trade in fabric, wines, spirits, and cattle. Like other innkeepers, Abraham quartered soldiers. Upon his request, and to allow him to keep the soldiers more comfortable, the mayor granted him the special citizen's price for firewood.

In 1812 the total population of Rottweil was 3,614, including fifteen Jews. Although members of the town council seemed to be treating Jews more positively, it nonetheless rejected the application of Abraham Leopold (who was born in Dettensee and had lived in Wankheim) when he tried to get protection in Rottweil. The council claimed that the town already had too many Jewish tradesmen and that the "cunning" Jewish peddlers, left uncontrolled by the police, damaged the trade of other craftsmen and tradesmen. The council did not believe Abraham Leopold's statement that he would not have a trade and expressed concern about his large growing family. Nevertheless, a few months later he bought one of the most important buildings in town, paying even more than Moises had paid for his house (4,400 gulden). The council, which had so recently rejected his petition for acceptance, ratified this house contract. Abraham Leopold adopted the name of his wife's hometown, Esslingen, as his family name. The Esslinger family became part of the community.

A short time later Natan Degginger and his family relocated from Mühlen am Neckar. Despite the protests of the Rottweil magistrate, Natan reported sufficient assets to become a protected Jew. In a bankruptcy sale, he bought Die Krone (the Crown Inn), across the street from Abraham Bernheim's inn. Upon his request the council granted him the special citizen's price for firewood.

The community was sufficiently large to apply to the Ministry of Internal Affairs for recognition as an official religious community. Abraham Bernheim and Abraham Leopold Esslinger, as trustees of the "church" fund, reported in their 1815 petition that four families supported the poor Jewish families through voluntary contributions and fines (collected for infractions of community rules regarding attendance at services and decorum). The ministry gave it permission to have a "church" and to set up a fund for the poor, both under its own local administration. The ministry stated that the synagogue and religious objects that Moises Kaz owned personally in his house were separate from the "church's" possessions.

The community, as an affiliate of the Mühringen community, was similar to the smaller communities at that time. It did not employ a rabbi; the cantor or learned men led the services. The individual families continued to be responsible for school fees for each child attending class in the Jewish school. This policy angered Abraham Bernheim, who, years later, complained that Moises, as by far the richest person in the community, with more than ten times the amount of assets of the other members, should have paid all the expenses for the school and teacher. Instead, Abraham claimed, Moises had made even the poor members pay those costs. Although the community advised the government that it wanted to build its own synagogue and cemetery, it did not have the funds to do so. Consequently, when a Jew passed away, he was buried in the cemetery in his original home village, and for this privilege, the community paid a small fee to each locale.

Some individuals, like Joseph David Berlizheimer and Moises Kaz, had made incredible strides in only a few decades. The growth and development of their Jewish communities in many ways paralleled the paths of their personal lives as they and their communities were becoming more established. In Rottweil and Mühringen, the future seemed secure and bright in 1815.

Hep! Hep! Riots

In view of the strides they were making in the early decades of the nineteenth century, it would not have occurred to the Jews that within a few years Christians would turn against them in the Hep! Hep! persecutions. Since the Middle Ages, no widespread overt anti-Jewish incidents had been reported, but that was to change dramatically. Hard economic times, political unrest, and an intensification of anti-Jewish feelings climaxed in rhetoric and riots over a broad geographical area.

When the Napoleonic Wars ended in 1815, soldiers returned to their villages to find that their jobs had been taken by other Christians and, very often, that their land had been destroyed by the armies. In 1811 the weather had caused havoc with the harvests, and four years later hail and frost completely destroyed the crops. Epidemics and diseases struck every home. Cycles of inflation, hoarding, and financial failures touched everyone during the Hunger Years of 1816 and 1817. Jewish peddlers and dealers were certainly not immune from the catastrophes. Their customers could not afford to buy their goods; farmers had few or no crops or livestock to sell; and the peasants often defaulted on their loans. After the death of King Friedrich at the end of 1816, his son, King Wilhelm I, enacted much-needed tax and economic measures to help the people and alleviate the situation. As the weather improved, the economic situation stabilized. But the political and social concerns remained unresolved.

During the Hunger Years the problems in the towns were very serious. Unemployment and inflation surged; beggars roamed the streets. Economic and political uncertainty led to direct and indirect repercussions aimed at the Jews. In Rottweil the magistrate sought to protect the merchants and craftsmen, and the town council refused to grant acceptance to Mendel

RURAL JEWS IN A FRANCONIAN VILLAGE   (Watercolor by M. D. Hartmann, 1817. Nuremberg, Germanisches Nationalmuseum, Inv. #HZ 5728.)

Degginger. The council stated that the citizens would be at a disadvantage if the number of Jews were to increase. The population of Rottweil was about 3,700, including 27 Jews, but once again the threat of adding even one more Jew alarmed the townspeople.

Jacob Kaz's request to marry a woman from Hechingen, in the neighboring principality of Hohenzollern, triggered a barrage of written complaints to the central government. Neither Jacob's future bride's very large dowry (3,000 gulden) nor his father's special status and financial wealth assuaged the town's anxieties. Rather, it fought to prevent the establishment of a new generation of Jews in the town.

JEWISH CATTLE DEALER   (Lithograph, 1820; Munich, Bayerisches Nationalmuseum.)

The town council's citizens committee, the tanners' guild, and the innkeepers each wrote long petitions to the central government. These groups complained that "the Jews squeeze the last kreuzer even from the poorest people" and that the Jews own the majority of the farmers' cattle (under cattle-renting agreements). The petitioners claimed that it was not just the local Jews who were causing the problems, but also those Jews who came by wagon from the neighboring states of Hesse and Baden and who went from house to house exchanging goods illegally for the farmers' cattle, skins, and leather, all the while saying they were the employees of

+ Beethoven in a letter likens a certain act by a person he is in conflict with as comparable to "Jewish trickery".

Portraits of Our Past

Rottweil's protected Jews. The shopkeepers, tanners, goldsmiths, and leather craftsmen wrote that they suffered the biggest losses when the Jews sold on quarterly installments and took the Christians' customers. The town leaders explained that it was "not the religion of the Jews, but only their attitude which was the issue," and added that if the Jews considered themselves "a tolerated Nation, they should behave like a tolerated Nation." The tanners' guild blamed the Jews for its members' miserable condition, with some lacking even bread to eat. According to its complaint, "the Jewboys are in every street in every village with heavy sacks, going from house to house selling cured leather and skins in exchange for anything from the peasants." Adding to the guild members' plight, they claimed, were the actions of the Jewish peddlers, who also snapped up skins that the peasants usually sold to the tanners in the town.[1]

Despite these complaints and the unsettled situation, the Rottweil Jews continued doing business in the town and even placed their usual advertisements in the newspaper. Although the magistrate did not grant him the necessary permission, Jacob Kaz nonetheless married Babette Maier from Hechingen. The very risky step of marrying without official permission was compounded by her status as a foreigner (and especially a Jewish foreigner) who needed permission to immigrate into the Kingdom of Württemberg.

The farmers could blame the weather for the crop failures, but that was an act of God so they could not express their anger. Jewish petty traders, cattle dealers, and moneylenders, on the other hand, were a ready target for their very real frustrations and fears. The Jews' business activities could have fed into that scenario since to a certain extent some Jewish grain and livestock traders might have contributed to the shortages and unstable prices by buying in quantities and exporting products to other countries. Adding to the Christians' perception of the Jews' increased influence was their new business as brokers and financiers in many land deals in the rural areas. Issued ostensibly to protect the peasants and uneducated masses from Jewish, conniving, a new decree ruled that Jews were forbidden to do commission trades or to speculate in land. Rather than helping the Christians, this new rule hurt the people who needed to sell their land to the Jews during bad economic times. No longer could they sell their land to the only ready buyers or get paid in cash on the spot; no longer did property buyers have the option of paying for new property by installments.

Jewish peddlers were encountering resistance and restrictions in many places. Sometimes they would appeal to the county authorities for relief, but generally the officials upheld the basic edict that Jews could only peddle goods not sold by local merchants. The situation became even more un-settled in Schramberg. Situated near the border with Baden, this market community of two thousand inhabitants was commercially important for the Jews in the Black Forest District. Tradesmen and peddlers from Mühringen and the surrounding villages would undertake the arduous six-hour trip through steep mountains to attend its four large seasonal cattle markets. These visits were allowed and even encouraged, but at other times all ped-dlers and traders needed special licenses from the administrator. Local edicts ordered the people to capture unlicensed peddlers. As an added in-centive, if it was the peddler's second offense, his captor would be awarded part of the value of the confiscated goods.

The situation of the Mühringen Jews was tense as well. The strain of years of war brought animosities to the forefront. In 1815, the village ad-ministrator wrote in a report to the county that since the Jews owned the biggest houses and were richer than the Christians, they should assume a greater (but actually unfair) responsibility for quartering soldiers.[2] Another Mühringen official was less sympathetic—this time in regard to the poor Jews—in his report to the government. He contended that the Jewish chil-dren left school still uneducated, and their uneducated parents used them for *schacher* trade and cattle dealing. He concluded that this background "bred an addiction to becoming rich in an immoral manner." The official at-tributed the Jews' increased level of poverty to two realistic problems: the disruption of trade and higher expenses for food and household goods. However, he then added two other causes for their dire situation: "the affec-tion of Jewish women for fancy clothes" and "the employment of Christian laborers to do the Jewish men's work."[3]

The generally miserable socioeconomic conditions spawned real or imaginary concerns. The guilds were concerned about competition, while apprentices and craftsmen worried about unemployment. Guild members viewed the 1809 edict regarding protected Jews and the guilds as an effort by the government to force the Jews upon them, to the benefit of the Jews and to the detriment of the members. Farmers, who were becoming increasingly indebted to Jewish moneylenders and cattle dealers, believed that the Jews were growing richer at their expense. The Christian merchants who still followed traditional sales techniques of selling only a single product and not extending credit to their customers were threatened by the Jews' more ingenious and versatile ways of doing business. The Jews were more visible and more involved with the non-Jewish world outside the confines of their villages than they had been for centuries.[4]

Political changes and uncertainty about the future exacerbated these concerns. Although statistically they remained a very small minority in Württemberg, Baden, and Bavaria, the increase in the Jewish population in the new political states alarmed the Christians. The Peace Congress of Vienna in 1815 tried to draft a constitution for the new German Confederation, including articles concerning the Jews' legal standing. Some states, like Württemberg, resisted, so the enactment of any changes regarding the Jews' status was left to the individual states. In the Kingdom of Bavaria, the *Matrikeledikt* (Registration Edict, also called *Judenedikt*) of 1813 gave the Jews civil rights if they left petty trade and *schacher* trade and went into a craft or farming. Those requirements were extremely difficult to fulfill, and other articles in the edict restricted the number of Jewish families allowed to live in each community. However, the mere possibility that Jews might be granted civil rights increased the Christians' concerns. In Baden an 1809 edict theoretically gave the Jews state civil rights but not local civil rights. The villagers were even more worried about the extension of local civil rights, which included the right to a citizen's share of firewood and pasture usage. Even a hint of change was upsetting to many, if not most, Christians.

When Napoléon abdicated and the French were defeated at Waterloo, Jews and Christians in some communities celebrated together in religious services. These victories, on the other hand, raised the level of consciousness of "German" nationalism. This atmosphere further excluded the Jews, who were still considered foreigners. The loose German Confederation, composed of thirty-nine independent states in 1815, was not equipped to bring any unified direction to resolve these issues.

Newly published literature reflected and, more importantly, fed this situation by articulating the anti-Jewish feelings of the common man. These demagogic writings defended the Christian-Teutonic ideal at the expense of any marginal group. Even though many people in the countryside could not read or did not have direct access to the anti-Jewish literature, the village priest or pastor, the local teacher, and some merchants and craftsmen would have bought the pamphlets and shared these ideas from the pulpit or in the taverns. The existence of these pamphlets and books, and even the rumors of what they might include, stirred up feelings, instigated smear campaigns, and encouraged Jew baiting.

Friedrich Rühs, a history professor at the University of Berlin, suggested, in "Ueber die Ansprüche der Juden an das deutsche Bürgerrecht" (On the Jewish claims to German civil rights) that the Jews, as foreigners, should be "compelled to accept Christianity, and through it, be led to a true acquisition of German ethnic characteristics, and thus effect the downfall of the Jewish people."[5] Jakob Friedrich Fries, a professor of science at the University of Heidelberg, advocated their expulsion from the villages and banishment from the country. He claimed that every farmer and city dweller hated and damned the Jews "when they corrupt the people through their depravity and steal their bread from them."[6] A popular farcical play, Unser Verkehr (Our crowd) by K. B. Sessa (a pseudonym), ridiculed Jewish social upstarts. ⟶ Manchester's title!!

The Rottweil newspaper in 1818 published a two-part article that was certainly in step with the times. The author described the Jews as "selfish, greedy, parasitic little worms who are obsessed with money and with the schacher spirit of haggling, usury, and cheating. They possess an incorrigible inner spirit." He warned that by giving the Jews the same rights as Christians, it would "transform a bad situation into an incurable cancer that could grow too quickly or eventually destroy the entire society."[7] A few months later the town council, concerned about the lack of fodder for livestock, enacted regulations to control when and where herdsmen could pasture cattle. The council included one other regulation: "The Jews will not be allowed to graze even one cow in the pasture."[8]

These factors led to a very volatile climate for the Jews. The situation resulted in the first violent riot at the beginning of August 1819, in the university city of Würzburg, Bavaria. At a public university event, a professor who had recently written something favorable about the Jews—supposedly in return for some payment by the Jews—was taunted with the cry "Hep-Hep" and forced to flee. Students, followed by the public, plundered Jewish businesses and homes. The rioters yelled, "Hep! Hep!" and screamed "Jew, drop dead!" Several Jews were killed in brawls or by fires set in the Jews' religious institutions. The mob was so out of control that to protect the remaining four hundred Jews, soldiers escorted them out of the city; they had to live in tents in the villages for several days until the tumult subsided.

The persecutions spread rapidly to cities and villages in many regions, and Hep! Hep! became the rallying cry. The slogan was inspired by the persecutions during the Middle Ages when the Crusaders had rallied their believers with the cry "Hierosolyma est perdita!" ("Jerusalem is destroyed!"). The shouted acronym reminded the Christians of these successful persecutions of the Jews, but it also had other elements that appealed to the common man: "Hep-Hep," was the sound of a he-goat, which was equated with the bearded goat and the bearded Jew; and "Hep" was slang for *Hebräer*, or "Jew." People created little ditties that they chanted and wrote on posters. In some places they decorated these posters with caricatures of a bearded Jew bent over from carrying an over-stuffed sack.

> Next Saturday the eleventh of the month,
> there will be a great Jew-Battle,
> so each "Hep" can be judged.
> Jew! Hep! Hep!
> Next Saturday they must die![9]

And:

> Jew! Jew! Hep! Hep! Hep!
> Pork meat is fat.
> Pork meat is good.
> And you are a stinking Jew![10]

While some incidents were reported in the newspapers and by the government, every Jew must have heard "Hep! Hep!" out loud or as an undercurrent, whenever he left his home.

Within weeks riots broke out in many cities, including Frankfurt am Main, Koblenz, Darmstadt, Hamburg, Karlsruhe, Heidelberg, and Berlin. The riots were especially severe in the university city of Heidelberg. Only about 350 Jews lived in the city of 10,000 people, but many tradesmen and merchants from other regions of Baden and the Black Forest did business there. The Jews doubted that any trouble would break out, but they were wrong. A mob of lower-class citizens and street people looted Jewish houses for three hours one day, causing such consequential destruction that the whole street was filled with bed feathers, furniture, and papers. Neither the police nor the armed citizen-guard stopped the looters, but three university professors and their students, armed with sticks and swords, routed the rioters. They apprehended some of the perpetrators and handed them over to the authorities.[11]

HEP! HEP! RIOTS IN FRANKFURT AM MAIN   The population in Frankfurt at the time of the riots in 1819 was 41,458, including 3,173 Jews. This contemporary copper engraving captured the fury of the mob and the violence perpetrated on the Jews. (By Johann Michael Voltz. Nuremberg, Germanisches Nationalmuseum, Inv. #HB 25820.)

The king of Württemberg received reports about the riots and, at the beginning of August, ordered certain counties south of Würzburg to be prepared if some families needed to flee. Despite these precautions, Hep! Hep! incidents occurred at the end of August in Künzelsau County, south of Würzburg. The events and the government's reactions were reported in detail by the county official.

On a Saturday evening, in a Catholic village with 158 Jews, some unmarried young men, including one soldier, yelled "Hep! Hep!" outside the house of Benedikt Isaac. The victim was a protected Jew whose son was serving in the Württemberg army. The men threatened to return the following day with more people to beat him up. The next night a larger group of young people threw stones at his shutters and doors, and also at the homes of Nachum Isaak, Löw Joseph, and Jacob Bär. One of the victims ran to the village administrator, but the official did nothing because he was afraid of being hit by the stones. In the end no one, including the neighbors and the night watchman, would corroborate the story. The government took no further action.

Around the same time, in a small Protestant village, a drunken ex-soldier, Joseph Schmetzer, yelled curses at Mendele Gumbal and Löw Hirsch Kahn, and, after following them to their village, stole their cow. Mendele returned to make a complaint to the administrator, but on the way, the soldier and two accomplices beat him up with their fists. They followed Mendele until he reached the administrator, who then ran to the neighbors to get help. After Schmetzer and his cohorts beat Mendele again, he finally escaped. A doctor examined Mendele the next day and reported observing only a few scratches. The county punished the participants in this "mischief." The ex-soldier was handed over to the military authorities; the others were condemned to a few days in the local jail and had to pay the cost of the investigation. The administrator was fined a small amount because of his negligence.

The county official reported that the Jews had complained that the administrators in the countryside had been passive and had even laughed about their dilemma. He ordered the administrators to punish such "mischief" and to protect the Jews against bad treatment. He forbade the use of the "Hep! Hep!" chant on pain of imposing a large fine (3 gulden) and asked the priests and pastors in the schools to punish delinquent boys.

The district government immediately issued a strong decree in the name of the king. The government would not allow disturbances of the public order or the endangerment of people, including Jews, who were under the protection of the state. It ordered the local and county officials to watch for unrest and to do all they could to prevent it. If such disturbances should occur, the officials were ordered to apprehend and punish the leaders. After the disturbances of August and September, no further incidents were reported, but the king's privy council was still concerned for several months.[12] The central government's intervention successfully quelled the riots, and the unrest did not extend to other sectors of society. The public order was maintained, and in the process the Jews were protected from further attacks.

Through the newspapers and the exchange of news at the markets and in the taverns, almost everyone knew about the excesses. One of the most anti-Jewish polemics was published and received widespread circulation just after the riots. Hartwig Hundt (who gave himself the aristocratic title of von Hundt-Radowsky), a German political writer and journalist, wrote *Der Juden-spiegel* (The Jews' mirror). His vitriolic diatribes were extremely anti-Jewish, even for those unsettled times:

> No people in the world have excelled from time immemorial through malice and vindictiveness, through cowardice, arrogance, and superstition, through usury, deceit, and treachery as the Jews.... I hold that the killing of a Jew is neither a sin nor a crime but only a police offense.... One should sell Israel's children to the English who could superbly use them on their Indian plantations instead of the Blacks.... So that the Jews will not reproduce, the men should be emasculated, and their wives and daughters should be lodged in houses of shame.... The best plan would be to purge the land entirely of these vermin either by exterminating them, or as the Pharaoh and the people of Meiningen, Würzburg, and Frankfurt did [in the Hep! Hep! persecutions], by driving them from the country.[13]

Mayer Rothschild threatened to leave Frankfurt if the .Hep! Hep! riots were not suppressed, an action that is said to have influenced the government.

Transitions

*I*n 1821 Moises Kaz, at seventy-one, still ran his businesses in Rottweil. The Hunger Years had taken their toll, however, on his financial affairs. Even when the economy improved, he could not recover from the effects of the debt defaults, grain and cattle shortages, and farm bankruptcies. As an important moneylender to the city and village governments, he suffered when the treasuries were depleted. He was going under financially.

Moises took steps to get his remaining assets out of his name to protect them from the courts and his creditors. He gave his houses in Rottweil to his wife Sara, his son Jacob, and his son-in-law Josef Hirsch Rothschild. Over the years Moises had entered into cattle-renting agreements with many individuals in the town. He ceded the ownership of these cattle (valued at 1,865 gulden) to his son-in-law Joseph David Berlizheimer in Mühringen and also transferred his house in Mühringen to Joseph David as a gift. On the evening of December 17, 1821, the county court in Rottweil inventoried his possessions; Moises Kaz was declared bankrupt.

As was the custom, the county court handled all the bankruptcy proceedings. It published the usual legal notices in the newspaper, advising creditors of Moises Kaz, Jacob Kaz, and the Moises Kaz [Trading] Company to file their claims. The town council appointed Dr. Burkhardt, a lawyer, as curator of the bankrupt company. The town recorder was appointed guardian of Sara; Abraham Bernheim became the guardian of Babette, Jacob's wife. Moises' possessions, including silver, men's and women's clothing, household goods, and considerable warehouse stock, were sold at auction.

The community at that time was composed of the families of Abraham Bernheim, Natan Degginger, Jacob Kaz, Josef Hirsch Rothschild, and Moises Kaz. Abraham, for one, could have felt slighted and abused by Moises'

"THE HOLY DAY" The scene depicted a family preparing for the Sabbath. (Watercolor by Hieronymus Hess, *Rüstung auf den Schabbis*, 1828. Basel, Öffentliche Kunstsammlung, Kupferstichkabinett, Inv. Bi. 259.29.)

treatment of him and the other members. Moises most certainly had enjoyed an exalted position in the community. After all, he had organized the community, and its members attended religious services in the synagogue located in his house. Of all the members, he had maintained the strongest connection with Mühringen, its principal community. Moises even chose to have Rabbi Adler perform his son's marriage ceremony in the Mühringen synagogue rather than in Rottweil. His inherited position as a *Kohen* also conferred upon him special rights and ceremonial duties.

Just three months after Moises went bankrupt, Abraham bought the ritual objects that had been in Moises' possession and used by the community. Abraham purchased a Torah with its case, the drapes and cloths, a table, a reading platform, and two brass candlesticks for a modest price (53 gulden 20 kreuzer) and then sold the objects to the community for the same amount. The sale was conditional on the members' accepting certain stipulations. Abraham's conditions were recorded in Hebrew and were translated by the teacher of its religious school.[1]

As a result of Abraham's conditions, some of Moises' power was transferred to the entire community: "all the married men residing [in Rottweil] were blessed for church affairs...to be undertaken without pay"; only a majority vote could decide any future purchases or approve the transfer of the prayer house to another home. All the members promised to contribute money to pay Abraham. The utensils to make matzos for Passover were also transferred from their private owners to the community. Future expenses had to be paid from capital funds, but if those funds did not suffice, the rest had to be paid by the members. The women's ritual bath, on the other hand, continued under private ownership, but Moises no longer owned his share of it.

Abraham's conditions also addressed how the members of the community treated one another. "If anyone now or in the future was not on friendly terms, this could not interfere with the way he was treated in the prayer house" or with the "allocation of mitzvot [honors]." Another article required that "only the person appointed to make that decision" could grant these honors. He would base his decision on the person's age, although the *Kohanim* would still be called to the Torah every Sabbath. If someone had the synagogue in his house and did not charge for that service, "he was not allowed to prevent any local or foreign Jews from attending services."

Despite these setbacks, Moises was still well regarded in the town. When he needed a letter of reference in 1824, the town council attested that Moises Kaz "deserved honor" since he often undertook "unselfish acts" on behalf of the town and private individuals. Two years later he was still involved in some business transactions. He ceded two promissory notes held by Christians to a third party in Stuttgart. A recent edict had prohibited the Jews from ceding notes to anyone, so the notes were confiscated. Moises appealed his case to the Ministry of Finance, but the government refused to change the law. Once again he was in the vanguard: two years later a new law eliminated that restriction.

Compared to the villages, the Jews in Rottweil demonstrated a higher level of business acumen and more involvement in the guild system. David

Joseph Rothschild (son of Josef Hirsch) and Moritz Esslinger (son of the deceased Abraham) were apprentices in business. Maier Rothschild (son of Josef Hirsch) was a student at the academic secondary school in Rottweil. Since Moises and Jacob were bankrupt, they were not in a guild. Josef Hirsch was in the printing trade.

Just as the men in Rottweil were more integrated in the Christian economic system, the twin daughters of Natan Degginger were more modern than their counterparts in the villages. Paulina Degginger apprenticed in Stuttgart and opened her own millinery business in her father's inn. Her specialties included creating new hats of gauze and silk, remodeling old ones, and washing straw hats. She attended the fashion trade markets, where she would purchase the latest women's accessories. With her twin, Fany, Paulina worked as a seamstress in Freiburg for a year. In their advertisements in the local newspaper, both emphasized their training and experience in those cosmopolitan cities.

The economy remained stagnant following the Hunger Years, so the Jews remained a target of recriminations. The Black Forest District sounded the alarm about a band of Jewish robbers and swindlers who had special hiding places in some villages and towns around Mühringen (including Hechingen, Haigerloch, Nordstetten, and Wankheim). The authorities warned the local officials to be vigilant during their markets, where the swindlers came to "practice their art." Assuming that these criminals would choose not to hide when they came to the villages, the authorities prohibited the lodging of "foreign Jews" in private houses or inns without the approval of the local officials, thus making it difficult for law-abiding Jews to find places to sleep. Although the government distinguished between foreign Jews and those that were known, its final decree ordered the local officials to "act cautiously and to prevent the Jews from becoming aware of these instructions," thus intimating that the law-abiding Jews were in collusion with the criminals.

Other incidents occurred in market towns when peoples' frustrations once again focused on the Jewish peddlers and dealers. The Rottweil and Schramberg merchants sent petitions to the government echoing the same complaints made in previous years. The merchant guild's leader in Schramberg also objected to the conduct of those dealers who refused to obey the operating rules of the markets. Natan Degginger, the owner of the Crown Inn in Rottweil, for instance, refused to set up his stall in the section of the market dedicated to fabric vendors. Several traders from Mühringen refused to set up their stalls in the back of the building, demanding instead that the other fabric vendors draw lots for the good locations. The situation escalated when the other vendors refused this plan, and the police had to be summoned. According to the authorities, the "Hebrew" Süssele, one of the Mühringen dealers, claimed he had the same rights and paid the same fees as the other vendors. He was allowed to set up in a good location, but the issue was referred to the county officials for resolution. While occasionally the head of the merchant guild cited Christian vendors for incorrect conduct, numerous complaints against the Jewish peddlers and dealers were recorded in the protocol books.

Both the son and Rottweil son-in-law of Moises Kaz were deeply and inseparably intertwined with his financial woes. His other son-in-law, Joseph David Berlizheimer in Mühringen, was only involved in the periphery of Moises' sphere of influence, so he was not brought down by the bankruptcy. Joseph David was the village's highest trade taxpayer, and in 1820 the Jewish community elected him as its president (*parnas*). It was not unusual for the wealthiest person to be elected as such; it was assumed that he would use his disposable assets to support the necessities of its institutions and its members. In some communities a family dynasty held the position for decades. In Mühringen the Kusel/Hilb family had done so, but their wealthy family members had left the village or had passed away.

Joseph David's eldest son, David, was one of the few Jewish men in Mühringen who had entered the guild system. He completed his apprenticeship in trade and then traveled outside his village as a journeyman. In the 1820s he opened a fabric shop with his father. The store was on the ground floor of the house Moises had bought in 1796. It enjoyed an excellent commercial location in the center of the village at the intersection of the roads running from Hechingen to Horb. David was part of the emerging middle class: he was now a merchant and shopkeeper.

It was time for David to marry. Given his financial situation and family background, he would have been considered a fine match. The customary matchmaking process, however, took an unusual path for his future bride, Fany Grünwald. A marriage had been arranged for her with Maier Auerbacher, the grandson of the former president and rabbi of the neighboring Nordstetten community. Fany's father, Samson, was a goods trader, the second-highest trade taxpayer in Mühringen, and the owner of a substantial house in the lower village; her uncle, Seligmann Grünwald, was a rabbi. It appeared to be a favorable match for both parties, but, in a rare reversal, the engagement was terminated. Fany's former fiancé's brother, Berthold Auerbach, remembered the events more than a half a century later. Auerbach recalled that his brother believed that Fany still loved him even after the engagement had been broken off; for a time afterward, he refused to pass through her village.

A marriage was immediately arranged between Fany and David Berlizheimer, and they married in 1826. Fany was twenty-seven and brought a substantial dowry (3,000 gulden) in property and money. Joseph David gave his son the same amount as his wedding gift. David used the assets to establish a small cotton-weaving factory. Since the family already dealt in fabrics and the weaving industry was expanding, a cloth factory was a viable option for increasing their business opportunities. Both the store and the factory were located in their house, and the couple lived upstairs. Exactly nine months after the wedding, Fany give birth to their son Simson, who was named after his deceased maternal grandfather.

Mühringen remained a feudal village well into the nineteenth century. Baron von Münch maintained his power and control over his villagers. He owned most of the land and the important buildings, which he rented out to the villagers. During the five-decade span from the 1770s through the 1820s, written debt obligations showed that the Christians in the village accrued more than sixty debts to the baron; they ranged from a few gulden to, occasionally, several thousand. The baron employed a rent and debt collector who was responsible for completing the documents and collecting the payments and interest.

In those years only a handful of Christians in Mühringen borrowed money from the Jews. One person had borrowed small sums from the court agent, Nathan Wolf Kaulla. Between 1817 and 1828 other villagers, including the owner of Zum Hirsch (the Deer Inn), borrowed up to several hundred gulden from the Guggenheim family, which owned the Zum Bären (the Bear Inn). Many small loans made for goods purchased on installment and cattle-renting agreements were not registered. Nevertheless, the baron was by far the largest creditor in terms of both the number and the size of the loans. These facts certainly did not support the public's perception that Jewish moneylenders controlled the economy.

The number and size of the debts the Jews owed the baron were equally large. The community still owed him almost half the amount it had borrowed to build its synagogue (2,850 gulden). From the 1780s through the 1820s, more than forty-five Jews had borrowed money from the baron in varying amounts (from 50 to 1,000 gulden). Most of them took out loans of several hundred gulden to buy the apartments and buildings that the baron owned. They used the same property as surety for the loan, so in case of default the baron would repossess his own apartment. Twenty debtors also listed their synagogue seat or seats as surety (the value ranged from 40 to 50 gulden per seat). Only the innkeeper Guggenheim borrowed money from a Christian other than the baron; his creditor was from Stuttgart.

Joseph David Berlizheimer was the second largest creditor of the Jews. In the same period eight people borrowed small amounts (12 to 110 gulden) from him. The only other lenders in the registers were the cantor, the gold dealer, and the president of the Nordstetten community; each made one loan in this period.

The opportunity of improving their occupation by entering the guilds had been available to the Jews since 1809. But even in the 1820s very few young men could achieve that goal. The obstacles were just too difficult to surmount. Guilds functioned in all the towns but not in the villages, forcing young men to enter into a guild system in a nearby town. Even for Christians, the entrance into certain popular guilds was carefully controlled, with preference given to members' sons. The rigid guild system demanded that boys spend three years as apprentices with official masters. The apprentices' families paid the masters for the privilege of having their sons learn the trades and for room and board. This system posed major problems for the rural Jews. Most did not have sufficient funds to pay for such an apprenticeship, nor could the families afford the loss of income while the boys did their three-year apprenticeships. Parents also had to pay extra money for board because their sons could not eat the nonkosher food served at the Christian masters' table. No Jews were yet masters, so the apprentices had to learn from Christian masters who, by personal preference or under pressure from the guilds, would rather take on Christian apprentices. After the apprenticeship each youth had to work in his trade or craft away from his village for a few years as a journeyman. The problems of keeping the Sabbath and observing the dietary laws made finding a position as a journeyman very difficult. Once a journeyman completed all the required training and work, the guild still demanded certificates of good standing and an unblemished family background, and subsequently a candidate had to pay acceptance fees and annual fees. Entering the guild system was expensive and time consuming, and the Christian guild members had no intention of making it any easier.

In addition to David and his brothers Marx and Löw, only two other young men in Mühringen were apprentices in trade; two others were tailor apprentices. Three youths were doing their journeyman travels: one as a shoemaker, another as a butcher, and the third as a trader. Since Mühringen did not have any guilds, all the boys were supervised by the guilds in Horb.

According to the 1823 trade tax payments, the villagers' businesses varied considerably in size: only two merchants had substantial assets while more than sixty-six people had minimal or no business assets.

Comparison of Occupations and Trade Tax Assessments: Mühringen (1823)

Jewish villagers	Christian villagers	Trade tax paid per person
1 cut goods dealer 1 goods dealer	[No Christians paid taxes at this level]	38 gulden 37 gulden
3 goods dealers 1 leather dealer 1 gold and jewelry dealer	1 mill owner	16 gulden each
7 cattle dealers and butchers 33 small-time dealers 1 pastry baker 3 innkeepers	1 innkeeper 4 bakers 1 locksmith, 1 miller, 1 ironworker 1 dyer, 1 carpenter, 1 shoemaker	3–15 gulden each
More than 30 small-time dealers and peddlers 1 shoemaker 1 innkeeper 2 kosher butchers and 2 laborers	30 small-time craftsmen and day workers	0–2 gulden each

In the 1820s, the population numbered 450 Jews and 550 Christians. In 1823 the Jews paid a total of 379 gulden in trade taxes compared to 105 gulden paid by the Christians. Adding these taxes together reveals that the Jews paid a third more in business-related taxes than the Christian villagers.

The Jews owned thirty of the 120 houses in the village and all but two of the thirty-four apartments. Home ownership in itself, however, did not necessarily attest to the wealth of an individual since in making a home purchase, a buyer often obtained loans and subsequently used that property as surety for other loans. Also, members of the extended family—often to three generations—lived together, usually sharing the burden of loan payments, house taxes, and expenses.

Unlike in other villages where Christians were more involved in agriculture, the Jews and Christians in Mühringen were beginning to compete against each other in certain trades. Young men, for instance, were being trained as apprentices and journeymen in the tailor and shoemaker guilds. Another increasingly competitive business was running the local inns because the Jewish inns were frequented by the Christians as well. The Catholic priest acknowledged that reality in his inspection report but added an anti-Jewish slant: the locals dance too much without asking permission, and the many Jewish inns are "always open for forbidden card playing and other excesses."

In these decades, the government was beginning to increase its control over the lives of its Jewish minority through edicts and decrees. In some instances the impetus would come from the Jews themselves. Other times the government's hand would seem to be forced by the conduct of the governments of the other German states. Its motivation would not be uniform, nor was it always completely clear: did it want to help the Jews, or did it want them to come under the same rules and regulations as the Christian majority? Not surprisingly, the Jews' reaction to the changes varied: some had already adopted the now-codified changes; others adapted to the new edicts without complaint; and still others resisted any efforts to interfere in their way of life.

In the late eighteenth and early nineteenth centuries, some western European countries, and some German states like Baden, Bavaria, and Prussia, had been influenced by the ideas of the Enlightenment, including those of the Prussian military councilor, Christian Wilhelm von Dohm. As the author of *Über die bürgerliche Verbesserung der Juden* (On the civil improvement of the Jews), published in 1781, he recommended granting Jews citizenship and "improving the Jews" through education.

Changes in Jewish education had already begun, to a great extent, with the ideas proposed by the leaders of the Jewish Enlightenment (Haskalah). Moses Mendelssohn's translation of the Hebrew Bible into the German language written in Hebrew characters was a concrete result of that movement. He undertook that momentous project in Berlin in 1778. Public distribution had been quite limited, and many traditionalists objected to the potential use of the sacred writings as a means of learning a secular subject, the German language. The Mendelssohn translation began to reach the village communities in the early 1820s. Rabbi Gabriel Adler, for instance, ordered several copies for Mühringen.

Until the 1820s, the children attended special Jewish schools that were funded, administered, and supervised by their local community or their parents while the schools serving the Christian children were funded by the government and supervised by the Protestant and Catholic school authorities. Fundamental changes in the system of grade school education for Jewish children in the kingdom began in 1817 when Isaak Hess, a book dealer and president of the Lauchheim community, asked King Wilhelm to set up a secular education program. The king ordered his minister to establish special school committees to look into the situation.

In 1818 the official for Mühringen's county presented a report on the education in the region to the government. He stated that the level of Jewish education was very poor since the Jews only employed private teachers who could not read and write German very well. His description was very critical of the situation: the children studied only Hebrew and religion; each teacher had too many pupils; and "overall in the schools, there is the greatest filth, disorder, and ignorance." The official noted that the teachers could not support themselves on their teaching fees. He criticized the rich families for employing foreign teachers (probably from Alsace or eastern Europe) for their own children and for denying a proper education to the poor people. He observed that all Jews mistrusted Christian teachers and would not hire a Christian teacher, even for nonreligious subjects. The official concluded his report by requesting that the state intervene to improve the situation.[2]

While the government was studying the issue, the Black Forest District under Mühringen's Rabbi Adler took strides to change the old system. He was forward thinking in his views and very concerned with education. Considering his ideas worthy of consideration at the highest level, he sent his proposal for educational reforms directly to the king. Rabbi Adler's most significant proposal was to prohibit Jewish parents from taking their children, male or female, out of school until they turned fourteen years old. At that time the rabbi would give the children examinations to determine their proficiency in several subjects, including the ability to read the Holy Scriptures, understand the Torah, read and write German and Hebrew correctly, and understand the basics of the Hebrew and German languages. He would also inspect the schools every two months.[3] No official response to this report has come down to us, but subsequent regulations would lead us to believe that his ideas were in line with the official thinking of the time.

In 1825 the Protestant and Catholic school councils issued their regulations for Jewish children. Both boys and girls would be subject to compulsory education until age fourteen. The education committee set up by the king had requested that the Jewish children attend the village Christian grade schools, believing that those schools were better than the Jewish schools and would facilitate the integration of the children into more acceptable professions. In spite of those suggestions, the regulations stipulated that the children could go either to Christian or Jewish schools. If they attended the Christian schools, Jewish children would not have to attend the Christian religion classes. Jewish religion classes, however, were not allowed during the school day. Moreover, the community would have to continue to pay all the costs and expenses of the Jewish school.

Since elementary education was closely associated with the church, the local pastor or priest of the predominant confession was responsible for inspecting the schools and giving examinations to the Jewish students, just as he did in the Christian schools. The Christian school councils, which selected textbooks for all the Christian schools, also chose books for the Jewish schools. The local pastor had the authority to examine the students, even in religious subjects; in practice, however, the district rabbis continued to be responsible for some parts of the curriculum.

The Mühringen community rented a schoolhouse (66 gulden per year) where an elementary school functioned. It started building a schoolhouse with money from two charitable foundations (350 gulden) but, lacking sufficient funds, did not complete the project. The community hired several teachers: one was from Mühringen, and another came from a village more than a hundred miles away. It also hired a local assistant teacher who had been a private teacher. Under the new system the Protestant council, representing the dominant religious confession in the kingdom, certified all the teachers. Their salaries (ranging from 80 to 100 gulden) were paid not by the community but from fees assessed on the parents of each student.

Rabbi Adler had suggested in his reform proposal that during his school inspections he would seek out boys who were capable and motivated in their study of the Talmud, and would encourage those students to improve themselves and continue their education at a higher level. These students could study at his small yeshivah in Mühringen or at the more prestigious yeshivah in nearby Hechingen. These Talmud schools were supported by private fees and contributions and not by the communities.

The writings of Councilor von Dohm had also urged governments to change the situation of all Jews by enacting edicts to control their most obvious outward signs of separation from the Christian world. One of his proposals, the adoption of surnames, was viewed as a prerequisite for any steps toward emancipation and assimilation. National governments issued these surname adoption laws over a long period of time: Austria in 1787, France in 1808, Baden in 1809, Prussia in 1812, and Bavaria in 1813.

While some Württemberg Jews at the economic level of the Berlizheimer and Kaz families had used surnames since at least the mid-eighteenth century, many peddlers and small-time dealers still went by their given names followed by their fathers' given names, for example, Marx Hirsch, Bär Isaak, Salomon Leopold. They saw no reason to abandon this system, which had been used since ancient times. As an interim step, the Württemberg government ordered in 1807 that Jewish families be publicly registered in the same manner as the Christian population. Jews often maintained a private register in the family prayer book or Bible. However, under the new system, the rabbi would keep a community family register, including birth dates and places, marriages, deaths, names of parents, and date of "confirmation" (Bar Mitzvah). While the registers had to be written in German, occasionally the Hebrew names were inscribed beneath the German entry. If there was no rabbi in the village, the pastor would be charged with inscribing the information.

Initially, Württemberg did not pass a law ordering its Jews to adopt surnames, but many did so anyway in the 1820s. It was an unwritten policy that the Jews should not adopt "Christian" surnames. A few years later, when the politicians codified the name-adoption process, the government ensured that Jews would not adopt the names of celebrities or famous people. The Christians worried that a non-Jew would be offended if he had the same surname as a Jew. To avoid those situations, Jews needed approval of the county government to adopt or change their surnames. Once the county authorities approved the new names, they published lists of the "old" and "new" names in the official gazettes.

Certain names, like Cohen, Kahn, Kaz, and Levi (names descended from the ancient tribes of Israel) were used throughout the German-speaking areas. Other names were derived from names of places, given names, occupations, features or qualities, or poetic descriptions. If someone adopted the name of a town or village, it did not necessarily mean that he or his ancestors had originally emigrated from that place, although it was often an indication of some connection. In Mühringen a number of families maintained the surnames that they already had been using:

Surnames Maintained

Name	Meaning or derivation	Name	Meaning or derivation
Berlizheimer	Probably from Markt Berolzheim, a village in Bavaria	Fellheimer	Fellheim, a village
		Grünwald	Green woods
		Haarburger	Harburg, a village
Degginger	Deggingen, a village	Petersberger	A village; also, Peter's mountain
Elsässer	Emigrated from Alsace in France in the eighteenth century		
		Rothschild	Red shield
Eppstein	A village	Schweitzer	Swiss
Esslinger	Esslingen, a city		

Other families took on new surnames derived from specific places or creative descriptions:

New Surnames Adopted

Name	Meaning or derivation	Name	Meaning or derivation
Bach	A village or a brook	Reinauer	Rheinau, a village
Feigenheimer	Feigenheim, a village	Rosenfeld	A village between Rottweil and Mühringen; also, rose field
Löwenthal	(One of the *Levi* families.) Common variation of Levi		
		Schilling	A village or a small coin
Perlen	Pearl, their ancestral given name		

In the early nineteenth century Jews voluntarily started taking on German-sounding given names by changing the spelling and the name itself. In those years, they did not adopt names commonly used by Christians or names connected with Christianity. The family fathers inscribed Hebrew or Yiddish names in the official family and birth registers, but in civil documents and in daily life individuals began to use the Germanized form. By the 1820s and 1830s, few if any of the younger generation in Mühringen or Rottweil used the older-style names. Some examples of the changes were: Baruch Berlizheimer to Berthold, Löw Berlizheimer to Leopold, Hefel Kaz to Henriette, and Voegele Kaz to Viktoria. Even within a family, parents would give some of their children traditional names, while others received modern, German-sounding names. Parents did maintain the Ashkenazic custom of naming their children in memory of deceased relatives.

The government enacted other new regulations that directly affected the Jews' lives. Previously they could sign documents in Hebrew, but the new laws ordered that all documents had to be signed in German. This new policy, and others relating to the use of German, posed problems for the illiterate or barely literate older generation. Even in the early nineteenth century, some Jews were unable to read or write at all. Officials or others would read civil documents aloud, and the parties would sign the papers, which would then be notarized. Consequently, even under the new regulations, wedding documents, real estate transactions, and inheritance divisions continued to be signed with shaky signatures in Hebrew and with symbols. While Christians who could not write signed +++, Jews rarely made the Christian sign of the cross, but rather wrote *ooo* or *xxx*.

In an effort to exert more control over the Jews' business transactions, the government demanded that they keep their books and receipts in German rather than in Hebrew or German written with Hebrew characters. The officials obviously could not read the documents written in Hebrew or in German written in Hebrew characters, a situation that made them quite uneasy. Christians also considered the speaking and writing of a different language a symbol of national separateness—a minority flaunting its differences in the face of the majority. Thus, the new requirements also stipulated that Jews use the German rather than their Jewish calendar. Still when they wrote to each other, they sometimes used German written in Hebrew letters. For instance, when a deceased member of the Mühringen community had had an outstanding debt owed to a Jew in the town of

Haigerloch, the president of Haigerloch's community sent a letter to Joseph David Berlizheimer, the president of the Mühringen community. The date, greeting, numbers, and his signature were in German characters while the rest of the text was in German written in Hebrew characters.

The financial arrangements of the Jews' marriages also came under the sphere of the government. By custom, engagement arrangements were written in Hebrew. After 1811, Hebrew-language engagement documents and the accompanying detailed inventory lists had to be translated into German. The local government then could check that the appropriate taxes and fees had been assessed, and that a couple had sufficient assets to set up a family in the village. Inheritance divisions of property also came under these rules. These documents were kept in the village archives, alongside the Christian marriage contracts and wills. Unlike other official registers that were organized by religious affiliation, these documents were filed strictly chronologically.

The government continued to be concerned about the poor Jews in the kingdom but did nothing to change the structure in place. The increased number of poor Jews in Mühringen burdened that Jewish community's financial resources. The drain on its assets was substantial, since approximately a sixth of its budget went to support the poor. One year the community paid for firewood and school fees for the poor families, as well as full support for one child from Schwandorf. It continued giving vouchers to "guests" (the beggars and wandering Jews) for meals in private homes. Some members of the community gave money to the poor, and the wealthier people supported their poorer relatives. However, the community felt that such outright payments of money to the poor was not a good system. It believed that the monetary support made poor people idle because they came to expect and depend on the support.

Even the Christians realized that the Jews did not request money, goods, or social services from the village poor funds or the government. The county government reviewed the status of Mühringen's poor Jews. The official reported that only a few families were still "wandering beggars," while some, who had been "born wandering beggars," had settled in the village and now begged only there. He stated that those beggars were not a burden for the state since the richer people supported them. Interestingly, the Christian official assumed that the "wandering Jews," the beggars, were a great burden since the Jews had to bring them "to their dining table, one after another." The official noted that he checked the passports of the foreign Jews because he wished to return those with improper papers to the border. How-ever, he understood that it was the "Jews' religious obligation" to take care of their poor, so he refrained from controlling the entrance or stay of the poor foreign Jews in the village.[4]

Just as the government began to exert more control on the lives of Jews, so did it use its authority to chip away at the power of the rabbis, the teach-ers and cantors, the community leaders, and the individual members of the community. Through edicts and regulations, little changes began to erode the basic structure of the community.

The new edicts circumscribed the power and the authority of the com-munity and of its president by placing them clearly under the ultimate su-pervision of the civil administration. Edicts ordered the president to swear that all the laws and regulations of the land would be observed in his com-munity. He became a quasi-government official. The Ministry of Internal Af-fairs even permitted the presidents to wear the royal emblem as a sign that they were performing duties under the aegis of the king. The government di-rectly involved itself in the previously private domain of the community by issuing an official edict stating that the president would be elected by a ma-jority of the members of the community and that the district administrative official must be informed of the results. Although the government now used the title "officer" or "leader," the presidents themselves and the local Chris-tian officials continued to use the traditional title of *parnas.*

The government also started to regulate practices that in the past had been entirely under the dominion of ritual law as interpreted by the rabbis. Since the Jews had no central organization to present their views to the gov-ernment, the government unilaterally enacted regulations. The government claimed in each case that its primary reason to issue such rules was to pro-tect the public welfare. Some of these rulings, however, imposed changes that conflicted with rituals and customs.

For example, when a Jew passed away, according to Jewish law he must be buried as soon as possible. In the late eighteenth and the beginning of the nineteenth century, real incidents or Gothic stories of live burials led the government to issue special regulations in 1780 and 1799 about the handling of the deceased. In 1820 the minister of internal affairs ordered the Jews to obey the regulations that were already in place for the Christians and put in place harsher penalties: a burial could take place only after forty-eight hours had passed. It was the responsibility of the Christian village officials to enforce the regulations. In the civil "register of corpses" in Mühringen, the officials noted the exact time of death, the certification by the doctor, and the exact time of the burial. In the summer months, if a corpse were decomposing, the officials sometimes gave a special dispensation for an earlier burial.

The government issued another edict regarding the danger of house fires during the week of Sukkot, the Festival of Booths. Jews would decorate a room in the upper floor or a booth next to their houses as a *sukkah*. They used flammable dried reeds and colored paper, and each evening they illuminated the booth with candles and lanterns. Based on an earlier fire law, they could be fined a considerable amount (for instance, 10 gulden in Rottweil, where such a fire had occurred) if they used candles or lighted tobacco pipes in the *sukkah*; if there were a fire, the individual would be responsible for all the damages. This edict did not affect the celebration of the holiday.

Even the women's ritual bath was not exempt from the far-reaching arm of the government. The government justified its involvement by claiming that it was concerned for the welfare of its subjects. At issue was the availability of warm water, especially in the winter, for the Jewish woman's cleansing after her menstrual cycle or after childbirth. A government medical official, a physician, stated that he had been informed that at least two women had suffered partial paralysis as a result of using the ritual bath. The report reached the minister of internal affairs, who ordered that because no religious reason existed against using hot water in the ritual bath, warm water must be available to all women for health reasons.

The technical logistics of having a warm-water *mikveh* were difficult and not inexpensive. The water had to be heated on the stove or in a fireplace and added to the ritually pure water. The cost of the wood and the fee for the attendant had to be paid by each woman. The government ordered the authorities, with the assistance of the rabbi and the community president, to ensure that everyone, even the poor women who could not pay, would have access to warm water.

The reaction of the individual communities to the ritual bath regulations varied with the financial situation of the members. In Rottweil, the *mikveh* was privately owned and maintained by four families. They already had complied with the law by making heated water available without payment to women who were poor or who did not live in the town. In Mühringen, the ritual bath was in the basement of the community house and had a fireplace to warm the water. The community paid many expenses of the poor, including firewood in winter so that poor Jewish women would have wood to heat the water. Other communities, which did not have the financial means to buy firewood for the poor or where there were privately owned baths, did not comply with the edict.

The early decades of the nineteenth century brought to the forefront many larger issues regarding the Jews' treatment and their place in society. In one instance, a Jewish leader asked the government for relief from the spread of anti-Jewish rhetoric. Hartwig von Hundt-Radowsky brought out a new edition of *Der Judenspiegel* in 1821. It had been confiscated and banned in Prussia, but it was still in circulation in some places, including Württemberg. The leader of the Sontheim Jewish community complained to the Ministry of Internal Affairs about the marketing of the book in the kingdom. He protested about the newspaper advertisements for this and other pamphlets that ridiculed, insulted, and persecuted Jews. His petition asked that police orders be issued to curtail the distribution of the book and that the offenders be punished. The ministry decided that the laws regarding censorship did not apply in this case and took no action.

Most of the time, however, it was just the small, everyday matters that really concerned the people. When Christian butchers in Lauchheim complained about the unauthorized slaughter of cattle by the Jews, the tax authority issued regulations to protect the butchers' trade. Jews would be allowed to slaughter a certain number of animals for their own consumption and would have to report the event to the cattle inspector or meat appraiser. Before they could sell those quarters that they were forbidden to eat, they would have to pay a tax. They would be fined severely (3 gulden 15 kreuzer) for any infractions or for selling meat by the pound.

The villages, on the other hand, resolved many small conflicts. For example, Joseph David Berlizheimer had a problem with his Christian neighbor over the storage location of the cattle dung between their houses; that issue was resolved by the village council. Another time the council fined a Christian for slandering a Jewish villager and, in the same decision, fined the Jew the same amount for slandering the Christian.

Very personal stories recounted in the memoirs of Berthold Auerbach may be the most telling of the times. Auerbach remembered vividly one experience that occurred when he was a young boy in Nordstetten in 1822. He had walked to the town of Horb to buy salt for his mother. She had warned him to beware of being cheated by the Christian shopkeeper, who might sell him salt that had absorbed water. His package was heavy, so he was unsure if there was water in the salt. He recounted the event in great detail:

> When I began the climb back to Nordstetten, I passed the brick shed and saw three young men lying around the woodpile, looking around and roguishly laughing, "Why don't you say 'Good Evening'?" I continued further on. I had a certain anxious feeling; something could happen to me even though the day was bright.... Suddenly I heard something behind me.... I draped my bag of salt over my head. It was wet and not so comfortable. Suddenly one young man stumbled toward me; my sack of salt fell on the ground.... "We don't want to fight with you Jewboy. We want you to kneel down and raise your hands and say, "Christ has risen." There must have been a mocking look on my face because the young men said, "So you deride today again our Holy Savior whom your ancestors crucified and martyred." [I answered,] "I didn't deride him." "Now we'll martyr you, we'll bind you if you don't immediately say 'Christ has risen.'" [I continued to refuse them.]... "Now that's enough," shouted the knife maker. "Look, I have enough cord, let's tie him up, the feet over each other. Hold him properly to bind him as crucified.... We'll spread his salt all around." They went away, and I was left, bound, fettered, and crucified.[5]

Berthold's Uncle Judel found him and brought him to Nordstetten. The local Christian boys avenged Berthold's treatment. From then on the men from Nordstetten had a "formal war" with the boys from Horb; one of the perpetrators lost the use of one leg. Berthold felt the incident would have been forgotten, but his father wanted a prayer of thanks recited in the synagogue because his son had been saved: "Then it was not private; it belonged to the community."

Auerbach also recalled his thoughts a few years after that incident when he, his mother, and his brother traveled to Friedrichstadt (a district just outside of Hechingen) where "I heard only Jews lived. That seemed to me a real paradise. How marvelous it must be to live with real Jews, not exposed to ridicule and hate!"[6]

Moving Backward

In 1827, 1,518,000 people lived in about 1,300 villages and towns in Würt-temberg. The 9,271 Jews were permitted to live only in about eighty of these places. In the two decades since the incorporation of the larger number of Jews into Württemberg, the government had exerted more control over the structure of the communities and the lives of its inhabitants. The more basic issues regarding the political, economic, and legal status of the Jews had not yet been addressed. Even the new Württemberg constitution of 1819 gave citizenship rights only to members of the Lutheran, Catholic, and Swiss Reform denominations, without even a passing mention of the Jews.

But changes were slowly coming to central Europe. The evolution from a feudal autocratic society to a bourgeois capitalist society was encompassing many fundamental reforms. The governments had been consolidating their power by removing the rights and privileges of the minority institutions, for example, the guilds and the nobles. In many states, the quest for the "civic betterment" and integration of the Jews was but one facet of the major metamorphosis of the state and society. As one of a number of autonomous groups, the Jews could not remain untouched by the transformation taking place around them. A token symbol of the burgeoning new era was the self-conscious use of "Israelite" or "Israelite believers" in the place of "Jew" and "Hebrew." Likewise, "Mosaic Belief" and "Mosaic Believers" were phrases used when referring to Judaism and Jews. Those Christians and Jews who were cognizant of political nuances adopted the new phrases in laws, decrees, protocols, petitions, and speeches.

Earlier in 1820, the president of the Württemberg Parliament had asked the king in a letter "to regulate the present situation of the Israelite believers in the state."[1] The very wording of the letter, however, was ambiguous. Did the Parliament want reforms or restrictions? The king took the letter as a request for reform. He immediately ordered the Ministry of Internal Affairs to draft a law that would be based on earlier edicts issued in Bavaria and Prussia as well as on a draft of a law that the Württemberg government had written in 1808. The ministry responded, however, with a hundred-page memorandum that described Jews in an unfavorable light. It referred to the hatred against their religion, highlighting the Hep! Hep! riots of the previous year. Many pages were filled with depictions of the Jewish nation as corrupt and with claims about the harmfulness of the *schacher* trade.[2]

Despite that negative beginning, the government asked five prominent Jews for their opinions about certain issues that would be addressed in the new legislation. The questions related to the transition of the Jews into acceptable professions, the education of the young, and the elimination of begging as a livelihood. Isaak Hess, Rabbi Gabriel Adler, two leaders of the Kaulla family (the court advisers and bankers), and the community president of Buchau each presented their suggestions in reports. Hess, a book dealer and president of the Lauchheim community, wrote a long memorandum that was also published as a pamphlet. He stressed that the Jews did not desire special rights or advantages but did want a normal life and an education for their children, who could then become beneficial members of civil society, according to the essence of the Mosaic religion. Rabbi Adler discussed the draft with the members of his five communities (including Mühringen). He included their suggestions in his memorandum to the Ministry of Internal Affairs. In their concluding report the five prominent Jews complimented the government for its noble intentions to put the Jews on a higher level but counseled it to consider the customs and the priorities of the Jews. The government acknowledged their input but did not incorporate any of their ideas in its preliminary legislation and report to Parliament in 1821. Three years later, the privy council wrote a draft for new legislation titled "The Law Regarding the Relations of the Israelites."

The government's draft legislation, and the speeches and reports accompanying it, reflected the times. The lofty ideals presented by the leaders of the Christian Enlightenment were undermined by the reality of the prevailing anti-Jewish feelings. There were several goals: to reconcile the relations of the Jews with the public policies of the kingdom by means of modern lawmaking, to improve their education, and to give them the opportunity to have citizenship rights. The government's enlightened rhetoric continued in the summary of the motives supporting the legislation. In this section, the government's stated objective was to tear down the wall between Christians and Jews in Württemberg society by ending the circumstances that caused the separation between the two groups, thereby increasing the mutual faith and unity between both parts of society so that they would exist as one united group of citizens.

Under the umbrella of seeking the best for the Jews, however, the accompanying speeches contradicted its commendable motives and the draft legislation. The government officials described in detail the reasons why Jewish society was different from Christian society:

> Aside from the peculiarities in his private life, the Jew believes he must pay attention even now to his "church" regulations, although these pertain to a long-past time and a far-distant clime. Apart from a national peculiarity, the majority of the Jews are immoral, and their injurious food habits separate them from the remaining inhabitants.
>
> The negative Jewish morals cannot be changed merely by laws and restrictions, but only slowly by education. The new law, therefore, must be an educational law aimed at improving the Jews in religious, moral, intellectual, and economic matters. The goal, the ideal, is the acquisition of a combination of education, culture, and morality (*Bildung*).... The route to this improvement will be the cleansing of the religion, reducing it to the Mosaic rulings.
>
> The Jews still consider themselves foreigners who only wait, according to the teaching of their rabbis, for the arrival of the Second Messiah, who is supposed to return them to the land of their Fathers and establish a new Israelite kingdom.[3]

The government, in its 1824 draft of the law and accompanying speech, specifically used the word *schacher*. According to common usage, the trades that were not *schacher* trades were called acceptable (*ordentliche*) trades. Weaving, blacksmithing, shoemaking, and farming were in this category of trained occupations considered to be productive and respectable. The higher levels of business were referred to as civil or citizen (*bürgerliche*) trades. Those people involved in business as merchants or shopkeepers, as well as trained professionals, belonged to this category. The government seemed to understand that the economic discrimination the Jews had suffered over the centuries had hindered them from entering these acceptable or civil trades, but it still described the Jews in negative terms:

> It deemed their religion as the cause of their moral and economic depravity. Because of their habit of laziness, the Jews always try to avoid any physical labor, and that was why they prefer the used-goods trade to an acceptable,

civil trade.... While all Christians work in labor-intensive occupations, only the Jews try to earn a living without physical labor. Although in former times the Jews had not been allowed to work in acceptable trades, over the past fifteen years, when they have been permitted to work in acceptable trades, they still, with some rare exceptions, carry on exclusively in the *schacher* trade....

Their religious traditions, including the Sabbath, kosher food, and other rituals, are mere hollow shells without religious meaning....

The Jews are disgusting, and their dirtiness can be seen in their entire appearance and in their degenerated language. These strange characteristics can be seen in all Jews, no matter whether they are born and trained [in Württemberg] or in a foreign country. They can be seen in Jewish children or Jewish adults.[4]

Despite this rhetoric the draft of the legislation included some parts that were positive advances for the Jews in business, education, and civil rights.

However, no action was taken in Parliament for the next three years. In 1827 the Jews took the initiative and established a special committee to represent all the Jews in the kingdom. Prior to that time individuals had petitioned the government to grant requests only for specific personal or community needs. This committee was the first unified action by the Jews in Württemberg.

Mühringen selected its president, Joseph David Berlizheimer, as its delegate. Seven other important Jewish communities had delegates on the committee, and six members of the important Kaulla family represented Stuttgart and the Neckar District. The small communities authorized the delegates from their district to represent their interests. The expenses of the local delegates were split among all the communities in each district. The Jewish Committee (as we will call it) sent a long, well-written petition to the king regarding the 1824 draft of the law. Each member, including Joseph David Berlizheimer, signed the document, which was subsequently published in the parliamentary record.

This petition, as well as subsequent letters and petitions, was carefully worded to be very respectful and subservient, according to the custom of the day. Suggesting a high level of political insight, the writers seemed on the surface to agree with many of the criticisms directed at the Jews. These leaders were not blind to the poor economic and educational condition of the Jews, but, by the same token, they knew that realistically the Jews could only improve their situation by having the same rights and opportunities as the Christians. They understood that the government saw itself as paternalistic; the state would give the Jews freedom gradually, after they passed through the necessary preparatory period. With this basic understanding of the situation in the early nineteenth century, the Jews worked to achieve new rights and reforms.

Couching its positions in a manner that would appeal to the authorities, the committee suggested that the new legislation would not only improve the situation of the Jews but also would enhance the welfare of all Christians, the society, and the state. Rather than comment on the number of Jews not involved in civil trades (2,600 of the 3,000 adult males), the committee used the statistics of an 1827 trade survey to highlight the 400 Jews working in or learning civil trades. It used those numbers to confirm that during the prior two decades the Jews who had struggled against the restrictions had improved their situations.[5] However, some older men included as masters in their craft or trade probably had not gone through the apprenticeship program but were listed as such due to the level of their business. In Mühringen, for instance, Joseph David Berlizheimer, Samson Grünwald, and several other middle-aged men were listed as masters when in fact they were probably too old to have gone through the apprenticeship and journeyman training system. Nevertheless, the committee claimed that if the law were enacted and the obstacles were removed, Jews would receive a positive start for the future. They would then become good members of the state.

The committee refuted the government's view that the Jews in the past had an easy way to earn their food and money. It described in detail the difficult life of the used-goods dealer, pointedly not using the word *schacher*:

> The Jew goes around with a cow or is loaded down with a big, heavy sack on his back. He always has the burden of caring for this animal or this sack in summer, in winter, during the day, and at night, without consideration of the heat and the cold, the thunderstorms and rain, from place to place, from house to house. His wandering is always the whole week from Monday to Friday. In full awe of his religion, he does not stray from the prayers of his religion or from the ceremonial food laws while he is wandering.... So it often happens that he comes exhausted and sweating or rigid from the cold to a Christian inn, and he scrapes together a meal of only potatoes and bread. This is his life. The next morning he rises up early for another journey. The proceeds from this used-goods trade are almost nothing, and caring for his family adds more worries to his already physically strained body. No one in

+ *Incredible, the millennial burden of ritual laws!*

his family can hope to do something better. How much happier is even the poorest Christian because the doors of earthly luck are not closed to him whenever he is skilled enough to go through them.[6]

Building from that emotional description, the committee went on to criticize the government for judging the Jews' willingness to work based merely on the limited changes allowed in the previous fifteen years. It claimed that it was not easy for an entire group of people to bring itself out of a centuries-old way of life. It asserted that whoever knew the Jews well would certify that they were hardworking.

Throughout the first sections of the petition, the committee very diplomatically stated how pleased the Jews were that after a long period of treatment as second-class citizens, their prospects seemed to look positive. It appreciated the initiative of the king and the intention of the proposed law to make higher education and better ways of earning a living available to the Jews. After assuring the king of its approval, the committee suggested changes to much of the government's draft. Each point was carefully supported by philosophical and factual background.

While the committee seemed to support the Christian premise of improvement through education to make the Jews become true citizens, its members undoubtedly hoped and planned that all Jews would be able to maintain their religious identity despite becoming closer to, and even part of, the German-Christian world. How did the Jews who were not part of the committee feel about these matters? Probably most supported the goals in theory, but they were more concerned with the effects of any new laws on their daily lives and on the lives of their children. Some traditional rabbis and very traditional rural Jews were concerned about the detrimental influence of further intrusion of the government into their lives and their inability to comply with the ritual laws under the potential new economic system.

+ In October 1827 a special parliamentary commission began reviewing the government's draft legislation. The proposed legislation became the subject of public discussion. The sudden proliferation of new anti-Jewish tracts and a new edition of Hundt-Radowsky's offensive *Der Judenspiegel* did not go unnoticed by the commission. When the commission issued its own draft of the law in early 1828, its changes reflected the public's open antagonism toward the Jews. Parliament's new draft seemed to take both the government and the Jews, who may have ignored the political atmosphere in the kingdom, by surprise.

Effective competition by a despised minority was always feared, it was the source of all sorts of restrictive legislation & decrees & eventually not alone in Germany but everywhere, even the U.S. it kept Jews 0 & of university... ...ties, medicine, law, heavy industry utilities (to this day!) In Hungary, Poland, etc. The success of Jews after emancipation was the source of their extinction

The parliamentary commission received more than twenty petitions from towns and cities. The most important cities of the kingdom, including Stuttgart, Ulm, the university city of Tübingen, and the former imperial cities of Schwäbisch Hall and Rottweil sent signed letters. These places for the most part allowed no Jews, or only a handful of carefully selected Jews, to live within their boundaries. The petitions, all very similar in their repetitious content and tone, demonstrated the perceived fundamental problem of trying to make the Jews productive. The townspeople, galvanized by the merchant guilds, complained that the *schacher* Jews forced unsuspecting buyers into wasteful spending and that the sellers used reprehensible business practices. At the same time, however, the petitioners were even more fearful of the competition that would hurt them if these same *schacher* Jews *did* become productive. Excerpts from the petitions formed a litany of economic fears, reinforced and exacerbated by basic anti-Jewish feelings:

> Jewish peddlers, both adults and children, are parasites doing the *schacher* trade and selling bad goods to unsuspecting peasants in the villages.... They will always choose the *schacher* trade to earn their livelihood, and eventually they will ruin the merchants.... Jews will not give up their cheating and their desire to do nothing for a very long time.... Their bad character is exemplified by their dealings with thieves who speak a language that only Jews could understand.... In other cities and states they have seized for themselves all the Christian trades as soon as they were given more rights and opportunities....
>
> Due to their tendency to engage in usury and *schacher* trade, the Jews are corrupt, cheat, and are very immoral. Their dirtiness and cheating lead to the result that no cheating is too dishonorable, nor is any crime too bad. The situation is more dangerous because no people in the world stick together more closely as they do.... When a Jew cheats a Christian, it is not a sin for the Jew.... No Jews will report a crime that a Jew perpetrates on a Christian.... False oaths are allowed....
>
> Jews only look after their own interests and want to triple these advantages but will not give anything back to the community. A century will pass before Jews will understand the term "citizen rights." Since Jews have only one aim in life—to make money and accumulate wealth—they will never be good citizens.... They can never hold an official position because their monetary interests are more important than the welfare of the state.... This part of the population will never be integrated into the Christian citizenry because of the Jews' superstition in their different ways of eating and drinking.... Even if one can believe that they can be honest and just, their superstition is the main shackle that has to be removed if there can be a community of Christians and Jews.... Jews will only change on the outside.... No matter what changes are made, Jews will always be Jews.[7]

Racial, not simply religious diagnosis a century later, Jews were among the **105** *leading citizens of Germany & even the world. Nearly 1/3 of Germany's Nobel laureates were Jews, Einstein included. German anti-Semitism, however, was little changed. Catholic leadership was about as anti-Jew as ever. Hitler was rising. In a few years, Holocaust.*

Coming from the most important economic and political centers, these petitions sent a very strong, clear message to their elected representatives: no one wanted any advantages given to the Jews that might in some way prejudice the interests of the Christians. No petitions came from the rural areas or from the villages where Jews had been residing for decades, if not centuries. Since these places did not have the political clout of the towns and cities, their conspicuous silence had no impact on the process.

Parliament scheduled for the end of February 1828 an extraordinary session of the lower chamber to discuss the draft legislation. The committee, on which Joseph David Berlizheimer still served, had no time to lose to stem the growing anti-Jewish movement. It sent a second petition to the king and Parliament. After perfunctorily thanking the government for its original draft, the committee angrily complained that Parliament's version had actually increased the limitations and restrictions on the Jews, and that the Parliament had acted contrary to the spirit of justice. Those changes would thwart the goal of the legislation to better the Jews.

The committee explained its concerns. If the parliamentary commission, composed of fifteen well-educated and respected men, had altered the draft so that its positive purpose had been destroyed, then the Jews had to fear that the full Parliament, composed as it was of members with much stronger anti-Jewish views, would place even more hardships upon them. The committee sounded the alarm that if those representatives who were involved in business held the same opinions expressed in the petitions, the mood of this Parliament would be like the negative atmosphere of previous centuries. The bottom line was that it might be safer and preferable if the present conditions were to continue and the new law were discarded. In desperation, the committee wrote, "The only true hope of the Jews is the king of Württemberg, who is a loving father of all his subjects [and] who makes efforts on behalf all the oppressed."[8] The men appealed to the king's wisdom, promising that their grandchildren would remember the blessing he could bestow upon his Jewish subjects and their descendants.

The site of the momentous debate was the elegant new Parliament building. The upper or first chamber (Kammer der Standesherrn), representing the nobility and the church, was not in session at that time. The lower or second chamber (Kammer der Abgeordneten) was composed of seventy representatives, mostly merchants and businessmen, who were elected from the counties and the large cities. Joining them were twenty-three privileged

INTERIOR OF LOWER CHAMBER OF THE WÜRTTEMBERG PARLIAMENT (Stuttgart,
Württembergisches Hauptstaatsarchiv, J 302, 1833.)

representatives from the ranks of the noble landowners, the Lutheran
Church, the Catholic Church, and the University of Tübingen.

The debate consumed ten days, and the speeches filled almost four
hundred pages of the parliamentary record. The Stuttgart newspaper, the
Schwäbischer Merkur, usually included news briefs about the events in Parliament, but due to the overwhelming interest in these debates, the editors
printed long, often verbatim excerpts of the speeches. Those of the representatives, especially the anti-Jewish representatives, received very thorough
coverage; the column space granted to the government's representatives
was much more limited.

On the first day, February 21, 1828, the narrow galleries were filled to
overflowing. After the president of the lower chamber, Dr. Jakob Weishaar,

inaugurated the session, the convocation speakers made their opening remarks. Several of them made special mention of a new anti-Jewish pamphlet, *Die Juden und ihre Wünsche* (The Jews and their wishes), by Rudolph Moser. In addition to repeating many of the views offered in the petitions, Moser had added a visual component to the complaints: "God forbid! The strong louts from Buttenhausen and Mühringen run around the markets and fairs showing off their tricks to the public, whistling like canaries and flapping their wings like quails."[9] That was not a good omen for the Jews.

Representative Karl Hofacker set the anti-Jewish tone of the debate. His forceful, demagogic speech went on for several hours; it filled twenty-seven pages of the parliamentary record. The Stuttgart newspaper gave his speech the most coverage of the entire debate: the man on the street heard what he had to say. Representative Hofacker began by pointing out that he wanted to speak about the "Jews," but nowadays one had to call them "Israelites," or "People of Israelite Religious Belief," or "People of the Israelite Denomination." His speech appealed to the emotional elements of the political debate:

> I feel sad about the rejected, despised, expelled "Jewish Nation" on which the visible curse of their God rests. I am weighing the advantages and disadvantages inflicted on the 1,500,000 Württemberg Christians by the 8,000–9,000 Jews. I speak for my beleaguered fellow citizens, the poor rural people whom the Jews have fleeced of their last [cent].
>
> The Jews for the past 1,500 years have been well known in Germany. They were always linked to each other by a network from city to city. But they were then, as now, hated and avoided. Only the kings or nobles liked them, but only for monetary reasons.... The Jews always had been separate and favored that isolation. They had remained strangers through their own fault since they never wanted to mingle with the mass [of Christians]....
>
> Before 1802 when practically no Jews lived in the Duchy of Württemberg, except for here and there a court Jew, it was a wonderful time, but these pleasant times unfortunately have disappeared.... It is technically not possible to throw the Jews out of the country because the neighboring countries will send them back under protest. Perhaps based on morality and Christianity, we the people will just have to keep these people [within our borders]....
>
> The Jews everywhere become richer than the Christians, and they reproduce themselves in a very unnerving progression.... The number of Jewish swindlers is increasing, and there is no way to stop them....
>
> The Jews are our burden through their sucking usury and *schacher* trade and rejection of an acceptable trade, through their moral and physical depravity, and through their religious and political separateness and hostile position....

> Sufficient proof that the government's draft is detrimental to the Christians is that the Jews praised the measures!... The new law should be about the Jews, not for the Jews; it should be promulgated on account of the Christians and to impede the Jews' damaging influence.[10]

Representative Christian Jakob Zahn, a lawyer and manufacturer in Calw (in the same district as the Black Forest District) and the author of a twenty-page anti-Jewish pamphlet in 1828, condemned the Jews and their beliefs in his speech to Parliament and more forcefully in his pamphlet:

> Above all I believe that absolutely no betterment of the Jews can be considered as long as they stick to the Talmud. The Jews should eliminate the dreadful contents of the Talmud from their religious services. The Jewish belief in the coming of the Messiah and their other religious beliefs prevent them from becoming loyal citizens and subjects of the king. How will the Jewish citizen fulfill his obligations to the king if the Messiah is to arrive? They are immoral, corrupt, and incapable of becoming Christian citizens.... The Jews, with their depravity, ruin the areas of the country where they have been allowed to settle....The 8,000 Jews rather than the 1,500,000 Christians should change their Sabbath from Saturday to the Christian Sunday.[11]

The legislation even called for the establishment of separate Jewish colonies in Württemberg. It would allow Jews to buy property to establish special colonies inside the kingdom. The 1828 petitions (also published as pamphlets) from Ulm and Stuttgart supported the idea. Moser's pamphlet advocated that those Jews who could not be coerced into emigrating should live and work in a specially created Jewish colony where they could work on Sundays.

During the debate Representative Hofacker explained the reasoning behind such Jewish colonies: the Jews did not work from Friday night to Monday morning and lost sixty to seventy more workdays than the Christians. On that limited schedule they just could not compete. Moreover, some representatives recommended the establishment of colonies for the poor Jews who were not working in a trade and were not being educated. In the colony, while living in government-built housing, they would farm, and the boys could be educated. Most representatives felt this was a very humane and positive idea, though in the end they decided that it would be very expensive and a huge effort to establish colonies for approximately six thousand Jews. In the final law of 1828, however, Article 20 "permits Jews to join together to set up separate colonies with their own administration and communal constitution. The state would guarantee that the Jews could purchase the necessary land and all basic facilities at reasonable prices."[12]

Not all the representatives agreed with these strong anti-Jewish views. The day after Representative Hofacker's speech, several representatives castigated him during the debate. They stated that Jews were now *"Württemberger"* not Jews or Israelites. Other representatives criticized the un-Christian characterization of all Jews as thieves, murderers, and uneducated people.

Chancellor Johannes von Autenrieth from Stuttgart presented the government's position. He belittled the representatives' exaggerated fear of the Jews. With sarcasm, he questioned whether they could actually be afraid that should the law pass, "the 9,000 Jews would immediately disrupt business and take away food from the 1,500,000 Christians?" The minister of internal affairs followed, reviewing the decrees that the government had already enacted. He pointed out that nobody had ever raised their voice against these statutes, but now he was alarmed that all of a sudden over the recent months so many voices, printed pamphlets, printed speeches, and published books had spoken against the Jews. He accused the representatives of raising an outcry against the Jewish "Nation," which in reality was scattered in eighty-four remote places in Württemberg, where it made up less than one two-hundredth part of the population and, with only a few exceptions, was its poorest segment. The minister's speech made a profound impression, as if a bolt of lightning had hit the chamber.[13]

The spectators and representatives openly expressed their reactions to the speeches and debates. Everyone laughed after a speaker remarked that one had to look at the Jews like a Hebrew book, reading from back to front. Laughter also erupted at the very idea that Jews might become professors of business and then give the Christians examinations. Emotions changed from one moment to the next. A contemporary witness described one such incident in his published review of the proceedings: "For me," the speaker concluded, "that is just why the *schacher* Jew is the most interesting (general laughter)—because, he is the most unlucky (profound silence)."[14]

At times the president of the chamber had difficulty just keeping order. He had to ring his bell loudly and often during the discussions of certain emotional topics. The spectators strained to hear the speakers during the fiery, and sometimes fierce and verbally violent, debates on the key issues of residence rights, bringing *schacher* trade and the *schacher* Jews under control, the Jews' potential participation in the state civil service, and Jewish immigration into the kingdom. On those days even more representatives attended the sessions, and the galleries and the diplomatic section were full. Only the first days of the debate, however, captured the interest of the public. Toward the end of the session, when the specific articles were discussed, the galleries were quite empty. On the final day a resurgence of interest again produced an immensely lively debate.

The Jews had become pawns in the struggle between the relatively weak and insecure parliament and the king and his ministers. The Parliament was an institution that had been restructured in 1819. Its power relative to the king and his government was in flux. Throughout the debate, whenever the representatives strayed too far from the government's draft, the minister of internal affairs would pointedly remind the chamber that the government did not even have to consult Parliament before issuing decrees and could withdraw its draft from consideration. The debate also highlighted the power struggle between the local governments and the central government. The representatives wanted the final decisions to be controlled by the village councils; the government wanted to maintain its powers. For their part, the Jews supported the central government's goal to maintain its authority since they knew from past experience that local control would be detrimental to their attaining any rights. The minister emphasized that despite "all the rage and chiding" he had witnessed, the government was not willing to redraft the law, and he expected the representatives to curb their passions and to seek the correct path.

Several representatives, who were officials in their local governments, supported the government's draft for the most part but wanted to grant the Jews citizenship gradually. It seemed that by citizenship, they meant becoming assimilated into the majority culture. One pointed out in his "friendly remarks" that there was not the smallest proof that Jews could follow the rules of civilization. Another representative asked how anyone could be surprised that the culture of such a "nation," which had been dishonored, discriminated against, and violated for 1,800 years, was not equal to the Christian culture. The mayor of Stuttgart, a lawyer, Dr. Wilbald Feuerlein, felt that hatred did not cause the resistance to the law; however, everyone wanted a guarantee that the religious and moral standards of the Jews would improve. The speeches of these representatives supported the basic tenets of the government's draft, but still exposed the fundamental anti-Jewish attitudes expressed by many representatives.

All the representatives agreed that only upon being improved and educated would the Jews gradually be granted citizen's rights. The new law adopted the long-term, open-ended, and subjective strategy of granting of civil rights in progressive stages. It was not set according to yearly plans or long-range projections. Rather, the government would grant rights based on its perception of the Jews' progress in restructuring their occupational patterns and acquiring acceptable cultural traits. This would be a step-by-step process that would reward the Jews after they had achieved certain goals. The final vote in the lower chamber demonstrated that the government had not convinced all the representatives to support the new law: sixty-one representatives approved the law, and seventeen representatives voted against it. Certain representatives were absent, including Representative Hofacker, the leader of the anti-Jewish faction.

Some members of the Jewish Committee, perhaps even Joseph David Berlizheimer, might have sat in the visitors' gallery and listened to the debates. What would have been their reaction? Probably no one was surprised. The men might have believed, as they had written in their official petitions, that times had changed in the nineteenth century. In their petitions they had acknowledged that some Jews had not had the opportunity to be educated or to learn moral behavior, but the members knew that given any prospects at all, these Jews would seize the chance to improve their lives as well as their children's lives. On that level, the committee recognized the need for change. The reality of the anti-Jewish culture Jews had lived in for centuries, the mere three decades Jews had been part of Württemberg, the anti-Jewish Hep! Hep! riots nine years earlier, and the anti-Jewish pamphlets and vitriolic petitions from the guilds in recent months would have forewarned them of what to expect. Although the Jews must have realized that the pamphlets and speeches had generalized about all Jews based on only a few, negative stereotypes, the reality of the anti-Jewish rhetoric must still have been distressing for all Jews in Württemberg—and for some, horrifying.

On April 25, 1828, eight years after Parliament's initial request, King Wilhelm I of Württemberg enacted the *Gesetz in Betreff der öffentlichen Verhältnisse der israelitischen Glaubens-Genossen* (Law regarding the public status of members of the Israelite faith). The final law was a compromise between the government and Parliament. The Jews were acknowledged as a part of the population and were no longer aliens who could be expelled at will. Württemberg accepted a measure of responsibility for the Jews who resided within its borders. The first article stated that "as far as there were no exceptions found in the law, the Jews living in the kingdom enjoy the rights of Württemberg subjects." The subsequent sixty-one articles, however, included so many exceptions that any potential improvement in the situation of the Jews was severely limited.[15]

Changes in the Families

The events of 1827–28—the new law and the rhetoric surrounding it—did not change the lives of the Jews in Württemberg overnight. Life in the villages and towns continued much as it had before. The Berlizheimer family maintained its position as one of the most prosperous families in Mühringen. Joseph David, now in his late sixties, still advertised that he sold a very good assortment of cotton and wool fabrics at very inexpensive prices. A few years later he slowed down, involving himself solely in a "not-important rural trade," according to the village administrative officer, and being supported by his sons.

The prosperity of the family was now in the hands of Joseph David and Gustel's sons David and Marx. They ran the Berlizheimer store that sold a large variety of fabrics. David continued to run his weaving factory, which stocked many colors of unspun cotton yarns. Twenty-five to thirty weavers worked in the factory, making it one of the more important businesses in Mühringen. In the course of their business David and Marx attended the regional markets. The sphere of David's business extended north some eighty miles to Tübingen and south to Lake Constance on the Swiss border. He often sold his goods on credit and made many small loans at 5 or 6 percent interest to both Christians and Jews. In an effort to diversify, David later started a match factory in the same building as the cotton factory.

In 1835 Marx, at age thirty-three, married Rosa Auerbacher. Rosa was from one of the most important families in neighboring Nordstetten. One of her cousins was the up-and-coming author Berthold Auerbach. She brought a large dowry (3,000 gulden, plus 800 gulden in gold and silver). Joseph David gave Marx the same amount for his marriage gift. Rosa's mother signed her name in Hebrew on the marriage contract. Joseph David signed the contract

Ansicht des Orts MÜHRINGEN von der Ostseite.

MÜHRINGEN 1838.

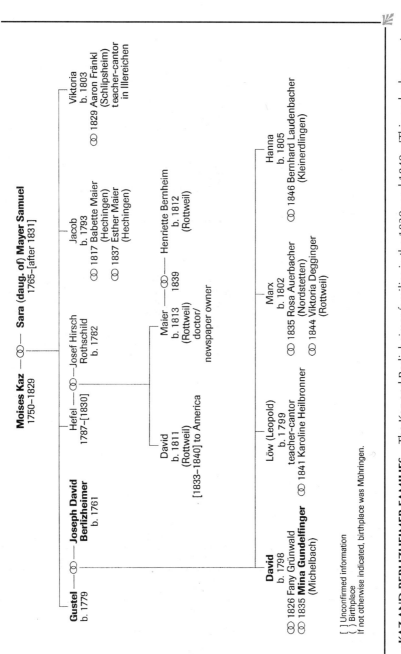

KAZ AND BERLIZHEIMER FAMILIES The Kaz and Berlizheimer families in the 1830s and 1840s. [This and subsequent family trees are presented in an abridged format.]

Moises Kaz 1750–1829 ⚭ **Sara (daug. of Mayer Samuel)** 1765–[after 1831]

Gustel b. 1779 ⚭ **Joseph David Berlizheimer** b. 1761

Hefel 1787–[1830] ⚭ Josef Hirsch Rothschild b. 1782

Jacob b. 1793
 ⚭ 1817 Babette Maier (Hechingen)
 ⚭ 1837 Esther Maier (Hechingen)

Viktoria b. 1803
 ⚭ 1829 Aaron Fränkl (Schlipsheim) teacher-cantor in Illereichen

David b. 1811 (Rottweil) · [1833–1840] to America

Maier b. 1813 (Rottweil) doctor/ newspaper owner ⚭ 1839 Henriette Bernheim b. 1812 (Rottweil)

David b. 1798
 ⚭ 1826 Fany Grünwald
 ⚭ 1835 **Mina Gundelfinger** (Michelbach)

Löw (Leopold) b. 1799 teacher-cantor ⚭ 1841 Karoline Heilbronner

Marx b. 1802
 ⚭ 1835 Rosa Auerbacher (Nordstetten)
 ⚭ 1844 Viktoria Degginger (Rottweil)

Hanna b. 1805
 ⚭ 1846 Bernhard Laudenbacher (Kleinerdlingen)

[ ] Unconfirmed information
( ) Birthplace
If not otherwise indicated, birthplace was Mühringen.

for himself and his wife Gustel. The village official noted that Gustel was blind and could not sign for herself. Did Gustel lose her eyesight from one of the eye infections or diseases that were common in those times, or did she have glaucoma, a disease that still affects her descendants? In any case, Gustel's unfocused gaze in the portrait that eventually made its way to America was thus explained. Blind by age fifty-five, she lived twenty-seven more years.

Joseph David and Gustel's second son, Löw, had worked as a journeyman in the clothes trade in the 1820s. At the age of thirty he entered the Esslingen Teachers' Seminary near Stuttgart. Either a deep commitment to teaching or an unsuccessful career in his father's trade had led him to this new career so late in life. In 1829 he enrolled as an older student who entered the seminary after receiving training with a private teacher (*Aesculant*). He did not receive any public funds during his three years of study. From that time onward, he used the name Leopold and often spelled his surname as "Berlitzheimer."

One of Leopold's fellow students was David Gundelfinger from Michelbach an der Lücke. David entered the Teachers' Seminary aspiring to study full-time, but first he had to join the younger students (*Hospitant*). He received a small stipend in his last year. Leopold and David stayed in contact during their teaching careers.

Teachers often served as marriage brokers for Jews, and sometimes for Christians as well. They had contacts in their villages of origin, with fellow students at the seminary, and in the villages where they worked. They used this network to arrange marriages between parties living in distant locations and received fees for those services. In 1834, Leopold and David most likely arranged the match of David's cousin, Sophie, with Salomon Ottenheimer in Mühringen. Usually the bride and groom brought comparable assets to the marriage, but on paper, at least, it seemed that Sophie brought considerably more assets. Why the match was made at all seems puzzling. Sophie (born Sara) was thirty and brought a medium-size dowry (1,480 gulden) to the marriage. Her future husband's situation, on the other hand, was questionable at best. On the positive side, the Ottenheimer family had lived in Mühringen since at least the early eighteenth century, coming from nearby Haigerloch, and Salomon, at age forty-three, was a protected Jew. However, he was plagued by financial problems: he declared bankruptcy in 1820, was on the list of Jewish beggars in 1830, and brought few assets (only 33 gulden, his clothes, and other small possessions) to the marriage. Sophie's father signed the translation of the marriage contract in German, and her mother signed in Hebrew. In subsequent years, Sophie would use her own funds to buy two apartments in the village. While most women owned their property jointly with their husbands, Sophie was listed as sole owner of the properties. Perhaps she was advised to protect her assets from potential creditors and from her husband's business dealings.

Meanwhile, David and Fany Berlizheimer's family grew to three sons and a daughter by 1832. Two years later Fany died. Typically, a widower with children was not a highly sought after marriage prospect because the potential groom wanted not only a wife but a housekeeper and mother as well. A match for a widower was usually made with a woman who would bring a small dowry, or who might be too old to find a more suitable match. The widower David needed such a wife-housekeeper-mother as soon as possible.

Sophie could have made the resulting match for David with her younger sister, Mina, or perhaps the two teachers—David's brother Leopold and Mina's cousin David Gundelfinger—arranged this marriage. Again, the match was a puzzling one. Why did Mina's father not make a better match for her with an unencumbered man? Her father was still working as a merchant and was a Jewish community officer in Michelbach, and she brought a medium-size dowry (1,400 gulden). At the time of her marriage, Mina, at twenty-eight, was working as a paid employee in service to a noblewoman in Mannheim in Baden.

Since it was David's second marriage, his deceased wife's assets were held separately for their children. Samuel Grünwald, Fany's brother, was the guardian who protected the interests of her children. David brought all his assets to this marriage. The wedding contract stipulated that if David should die, the four children from his first marriage would divide their deceased mother's dowry (2,250 gulden). According to the contract, David would pay the full costs of the wedding but not any transportation costs incurred by Mina's father. As was often the case with widowers with small children, the engagement period was brief, only three months. In July 1835, Mina became David's wife and the stepmother of Simson, Nehemia, Hanna, and Isaak.

Sophie and especially Mina found their new home to be a very different environment from their own background. Mühringen was a renowned and wealthy Jewish community, and the Berlizheimer family was one of the leading families in that community and in the village. Mina and Sophie's family circumstances and the history of their Jewish community, on the other hand, were typical of the smaller and poorer Jewish communities. Their great-grandfather, Jakob Gundelfinger, had settled in Michelbach before 1731, coming from the village of Gundelfingen an der Donau. Jews had lived in Gundelfingen from the end of the thirteenth century and were persecuted during the time of the Black Death. In the eighteenth century Gundelfingen did not have an established Jewish community, so after his marriage to Fradel, daughter of Salomon, Jakob settled in Michelbach. Fradel had lived in the Jewish community in Fischach, but perhaps the newlyweds could not get permission from the barons of Burgau to establish a new family there.

The Michelbach Jewish community had been established when the Jews were expelled from the imperial city of Rothenburg ob der Tauber during the sixteenth century. Many Jews retreated to the feudal estates outside its territory, from which they were able to continue doing business in the city. Michelbach an der Lücke derived its name, an der Lücke, from its location at one of the *Lücken* (gaps) in the artificial border that surrounded Rothenburg. During the Thirty Years' War in the seventeenth century, the kaiser of the Holy Roman Empire rescinded a disloyal ruler's rights over Michelbach and granted the rights to Count Georg Ludwig von Schwarzenberg as a reward for his good and spirited service. Although the von Schwarzenbergs were Catholic, the village remained Protestant. The count allowed Jews to live in his territories and even issued an official document giving the Jews permission to acquire houses and build synagogues. By 1732 the community had grown so rapidly that Jews owned thirteen of the forty-seven houses in the village.

In 1762, when Jakob and Fradel's son Elias was twenty-five, a marriage was arranged with Behle, daughter of Simon. Behle, at twenty-one, left a twenty-family Jewish community in Feuchtwangen. Jakob and Fradel's other son, David, married Sara, daughter of Bär, who lived in Michelbach. Unlike Elias and David's own father, their wives' fathers did not use surnames. Bär and Simon were most likely peddlers or small-time dealers.

The Michelbach cattle dealers, peddlers, and small-time brokers (schmoozers) went to the markets in nearby Hengstfeld, Niederstetten, and Rothenburg ob der Tauber, and to regional cattle, grain, and wool markets. By 1781 four Jewish families, including those of Elias and David, had amassed considerable assets (900 to 1,000 gulden), and six families had some assets (300 to 750 gulden). But it was a particularly poor community. Seven of the seventeen Jewish households did not own any property and had to pay only a token tax payment. Only eleven of the twenty Jewish families in 1788 could afford to pay protection money.

While trying to survive and provide for their families, Michelbach's Jews searched for ways to follow their longtime traditions. They used the same

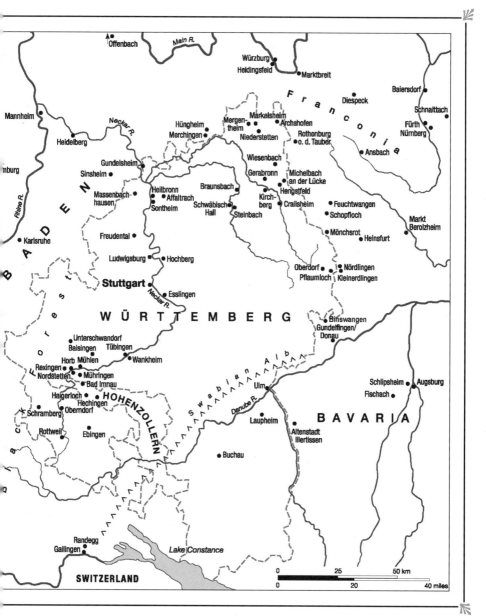

SOUTHERN GERMANY IN THE MID-NINETEENTH CENTURY   A geographical guide to the history of the Kaz, Berlizheimer, and Gundelfinger families.

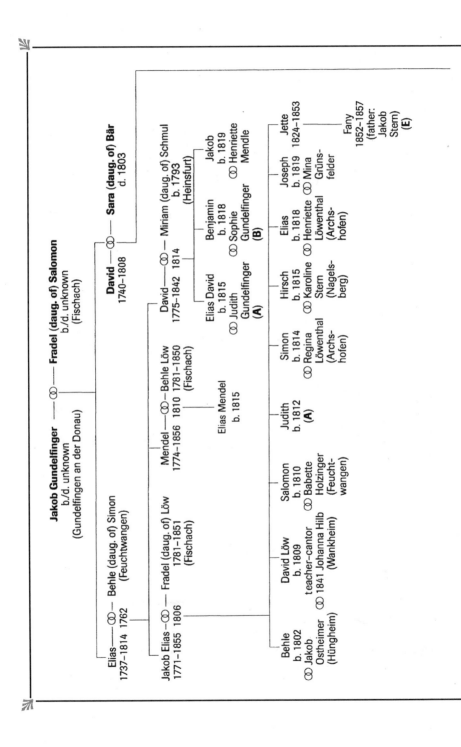

Jakob Gundelfinger ——— ⊗ ——— Fradel (daug. of) Salomon
b./d. unknown   b./d. unknown
(Gundelfingen an der Donau)   (Fischach)

Elias ——— ⊗ ——— Behle (daug. of) Simon
1737–1814 1762   (Feuchtwangen)

David ——— ⊗ ——— Sara (daug. of) Bär
1740–1808   d. 1803

Jakob Elias – ⊗ – Fradel (daug. of) Löw
1771–1855 1806   1781–1851
                    (Fischach)

Mendel ——— ⊗ — Behle Löw
1774–1856 1810 1781–1850
                 (Fischach)

David ——— ⊗ — Miriam (daug. of) Schmul
1775–1842 1814   b. 1793
                       (Heinsfurt)

Behle
b. 1802
⊗ Jakob
Ostheimer
(Hüngheim)

David Löw
b. 1809
teacher-cantor
⊗ 1841 Johanna Hilb
(Wankheim)

Salomon
b. 1810
⊗ Babette
Holzinger
(Feucht-
wangen)

Judith
b. 1812
(A)

Elias Mendel
b. 1815

Simon
b. 1814
⊗ Regina
Löwenthal
(Archs-
hofen)

Elias David
b. 1815
⊗ Judith
Gundelfinger
(A)

Hirsch
b. 1815
⊗ Karoline
Stern
(Nagels-
berg)

Benjamin
b. 1818
⊗ Sophie
Gundelfinger
(B)

Elias
b. 1818
⊗ Henriette
Löwenthal
(Archs-
hofen)

Joseph
b. 1819
⊗ Mina
Grüns-
felder

Jakob
b. 1819
⊗ Henriette
Mendle

Jette
1824–1853

Fany
1852–1857
(father:
Jakob
Stern)
(E)

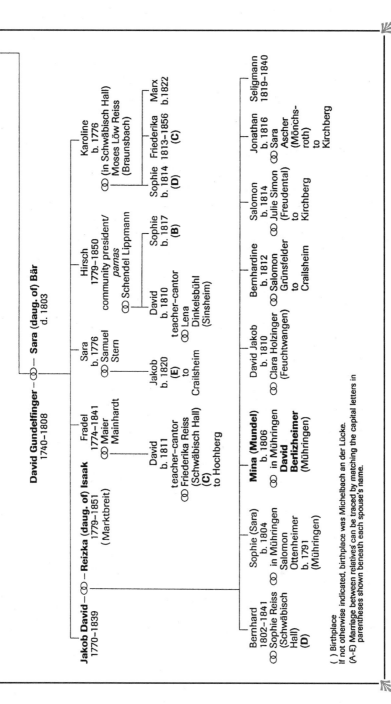

GUNDELFINGER FAMILY The Gundelfinger family traced back to the beginning of the eighteenth century.

David Gundelfinger ⊗ Sara (daug. of) Bär
1740–1808   d. 1803

Jakob David ⊗ Reizka (daug. of) Isaak
1770–1839   1779–1851
                 (Marktbreit)

Fradel
1774–1841
⊗ Maier Mainhardt

David
b. 1811
teacher-cantor
⊗ Friederika Reiss
(Schwäbisch Hall)
(C)
to Hochberg

Sara
b. 1776
⊗ Samuel Stern

Jakob
b. 1820
(E)
to Crailsheim

Hirsch
1779–1850
community president/
parnas
⊗ Schendel Lippmann

David
b. 1810
teacher-cantor
⊗ Lena Dinkelsbühl
(Sinsheim)

Sophie
b. 1817
(B)

Karoline
b. 1776
⊗ (in Schwäbisch Hall)
Moses Löw Reiss
(Braunsbach)

Sophie   Friederika   Marx
b. 1814   1813–1856   b. 1822
(D)   (C)

Sophie (Sara)
b. 1804
⊗ in Mühringen
Salomon Ottenheimer
b. 1791
(Mühringen)

Bernhard
1802–1841
⊗ Sophie Reiss
(Schwäbisch Hall)
(D)

Mina (Mundel)
b. 1806
⊗ in Mühringen
David Berlizheimer
(Mühringen)

David Jakob
b. 1810
⊗ Clara Holzinger
(Feuchtwangen)

Bernhardine
b. 1812
⊗ Salomon Grünsfelder
to Crailsheim

Salomon
b. 1814
⊗ Julie Simon
(Freudental)
to Kirchberg

Jonathan
b. 1816
⊗ Sara Ascher
(Mönchsroth)
to Kirchberg

Seligmann
1819–1840

( ) Birthplace
If not otherwise indicated, birthplace was Michelbach an der Lücke.
(A–E) Marriage between relatives can be traced by matching the capital letters in
parentheses shown beneath each spouse's name.

+ Recall Fred Brock's "idiom:" Stinks worse than a dead Jew." He
said there was "nothing anti-Semitic" about it!

cemetery in Schopfloch that many small communities in the area had used since 1612. The ten-mile journey southeast to the cemetery was difficult for the mourning family and the accompanying members of the community who traveled the long route with the coffin. In the eighteenth century the journey was expensive as well, since everyone—including the corpse—was charged the Jewish body toll when they crossed territorial borders. A wry expression, still a regional idiom, was coined during those years: "It's not worth going to
† Schopfloch for only one Jew."

Until 1756 the Jews worshiped in a private house. When the community wanted to build a synagogue, it sent Prince von Schwarzenberg an official petition asking his permission to build a synagogue. The community pointed out that the prince had previously allowed another community in his domain to build a synagogue, and that the building would provide an additional source of tax revenue for him. The prince approved the construction of the *"schule."* The newly constructed synagogue stood higher than the other houses, although the steeple of the Protestant church at the other end of the village rose even higher.

Michelbach followed the custom of most European villages and towns, naming streets for their most important characteristic. A castle gave Schlosstrasse its name. In much the same way, the location of the synagogue gave rise to the Jews' Lane (Judengasse).

With each new generation, the Gundelfinger family took on an ever-enlarging role in community life. The community elected Elias as its president around 1788. Years later, it elected David's son, Hirsch, to serve in that position. Jakob David peddled fabric in the area of Kirchberg, a nearby walled-town. Several Gundelfingers bought houses in the Jews' Lane (where Christians also owned houses). Other Jews bought houses throughout the village. Usually they shared their houses with relatives; the houses cost less than in Mühringen (250 gulden for half a house). The Jews also bought small parcels of land to use as cabbage gardens or potato fields.

To find suitable spouses for the children of Elias and David, matchmakers or relatives drew on their business and social connections over a large geographical area. David's son Jakob David married Reizka, daughter of Isaak, whose family was part of the large Jewish community in the market town, Marktbreit. Reizka's mother was from Heidingsfeld, which had become an important and large Jewish center when the Jews had been expelled from nearby Würzburg in the sixteenth century. David's daughter Karoline married a widower with children who lived in Schwäbisch Hall. Elias's sons married women

30 miles away r. 20 days

MICHELBACH SYNAGOGUE   The synagogue, constructed in 1756, was light and harmonious. At the eastern wall (facing in the direction of Jerusalem, the site of the ancient Temple), stood the Holy Ark for the Torah; it protruded from the exterior wall. Above the rounded entrance was a carved arched lintel with a Hebrew inscription "House of Assembly, Michelbach an der Lücke." On the wall to one side of the entrance they crafted a wedding stone, a frieze of the Shield of David, an unadorned six-pointed star. (In Paul Rieger, *Jüdische Gotteshäuser und Friedhöfe in Württemberg* [Stuttgart: Oberrat der Israelitischen Religionsgemeinschaft Württemberg, 1932], 102.)

from Fischach (his mother's village) and other distant villages, and his daughters moved to villages more than twenty-five miles from Michelbach.

By the end of the eighteenth century, the village had grown to 549 inhab- +
itants, including 150 Jews (twenty-six families). Compared to the relative stability of Mühringen, the political situation in Michelbach changed frequently. In 1796 Prussia acquired several feudal estates that included Michelbach. Ten years later, by a treaty with Napoléon, Michelbach became part of the Kingdom of Bavaria. The next year it became part of the Kingdom of Württemberg.

+ Much higher % than one finds in the Palatinate Towns villages.

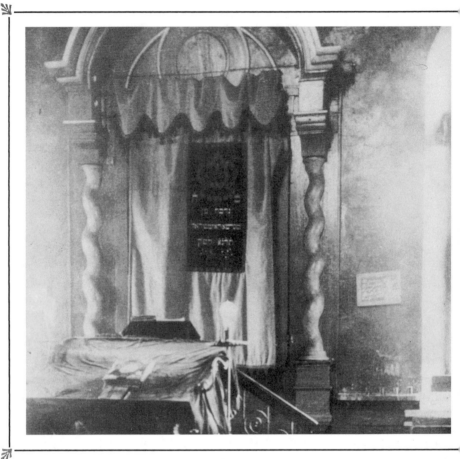

MICHELBACH SYNAGOGUE, INTERIOR   The interior walls were richly decorated with geometric patterns painted in pastel colors. (Kreisarchiv Schwäbisch Hall, 1930.)

As a result of these changes, the village lost parts of its territory, so it had few communal assets by the beginning of the nineteenth century.

Even as the Jews established themselves and continued to develop a livelihood in the village, the Christian authorities were voicing complaints and anti-Jewish sentiments. In 1808 the Bavarian king sent a report to the deacon in the nearby city of Crailsheim after its parish office had complained about the "mischief" caused by the Jews on Sundays and holidays before church services when, as reported to the police, they engaged in trading. A few years later, Protestant Pastor Friedrich Zink's official report, titled "Die

[handwritten: Current black Jew-haters use nearly identical language or worse.]

Changes in the Families

moralischen und religiösen Zustände der Gemeinde Michelbach" (The moral and religious conditions of the Michelbach community) described the Jews in very unflattering terms:

> One could with full support be satisfied with the religiousness of the community....But, based on personal observations and the experience of others, in most places where Jews live morality has declined. The conduct of this mostly *+* lazy, cheating, and profit-sucking nation is infectious.... In particular, the vice of sensuality, has increased in high measure by the abolishment of the fornication penalty; of the 31 children born in the previous year, no less than 11 were illegitimate.... [A]nd—*o tempora o mores*—an irresponsible prostitute who already had two illegitimate children got involved with an unmarried Jewish man in a sinful relationship and had a son on June 30th of the previous year.[1]

Michelbach did not escape the hard times of the Hunger Years, and some of the Gundelfingers were involved in activities that could have contributed to the area's economic difficulties. One time in 1812, a local tax official had given a Gundelfinger permission to deal in horse trading outside the kingdom, although the central government had forbidden such trade during wartime. He was not punished for this offense, but the minister of internal affairs fired the local tax official a few years later for his negligence. In another incident, the district government accused a Gundelfinger of conducting forbidden trade. He had contracted with a farmer to buy grain that had not yet been harvested. Both parties declared that they did not know that such activity was forbidden by law. The farmer claimed he was in debt to the Jew and was afraid that if he did not fulfill the contract, he would be forced to sell his land. The government decided not to punish either party, but the village head official, who had approved the contract, received a warning.

Nonetheless even in these difficult times, the Jews were very much a part of the village. The Protestant pastor reported that the Jews helped the Christians harvest their crops in 1816 and 1817. He also recorded that many Jews attended a special service organized to pray for a good harvest, noting that the ritual made the Jews very emotional. *[handwritten: "It was the best of times, it was the worst of times." By 1940–45 in Europe, it was only the worst.]*

While the size and wealth of communities like Mühringen could support both a rabbi (shared with other communities) and a cantor, one person filled the two positions in Michelbach. In 1815 the Jewish community signed a contract with a new rabbi-cantor, Schlomo Katz, from Diespeck, Bavaria. The contract stated that the entire community gathered "at the home of the wealthy community leader Hirsch G'P [Gundelfinger]" to hire a rabbi by a majority vote for a period of three years.[2]

The contract listed exactly what Rabbi Katz was allowed to do: serve as the cantor and rabbi; decide questions of permission and prohibition; perform marriages; and act in all ways fitting for the rabbinate. He was to lead prayers on the Sabbath, holidays, and weekdays. Rabbi Katz earned an annual salary (150 gulden) and was given an apartment in the community

Fees for Services as Rabbi and Cantor

Service or ritual performed	
For the honor of being called to the Torah on the Sabbath or a holiday	4 kreuzer Poorer men: 2 kreuzer
Read Book of Esther on Purim	1 thaler (1.76 gulden) extra, paid from the charity fund
Write engagement documents	1/4 thaler
Write wedding contract	1 gulden
Sing prayers on behalf of a groom before marriage and on behalf of a woman after childbirth	1/2 kreuzer

Services performed in connection to the women's ritual bath (*mikveh*) by the cantor and his wife	
For a bride's first visit	1 gulden
For a bride's second visit	30 kreuzer
For each monthly immersion	4 kreuzer

Services performed as the ritual slaughterer (*shoḥet*)*	
Large animals	The heart fat and two legs (The heart fat was used to make candles and soap.)
Small animals	The heart fat and four legs
Calves	Three legs
Slaughtered animal—not belonging to a Jew	The legs (He did not have the right to the heart fat if the animal was not kosher.)
Travel outside the community on behalf of a member	1/2 kreuzer per hour of travel time
Slaughter an animal outside the town on behalf of the whole community	The heart fat and the legs, but no travel money

Fees were paid for every animal slaughtered, whether it was found to be kosher or not.

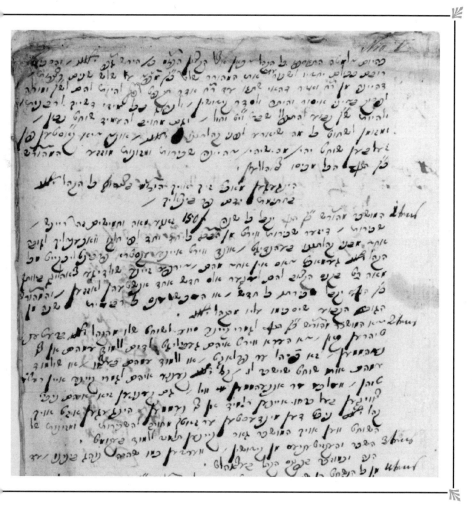

PAGE FROM RABBI'S CONTRACT, 1826   About 80 percent of the contract was in Hebrew, with the rest in German written with Hebrew characters. Numbers written in Latin script designated the order of articles in the contract and the amount of his salary. All the signatures [not shown] were written in Hebrew: Hirsch Gundelfinger, followed by his title, president of the regional community; Schlomo Katz, Mendel Gundelfinger, and twenty other members. (Ludwigsburg, Staatsarchiv E212 Bü 219, Contract 1810/1835; photo: Haupstaatsarchiv Stuttgart. All rights reserved.)

house and the use of its garden. Every week each family had to pay its corresponding portion to the payment collector, who would then pay the rabbi every month, or at least every quarter. The contract described in detail the services the rabbi could perform and the fees he would receive.

An unusual fee listed in Rabbi Katz's contract (perhaps charged by other cantors) was collected from itinerant peddlers or beggars. When a "guest" slept in the community house, he had to pay Rabbi Katz 1 kreuzer. In return, the rabbi had to provide the straw on which the visitor would sleep. Rabbi Katz earned about the same as other cantors who served in poor or small communities.

Michelbach remained a poor village, and the status of the Jews reflected that overall economic and political condition. The Protestant pastor wrote in another report (this one in 1818) that the Jews had no inclination to have a civil, acceptable trade; rather, they only did peddling and schmoozing and were very active subdividing and reselling real estate. He reported that some of them were still involved in land deals, although Jews had recently been prohibited from dealing in real estate. To get around that law, the pastor remarked, some brokers used Christians as fronts for their contracts. In an effort to curtail that practice, the county court issued an official order outlawing fictitious contracts under threat of severe punishment and ordered the village councils to examine each contract for false buyers.

The Gundelfingers had been using their surname for at least a century. Although the Christian noble Gundelfinger family and Christians from the several Gundelfingen villages also used that surname, the Jewish Gundelfingers had been allowed to retain the name. Several other Jews in the area were already using surnames in the 1820s:

Surnames Maintained

Name	Meaning or derivation	Name	Meaning or derivation
Elkan	Elchanan, biblical name	Landauer	Landau, a village or meadow
Grünsfelder	Grünsfeld, a village or green field	Stern	Star

Other families took on new surnames derived from specific places or creative descriptions:

New Surnames Adopted

Name	Meaning or derivation	Name	Meaning or derivation
Leininger	Leiningen, a village	Rosenthaler	Rose valley
Löwenberg	Lion mountain	Schönmann	Handsome man
Mainhardt	A village	Strauss	Bunch of flowers
Ries	A geographical area around Nördlingen	Unterdörfer	Lower village
		Wassermann	Water man

Changes in the Families

As was customary, the given names of the Gundelfinger male cousins honored their deceased forefathers, so many names were combinations of David, Jakob, and Elias. The family continued to use these traditional given names throughout the nineteenth century. The Gundelfinger girls, on the other hand, took on more modern given names by the 1820s: Mundel to Mina, Sara to Sophie, Behle to Babette, and Fradel to Friederika.

In the 1820s Michelbach had only three journeymen among its 175 Jews. One was a butcher, another a shoemaker, and Mina's brother, David Jakob, was a saddler. Hirsch's only son became a private teacher in Sinsheim in Baden, which had seventy-five people in its Jewish community. While many of the Gundelfinger women moved to other villages, the number of cousins grew so that by the 1830s, the Gundelfingers made up more than a fourth of the Jewish population of Michelbach.

What a change Mühringen must have been for Sophie and Mina when they married into such a prestigious and wealthy community! While Sophie married into a smaller, poorer family in an important community—itself an adjustment—Mina's new family was clearly economically and socially above her family and life in Michelbach. Aware of her new surroundings, she was careful not to jeopardize her standing. Years after her wedding, Mina admitted to her siblings that she had contributed her earnings from her years in service to her dowry, but she never shared this fact with her "new house." Her lower status as second wife and stepmother might have made for difficult times. At least Sophie and Mina had each other's company, and they maintained close ties with their relatives back in Michelbach.

In contrast to the continued prosperity of the Berlizheimer family in Mühringen, the Kaz family in Rottweil remained weakened after its bankruptcy. The newspaper announced the death of tradesman Moises Kaz, eighty-nine years old, on January 17, 1829. He had served as the local supplier and banker for the town of Rottweil for fifty years and had become very wealthy and important. However, unlike the court agents, who saw their wealth and power increase, Moises' son and son-in-law had not expanded their businesses. Jacob Kaz and Josef Hirsch Rothschild seemed to lack his drive, initiative, and business acumen. According to the town council, as a result of his bankruptcy in 1821, Moises died in great poverty. Since there was no cemetery in Rottweil, he was buried in his native village of Mühringen.

[handwritten annotations: "So Moses was 63 when he was born in the... 1860? 1798~ Why did Jews work... they have many children from ~1798"]

A few months after his death, Moises' youngest daughter, Viktoria, married at twenty-six. Moises' son must have tried to make a suitable match for her, but the bankruptcy could have restricted his efforts. Young women with small dowries often could marry only schoolteachers, who also brought but a small amount of assets to the marriage and had limited future earnings. Viktoria's dowry (1,000 gulden) was an acceptable size, but perhaps the potential debt claims against her father's estate precluded a better match. In any case, she married Aaron Fränkl, age thirty, a teacher in Altenstadt, which was the predominately Jewish section of Illertissen, Bavaria. Aaron (born Ascher) grew up in a Catholic hamlet, Schlipsheim, near Augsburg, Bavaria, which had a small Jewish community. His widowed mother owned one of the nine apartments in the Jewish House (*Judenhaus*). Aaron had just become the Jewish community's first trained religious and elementary school teacher. Most of Altenstadt's four hundred Jews lived in the streets around the large synagogue; the teacher and his family lived next door in the new building. *[handwritten: ~39 when Viktoria born.]*

Moises' death placed more responsibilities on his sixty-five-year-old widow, who, like Moises, signed documents only in Hebrew. After Moises' death, one of his houses was sold to buyers outside the family. Sara sold the remaining half of the other house to her daughter-in-law Babette. That contract stipulated that Sara could keep one room at the back of the house and had the right to use the kitchen for the rest of her life. Josef Hirsch owned the other half of the house. Jacob and Josef Hirsch shared the store and office. One room in the house continued to be used as the synagogue.

[handwritten: + "Contract". Evidently all sorts of arrangements were governed by Contracts, even within families. Rather odd by current standards]

MOISES KAZ'S HEADSTONE, MÜHRINGEN JEWISH CEMETERY   The scalloped headstone was chiseled in deeply cut Hebrew letters, but only two fingers of the symbol of the *Kohanim* remain visible. The inscription "Moises Kaz. Son of Leopold. From Rottweil" appears in a semicircle tracing the rounded shape of the stone. The lower part of the inscription was an acrostic, using the first letters of his name:

> From the righteous family of priestly lineage.
> A great community representative for far and near.
> Who satisfies the hungry and thirsty with goods.
> All his deeds were in faith and love.
> A confident envoy in good days.
> May his soul be bound up in the bond of everlasting life.

(Mühringen Jewish Cemetery, Grave #409, Stadtarchiv Horb; photo: Marek Leszczyński.)

ה
פ"נ

בוגזע ישרים בתים השובים
שומדין גדול לרחוק ולקרבי
הישב"ים טוב ובמאורעים
בכל מעשהו באמונה וחביים
ויראו נאמ'בניםטובים
תנצבה

KOHANIM HEADSTONE The symbol of the *Kohanim*, two hands giving the sign of benediction, adorned the stone. The descendants of the tribe of Aaron, priests of the ancient Temple, blessed worshipers on particular occasions. During these ceremonies, neither the priests nor the worshipers were permitted to look at the priests' hands as the *Kohanim* raised them over their heads, fingers separated to form openings through which the blessed radiance of God streamed down on the worshipers. (Mühringen Jewish Cemetery, Grave #272, Stadtarchiv Horb; photo: Marek Leszczyński.)

Moises' financial situation before his death continued to have repercussions for Sara. When the town council made a claim for an outstanding
debt (640 gulden), Sara went to the council personally to ask them to lower
the sum she owed. She supported her petition by stating that the town
should recognize that her husband had provided excellent services for it,
especially during wartime. The council acknowledged the contributions he
had made thirty years earlier and lowered the sum by a third. No other
claims from the Württemberg government or from private individuals
against Moises Kaz were ever repaid; according to the decision of the town
council, his few remaining assets belonged to his widow and children.

After the bankruptcy in 1821, Jacob regained some of his assets and
retained his house and store. In 1835 Jacob's wife died, leaving him with
three young children. Babette was not buried in the cemetery in her birthplace, Hechingen, but rather in the Mühringen cemetery, directly up the hill
from her father-in-law's grave. Babette left a large estate (4,000 gulden) to
her three children. Within eighteen months Jacob married Babette's sister,
Elise (Esther). She gave birth to seven children, but only two of them survived infancy.

Unlike Jacob, Josef Hirsch Rothschild never recovered from the bankruptcy. His wife died around the same time as her father and sister-in-law,
and Hefel was buried in the Mühringen cemetery next to their graves. Her
four grown children inherited her estate (3,000 gulden), which was used in
part to pay their apprentice fees and school payments. In 1830, at age forty-
eight, Josef Hirsch sold many of the family's possessions. Besides silver, jewelry, and household goods, he also advertised the sale of a very fine piano.
Josef Hirsch's poor financial situation may have pushed his son, David, who
had apprenticed in business, to immigrate to America sometime between
1833 and 1840.

Josef Hirsch's precarious position was also a problem for his other son,
Maier, but this son's activities increased his father's financial difficulties.
Maier became one of the early Jewish university students. Even before 1828,
no law precluded Jews from attending university in Württemberg, and a
handful of wealthy foreign and Württemberg Jews did attend its only
university, the University of Tübingen. The law of 1828 opened educational
opportunities to young Jews who, just the same as Christian youths, were
now officially allowed to attend university in Württemberg. By 1833 more
Jewish young men were studying at the University of Tübingen: fifteen,
including Berthold Auerbach of Nordstetten, studied "Mosaic theology";

two studied medicine; three studied law; and eight were in the humanities. Other than the university students, no Jews lived in the city of Tübingen, which only a few years earlier had sent anti-Jewish petitions to the Parliament.

Maier must have shown intellectual promise from an early age. After he graduated from the academic secondary school in Rottweil, he obtained permission from the government to begin medical studies at the University of Tübingen in 1831. He was only the eighth Jewish medical student to attend the university. Emil Auerbach from Nordstetten was the only other Jew in his class of about a hundred students. It was not unusual for some students from towns like Rottweil to face academic difficulties at university. For unknown reasons, Maier had a very weak and uneven scholastic record. His grades in the traditional medical courses ranged from one "very good" to "incomplete knowledge" to "insufficient efforts."

Maier's financial situation was even more difficult, but he seemed to have contributed to the severity of the problem. Over the years in Tübingen, he boarded in the homes of a Christian surveyor, a lathe operator, and a saddler. At times he was unable to pay his rent or for his books, course fees, food, medicine, and other goods. Maier also accrued seemingly frivolous debts that he owed to various service people (including a ballroom dancing instructor, a tailor, a shoemaker, and a driver). His personal financial situation deteriorated to such an extent, and he accumulated so many debts (more than 500 gulden by 1835), that he had to leave the university. His father, at fifty-four, had no assets and so could not solve his son's dilemma. When Maier returned to the university, the officials informed him that he could not take his examinations until he paid off what he owed.

Eventually Maier paid off enough debts to be allowed to take the official state examination. His written paper discussed children born with birth defects and how those children developed. The results of the examinations were unsatisfactory in all subjects. The university advised him to take no more examinations at that time; after a year, he would be allowed to take the examinations again. The next semester he stayed in Tübingen and was tutored in nearly all his subjects; his effort was recorded as diligent. When he took the examinations again, the results were satisfactory in all subjects. Maier passed the state medical examination, but he still had a lot of outstanding debts. Josef Hirsch's four children sold their half of the house to the children of Jacob's first wife. Maier must have used his share of the proceeds from the house sale to pay off his debts.

In 1838 Maier began to practice medicine in Mühringen. Prospects for attracting patients were favorable since the Jewish population there, and in the other nearby villages of the district, was large. Maier's family was also already well known, given that his father and maternal grandfather were originally from Mühringen; he still had many cousins in the community. Maier married Henriette, the daughter of innkeeper and trader Abraham Bernheim of Rottweil. We can only surmise that they decided not to settle in Rottweil because of concerns that a Jewish doctor would not be accepted in the town. The grandson of Moises Kaz had come a long way, but perhaps, like his ancestor, he was ahead of the times.

The New Jewish Community

J oseph David Berlizheimer's life spanned decades of change in the Jewish community. He grew up in a closed autonomous community that was segregated and separated from the Christians and the central government. In later years he was involved in leading his community as the government chiseled little chinks in the Jewish community's invisible walls. These changes were relatively minor compared to the reforms and developments that he participated in during the 1830s and 1840s.

The basic organization of Württemberg Jewry was transformed after 1828. Before then, autonomous communities joined together into district organizations. In 1821, the government had wanted to set up the system used in other European states: one rabbi as chief rabbi (*Oberrabbiner*) representing all the Jews in the kingdom. Rabbi Adler of Mühringen had explained that the community officers in his Black Forest District (including Joseph David Berlizheimer) believed they did not need a chief rabbi because they already had a rabbi who could perform all the necessary duties. The Jewish leaders conferred in 1821 and, with the exception of one court Jew, were against the government's plan. Some of them felt there was no need for a hierarchy; others just did not want to pay for it.

The government's 1824 draft legislation discarded the idea of a chief rabbi but did set up a superior authority composed of a government commissioner, a Jewish religious expert, and at least four other Jews as regular members. The 1827 Jewish Committee reacted positively to the concept but suggested that the Jews should have direct input into the selection process. The Jewish teachers, on the other hand, were against any increase in the power of the rabbis. In their petition they urged the government to choose the members so that those officials would not be subject to undue influence.

While Parliament and the general public debated the economic and political issues at length, the articles relating to the relationship between the Jews as a religious group and the state quickly passed in the lower chamber with hardly any discussion. Parliament accepted the establishment of a political organization placing the Jews within the Christian government system. The representatives believed that the changes would result in more control over the Jews and would make them more "German."

The government established the Königlich Israelitische Oberkirchenbehörde (Royal Israelite Supreme Ecclesiastical Authority, which we will call the Jewish Board). The Jewish Board would be responsible for overseeing the Jewish community, including carrying out regulations regarding the poor. The Protestant and Catholic Church Authorities, and now the Jewish Board, reported to the Superior Church Authority. The Superior Church Authority reported to the Ministry of Internal Affairs; the Jewish Board thus had official status in the secular government. The board was charged with enforcing the changes stipulated by the Law of the Israelites (as the 1828 law regarding the public status of members of the Israelite faith was called).

Parliament ignored the suggestions of the Jewish Committees regarding the selection process. The board was finally constituted in 1831. Since Jews were not allowed to be government officials, the position of president went to a Catholic judge who was also a member of the Catholic Church Authority. The government chose Dr. Carl Weil, the private academic teacher of the Kaulla family of court Jews, as secretary. Dr. Weil was a foreigner from Frankfurt who had only recently received Württemberg citizenship rights. He held a doctor of philosophy from the University of Heidelberg and had passed the Württemberg state examination. He had worked as a journalist and had authored the letter the teachers had sent to Parliament and another pamphlet on Jewish rights. His appointment reflected the power of the Kaullas.

The selection of the theological member was more delicate and more difficult. The influence of the Kaulla family was again evident with the appointment of its family rabbi, Dr. Joseph Maier. After attending the Fürth yeshivah, he studied theology at the University of Heidelberg, and earned his doctorate from the University of Tübingen. Although he was an ordained rabbi, he used the title "Doctor." From the outset of his tenure, some communities were skeptical and even antagonistic toward Dr. Maier because of his secular background and his uncompromising push for reform. Since many of these same communities also resented and resisted

+ Obviously, wealth = influence. But now, one supposes, diluted.

the very existence of the Jewish Board, Dr. Maier's appointment intensified their concerns.

The twenty-five articles of the 1828 law regarding taxation, community officers, and the employment of the rabbis generally stripped more powers from the local communities. One change called for a "church" tax, modeled on the central government's traditional church tax, assessed on every individual, who by law had to belong to a Christian church. The board set up a two-tier tax system, and even in the official government documents and forms, the taxes were called by their Hebrew designations. A personal tax (*rosche bajis*, or head of household) was assessed on each married head of a household (6 gulden) and on widows (3 gulden). In a few instances the community officers approved individual discounts or full exemptions from the personal tax. In Mühringen many very poor members did not pay any personal tax.

The other tax was a tax assessment on a portion of a person's assets (*erach*, or asset value). This was a tax calculated so that the wealthier Jews would pay a larger amount. The members' total assets were figured by one of the community officers and discussed at a community meeting. That meeting was often quite heated, but since it was impossible to hide anything in a small village, equitable amounts were usually assessed. The funds collected by these two taxes went directly to the treasury of the Jewish Board, which then paid the rabbis, the teachers, its own officials, and apprentice stipends. It returned a portion to the local communities for their synagogues and poor funds.

The law of 1828 changed the system of community administration that had existed for centuries, in which a president governed with a board of officers. Under the new law the administration was composed of the rabbi or the cantor and at least three men elected by the community and *+* approved by the government. These community officers were responsible for carrying out "church" regulations and other community business and for seeing that their members complied as well. The officers could only levy small fines that would go to the "church" community treasury. The officers or the rabbi were forbidden to levy other "church" punishments, and if they did so they could be severely penalized. This new system appeared to be more democratic, with power and responsibilities shared among several officers. In some communities where one person or family had wielded autocratic omnipotence for decades, it was a welcome improvement.

Portraits of Our Past

In Mühringen, Joseph David Berlizheimer remained president of the community until 1832, when he, the village administrator, Rabbi Adler, Cantor Salomon Löwenthal, and the treasurer began the process of establishing a new administration. Because the community consisted of more than four hundred people, it had to elect five members as officers. Twenty-nine of the eligible forty-nine members cast their votes, and the results were quite close. Joseph David was elected as an officer, although he did not receive the highest number of votes. When two men tied for the last position, the administrator ruled that the older candidate had priority. Rabbi Adler and the officers formed the supervising council. Of these five officers, two members were appointed to care for the "church" and another was appointed to be the treasurer.

The responsibilities of hiring, dismissing, and paying the local rabbi were transferred by the Law of the Israelites to the board and the government. The 1827 Jewish Committee acknowledged the need to make some changes to the existing system so that qualified rabbis would be hired. The committee suggested to the government that having the rabbi's salary come from the central Jewish "church" treasury rather than the individual communities would be beneficial. Such a system would ensure that the rabbi's salary would not be dependent on the financial circumstances of each community; in this manner, even poor communities could have a well-educated rabbi. Another benefit of a fixed salary would be that the rabbi would not be dependent upon the donations of certain wealthy members, which, the committee admitted, had led some rabbis to act dishonorably. These suggestions were adopted in the law of 1828. Also included were regulations that the rabbis could not serve as ritual slaughterers or, like the Christian clergy, hold another official position or be involved in trade. In subsequent years the salaries of all the rabbis became more equal (500 to 590 gulden), but their income from other services still varied depending on the size and wealth of the communities they served.[1]

Previously, rabbis in Württemberg were chosen for their erudition, wisdom, and knowledge of the Torah, Talmud, and Jewish laws and rituals, all of which they had gathered over years of religious study. The government sought to transform the rabbis into functionaries similar to Christian ministers by bringing the rabbinical qualifications in line with the credentials required of the Christian clergy. The government in 1821 had suggested that the rabbis should have a general background in science or philosophy. The prominent Jews requested that the study of philosophy at the university level not be required because school and lodging fees and the problem of kosher food would make attending the university difficult. The Jewish leaders stated that only the knowledge of German, rhetoric, and logic should be required, but the government rejected these suggestions. The Jewish Committee of 1827 was very concerned about the qualifications for the rabbis as outlined in the government's draft. It pointed out that study at a yeshivah in Frankfurt, Fürth, or Würzburg, coupled with some years of experience, should be satisfactory. The government ignored the committee's concerns. The Law of the Israelites and subsequent regulations required new rabbis to study Mosaic theology, pursue general studies at a university, provide good references, and pass a state examination.

The committee was also worried about the requirement that current rabbis pass a qualifying exam. It described eloquently the potential plight of the elderly, revered rabbis who might not be able to learn the necessary material in time for the qualification exam because of their age or because they were working. The committee strongly warned that it would be immoral for those rabbis or cantors to lose their positions because they depended on the "church" community and lacked sufficient assets to support themselves.

A special commission carried out the Württemberg state requirements. It was composed of the Jewish member of the board, Dr. Joseph Maier; one professor each from the Protestant and Catholic theology faculties; four philosophy professors; and Rabbi Grünwald of Mühringen, who had studied at the Fürth yeshivah and at the University of Würzburg. Some of the rabbis had no difficulty with the oral and written examinations. Rabbi Adler of Mühringen took the examinations in 1834. He wrote nine long essays in German, with notations in Hebrew. One essay was a written translation of the section of Talmud dealing with marriage between relatives. Rabbi Adler received impressive results in rabbinical law, preaching, sermon delivery, pedagogy, Hebrew Bible, Talmud and ritual law, and Mosaic belief and customs.[2]

The fate of Rabbi Joseph Maier Schnaittach of Freudental, on the other hand, represented the failure of the rigid system. At age sixty-seven, Rabbi Schnaittach was revered throughout the region as a talmudic scholar who was well versed in Kabbalah, the study of mysticism. It was not surprising that he scored poorly in the examination in business and sermon delivery because he had never needed those skills. His unsatisfactory grade, however, in Mosaic belief and customs—an area in which he clearly had a very high level of proficiency—caused him to fail the examination. Based solely on the results of his examination, the board fired him. He subsequently remained in Freudental living on a meager pension from the board.

Rabbi-Cantor Salomon (Schlomo) Katz in Michelbach was also affected by the new rules. His situation could have been viewed as either the necessary removal of an unqualified rabbi or the arbitrary use of the law to thwart the wishes of a community. Perhaps because of his age or his limited educational background, Rabbi Katz did not take the rabbinical or the cantorial examinations, and he was advised that he could not continue in his position. The community presented petitions in support of its rabbi, pointing out that Rabbi Katz had held that office for twenty years, and expressed its concern that at age sixty-three, with a wife and seven children who were still not self-supporting, he had no trade and few assets. The Protestant pastor also wrote a very positive reference about Rabbi Katz's behavior. The community members, including three Gundelfingers, signed the request. Rabbi Katz also sent petitions to the board, but it refused to change its decision. It ruled that the community could employ Rabbi Katz only as an additional cantor or deputy rabbi at its own expense, but of course such an action was not feasible in that poor community. After Rabbi Katz's dismissal, Michelbach no longer had a rabbi who resided in the village; its teacher served as the cantor. Rabbi Katz and his family remained in the village and received a tiny annual pension. He served as a judge for ritual matters there and in the nearby communities and for these services, according to the board, he could be paid privately. Michelbach's new rabbi served several communities from his district office in Braunsbach, twenty-five miles west of the village.

The requirement of a university education for rabbis was the death knell of the centuries-old Fürth yeshivah, where most of the Württemberg rabbis had studied. By the 1820s, dissension and uncertainty concerning its role in the formation of future rabbis, cantors, and teachers in the south German states led to chaos within the school. Although it still had eighteen teachers and more than eighty students, the Bavarian government closed the yeshivah in 1829.

Within only a few years, the Jewish Board reorganized the sixty-nine communities into thirteen rabbinical districts, with one rabbi for each district, and it dismissed forty-five rabbis for lack of proper educational qualifications. The central organization wanted to capitalize on its new power. Some communities, however, did not acquiesce. They fought to maintain control over their rabbis and teachers. The experiences in Mühringen in the 1830s demonstrated the tug of war between the local community and the board.

Rabbi Adler's contract was up for renewal. His strong credentials should have assured his tenure. He had passed the state examinations and had been appointed one of the district rabbis. He was considered a talmudic scholar whose inquiries were mentioned in the responsa of Rabbi Wolf Hamburg, the head of the Fürth yeshivah. His status was enhanced by the position of his younger brother, Nathan, first as chief rabbi in Hanover and later as chief rabbi of Great Britain and the British Empire. Still, Rabbi Adler was concerned about his future in Mühringen, and he wrote a letter to the board stating that he was sure he enjoyed the trust of the community.

By that time Joseph David Berlizheimer's son, David, was a community officer and was involved in the efforts to retain Rabbi Adler. The teacher, Michael Hirsch, wrote a letter of support that was signed by the officers from the five communities in the district. It formally requested that the board use its best efforts to renew Rabbi Adler's contract, citing his untiring efforts in all five communities over the past twenty-two years. Despite these efforts, the board transferred Rabbi Adler from the Black Forest District, with its 1,576 Jews, to the smaller, less prestigious Oberdorf District, which had only 1,104 Jews. Dr. Joseph Maier might have wanted and needed to show his new power over all the Jewish communities by going against the wishes of the important Black Forest District. He also may have wished to install one of the new breed of young, university-educated rabbis in this important rabbinical district.

Rabbi Moses Wassermann became the new rabbi in the Black Forest District. His father, a private teacher, had served later in life as the rabbi in Laupheim and Mergenheim. Moses Wassermann had graduated from the academic high school in Ulm, studied in Laupheim and in Ansbach, and attended the University of Würzburg. He had earned a university degree in Jewish religious studies (studying philosophy and theology) from the University of Tübingen. During his academic years he became friends with a young Kaulla who was studying law. Rabbi Wassermann had served in Mergenheim for one year when Dr. Maier transferred him to Mühringen. He was only twenty-three. He served for two years as provisional rabbi; after his second examination he became the permanent rabbi for the Black Forest District.

Not long after his arrival, a situation developed that tested the rabbi, the community, and the new bureaucracy. Rabbi Wassermann had been placed in a community against the wishes of that community, and his authority was derived from the board rather than from the community officers. When Rabbi Wassermann felt that his housing was unsuitable for him and his family, for instance, he complained to the county and subsequently to the board. He explained that the rabbi's quarters in the community house in Mühringen received little sunlight and overlooked the neighbor's out-house. The structure was weak and in very poor condition; all the rooms, but especially the community room, were infested with bedbugs. He needed a suitable house with heated rooms to use as his home and district office. The county government agreed with his petition, but the question of fi-nancing the project remained. Rabbi Wassermann probably underestimated the community's will to fight and overestimated its allegiance to its new young rabbi. The officers, including David Berlizheimer, commissioned a professional architectural rendering of the existing building and its sur-roundings and included it in their response. In the officers' opinion, the rabbi's complaint was unwarranted since two other rabbis had lived there previously without any problems. They suggested, with a note of sarcasm, that since the government was paying part of the rabbi's salary, it should pay for his new housing as well. The community criticized Rabbi Wasser-mann for requesting expenditures when he knew it could not pay for them. They explained the rabbi knew that sixty community members paid the stan-dard personal tax, but the other half of its members, who possessed few or no assets, could not afford to pay the church taxes. The officers requested that the authorities tell the rabbi to calm down and be patient. The author-ities did not order the community to build a new house. In that instance the Mühringen community won.

At times several issues seemed to be intertwined. Some conflicts that came to the attention of the authorities in Michelbach illustrated the re-sentment of the changes brought on by the law of 1828. One issue related to marriage ceremonies. Ritual law did not require a rabbi to perform marriage ceremonies, but the new law ordered that the rabbis had to perform all such services. To offset the costs, two marriages or other religious ceremonies often were scheduled together. Even then, according to petitions of several disgruntled grooms in Michelbach, the rabbi's fee and the transportation costs to bring the rabbi from a distance of several hours resulted in one Jew-ish couple spending the amount (17 gulden) that three to four Christians couples would spend to get married.

Compounding the issue was the animosity between the district rabbi and a community that had so recently lost its own rabbi. One such incident involved the Gundelfinger families. Two couples had arranged to be married on the same day. Since it was a pleasant March day, their fathers had sent an open buggy to fetch Rabbi Naphtali Frankfurter from Braunsbach. The rabbi refused the buggy, claiming that due to the long distance he needed to have a covered carriage. He rented a carriage and charged the families double the usual transportation cost (9 gulden). The two grooms presented several petitions to the county government and then to the board. They criticized the rabbi for his unwarranted pretensions of superiority, stating that other government employees did not mind using an open buggy with one horse. Michelbach's cantor, a Gundelfinger cousin of one of the grooms, supported these petitions. The board ruled that the families only had to pay transportation costs for the rabbi based on the fares for the lowest class of transportation, or else they had to pick him up and bring him back in a suitable carriage.

In another situation in Michelbach, two couples complained about the new rabbi, Rabbi Maier Hirsch, who had officiated at their wedding. For a year and a half the parties wrote complaints and declarations about monies owed or overcharged for the rabbi's transportation, food, and fees. One groom, Salomon Gundelfinger; his brother, David, then a teacher in Wankheim; and his brother-in-law, Jakob Ostheimer of Mergenheim, testified how they had tried to accommodate the rabbi by using Salomon's carriage and driver. They also brought up a discrepancy about the standard fee versus Rabbi Hirsch's fee. The statements on both sides were strong, and the rabbi even accused Salomon of telling a lie. In the end the board ruled only that Rabbi Hirsch had overcharged his fee by one-third and thus owed the couples that amount (3 gulden).

The Law of the Israelites also brought the centuries-old system of education into the modern world. The old system of private teachers had many problems that might have been resolved over time without the intervention of the central government. Nevertheless, the new law did provide a much-needed uniform structure. Most of the articles adopted were contained in the regulations formulated earlier in 1825.

The Upper School Authority supervised all the schools in the kingdom. That group reported to the Ministry of Religion and Education. After 1828 the Jewish schools came under the jurisdiction of the Jewish Board under the Upper School Authority. Therefore, the Protestant authorities regulated the secular as well as religious curriculum and the selection of textbooks. The local vicar, as the school inspector, supervised the schools. Some Jews might have believed that the system was inherently insensitive to their particular needs. The teachers in 1827, however, presented a petition supporting the government's plan. Those people who were eager for a strong secular education for their children would also have appreciated the benefits of being part of the kingdomwide system.

Two educational programs were available to the communities. If a community had less than sixty families, the children would attend the local elementary school. They also had to attend a religious education school for eight hours each week. The children in Rottweil, for example, were under that system. They attended the predominately Catholic elementary school but were excused from catechism class. Nevertheless, throughout the school day they were exposed to a curriculum replete with Christian subject matter and would just sit quietly when all the other children prayed aloud.

In places with more than sixty Jewish families, the Jewish community could choose to have its own elementary school. While the state supported the Christian local schools, it did not contribute any money to the Jewish schools. To cover the costs of rent, teacher, and materials, the community collected taxes from each household and an additional fee from the parents of every student.

The Law of the Israelites also stipulated the qualifications for the Jewish teachers. All teachers were required to be subjects of Württemberg and to fulfill their duties to the state. All prospective teachers would be examined on the same secular subjects by the Protestant School Authority; in addition, Jewish teachers and cantors would be examined on Hebrew and music by rabbis. Since 1820 the government had allowed Jews to be trained at the Protestant Teachers' Seminary in Esslingen, near Stuttgart. The three-year course of study was free. Needy students received stipends for living expenses and board; the Protestant students generally received larger stipends than the Jewish students. Each class in the Jewish section had only one to three students.[3] The Jewish students studied the Hebrew Bible with the Protestants and then studied Hebrew for three hours each week.

Unlike Jewish teachers in some other German states, the Jewish teachers in Württemberg were officially recognized by the government and received the same salary as Christian teachers. The board had the responsibility for teacher placement in the various communities and dealt with any problems that arose between the community and its teacher. A few years after the enactment of the law of 1828, a Jewish Committee reported rapid improvement in the level of education. It assured the government that they had a sufficient number of well-qualified teachers to set up schools in all communities in the kingdom.

On paper, it appeared that the teachers had been given the status and control they wanted, and that the new system was working smoothly. The reality was that some communities found the new system a financial burden and resented the board's control over their schools and their children. At the same time, some teachers felt that they were underpaid and that they did not receive the respect they were due. The experience of Joseph David Berlizheimer's son Leopold as teacher-cantor illustrated the problems and conflicts that arose in the small poor communities. Other protocols and memoirs confirm that his experiences were certainly not unique and even could have been quite common.

In 1835, at age thirty-five, Leopold took the teacher's examination and obtained his certificate. He immediately applied to the board for a position as a cantor-teacher and reapplied while he was working as a teacher's assistant. The community officers in Massenbachhausen and its district rabbi requested that a cantor-teacher be assigned to its community. Leopold was assigned to the community in Massenbachhausen as a provisional cantor-teacher. He received a salary (150 gulden) plus free room and board.

Massenbachhausen was a typical village with a small Jewish community; it was a Catholic village with a population of 1,104, including 46 Jews (nine families). Jews had lived there since the 1700s. At the beginning of the nineteenth century, most of the men were in the *schacher* trade; three decades later, three were butcher masters, several were wine distillers, and the rest were cattle and grain dealers, petty traders, and rag collectors.

One winter the community had a problem that was certainly not unusual. According to the religious school regulations, school-age children had to attend seven to eight hours of religious teaching each week. During the cold winter months, however, the children were unable to attend the religious lessons because they did not have sufficient warm clothing. The community officers claimed that Cantor Berlizheimer taught only half the required hours during the winter, and they reduced his annual salary (by 25 gulden). The board approved the reduction.

Another typical issue was accommodations. Leopold was not satisfied with his lodgings and presented his case to the board. He said that he needed an apartment commensurate to his standing. While the community had promised him an apartment in his contract, he had to satisfy himself

MASSENBACHHAUSEN SYNAGOGUE   Built in 1826, it was typical of the synagogues in the small Jewish rural communities. The rustic building (about 40′ by 35′) was used as a prayer hall and school. (In Paul Rieger, *Jüdische Gotteshäuser und Friedhöfe in Württemberg* [Stuttgart: Oberrat der Israelitischen Religionsgemeinschaft Württemberg, 1932], 100.)

with a room. He had considered fighting the community, but he thought they might take away his free meals. He added sarcastically that he was sure that there was more to an official's quarters than one room, and he contended that the community was rich enough to buy housing for him. Since he had decided to get married (to the daughter of a petty dealer and an illiterate mother in Mühringen), he needed a larger apartment. He asked the board to order the community to provide appropriate housing and furnishings for him.

The board agreed with Leopold, so the community gave him a new contract and rented an apartment for him. Then Leopold complained that the community had reduced his salary even though his needs had increased because of his marriage. He observed that, compared to other cantors, he made only a tiny sum (3 gulden) from performing extra services. The community and Cantor Berlizheimer finally agreed on a compromise on the two issues: he would receive an increase in his salary (15 gulden). In return, if he could not do the instruction for seven to eight hours weekly because of the weather, he would have to make up the time with the children.

Another change in the traditional community involved the treatment of the poor Jews. When in 1821 the government asked for ideas about how to deal with the poor, Rabbi Adler reported that his district wished to continue with the existing system, which took the form of individual contributions and meal vouchers. The most contentious part of the issue was the division of the costs between the local Jewish communities and the central government fund. The representatives in Parliament unanimously agreed that they did not want any money or goods from Christian funds at any level of government to be dispensed to benefit the Jews. The law of 1828 established special Jewish community funds to support the "church," the school, and the poor. Only if the Jews could not support their poor would the local government be obliged to take over responsibility for up to two-thirds of the total costs involved; the Jewish Board would pay the remainder.

The officers and the members of the Mühringen community had intense discussions about the support of the poor and community taxation in the 1830s. The issues went from the community, to the county, and on to the board. A poor fund was set up, funded by half of the donations to the synagogue and by voluntary payments given for the honor of being called to the Torah. The poor fund distributed money for firewood and paid for medical care.

Although charity was becoming more institutionalized, individuals continued to donate to the less fortunate. A middle-aged Gundelfinger, for example, requested in his will that the community officer auction all his clothes (except his coats and two finest jackets). A small amount of the proceeds (3 gulden) was to be donated to the church committee for the Christian poor, with the rest to go to the Jewish poor. He stipulated that the remainder should not be given equally but divided based on need.

The care of Jewish orphans was also removed from the communities, but as with the schools, the Jews had to pay all the costs involved. In 1831 Isaak Hess, who had been involved in the Jewish Committees of the 1820s, organized in Esslingen the Association for the Care of Poor Israelite Orphans and Neglected Children. He set up a committee that was recognized by the Ministry of Internal Affairs. The king was well disposed toward the organization and made a one-time contribution from his treasury (300 gulden). Ongoing support came from special contributions solicited from all the communities on the Sabbath before the Day of Atonement and from voluntary donations to honor special personal occasions.

From 1831 to 1840 the association supported fifty-five boys and girls of ages six through thirteen. Orphaned children or children of widowed mothers who could not support them were placed in foster homes with teachers all over the kingdom. Michael Hirsch, the teacher in Mühringen, took in children from several different villages, while five young children from Mühringen stayed with teachers in distant communities. By 1842 the association had collected sufficient funds (14,800 gulden) to buy a large building on a hill above Esslingen. It named the orphanage the Israelite Orphan and Education Institution "Wilhelmspflege" in honor of King Wilhelm.

Fundamental changes had come to the Jewish communities: the invisible walls that had surrounded the communities were broken down; the autonomous communities were now under the jurisdiction of the secular governments; and the autocracy of the wealthy Jewish elite was replaced by more democratic representation. The Jewish communities were moving into the modern world and the modern age. Nevertheless, members of the Berlizheimer, Gundelfinger, and Kaz families continued in positions of leadership. They worked under the new system—at times supporting it and at other times fighting it.

Leaving the
Schacher Jew Behind

During the 1830s and 1840s, as well as serving as a liaison between the individual communities and the central government, the Jewish Board gave Württemberg Jewry an official presence in the governmental structure. This represented an important and long-lasting improvement in their political status. The Jewish members of the board also formed the nexus in the ongoing struggle for equal civil rights: Dr. Weil and Dr. Maier wrote petitions that were sent to the king and to the Parliament. At times they joined with members of the Kaulla family and community leaders. Unlike the 1827 and 1828 committees, the members of these new committees were not selected by their communities. Nevertheless, when the important Kaulla family and the community officers signed these petitions, the Jews appeared as an organized, united, and official front to the government and to all the Christians. No longer were the Jews without a voice; the board made that new voice heard at the highest levels of government. Over the next four decades, these ad hoc committees continued the efforts begun in the 1820s to fight for the improvement in the conditions of all levels of Württemberg Jewry.

In the 1830s, 93 percent of the Württemberg Jewish population was still living in rural areas. Compared to the other German states, the kingdom had the highest proportion of rural Jews. More than three-quarters of the adult males made their living as petty dealers and were involved in the *schacher* trade. The Law of the Israelites implemented a two-pronged plan to eliminate this trade. Since the law was based on the premise that Jews actually chose to work in the *schacher* trade to the exclusion of the acceptable trades, one facet of the law punished participants and restricted the *schacher* trade to make it unattractive as a way of life.

The special restrictions placed on the *schacher* Jews made their difficult lives even worse. Jewish men usually married in their early thirties (as did Christians) because they needed enough assets to comply with the general marriage regulations in Württemberg. By the Law of the Israelites, however, *schacher* Jews were allowed to marry only at the age of thirty-five. Since all marriages had to be approved by the local authorities, a number of specific situations came to the attention of the local and ministerial authorities.

In Mühringen in 1839, a peddler petitioned the government for a dispensation from the marriage-age restrictions. The peddler explained that he, at thirty, belonged to the group of unlucky Jews forced by bad conditions to peddle to support his poor parents and younger sisters. He wrote that when he had been permitted to learn another trade after 1828, he could not do so because he was too old and too poor to become an apprentice, was about to be drafted into the army, and, most important, had to support his parents and sisters. He asked the government to consider that he had been engaged for two years to a fine girl from Mühringen who would bring a sufficient dowry (850 gulden) and who was practical, sewing clothes to support her family. The Ministry of Internal Affairs denied his petition, pointing out that if it granted his dispensation, then everyone else would want an exception as well. He married when he turned thirty-five. Another case involved a peddler who supported his widowed mother and five unmarried sisters. His petition to marry at thirty-three was also denied.

Another incident illustrated the government's meticulous adherence to this law. In 1846 Rabbi Wassermann made the required announcement of the pending marriage of the *schacher* trader Julius Levi just before the groom turned thirty-five. A county official presented an official complaint against the rabbi, who immediately fired off a response. Rabbi Wassermann admitted that he was furious because he had made the wedding announcements in this manner for years. The law of 1828, he pointed out, stated only that the marriage had to take place after age thirty-five but said nothing about the announcement date. Under ritual law, he analogized, a widow or widower could not marry earlier than twenty-six weeks after the death of the spouse, but that too referred to the date of the marriage, not that of the announcement. The district government interpreted the law to include the date of the announcement and ordered the county government to inform Rabbi Wassermann that he should not make an early announcement again.

The law of 1828 placed yet another restriction upon young men. If they were not engaged in a productive trade or in academic training, they would not be allowed to pay for a substitute to do their military service. The 1833 Jewish Committee pointed out the potential hardships for very religious families, or for families that needed the financial support of their sons. It suggested that perhaps the government could decide each case on its merits, but this idea was not included in the final law.

The committee asked that an exception to the law be granted to sons who had to take over their fathers' trades when the fathers were old, sick, or deceased. Again the Parliament refused to make any changes in the 1828 law, and the poor Jews suffered. In Mühringen a young rag dealer, Gabriel (Gustav) Levi, petitioned the county government to be able to continue that trade. Before 1828 he had been a rag dealer, but after the law was enacted, he trained as a cabinetmaker. His apprenticeship had been interrupted when he was drafted into the army where he was in the infantry. Now Levi needed to return to his earlier trade because he and his brother had to support their parents and six siblings. The village council verified his situation, pointing out that he had shown good behavior, had no property, and was in great need since he supported the family. A report was sent to the district government and to the Ministry of Internal Affairs. The ministry denied the petition. Another young peddler, Salomon Schilling, faced the same problem. The teacher in Mühringen wrote Salomon's petition, which Salomon's father, Moses, signed in Hebrew. The father stated that his son had finished his military service and wanted permission to peddle rags. His father explained that he was old and ill, his wife was ill, and his five sons and two daughters had no jobs and were unsupported. The ministry rejected this petition also.

When it passed the Law of the Israelites, Parliament had also decided the punishments that would be assessed if the Jews claimed they were in the wholesale trade while they were actually involved with the *schacher* trade. For the first offense, they would be fined a large fine (10 to 75 gulden). A repeat offense would result in imprisonment for at least fourteen days.

Two other restrictions put forth by the government struck at the very survival of the poor Jews. Customarily the peddlers sealed a business deal orally or with a simple receipt. This method had worked well because many farmers could not write but often had dealt with the same Jews and their families for years. The 1824 draft legislation included sections stating that those Jews who did not engage in civil professions did not have the right to make their claims based on normal receipts or invoices. Instead, like third-party creditors, these Jews had to prove their claim. In a similar vein, another article stated that a court did not necessarily have to accept the testimony or the sworn written assurances presented by the *schacher* Jews.

The Jewish Committee of 1827 had been very upset by these dire prospects. In its response it maintained that Christians could just refuse to sign, or could deny that they had previously signed any documents. After the parliamentary special commission made that 1828 legislation even stricter, calling for two witnesses to support any claim, the 1828 committee fought even harder to delete the restrictions. Direct criticism and even sarcasm replaced the polite suggestions of the 1827 petition. This time the committee used the word *schacher*. The word was pejorative and anti-Jewish, but in that petition, the committee legitimized the term and played down its inherent anti-Jewish connotation. The committee stated that all Jews making a living from the *schacher* trade would have to close down their businesses. It asked: "What would happen if the peasant did not have two neighbors who would testify to the transaction? Or what would happen if one of the witnesses died?"[1]

The committee of 1833 focused its harshest criticism of the 1828 law on the treatment of the *schacher* Jews, claiming that the goal to end the *schacher* trade could not be pushed so far that people, who despite their best intentions could not find other employment, were robbed of their means of livelihood. It built upon earlier eloquent writings:

> One cannot accuse the Middle Ages of being positive toward the Jews when they were ill-treated in those barbaric times without laws. [However], even in the Middle Ages there was no law of any state that claimed Jews should live without the means of earning a living. In those times the Jews had been sent away and had been killed, but at least they rested in peace! Do these rules that in essence give Jews their lives but take away their means of supporting themselves fit into the political and ethical climate of the nineteenth century?[2]

The committee was clearly alarmed at the growing poverty in the villages. It claimed that the restrictive articles were killing the existing *schacher* trader and warned Parliament about the inevitable ruin of many families and some Jewish communities that would result from this rule. Parliament discussed the committee's 1833 petition but did not amend any of the articles relating to peddling or *schacher* trade. The committees of 1836 and 1837 again appealed to Parliament to revise the articles, maintaining that they caused problems for the poorer Jews. In both years Parliament, while acknowledging the diminishing number of *schacher* Jews, refused to remove any of the restrictions. In 1836 another group of Jews, composed of representatives from the several political districts, petitioned the king, asking the government to lower the peddling license fee for those young men who were sons of peddlers and who had to support their old or sick parents and siblings.[3] These efforts were unsuccessful. Although the districts claimed that they made numerous exceptions in the special cases of sons of older parents, the restrictions left the poor families with even fewer means of immediate support.[4]

An elderly Gundelfinger in Michelbach complained that he was too old to begin a new life and learn a new trade, and it was not fair to force him to do so. The county government official was not sympathetic: "While the Jews pretend they are selling fabric, they are really peddling. These Jewish peddlers pester everyone but especially newlywed couples, and mourners to whom they sell mourning clothes. The peddlers pursue these people and accept foodstuffs and grains if they cannot receive payment in cash."[5]

The concerns of the Jewish leaders were not unfounded. The law of 1828 did not help the poor families improve their standard of living. Rather, the restrictions made it even harder for those who were just eking out an existence. In Mühringen in late 1828, Joseph David Berlizheimer presented an official report on the status of the community to the county government. Compared with just over one hundred self-supporting families, forty-two families and fourteen widows were poor and destitute. Two years later Joseph David compiled a detailed list of those heads of families and widows who could not support themselves. They were listed by name, with remarks that some were poor beggars and some lived off public support or private donations. Thirty fathers and seven widows were on the list in 1830. The poor fathers remained peddlers, rag collectors, cattle dealers, and petty dealers. Of the fifty fathers whose sons were listed from 1837 to 1848 in the apprenticeship register, thirty fathers were described by the county official with the remarks "very poor," "poor," "no assets," or "few assets." In 1845 the number of Jews involved in peddling or the *schacher* trade was still high, with twenty-eight men exclusively doing the *schacher* trade while thirteen were doing it principally or combined with another occupation.

The second focus of the law of 1828 was to train the Jewish youth in acceptable trades so that they would not enter the *schacher* trade. If seen as a purely educational or training law, the Law of the Israelites was successful because young men were trained in civil trades. Whether the law was *necessary* was questionable. Most Jewish boys would have learned these or other trades voluntarily if the opportunities and financial help had been available.

The Jewish Board supervised the program, and the county governments monitored the placements of the young men. Part of the funds collected from the annual personal "church" tax assessed on each Jewish married man funded the apprenticeship program. While poor Christian apprentices received money from local funds, the Jewish boys could now look to the board for money for fees and kosher meals. The Ministry of Internal Affairs officials provided the board documentation about each boy, his family's circumstances, and his references. The applicant had to sign a letter promising to pay back the amount given to him if at any time he left the craft he had learned or went back to the *schacher* trade.

From 1830 to 1832, the board paid stipends in varying amounts (15 to 50 gulden) to twenty-nine boys who were training to become, for the most part, shoemakers, weavers, tailors, bookbinders, carpenters, and soap boilers. It received so many applications for stipends that it had to issue new regulations in 1833. Applications for the trades of butcher, tailor, and baker would not be favorably received unless the applicant was physically unable to enter another profession or the village supported the application with a letter stating that those professions were not yet overcrowded. The boys going into the more difficult trades of blacksmith, locksmith, bricklayer, carpenter, and wagon maker, on the other hand, had a better chance of receiving a stipend. During the years 1832 to 1840, the board paid out funds (12,922 gulden) to 177 young men.

For the young men in apprenticeships, as well as those attending schools in distant towns, a major concern and problem was observing the dietary laws (kashrut). In his old age a teacher recalled his days as a student in the 1820s:

> We Jews in school fared wretchedly in regard to board. Since there were no resident Jews, there was no kosher market. Meat was brought once a week from [another village]. In the summertime it was often spoiled, and once it smelled so bad that it went directly to the garbage heap. In one stretch we had no meat-broth for two months. My mother sent me victuals made of flour, along with cold meats. My colleagues ate smoked meats. They looked fine, while I, accustomed to better food, looked sick and scrawny.[6]

The apprentice program had an immediate impact on young Jewish men. In Mühringen just five years after the enactment of the law, three men had become master butchers, and one became a master wine and spirits distiller. Five men made their living partially from agriculture. Joseph David Berlizheimer wrote in the official register that no young men could become full-time farmers because Baron von Münch still owned almost all the land. Some young men whose fathers' trades were listed officially as peddlers, rag collectors, butchers, and dealers completed apprenticeships in the village crafts under Christian and Jewish masters in Mühringen and in nearby villages. Several stipends from 1830 to 1832 went to sons of poor fathers for their apprenticeships with shoemakers, a weaver, a bookbinder, and a tailor. Even those families with special needs were assisted. A poor widow's son, who had been placed in a foster home under the auspices of the Association for Israelite Orphans and Neglected Children when he was six years old, later trained as a knife maker. Another poor peddler's son pursued a scientific profession in a school in Hechingen.

Some of the better-off Jews—the cantor, the jeweler, and the innkeeper—had higher aspirations for their sons and could afford to pay larger apprenticeship and board fees. These young men studied business, architecture, and technical studies in trade schools in Stuttgart, Heidelberg, and Karlsruhe.

The Christians' fears that the Jews would keep up their "lazy" *schacher* trade turned out to be wrong. By 1845 it was clear that the old age or death of the *schacher* Jews, coupled with the increased number of men who entered the acceptable trades, had dramatically changed the economic composition of the Jewish minority. The board reported the employment statistics to the Ministry of Internal Affairs.[7]

Jewish Men Involved in *Schacher* Trade and Cattle Dealing*

Trade	1828	1845
Schacher traders	2,600	860
Cattle dealers	Included in *schacher* trade	445 (some cattle dealers might have been in *schacher* trade)
Butchers (many were cattle dealers as well)	150	412
Total of *schacher* traders, cattle dealers, and butchers	2,750	1,717

*1828 survey included 3,041 men over age 14; 1845 survey included 3,930 men over age 14.

The statistics, while certainly demonstrating a marked change, also showed that a good number of petty traders still plied their trade. The 1828 law had specified that only cattle-renting was considered a *schacher* trade, so subsequent trade surveys listed cattle dealing as a separate category from *schacher* trading. Under that system the number of *schacher* traders seemed to have decreased dramatically. If, on the other hand, we assume that some cattle dealers and a lesser number of the many new butchers engaged in *schacher* trading as a principal occupation or as an additional occupation, the statistics do not shed such a positive light.

The blurred lines separating an acceptable trade from a *schacher* trade in the apprenticeship program also resulted in conflicts between parents and authorities. Some parents, especially those who could not afford to be without their sons' help for more than four years or to pay the apprenticeship fees, tried to circumvent the apprenticeship system. In Mühringen, for instance, ten boys did their apprenticeships with their fathers as butchers, cattle dealers, cotton weavers, bakers, or tradesmen. The board and the county officials noted their concerns that these apprentices were not learning from trained masters and were not actually learning a productive trade, but the boys remained with their fathers. A similar situation occurred in Michelbach with those young men who were supposed to be learning to be farmers. When a cattle dealer told the authorities that his sons would work in agriculture in his fields, the officials responded that the fields were too small to give credibility to that plan. Three years later the father admitted that one son was a cattle dealer. Another cattle dealer told the authorities that his sons worked in agriculture on his sizable property. The officials stated that they did not believe him since they knew that the Christians worked his fields while he and his sons were actually cattle dealers. The board worked with the government authorities by threatening stiff penalties if the young people only pretended to learn a trade when they were really engaged in *schacher* trade.

In 1836, only five years after the new programs began, a county official in the university city of Tübingen (where many Mühringen Jews went to trade and to the markets) used anti-Jewish stereotypical descriptions to proclaim the failure of the new system:

> One had expected that the Jews would be thankful for the opportunities the Law of the Israelites had opened to them. But this is not the case in his [personal] experience. The majority is not thankful, and feels that it is restricted by the law. The majority of the Jews who live from the *schacher* trade and who

are no longer allowed to train their children to do this trade regard this law as a mistake and a misfortune. Most Jews do not wish for an equal position with the Christians because then they would lose their right to laziness, begging, wandering, and stealing. It is false to say that the Jews had been dissatisfied with their situation before the law and that they wanted a nice quiet way to earn their livelihood. They would much prefer to wander around and stick their noses in the wind to find all the ways and means to steal from the Christians.[8]

Not surprisingly, the Jewish Board consistently presented the situation of the Jews in a more positive light in its reports. In 1845 it described the new breed of dealers who did not go from house to house through the towns, carrying sacks, offering a variety of articles, and accepting used clothing as payment, as had earlier been common among *schacher* Jews. It pointed out that the trade was now transacted more in the cities, and that communications and travel were better. The board explained that now the peddlers carried more proper, sometimes even significant, inventories of goods—admittedly cheaper fabrics—and they visited fairs and markets here and in foreign lands, where they offered their wares for sale in small shops.[9]

Restrictions on the type of business the Jews could do also placed limitations on their source of livelihood. They were still not allowed to work in the real estate trade, and this directly affected the small-time traders. As early as 1833, the committee requested that Parliament revoke the restrictions that had been in force since 1818:

The prohibition to deal with real estate is a double burden since it questions the Jew's honor, but it also goes against his financial interests.... Just like the Jewish dealers, Christian real estate dealers take advantage of rural people. Both Christians and Jews before 1828 had been involved in profiteering, but since there had been more Jews in that business, it followed that Jews were implicated more frequently in usury. Since 1828, court files show that the number of cases of profiteering has not diminished although only Christians are allowed to pursue that trade.... Since the competition of the dealers was severely limited, there are now more disadvantages than advantages to the public. The law has hit respectable and honest dealers very hard, and those dealers can no longer make a living....

The Jews have [also] lost the opportunity to become farmers—a basic goal of the law that received so much lip service during the debates. Since a Jewish farmer could not sell his farm for three years even if he had no success in the precarious first year, only few people would take the risk to attempt to be farmers.[10]

These points were repeated again in subsequent petitions to Parliament in 1836 and 1837. The parliamentary representatives claimed that an increasing number of Jews were getting rich in real estate to the detriment of the local people. The representatives used the more polite phrase "farm butchery" (rather than the commonly used phrase "farm slaughtering") to describe how the Jews cut up the peasants' land. In the debate, one representative did admit that Christians engaged in that type of unscrupulous trade as well. Nevertheless Parliament refused to change the restrictions. Officially the real estate business remained the exclusive domain of Christians.

Many Jews still worked as brokers, but if apprehended they were punished. Seligmann Löw Emmanuel of Mühringen, for example, was a farmer's helper in an area far from his village. When the authorities caught him engaging in buying and selling land, he was sentenced to four days in prison and a fine equal to a fourth of the court costs (22 gulden). Several Gundelfingers were also in the business. Mendel and David were working as land brokers, schmoozers, in Bavaria. Michelbach's county authorities sentenced them to four days in prison and fined them double the broker's fee (*Schmusgeld*). Mendel and David asked the authorities to waive the prison sentence but were refused. Another time, two Gundelfingers asked for a dispensation to sell some real estate. In their petition, which went to the Ministry of Internal Affairs, they explained that they had wanted to buy only a small field of about two acres, but in the transaction they had to buy property that was nineteen times larger. The ministry refused to give them the necessary dispensation.

Other restrictions spelled out in the law of 1828 limited the aspirations of those Jews who wanted to move into other businesses. Jews could not start retail stores or buy stores from Christians without the explicit permission of the local government council. Jewish craftsmen could sell products purchased from other craftsmen only if they were working in that craft themselves. Jews could only open a pharmacy or an inn in a place where a Christian already had such a business. The prospect of a Jewish pharmacy in their town had incensed the parliamentary representatives, who claimed that one could not force a Christian who was sick to buy medicine in a Jewish pharmacy. The representatives supported their decision by stating:

> There are two reasons to keep the public away from Jewish pharmacies. One of them is the known uncleanliness and lack of punctuality of the Jews. The

other is their inclination and tendency to always buy bad merchandise because they are cheap, and it is easy to cheat.[11]

It was not surprising that very few, if any, Jews became pharmacists. Even
the Christian politicians admitted that potential Jewish pharmacists still met
resistance in 1845 when they tried to enter the pharmacists' guild.[12]

The basic limitation on changing one's place of residence was the
broadest restriction hindering improvements in the lives of the Jews. The
young Jews and Christians were all learning the same crafts and trades. In
Mühringen, for instance, the number of masters increased sixfold from 1828
to 1845. Most of them, however, were involved in the usual guild trades. In
Michelbach the options were even fewer. A few young men became master
carpenters, tanners, soap boilers, and butchers, but most continued working
as cattle dealers.

How many shoemakers, tailors, or butchers could a small village support? While Christians with sufficient assets could move to another village
or to another German state, the Jews had to stay in their villages and face
stiff competition from the Christians who remained and from other young
Jews who also were not allowed to relocate.

Despite these restrictions and limitations, by the 1840s Jews were
emerging as a viable middle class, a new direction from that of the Jews of
the previous centuries.[13]

Occupations of Jewish Men*

Trade	1828	1845
Professionals	7	201
Farmers	32	68 (as their only occupation) 83 (as their main occupation)
Merchants	106	349
Shopkeepers	33	557
Manufacturers	—	21
Craftsmen		
Cloth-producing	8	266
Butchers	150	412
Other	124	729
Subtotal of craftsmen	282	1,407

*1828 survey included 3,041 men over age 14; 1845 survey included 3,930 men over
age 14.

The government and Parliament recognized the great strides the Jews had made in such a short time. During the parliamentary debates of 1845, representatives agreed that the Jews now worked in most of the same trades as Christians. A Protestant prelate pointed out that the Jews in the past seventeen years had become more productive and moral—in short, more like citizens. The committee of 1845 articulated what the rural Jews knew: that the many outstanding restrictions were completely unwarranted and unnecessary. But new legislation would not come easily. The issues were just too complicated and too emotionally charged.

Even Keel

During the 1830s and 1840s, the Jewish communities in Mühringen and Michelbach grew, and the lives of the Berlizheimer and Gundelfinger families improved. The portraits of Joseph David and Gustel were most likely painted during these years. The decision to have the paintings commissioned indicates that the family had sufficient assets to spend money on such a project. Although the name of the painter has not come down to us, these portraits were not done by an itinerant artist who just painted an individual's head above a model body and set background. The dress depicted in the paintings also supports the conclusion that the family enjoyed a middle-class or even upper-middle-class status in the village. Joseph David's silver snuffbox is certainly the symbol of a German burgher.

Marx Berlizheimer and his family lived in an apartment above the Deer Inn, next to his brother's house and their store. His wife died in 1843, leaving him with four young children. Like other widowers, he needed a mother for his children. Within fifteen months of his wife's death, a marriage was arranged with Viktoria, daughter of the elderly innkeeper and peddler Natan Degginger of Rottweil. She was thirty-four and brought a smaller dowry (1,000 gulden) than his first wife had. Marx was never as financially solid as his father or his brother, David.

David Berlizheimer continued to operate his successful cloth shop and weaving factory. The weaving industry was thriving in all the German states; increasing numbers of young men, including more than two hundred Jews, worked as weavers. With the money Mina brought to the marriage, David and she enlarged their house and purchased a small adjacent building and a small field. David replaced his father as the largest creditor in Mühringen after the baron. He made a number of medium-size loans (100 to 300 gulden at 5 1/2 or 6 percent interest) to four Christians, and one Christian ceded a debt to him. David was well respected in the community. He served as a Jewish community officer, and several people selected him in their wills to represent their heirs.

Mina and David's family grew in spite of the deaths of several infants. One son, named after his paternal great-grandfather, Moises Kaz, died before he was three months old. Another son, Jacob, named after maternal ancestors, died after only a few weeks. His parents buried him in the main part of the cemetery, rather than in the special children's section, and erected a nicely carved headstone. Their next three children survived.

Meanwhile, David's children by his first wife were now adults. Nehemia, the second son, started working with his father at fourteen and continued until he became a journeyman. When David's third son, Isaak, was fourteen, he started his apprenticeship with a watchmaker and goldsmith in another town. Within a year Isaak quit because of mistreatment and subsequently entered an apprenticeship as a cotton weaver.

While some Jews were beginning to emigrate from a few other Württemberg Jewish communities in the 1830s, it was only in the next decade that Jewish emigration from Mühringen began. All of these emigrants were in difficult situations. An unmarried mother immigrated to America at age thirty-six with her two illegitimate sons (ages four months and seven years), taking with her considerable travel money (800 gulden). The daughter of a poor widowed mother also left. The family of Salomon Öttinger traveled to America just after he sold his debt-ridden Deer Inn to Matteus Hertkorn for a small amount of cash. His brother, a poor butcher, emigrated with his four children and his niece; he sold his house to pay for his passage from Strasbourg, France.

Immigration to America entered into the story of the Berlizheimer family in a most dramatic and unexpected way. In 1845 a match was made between Joseph David's forty-year-old daughter, Hanna, and Bernhard Laudenbacher. Bernhard, who was only twenty-five, lived in Kleinerdlingen, located just outside the fortified city of Nördlingen in Bavaria, eighty miles northeast of Mühringen. The village was similar to Mühringen, with 250 Jews and an equal number of Catholics. Bernhard's father held the important and respected position as the royal lottery collector and had owned a substantial house since 1806.

Even Keel

Bernhard was a master in trade and dealt in notions. He received a medium amount of assets from his father (2,000 gulden), and the village council gave written testimony attesting to his assets and to his good moral and ethical reputation. Hanna brought a large dowry (3,000 gulden) plus a promissory note (1,000 gulden) to be paid to her within six months. This dowry was a third larger than the amount her brothers had received as their wedding gifts. She also brought a suitable trousseau of clothes, linens, jewelry, and nightgowns (valued at 1,465 gulden). Usually the marriage was held in the groom's village, but, for some reason, Bernhard and his two brothers traveled to Mühringen for the wedding. The couple then returned to Bernhard's village.

The sterling testimonies that Bernhard received from the village council before his marriage failed to mention the actual state of his financial affairs. The district court had declared Bernhard bankrupt in 1845; he had huge debts (5,000 gulden) and only a very small amount of assets (400 gulden). His lawyer later explained what had happened. Bernhard did not want to inflict losses on any of his creditors. Since his relatives could not afford to help him, he had to look elsewhere for resources to satisfy his creditors and ensure his future. His solution was to marry a wealthy woman, and his plan succeeded with his marriage to Hanna. The lawyer did not add, or perhaps it was just assumed, that Bernhard had to find a family that was quite desperate to arrange a marriage. Hanna, at age forty, certainly would have been considered an old maid. His lawyer reported that to comply with the bankruptcy proceedings, Bernhard immediately took almost two-thirds of his wife's money to repay some of his creditors. Another legal report stated that he wasted Hanna's entire dowry within a few months and even sold her jewelry and their household goods—pewter, the mattresses, and other possessions—to cover his insolvency. Ten months after their wedding, a civil divorce proceeding was opened because Bernhard fraudulently had declared that he owned assets. A short time later Hanna declared that Bernhard was officially missing. Not even his mother or sisters knew his whereabouts. Bernhard had fled to America; he even used part of Hanna's dowry to buy his passage!

Hanna's lawyer claimed that Bernhard had committed deception and fraud when writing the marriage contract. Her lawyer supported his client's divorce petition with the legal principle that if it were shown that the husband were unable to feed his wife suitably, the marriage could be declared null and void. The lawyer then turned to Jewish religious law, in addition to the already established Bavarian civil law. Jewish law stated that the wife could seek a divorce if the husband was not able to provide her with free board and other maintenance.

Unfortunately, it was probably not coincidental that at the beginning of 1848, Hanna's elderly father took out several large loans from three lenders in different towns and a larger one from a credit institution (totaling 1,123 gulden). For years Joseph David had been selling only goods leftover from David's store, so he had limited sources of income. He might have needed to borrow money to pay for the legal and court fees and for Hanna's support.

Despite the long distance between Mühringen and Michelbach, Mina Berlizheimer and Sophie Ottenheimer were able to maintain close contact with their family. Their brother, Salomon Gundelfinger, spent time in Mühringen. After he finished his apprenticeship and journeyman year with a merchant in Fürth, he obtained his master's certificate in business in nearby Horb. He did enough business in Mühringen to pay trade taxes to the village. Salomon's special situation also warranted a ruling on where he should pay his "church" taxes. The Jewish Board decided that since his family remained in Michelbach, he would pay the fixed personal tax there, but he would pay the variable asset tax in Mühringen.

Two of Mina and Sophie's brothers died at young ages. One brother, Seligmann Gundelfinger, died at twenty-one. His father had just bought him several expensive fields that he was farming. Another brother, Bernhard, died a year later, at thirty-nine. An active tradesman and moneylender, he left a large estate. Subsequently his widow and their two children lived with her parents, Karoline (born Gundelfinger) and Moses Reiss, in Schwäbisch Hall.

Karoline's husband, Moses Reiss, had been a cattle dealer, mortgage broker, and goods dealer for thirty years in Schwäbisch Hall. He applied to the government tax authorities to open an inn in the city to serve food and offer overnight facilities for his coreligionists, and also to serve wine, beer, and brandy to the general population. His petition was denied for three reasons: the innkeepers feared more competition; there was concern that unknown people would stay in the city; and in neighboring Steinbach, which had a larger Jewish community, there was already an inn for Jews. A few months later, his renewed application was approved, based on the location of the inn at the new southeastern city gate, where no inns already served the public. The authorities, however, permitted him to serve food, wine, and beer only to Jews. It is hard to envision that such a rule was actually enforced. Moses and his son ran the large Zum Waldhorn (the Forest Horn Inn) for decades.

Mina and Sophie's father, Jakob David, a peddler in Kirchberg, also met with resistance when he wanted to establish an inn that served food in Michelbach. The officials explained their reasons for prohibiting another inn: Michelbach was unimportant and was not located on a main road, so it did not have any opportunities for trade; it already had two inns, three brandy distilleries, and a Jewish inn that served wine; and its inhabitants were poor—therefore, there was no need for another inn. Nevertheless they granted him an exception because his building already had the concession rights for an inn.

A few years later, Jakob David died at age sixty-nine. He was buried in the old Schopfloch cemetery, several hours from Michelbach. His widow, Reizka, took over many of his business transactions. It was not uncommon for women, especially widows, to be involved in moneylending and other businesses. Reizka made various small and large loans, usually at 5 percent interest, to both Christians and Jews in the village; in Kirchberg, where her husband and then her sons did business; and in the surrounding areas. She always signed documents in Hebrew.

Another of Sophie and Mina's brothers, David, a master saddler, bought a building at the opposite end of the village from the Jews' Lane. He petitioned the village administrator to open an inn that would serve food. The petition was initially rejected because his mother was still running her deceased husband's inn, and there was no need for another one. Reizka responded that her house was not well suited for an inn and gave up her rights for the benefit of her son. The official gave David permission to serve drinks of all kinds, to serve food to guests, and to stable cattle during the day. David also received official permission to hold dances, host Jewish marriages, and serve the celebration meal after a circumcision ceremony. David later bought the bakery next to his inn; he baked the matzos for the community every Passover. The inn was known as the Jewish Inn (Judenwirt).

Poor financial and business prospects forced several Gundelfinger cousins into the teaching profession. While Sophie and Mina's cousin, David, was teaching in his first position in Affaltrach, the parents of an eleven-year-old girl accused him of mistreating their child. The board decided that he had not overreached his authority, and since it was not proven that the student's sickness was a result of the punishment, David did not have to pay any of the doctor's bills. A few years later, the board transferred David, his wife, and the couple's three children to Wankheim, in the same district as Mühringen. Most of its 179 Jews did business in the university city of Tübingen. David complained that because his community was so small, he earned no extra income from other fees and did not receive the usual free board. His salary (195 gulden) barely covered the rent (34 gulden) and his other expenses. Despite these problems, he remained in Wankheim for several years and continued teaching in a few other villages.

Another cousin, David Mainhardt, was the poor son of a widow. David attended a preacademic high school and then a yeshivah in Ansbach, and at age nineteen he entered the Esslingen Teachers' Seminary as a full-time student (*Seminarist*), receiving annual stipends (25 to 50 gulden). The board may have taken his special family situation under consideration when placing him in his home village. A few years after David become its cantor-teacher, the Michelbach community established its own elementary school. Classes for twenty-four children were held in a small annex built onto the synagogue. In addition to his salary (229 gulden), David received an additional sum (52 gulden) for teaching part-time in Hengstfeld, about a mile away. The Christian district school inspector and the district rabbi gave him excellent recommendations. After sixteen years in the village, David applied for the position of teacher and cantor in Hochberg near Stuttgart because, according to his application, he had health problems and wanted to go to a milder climate. It was a very desirable position, and he won the appointment over the many teachers (including his cousin David) who applied.

Several of Sophie and Mina's cousins married other cousins. In certain villages, and indeed in certain extended families, it was not unusual for cousins to marry. It was not illegal under German law to marry close relatives, but this practice was much more common among Jews than Christians. The proportional number of marriages among the Gundelfinger relatives was very high. The reasons varied in each situation, but some common motivations occurred in these marriages: the familiarity with the family, the ease of making a match, acquiescing to a love relationship, the lack of a substantial dowry to make a better match, or the preservation of property and money within the family. In one instance, two cousins married two sisters who were also their cousins. The sisters, Sophie and Friederika (Fradel) Reiss, were the daughters of Karoline Gundelfinger and Moses Reiss, and grew up in Schwäbisch Hall. One married Bernhard Gundelfinger and the other married David Mainhardt; both men were Karoline's nephews. Each couple paid a small sum to the court for a dispensation.

In another line of the family, children of cousins married. Sophie's and Benjamin's fathers had died, and their families were very poor. The groom's mother signed the wedding contract with her mark, and the bride's mother signed her name in Hebrew. The bride and groom brought very few assets and possessions to the marriage (300 gulden each). Benjamin had received a stipend for his training as a shoemaker; he also worked as a cattle dealer. The couple lived in the house that he bought from his parents. Another marriage took place between cousins, but in that case, both Judith and Elias David owned a medium amount of assets and possessions (1,500 and 500 gulden, respectively). When they married, Judith was forty. None of their children survived infancy or childhood.

The Berlizheimer children, and especially the numerous Gundelfinger offspring, made up part of the growing school-age population in the 1840s. The Michelbach and Mühringen Jewish communities saw the immediate need for larger facilities. Given that the Württemberg government had begun contributing financially to the Jewish schools in 1840, the option of improving the schools appeared viable. The Michelbach community applied to the Jewish Board for new facilities, pointing out that the present school was very uncomfortable and unhealthy because of cellarlike humidity. The community explained that the financial situation of its members precluded them from paying for the new construction. The members owned only a very small amount of land; one-third of them were considered poor, one-third had barely moderate incomes, and the remainder were well situated enough that they could pay some of the costs. The one-story building, completed by 1846, housed the school, the teacher's apartment, the women's ritual bath, and an outside lavatory. The government gave the requested funds to the community (450 gulden of the 3,800 gulden total cost).

In Mühringen, sixty-eight children studied in the Jewish elementary school, and forty of them attended the voluntary religious school program on Sundays. In 1845 the community bought the Deer Inn from Matteus Hertkorn. It was one of the most expensive buildings in the village (3,572 gulden). The building, located next to David Berlizheimer's house and store in the middle village, provided large enough rooms for the elementary school and living quarters for the rabbi and the teacher. The spring in the basement, which had previously supplied the water for the beer brewery, now supplied the water for the ritual bath. The contract included a clause stating that the new owners had to fulfill the prior contract between the seller and his neighbor, David Berlizheimer, to move the lavatories to the other side of the house. Since the building had been an inn and brewery, it needed major remodeling. The community applied to the Ministry of Internal Affairs for funding (500 gulden). In its application, the officers explained that it was the largest community in the kingdom, but its members were unfortunately in bad financial straits: of the 110 families, only 4 were well-off, and one-third were very poor. The ministry gave the community about one-fifth (300 gulden) of the funds needed for the remodeling (1,467 gulden).

The construction of these new schools would not have been undertaken without the officers' belief in the long-term projected growth and stability of their rural communities. The Jews were investing in their future in the German countryside.

Fighting for Civil Rights

A long with the struggle for equal economic rights and opportunities, the Jews were also fighting for equal civil rights. After the 1828 debates, neither the Christians nor the Jews ever seem to mention the articles in the Law of the Israelites regarding the establishment of special colonies, and certainly none were set up in the nineteenth century. The other articles relating to civil rights, however, were the subject of many discussions and debates.

The law of 1828 abolished the civil designation of protected Jew, and all Jews were made subjects (*Untertanen*) of the king. In Württemberg the distinction in civil status between citizen (*Bürger*), partial citizen (*Beisitzer*), and inhabitant (*Einwohner*) was integral to the functioning of the villages, towns, and cities. On a material level, citizens received the use of certain common assets owned by the village. In villages like Mühringen, citizens received the use of plots of land in the common forest for cutting firewood, and the use of the common pasture where they could graze their livestock. The communal land was divided into tracts, and each citizen received some plots of each kind. In towns like Rottweil, citizens could buy firewood at a special citizen's price, and they could use the common pasture. Only citizens could vote or hold office. The status of citizen brought respect and security, both extremely important in all villages and towns. Partial citizens had limited rights, but they could not receive the important benefits of the citizen communal rights. Community officers and members of the Jewish Board had to be partial citizens or citizens. Inhabitants could not be expelled from their village or the kingdom but had no other rights.

The new law ordered that each Jew had to belong to a specific civil municipality as either a citizen or partial citizen. Those Jews who previously were only categorized as inhabitants would have to receive partial-citizenship rights in the towns and villages where they lived at that time. The elevation to the status of a partial citizen was in no way automatic, but was predicated on each local municipality's decision that the individual worked in an acceptable occupation.

The law of 1828 also gave full control to the village councils to accept or reject new Jewish residents. The village council would have to accept a Jew only if he stated that he would not do *schacher* trade, that he would earn his living as a farmer or a craftsman, and that he had been working in an acceptable trade for ten years. The representatives believed that after such a long period of time, the Jews would never wish to return to the *schacher* trade. In addition, the final version of the law stated that if a municipal government decided that the trades were overcrowded, Jewish bakers, butchers, and tailors could also be refused acceptance. The law awarded the guilds and tradesmen the protection they had fought so hard to maintain. The Jews would not be able to settle in new locations any time soon.

The application of the law resulted in different treatment from location to location, depending on the local government and the attitudes of the Christians in each place. In many instances the Jews were forced to appeal to higher levels of government when the local governments refused their petitions. Often individuals would appeal their cases to the county governments, and in some cases they brought their appeals all the way up to the Ministry of Internal Affairs. In all cases, however, the government officials upheld the articles of the 1828 law.

In Mühringen the local government was quite reluctant to extend civil rights to its Jewish inhabitants. In 1835 Marx Berlizheimer became the first Jewish citizen in Mühringen, officially receiving his citizenship on his wedding day. He had been working as a master tradesman for at least ten years. As a citizen he received the use of four parcels of communal pastureland and one parcel of communal forest. For the next sixteen years he was the only Jewish citizen in the village.

Acceptance as a partial citizen in Mühringen was easier. For instance, a gold dealer received partial-citizenship rights when he informed the village council that he had given up unauthorized peddling in 1833 and had a license to prove it. When Mina Berlizheimer's brother, Salomon Gundelfinger, was working in Mühringen, the village council accepted him as a partial citizen in 1838, based on his considerable assets (3,000 gulden) and good references.

Individuals in Michelbach, on the other hand, gained citizenship rights based on their birth in the village. Many were accepted as citizens in the 1830s, although some remained partial citizens. This change in status did not please everyone, including the Protestant pastor, who wrote in his 1831 inspection report regarding the "spiritual characteristics of inhabitants of Michelbach": "With the greater portion of the Jews, who are in increasing numbers working as cattle traders, it is always active in the place, as you probably would expect. The spiritual nature of the Jewish inhabitants is: cunning, deceit, taking advantage of others, and not keeping today the oral promises made yesterday."[1]

Becoming a partial citizen or citizen was more difficult for Jews in towns like Rottweil. In the 1820s, about 85 percent of the Christians in Rottweil were citizens rather than partial citizens. Rottweil accepted a larger percentage of applicants as citizens than did other towns because, given its weakened economic condition, fewer potential citizens wanted to move there. Its treasury also needed the funds generated by the acceptance fees. Nevertheless, in regard to the Jews, the authorities and citizens upheld the stringent law of 1828.

Abraham Bernheim's quest for citizenship rights illustrated the difficult obstacles the Jews faced in Rottweil. He had owned his inn there for more than twenty-five years when he requested acceptance as a citizen in 1830. The town council refused his petition, saying it would not accept any Jew as a citizen because it would be disadvantageous for the town. It was only at this point—two years after the law's enactment—that the council decided to purchase a copy of the law of 1828 from a bookshop in Stuttgart. Abraham then applied to the county government, which reviewed his trade history, including his prior years as a *schacher* trader and protests by the guilds and council against his business practices. The county also refused to give him civil rights. Abraham persisted and presented his petition to the Black Forest District government, which approved his petition and granted him citizenship rights. The town council appealed the district government's decision because Abraham had not renounced the *schacher* trade but traded with all types of goods at lower prices, thus damaging the respectable civil trades. Only after receiving an order from the district government did the town council give him civil rights, but only as a partial citizen. Despite his subsequent petitions and complaints, he never became a full citizen.

When Moritz Esslinger, a young master in trade and shopkeeper of a notions store in Rottweil, petitioned for citizenship rights in 1830, the council refused him, based on its refusal to grant his father, Abraham Leopold, acceptance in 1813. The magistrate even suggested that Moritz should return to the village where he was born. The county government got involved, and after many petitions and appeals, he finally became a partial citizen. His wife, Paulina, daughter of Natan Degginger, became a partial citizen as well, based on Moritz's status. In the 1830s the town council also accepted Natan Degginger's son Adolf and Abraham Bernheim's son Benjamin as partial citizens.

In 1834 Moritz Esslinger again sought citizenship, but this petition was also refused. The town council based its decision on the article in the Law of the Israelites that stated an applicant needed to work in an acceptable trade for ten years. After the required ten years, Moritz presented yet another petition, but the council again refused him. Although he had the necessary references and certificates, the town council claimed that an agreement he had made with his creditors had given him a bad reputation and that he had undeclared debts. After the county examined his official business books, Moritz was accepted as the town's first Jewish citizen in 1841.

The next year Dr. Maier Rothschild, son of Josef Hirsch Rothschild and grandson of Moises Kaz, asked the council to grant him citizenship rights. He had returned from Mühringen and was practicing medicine in Rottweil. After seeking legal advice from higher government authorities, the town council refused his petition, citing the same article it had used in rejecting Moritz Esslinger's application. Dr. Rothschild did not accept this decision, and he sent a complaint to the Ministry of Internal Affairs. He contended that the ten-year rule applied only to those Jews transferring into a new area, but Rottweil had always been his native town, even when he had studied at university and had practiced medicine in Mühringen. Dr. Rothschild added that he had thought that the time of prejudice against Jews had ended. The ministry did not support his contention, noting that he had only worked in his profession for four years. It did not count his years of university study. Three years later Dr. Rothschild applied again, and the town council refused the application without explanation. Just as the Jewish Committee had predicted in 1828, the law was used to the detriment of even a university-trained medical doctor, treating him the same as a *schacher* Jew.

The strict 1828 law posed difficulties for the Jews who wanted to move into places where no Jews were living. Though the law clearly set up the criteria for admittance, the local civic councils, controlled by the trade and guild leaders, worked hard to thwart the Jews' efforts. Jakob David Gundelfinger had peddled cloth in Kirchberg for thirty-four years, traveling the short but hilly road from Michelbach. Finally, in 1833, Kirchberg accepted him as a partial citizen, but officials prohibited his family from living there and from applying for acceptance. That meant that only Jakob David could live and do business there. Upon his death his son, Salomon, inherited the business and needed to receive partial-citizenship rights. In 1840 the town council and the citizen committee both rejected his application. Michelbach's ruler, the prince of Hohenlohe-Jagstberg, however, decided that Salomon could get partial-citizenship rights in Kirchberg while retaining his citizenship rights in Michelbach. The citizen committee of the council and several tradesmen complained without success, and by 1841 Salomon had received his partial-citizenship rights.

Salomon expanded his business and bought a substantial house just outside the castle wall on the central market square, where he set up a store. When business boomed, he enlarged the store, built a stockroom, and added some employees. Salomon then advised the town administrator that he was bringing his wife and small sons to live in his house. In short order his partial-citizenship rights were revoked because the right applied only to Salomon. Subsequently he sent a fifty-four-page, professionally written memorandum to the district government in which he detailed his business situation and his prospects. He delineated the large financial investment he had already made and his financial risks if he lost his rights. He appealed to the authorities on an emotional level; he said that he felt hurt by the unfair treatment he had received.

Salomon's lawyer in Stuttgart sent his petition to the king. The district government sent its own memorandum to the Ministry of Internal Affairs, attaching certificates of Salomon's status as an owner of a business and as a member of the merchant guild, and the police and the county authorities submitted character references. The Ministry of Internal Affairs ruled that the town council had made a legal error: Salomon should be allowed to be a partial citizen. A small side comment noted simply that it was not fair to separate a family. In 1846 Salomon's wife and three children moved to Kirchberg, and the Gundelfingers established a tiny new Jewish community.

An 1832 German encyclopedia noted: "Emancipation, that is, the Jews' coming of age, takes place on two levels, from within outward, and from outside inward. The German Jews, have, as it is proper, thus begun to emancipate themselves before making demands that the civil restrictions place upon them be removed."[2] This definition included the fundamental social and religious changes that paralleled the new economic and political developments. Education, language, religion, and societal norms were in flux. Some transformations came from the people themselves, while the government instigated other reforms. The Jewish Board was the leader or the conduit for most of the changes. Sometimes the articulated reasons for the new ways of life did not amply describe the hidden or subconscious motivations. Rather, the issues were layered, so it was difficult to discern their true meaning.

The schools and the newly trained schoolteachers were the main agents of change. The improved schools opened new opportunities. Some teachers still taught German written in Hebrew characters so that the children would be able to correspond with their older relatives, but the young people were most comfortable using German. The use of Jewish-German calendars, prayer books, and women's popular books declined more rapidly each decade. Girls now attended school through age fourteen. Although they usually worked in service or as seamstresses, those years of schooling exposed them to the basics of German education and culture. Some parents gave their daughters additional training in the domestic arts of cooking and needlework.

School inspections in the 1830s by the Protestant pastor in Michelbach, who usually was very critical of the Jews, consistently gave the Jewish children higher grades, commenting that compared with the Christian children, the Jewish students nearly always came out better in almost all school subjects, especially in school discipline and arithmetic. Amidst these positive assessments, however, the pastor did note that "when the Jewish children attend the common [village] school, they forget their secret hate towards the Christians that the Jewish teachers—prompted by the Talmud—always fomented."[3]

While we certainly cannot jump to the conclusion that all the Jewish children were model students, it is clear that most were receiving a better education than had Jewish students at the beginning of the century. Most of them (just like the Christian students) completed only the minimal required years of school before they started their apprenticeships. By 1845, only two hundred of the almost four thousand adult men had received higher education and worked in higher-level professions.

Other changes encompassed many aspects of religious and social life. Little by little the Jewish community began to emerge from its isolated feudal community and enter further into the secular society. Several village traditions may have developed in these decades. In most villages, for instance, the children ceremoniously delivered matzos, which everyone called "Easter cakes," to their neighbors at Passover. The children would carefully carry a packet wrapped in napkins to each family. The packet contained one, two, or three matzos, depending on the number of people in the recipient's family. The children walked to the homes of the village administrator, the mayor, the village council members, the farmers, the craftsmen, and the vintners. At each place the children would recite a little speech, explaining that their parents offered them a matzo or Easter cake just to try. By custom, the Christians would pretend they were really surprised, and some would go into another room and return with one or two eggs that they gave the children as a little present to take home. The giving of the matzo marked the Jews as good neighbors, so the children were very careful not to forget anyone. The Christian neighbors showed their respect and understanding of the Jewish dietary laws and the special Passover rules by giving the children the uncooked fresh eggs.

In turn, the Christians reciprocated by giving their Jewish neighbors special cookies on Christmas. Also, in Catholic villages on the holiday of Corpus Christi, the Jews decorated the fronts of their houses with greenery and tree branches. In that way, when the priests carried the church icons in long processions around the village, greenery would be seen along the entire route. In some places Christians and Jews would share the joy of village wedding celebrations and the sadness of funeral processions.

Music was an integral part of life in the villages and a vehicle for further social contact and exchange. Jewish musicians played at Jewish weddings and other celebrations, but they also played at the taverns and dance halls in the village. Everyone enjoyed playing and hearing the boisterous music of the brass bands playing marches and polkas. Jewish folksingers entertained all the villagers in the inns and coffeehouses. They often composed humorous ditties in a mixture of High German, the local dialects, and some familiar phrases of Jewish-German.

Some religious rituals, perceived by Jews as hindering their efforts to reach their goal of becoming citizens, were reformed. The Jewish Board, under the control of its theological member, Dr. Maier, undertook a conscious effort to create a more Germanlike, "civilized" atmosphere in religious practices. Just as the new board restructured the communities, it also set out to refine some religious rites.

All these and other issues were part of the public debate in the German states. In 1837 several rabbis, including Dr. Maier, the religious members of the board, and Rabbi Wassermann of Mühringen, attended a preliminary rabbinical conference organized by Abraham Geiger, the progressive rabbi of Wiesbaden. In 1844 Dr. Maier was elected president of the first official rabbinical conference and was selected to chair its most important liturgy commission. Although Dr. Maier was not known as a great intellect, the members recognized his record of pushing through reforms and his skills as a mediator and administrator. Rabbi Wassermann and other southern German rabbis were absent. Perhaps the traditional south German communities, like Mühringen, boycotted the conference. Dr. Wassermann may have felt that local politics prevented his affiliation with the advocates of reform, or perhaps he did not agree with the reforms under discussion. Frankfurt am Main was the site of the 1845 conference. Dr. Maier again led the very important liturgy commission. And again Rabbi Wassermann and the other south German rabbis did not attend. The rabbis resolved to call its society the Conference of German Rabbis. Many urban and northern German communities sent letters of support. The following year another conference was held, this time in Breslau. This group of rabbis and the conferences formed the foundation of the Reform movement.

The Law of the Israelites included new responsibilities for the rabbi and the cantor as well as new practices for congregations. At every Sabbath morning service, the cantor had to give a German-language sermon about the regulations of the religion and ethical teachings. The goals, according to the law, were to morally uplift the adults and educate the young people. All women were ordered to listen to the sermons.

In 1838 the Jewish Board, under the supervision of the central government, issued detailed new regulations. The Jewish authorities in other states had already issued similar decrees during the previous decades. The goal was to make external changes and eliminate some practices that the Christians might consider socially unacceptable—to prevent any pretext to arouse malice or anti-Jewish feelings (*risches*) among non-Jews. Certain rules applied to the religious services in the synagogue: no loud praying, no noisemaking when reading the Book of Esther on Purim, no noisy processions on the seventh day of Sukkot, and no stocking feet on Tishah be-Av. The religious services were shortened by abridging the religious poetry (*piyyutim*) and by encouraging shorter and more decorous processions with the Torah. All mourners would say the prayer for mourners (*Kaddish*) in unison. In addition to the weekly sermon in German, German songs and prayers were allowed during services. While special prayers for government leaders had previously been added on certain occasions, a new German prayer for the government was now included in every service. The number of honorees called to the Torah was limited, and these honors could no longer be auctioned off inside the sanctuary of the synagogue. A new ceremony, Confirmation, was introduced for both boys (as a supplement to the Bar Mitzvah) and girls. The service would be held in the synagogue and was based on the Christian confirmation. The new orders also included the addition of an organized children's choir. With respect to decorum, chewing tobacco and spitting on the synagogue floor were both forbidden.

The communities interpreted these new regulations in different ways. Some of the new rules, like the one prohibiting any extraneous noise during religious services, were carefully regulated. Once, in Mühringen, one of the community officers spoke too loudly to the ushers. The rules committee fined him (18 gulden), and he paid the sum without complaint. The same rule had different consequences for Leopold Berlizheimer in Massenbachhausen in the 1840s, when the community officers and sixteen members asked the board for permission to terminate his contract as their teacher and cantor. The community complained that Cantor Berlizheimer had been sick for a few years and had to excuse himself at least twice during each service because he had difficulty breathing. A full investigation by the board and the district rabbi, Maier Löwengart, ensued. The rabbi attended a religious service, wrote an official report, interrogated Leopold, and deposed the community members. Leopold claimed that his physical condition forced him to leave the services from time to time. His performance at the Sabbath morning service observed by the rabbi certainly helped Leopold's case. That day he did not leave the service even once, and he led the service well. Rabbi Löwengart ordered rules to be written stating that at every religious service, everyone should maintain the reverential decorum; no one was to leave the synagogue before the ceremony ended. He decreed that if someone disobeyed, the community officers would give the person a warning; after a second offense, he would receive a monetary fine set by the officers, and they would send a report to the district rabbi. With the rabbi's support, Leopold was able to keep his position.

Denkspruch am Confirmationstage

für *Bernhard Berlizheimer in Mühringen*

geboren den *9ten April* 1838

konfirmirt den *6ten Juni* 1851.

T. *Rabbiner Dr. Wassermann*

Der Herr thut, was die Gottesfürchtigen begehren, und
höret ihr Schreien, und hilft ihnen. (Psalm 145, 19.)

Verlag von Wilhelm Lubrecht in Blaubeuren.

BERNHARD BERLIZHEIMER'S CONFIRMATION CERTIFICATE

A Remembrance Verse on Confirmation Day

> *For* Bernhard Berlizheimer in Muhringen
> *Born the* 9th of April 1838
> *Confirmed the* 6th of June 1851
> *Signed* Rabbi Dr. Wassermann
> *He does what the God-fearing desire; and hears their cries and helps them.*
> *(Psalm 145, verse 19)*
> *Published by Wilhelm Lubrecht in Blaubeuren*

Bernhard kept his certificate with his personal papers. Christians received similar certificates on their Confirmation and wedding days with a particular personal biblical passage. They also saved these certificates with their personal mementos. (Private collection, Janet Iltis.)

Some Jews resisted the changes made by the board. Honors continued to be auctioned in the synagogue. After several communities strongly objected to the Confirmation rite, it was changed to a ceremony marking the children's graduation from religious school and was no longer held in the synagogue. Fewer than ten villages instituted the choir, and girls were not included. When the board issued a new "hymn" book, Rabbi Wassermann noted that several families refused to buy the book for their children. The board responded that the book's aim was education and higher culture, and ordered him to require everyone to buy it. The purchase orders confirm that everyone complied.

The board also tried to impose modern ideas on the old tradition of the women's ritual bath. Some communities had not complied with the government edicts of the 1820s to provide hot water in the *mikveh*, and new issues were also being addressed. The Christian authorities claimed that the ritual baths in basements were flooding and were unhealthy, that women were actually drowning in the deep water (which seems hard to believe), and that women were suffering in the cold water. The authorities referred to the new ideas presented at the 1845 Frankfurt rabbinical conference, which stated that the reason for the ritual regulations was merely cleansing. The next year the board issued stringent regulations controlling the bath's construction, water quality, and water temperature, all of which the local governments were to enforce. According to the board, if an Israelite woman had a submersion bath using a simple bathroom tub, she would comply with the talmudic laws. Some traditional rural communities refused to accept the very avant-garde idea of using a bathtub instead of the *mikveh*. Michelbach, for instance, built its first public *mikveh* in the 1840s, and Mühringen built a new one in the basement of its new school in 1848.

Modern medicine also brought changes to the ancient ritual of circumcision (*berit milah*). In 1847 the board issued new regulations about the ritual, basing them on the government medical committee's memorandum that addressed health concerns previously discussed in other German states. The changes focused on the medical issues and the decorum of the ceremony. Under the new rules the circumciser (*mohel*) needed certain qualifications: he should come from a good home, have a good reputation, be at least twenty years of age, and provide good references. An old man whose hands shook or who could not see well, or someone who had an infectious disease or a diabetic condition, could not perform the ritual. A candidate had to be trained and tested by both an experienced circumciser and a physician. He was no longer required to say prayers in Hebrew; instead, the rabbi or cantor could recite the prayers. A medical doctor needed to attend the "operation." If it were not too expensive, the doctor should remain for six hours afterward to attend the infant; otherwise, the circumciser should do so. The final regulations did not include two other suggested recommendations: that the circumciser should not wear a tall stovepipe hat and that he should refrain from using snuff!

Other regulations favored the well-being of the infant over customary rituals. The *berit milah* had traditionally been performed in the synagogue, but the authorities were concerned about the threat to the eight-day-old infant's health from the cold, unheated sanctuary. According to the new rules, during winter the ritual was to be done in a warm room. If the family lived a long distance from the synagogue, the circumcision ceremony could be performed at home. The ritual could be delayed up to nine months if the infant were in poor health. Further regulations ordered changes that were based on modern medical knowledge. The board ruled the sucking of the blood (*metzitzah*)—required according to the teachings of the Talmud—was not necessary, citing statements of well-known physicians to the effect that this procedure did not help the healing and could be medically dangerous for the infant and for the circumciser. The board supported its ruling by referring to certain "educated rabbis" (those who attended the rabbinical conferences), who agreed that new measures were necessary. The board endorsed the use of medically approved clamps to stop the bleeding.

The communities did not adopt all the new rules, and some fought the authorities when they believed it was necessary. Some people welcomed the changes, while others resisted any modifications of their traditional customs. Several questions are difficult to resolve. Were the Jews resisting the new rules or the secular authorities' growing interference in their religious life? Were they actually adhering to the new rules and giving up their old traditions?

The Jews also began to make considerable efforts to appear more like the Christians in terms of their appearance and language. For example, by the 1830s many men were beginning to cut their beards shorter. These changes did not go unnoticed, as evidenced by a cruel, anti-Jewish article published in the Rottweil newspaper in 1831:

Anecdote: Why Do the Jews Rarely Have Long Beards Anymore?

A prince bought four beautiful horses from two Jews at very high prices. He felt he was heinously swindled when he found flaws soon afterward, although the Jews had protested the opposite with body and soul. The prince, a very jovial sort, decided to exact a small revenge and invited them back under the pretext of giving them a new contract. When they appeared he put in front of them several bottles of wine. The Jews drank quite a bit. The prince complimented them on their beautiful long beards, and then proposed that if they tied their beards together so that their noses touched, the prince would give each of them a small sum of money, a louis d'or [about 10 gulden]! They agreed to the wager...but the prince failed to mention that he had laced the wine with a vomiting powder. Immediately the Jews became violently ill, and they wanted to rush out the door, but since they were tied together they could not move.... They ended up spitting into each other's faces so that they could not see and they yanked themselves around for a long time—vomiting and screaming—until their beards were finally pulled apart. The prince wanted to burst with laughter. He handed over the agreed-upon money. After this experience the two Jews had their beards cut, and from that time onward, out of fear no Jew would wear a long beard.[4]

Some Jews certainly would have been met with such reactions to their early efforts to take on the outward signs of German culture, but they did continue to make changes in their lives.

The Jews did not emulate one growing trend among Christians. The government and the clergy considered illegitimate births among Christians a grave social and moral issue. Because of the Württemberg requirements that before marriage the bride and groom each needed to possess a certain amount of assets (300 gulden each), many Christians could not, or just did not, marry legally. The villagers themselves did not seem overly concerned, but instead produced numerous out-of-wedlock children. The priests who registered all Christian babies maintained detailed records, as did the rabbis, who duly inscribed similar information when necessary in the Jewish birth and family registers. When the Jewish boys were inscribed in the official apprenticeship register, the marital status of a single mother was included as well. Very striking and significant was the statistical difference between the number of births of illegitimate children in the middle decades of the century. The average proportion of Christian illegitimate births in Württemberg was just over 13 percent of all births, while for the Jews it was only 1 to 2 percent. Many of the Christian children became a burden for the municipal social services, which aggravated the problem for many poor municipal governments. The Jewish families and communities, on the other hand, took care of their charges. Not even the most vociferous opponent could deny the high Jewish morals and sense of responsibility, compared to the general population, in this one facet of life.

The experiences in Mühringen were probably typical of the times. In the 1820s only one Jewish illegitimate birth was recorded. An older woman had a baby girl; the child remained in the village and later married there. A few years later Joseph David Berlizheimer, as the president of the community, tried unsuccessfully to help the foreign father of an illegitimate baby by offering him employment so he could remain in the kingdom. Only a few unmarried women had babies in the 1830s and 1840s. One of them worked in Heidelberg (probably in domestic service), and another worked in domestic service in Tübingen. An unwed mother of two boys was one of the early immigrants to America.

In the Protestant village of Michelbach, the number of out-of-wedlock births was extremely high (between 30 and 35 percent of all births) during this difficult economic period. Very few illegitimate births occurred there among the Jews, but one such birth did involve two Gundelfinger families. Jette Gundelfinger, at twenty-eight, had an out-of-wedlock child by her cousin Jakob Stern. In the family register, her baby, Fany, was inscribed on the page listing Jette's father's own children, under the heading, "Fany, from Jette." Jakob's name was not included in the family register. Jette died seven months after Fany's birth. Later, when the infant's grandfather died, Fany was listed in his will as his deceased daughter's out-of-wedlock heir. The baby's guardians, her two uncles, and her father then drew up very detailed documents. Jakob Stern had to pay a one-time payment to her guardians (340 gulden), who would draw small sums for her food, clothes, and care while she lived in her uncle's home. When Fany was three, her father married a woman from a nearby village and moved to the nearby town of Crailsheim, where he started a new business. Fany died when she was five years old.

The changes the Jews made in their lives to become more accepted by Christian society had an ancillary consequence by the middle of the nineteenth century. As a result of these transformations, the differences between German Jews and the Jews living in eastern Europe became more pronounced. The eastern European Jews, with their long coats and beards, their public use of Yiddish, and their traditional, "unrefined" religious services and rituals, became more removed from the German Jews. The

German Jews were very concerned that the eastern European Jews, who peddled or traded in the German states, would undermine their efforts to become equal citizens. The eastern European Jews, on the other hand, viewed the German Jews as not sufficiently Jewish or religious. They looked askance at the German Jews' more secular lifestyle, giving rise later to their custom of calling them "Yekkes" because they wore German-styled jackets (*Jeckes*) rather than long coats.

Despite the transformation the Jews and their culture underwent after the law of 1828 was passed, the rural Jews neither became Christians nor assimilated into Christian society. They did not give up their Sabbath, dietary laws, or holidays. The changes they did make, which involved their trades, language, and appearance, nevertheless gave them timely and important ammunition in their ongoing quest for equal rights and opened new paths for their lives.

While a number of Jews fought individual battles to acquire the rights they believed were their due, some basic civil and legal rights issues, not resolved by the 1828 law, concerned Jews of all economic and social levels. The special Jewish oath required in court proceedings continued to separate Jews and Christians. The 1824 draft of the Law of the Israelites had proposed administering the same oath to everyone in the kingdom. During the parliamentary debate in 1828, the representatives had been divided on this issue, and many misconceptions and ignorance of the Jewish religion had been expressed on both sides. The minister of internal affairs stated that he did not see any difference between a Christian and Jew, nor did he see why a Jew would not give truthful testimony. He pointed out that there were good and bad people among Christians as well as among Jews.

The extremely anti-Jewish representatives, adamantly against one oath, argued vehemently that a Christian was ruled by his conscience and would not give false testimony, whereas the Talmud specified that Jews who gave testimony in favor of a Christian would be banned from the Jewish community. The representatives claimed that the Jews' rituals negated any oath made to Christians. One representative quoted from an "expert" to show how the *Kol Nidrei* liturgy on the eve of the Day of Atonement meant that all promises, duties, and oaths Jews took during the prior year were not binding.

The exact Jewish oath and procedures were subsequently enacted in 1832. These modifications supported the representatives who did not trust

Jews. When a Christian swore an oath at that time, the judge gave him no admonition or instructions. In the courtroom he would raise his right hand and repeat a one-sentence oath to tell the truth. Before a Jew could swear an oath in court, however, a rabbi or his substitute (a cantor or religious teacher), or two Jews with good reputations, would have to instruct the Jew on the nature and holiness of the oath and also on the consequences of a falsehood. The text of these instructions was given to all the rabbis, but they were ordered to use other means of instruction as well, depending on the circumstances. The civil official then would instruct the Jew on the specific nature of the oath so that there was no doubt about the consequences of keeping secrets or falsehoods.

When a Jew took the oath, he would place his right hand on the Five Books of Moses and read a German copy of the Hebrew Bible verse that ended with "The one who lies will be punished." If he could not read German script, he could read the oath in German written in Hebrew characters; if he could not read even that writing, he could repeat the oath orally. In accordance with the statutes of the 1832 law, God's name was written in Hebrew, so that all oath givers would say that word in the sacred language.

The law of 1832 allowed for even more stringent oath requirements for Jews. The judge could order that the oath be taken in the synagogue. He would also decide who would have to bear the extra costs. In the synagogue the rabbi, his substitute, or two witnesses would place the Torah on the right arm of the oath taker, who would then place his left hand on it while swearing the oath. The special oath, admonitions, and instructions were the cause + of recurring humiliations and frustrations for the Jews of Württemberg.

The issue of the Jews' right to vote had not even been considered by the Law of the Israelites. The Jewish Committees of 1827 and 1828 had not asked for those rights, and Parliament had not discussed the possibility of Jews voting or being elected. The Jews probably realized that it was premature to raise this issue in the 1820s. If the word "emancipation" had been spoken at all, it was uttered only rarely, and only by those people, like the merchants in Tübingen in 1828, who were vehemently against even considering it.

Only five years later, however, in its petition to Parliament, the committee of 1833 forcefully urged the representatives to give the Jews absolute parity with the Christian members of a municipality, asking for the right to vote and the right to be elected to the local councils and to Parliament:

pare with Mark Twain's description of the Austrian
Parliament in 1896, 760 yrs later, a scene of violent, obscene
Semitism.

Fighting for Civil Rights

The very rapid changes in a period of barely five years prove that the legislation had helped the Israelite population, in many respects, to reach the
same status as the Christians.... The more men have increasing moral and
religious education [*Bildung*], the more they are aware of the slights and the
feeling that they are second-class citizens who are treated like foreigners
compared to the Christians who have more rights. The Law of the Israelites
has given the Israelites more self-confidence and independence by removing
obstacles, by allowing them to do respectable jobs, and by developing civic
consciousness. The Israelites are completely integrated, pay their taxes, and
perform all their duties, but are still denied their civil rights....

The religion of the Israelites is not an obstacle for voting or being
elected because their religion tells them clearly what their obligations are in
regard to their country. The Israelite citizen who is elected to a public position will be so well known and honored that even the Christians would vote
for him. If he were elected to the State Parliament, he would be welcomed as
a desired example of the equal rights in the country. The elected person will
not undermine the honor of Parliament, and each Christian member of Parliament would reach out his hand in a brotherly manner to the Israelite in
the seat next to him....

If the government were so wise as to grant this wish, it would raise
the status of the Israelites, enhance their incentives to educate themselves,
and deepen their loyalty to the Fatherland.[5]

In 1833 the upper chamber of Parliament debated the Jews' petition.
While acknowledging the higher numbers of young men in civil trades, the
representatives stated that an insufficient number of Jews were working in
productive trades. The representatives still mistrusted the Jews and accused
them of becoming richer in the last five years to the detriment of the Christians. They refused to grant any changes in the law of 1828 because they felt
that the basic religious and moral problems of the Jews could not have been
resolved in such a short period of time.[6]

Again in 1836, the committee sent a petition to Parliament with several specific requests: revise or revoke some articles of the Law of the Israelites, amend the 1819 constitution to allow Jews to hold positions in the
government, and grant them equal rights since they had fulfilled all their
duties and obligations. Its petition included substantive supportive
arguments:

The situation has changed so drastically since 1828 that the law is no longer
valid. More than eight hundred Jewish young men work in civil trades and
agriculture, and the Israelite schools are considered better than the Christian schools. More rabbis, teachers, and cantors have been trained, and all Israelites pay their "church" taxes [30,000 gulden in total] that support their

schools and their poor. The Israelites are using German in their religious services, and they now have a more moral and ethical attitude.

Once the Israelites were emancipated, no one would speak about them any more. The question of the Jews would cease being a theme, and the problem of the hatred of the Jews would go away. The disadvantages and damage that one feared in 1828 are not taking place. Rather all the improvements would be successful, all the resistance would disappear, and all the best is coming.[7]

Some reports sent to the government from the county officials showed a significant change compared to the 1828 petitions from the merchants. The county officials in Rottweil and Gerabronn (where Michelbach was located), for example, wrote about the improvement in the status of the Jews and advocated giving the Jews civil rights since they already performed their duties and supported their poor. However, the county official in Tübingen informed the government that its tradesmen were jealous, and they still were against the rights given to the Jews in 1828. The tradesmen in Tübingen felt that the situation would not improve and that it was too soon to revise the law.

During the discussions in Parliament in 1836, the parliamentary representatives reported that the Jews had come a long way in reforming their religion in regard to rituals and culture, and they had trained their teachers well in the seminaries. The new trade statistics impressed the representatives. Compared with those of earlier years, the debate brought out a wider range of opinions. One liberal supporter actually used the word "emancipation," stating that it was the Christian's duty to use his tolerance and love of all religions as a basis for accepting the Jews' equality. A few other representatives affirmed that the Jews had been treated like foreigners, but these same representatives went on to say that they did not feel the Christians were ready to accept any changes. Most representatives agreed that the people in the villages and towns still feared competition, and that their hatred of the Jews, inherited from past generations, had not dissipated. Parliament nevertheless asked the government by a vote of 80 to 3 to consider revising the Law of the Israelites. The government did nothing.[8]

Less than a year later the committee sent another petition to Parliament. In this petition it used philosophical and legal arguments to show why, under the constitution of 1819, the Jews should have equal civil and political rights with the Christians. The committee argued that the Law of the Israelites contradicted the constitution. Parliament did not debate any of these issues in 1837.

The Jews in all the German states had been aided since 1837 by another voice in their fight for equal rights. Rabbi Ludwig Philippson, editor of the new weekly newspaper *Allgemeine Zeitung des Judenthums* (General newspaper of the Jews) continually published articles chronicling the emancipation efforts being made in the various states.[9] A number of people in each community had access to this source of information.

Five years later the committee—composed of Dr. Maier, several Kaullas, several rabbis, and community officers (including David Berlizheimer)—sent a long petition written by Dr. Carl Weil to the king. It appealed to his wisdom as the father of the country to support equal rights for the Jews. The petition reviewed the events of 1836 and concluded that it was time to take action. Nothing happened.

In 1845 another committee wrote the king with the same requests. This time, the committee claimed that the government's draft had not been properly debated in 1828 because only the lower chamber had been in session. The committee cited once again the great improvements that the 11,600 Württemberg Jews had made. They promised that their Jewish faith would not be an obstacle to their being good citizens or to their being loyal to the king.

The political climate and opinion about the Jews had changed considerably in recent years. The *Schwäbische Chronik* reported in a more balanced manner on the Jewish petition and presented both sides of the 1845 debate. The lower chamber received the petition quite positively, commenting on the good experience of the past decades. One representative said that he hoped he would not hear the words of hatred that had been heard in the chamber seventeen years earlier. Another representative thought that the laws which had been promulgated had given the Jews some rights but noted also that the restrictions in the law, in reality, took away those same rights.[10]

Other representatives, however, still worried that the Jews would dominate the local government in the few villages where they made up a majority, or close to a majority, of the population. The Christians' fear of competition if the Jews moved into new places made any new measures unpopular. The feelings that the Christians had about the Jews in 1828 had developed over hundreds of years, and those emotions were still strong. The roadblocks to equal rights were no longer concentrated on the *schacher* Jews and usury. Once again, in 1845, the government did not take any action, and the Law of the Israelites remained unchanged.

No matter how successful he became in business, or how honorable and moral a reputation he enjoyed, the Jew still was treated as an untrustworthy and second-class person. This treatment not only highlighted the differences between Christians and Jews, but also prolonged their segregation and perpetuated anti-Jewish feelings. In the 1830s, political advocates of gradual emancipation had discussed the "question of the Jews." Within only a few years, the phrase was adopted and adapted by the anti-Jewish faction: the "Jewish Question," or *Judenfrage*, was definitively introduced into the political and social milieu.

Years of Turmoil

The dramatic and rapid deterioration of the economy in Württemberg and the other German states in the 1840s led to social and political unrest and to the Revolution of 1848. Small businesses and handicrafts sectors had become depressed; the textile and wine industries were hit the hardest. Land, fragmented through generations of inheritance divisions, proved even more inefficient to cultivate. Prices of agricultural products began to rise in 1841. However, four years later an unusually warm winter throughout Europe brought on a blight that ruined the potato crop. The next year the weather ruined both the potato and grain crops, resulting in famine and crisis.

Money and credit were scarce. News of bankruptcies and business failures filled the local papers, with one foreclosure for every 250 families in Württemberg from 1840 to 1847. Both unemployment and underemployment increased in the countryside and, as farmers and farm laborers fled to the cities, in the urban areas as well. Bread riots in the cities became increasingly common. The cost of goods rose higher than during the Hunger Years of 1815 to 1817. Beggars and criminals formed bands; public order was breaking down. Once again the threat of Jewish criminals coming from Alsace alarmed the officials in Württemberg. Carrying French passports under false names, these criminals committed burglaries and used fake jewelry to swindle people. New regulations were issued based on those of 1816 and 1823; any Jew with improper documents was to be reported to the county authorities.

Unlike during the Hunger Years, some of the tension was mitigated by emigration. From 1840 to 1843, only about 11,000 people left Württemberg. That figure jumped to approximately 38,000 in the years 1846 to 1849. Many people just sold their property and left the country (perhaps with outstanding debts) without filling out official forms or informing the government. Local governments often paid the passages of the poor potential emigrants (about 60 gulden) rather than continue to support them. Everyone in the villages knew that their neighbors were leaving for America. Letters began to arrive from the new settlers extolling the absence of police authorities, government officials, taxes, and feudal restrictions on hunting and fishing, as well as the abundance of land, firewood, and food. These descriptions made the reality of multiple and high taxes, tiny farms, and unemployment seem even grimmer.

Economic turbulence led to more volatility in the rural areas. It was easy for Christian farmers and craftsmen to identify Jewish creditors as their exploiters and the cause of all their problems. The peasants and petty bourgeoisie turned against the Jews once again. In Rottweil, where still only about thirty-five Jews lived, the local newspaper, the *Rottweiler Anzeiger*, published an anti-Jewish polemic under the "Political Overview" column in February 1848:

> This would be the time to put an end to the peddlers, namely the *"schacher* Jews." These "people" sneak from house to house and prey obtrusively like leeches; they know very well on which part of the body to grab each person. It is not too much for them to try a hundred times in vain because, finally, they will get something. Then they come again and again until they make themselves indispensable and have filled their "moneybags" with the sweat of whole families—especially the poorest [Christians], the ones who are hard-pressed, the ones fighting for their existence.... The poor face this despicable cheating when they do not know another way out of a situation! Even the "beggar-Jew" accumulates money if there is a way to make money from the "Goyim" [Yiddish for non-Jews]. When a Jew writes a contract, he puts down 20 instead of 10 to cheat the other person.
>
> Those who declare yourselves enlightened and preach humanity should not speak about the emancipation of the Jews all the time. Instead, the poor [Christian] population should first be emancipated from their *schacher* spirit that sits like a scorpion on the neck. Town officials close one eye and let peddling and *schacher* trade go on year after year without any restrictions. Everyone needs to look at this evil situation![1]

Unsettling events were occurring all over the kingdom. During the same month, for instance, local officials took arbitrary measures to restrict the business of Jewish cattle traders in the Michelbach region. The police published a decree in the local newspaper that prohibited Jews from conducting cattle trade in all the villages they usually reached by foot; they could trade only where they resided. The decree specifically referred to one Protestant village located a few miles from Michelbach, just outside of Kirchberg. Elias Jacob Gundelfinger, who had been a cattle dealer in that village all his life and had the necessary police permits to trade cattle in Württemberg, Bavaria, Baden, and Hesse, immediately sent a strong petition to the county. He pointed out that if he were not able to do cattle trade, all the Christian farmers and cattle breeders would be unable to sell, trade, and do business. In its petition to the district government, the county claimed it was well known that the Jewish trade was disadvantageous to the peasants and that the farmers became dependent on the Jews. The discontent of the rural people was the reason that the business of the Jews had been forbidden. A few months later the district government rejected the claims of the county government and supported Elias Jacob's petition. The government ruled that cattle dealing was an acceptable trade and that going from place to place fell under the parameters of such trade.

Unrest in Europe reached a critical point when, on February 24, 1848, French revolutionaries burned King Louis Phillippe's throne on the Place de la Bastille. This event was the trigger that unleashed revolutions all over Europe during the early spring. In the cities, the underclass looted pawnshops, factories, and tax offices. People died at the barricades in the streets of Paris, Berlin, Vienna, and Prague. Peasants revolted against their feudal masters and those masters' representatives.

On March 5 fifty-one politicians, primarily from the southwest German area, met in Heidelberg to plan what actions should be taken to establish a united national German state. On March 31 almost six hundred individuals convened as the Preliminary Parliament (*Vorparlament*) in Frankfurt's St. Paul's Church. They accepted the principles of equality, full emancipation, and enfranchisement for all people; and called for elections. Thereafter, March 1848 became a symbol of the revolutionary spirit, and "March" was adopted as the name of the many organizations started by the proponents of these revolutionary ideals.

This revolutionary Frankfurt Assembly had the attention of Jews in all the German states. A Jewish politician, Gabriel Riesser, served as its vice president, and several Jews were chosen as deputies. While about half of all Jews were politically conservative, many others supported the ideals of liberalism, nationalism, and socialism. The actions in late 1848 and 1849 of the subsequently elected German National Assembly in Frankfurt were encouraging. Petitions presented by the lower classes, however, marred the aura of revolution and equal rights. These petitions described the Jews as usurers and hagglers. A leftist deputy from Stuttgart, Moritz Mohl, proposed a plan to continue anti-Jewish discrimination. Riesser successfully argued that laws administered uniformly toward all religious denominations would prove more successful in combating such evils. Mohl's anti-Jewish amendment did not even marshal enough support to merit further deliberation or a vote.

Even as the hopes of the Jews were raised, reality slapped them down. The early turmoil of the Revolution of 1848 incited anti-Jewish feelings that had been fermenting. The places with Jewish populations reacted. In Pressburg (Bratislava), Budapest, and Prague, and in villages throughout the German-speaking lands, including Alsace, Baden, Bavaria, and the Rhineland, violence erupted against the Jews. The Jews were a visible and handy scapegoat.

Mühringen did not escape the unrest and anti-Jewish agitation. Events there were typical of those places where the feudal system prevailed. Baron von Münch still owned much of the village, and the people owed him money for debts, rentals, and some feudal fees. In a rare parish report, the priest described what happened in March 1848:

> The March wind of this year brought to begin with a small anti-Jewish riot during which they escaped with a fright without more violence being carried out against them. The powerful Baron von Münch's rent collector Heiler also found it advisable, following a demonstration by the citizenry, to abandon his place of residence in the castle for Horb.[2]

These currents continued to agitate the Christians in Mühringen. The issue of communal rights and benefits came to the fore. The monetary value of these benefits was relatively low (about 20 gulden per person), but the emotional value was very high indeed. Later in 1848, the village council and the citizen committee decided to distribute all the pasture and forest properties among the active citizens. Their reasoning was recorded in the village protocol book:

> In the future it is uncertain whether the Jews will receive emancipation and would as a result participate in the same benefits as the other active citizens. If this law materializes, it would greatly harm the village because it has

A CARICATURE FROM 1848   "Attention! Pay Attention!" The banner reads "Profit. Equal Rights with the Christians." The Christians are depicted as beasts of burden carrying a Jewish leader and pulling the plow for a Jewish master. (In Eduard Fuchs, *Die Juden in der Karikatur* [Munich: Albert Langen, 1921], 117.)

about seventy Jewish partial citizens. The Jews would then also receive their share of the communal properties.

The Jews were placed here by the baron who collected their taxes, partial-citizen fees, and protection money. The village receives no benefit or advantage from them. As a result it would be a great injustice if we would be forced to divide our property, which has been owned by our ancestors as the citizens' property.

The council decided that the village needed the money to pay debts, and concluded that with the [potential] distribution [of the benefits to the Jews] the entire citizenry would perish.[3]

The council expressed very basic resentments that had festered for centuries: the baron, not the villagers, had invited Jews into their village. When the county government became aware of the council's plan, however, it protected the status quo and prevented the sale from taking place.

195

Serious anti-Jewish riots rocked another village in the Black Forest District. Baisingen was a small village with 719 Catholics and 238 Jews, about two hours from Mühringen. The Jews, who had lived in the village for two centuries, in 1848 were spread across the economic spectrum. Some of the Jewish homes were clustered around their simple house-style synagogue in the Jews' Lane. They used the cemetery in Mühringen, and Rabbi Wassermann served as their rabbi. Marriages connected the two communities on a personal level as well.

According to a Baisingen Jewish community leader, animosity existed between Christians and Jews. The local priest accused the Jews of goading the Christians by telling them that the Jews would be like them: they would be emancipated; they would be able to elect members to the town council; and they would be able to share in the Christian poor funds. The nervousness of the Christians increased with all the talk of emancipation in the village council meetings. During these meetings quite a few people made anti-Jewish remarks, and the officials fueled the emotional atmosphere. The Christian teacher also admitted that he read aloud a document stating that the Jews were "not capable of being emancipated."

At the beginning of March 1848, Christians from the neighboring villages attacked ten houses in Baisingen, smashing the windowpanes and breaking into the yards. The victims reported that their neighbors and the night watchmen stood by or even helped the attackers. Some Jews fled to neighboring villages, including Mühringen, and some moved into the homes of Christians whom they could trust. The Jewish community hired additional Christian and Jewish night watchmen, and the village appeared to be calm for a few weeks.

On the evening of April 25—Easter Monday and coincidentally the last night of Passover—the local villagers gathered as usual at the Zum Löwen (the Lion Inn). About forty single and married men drank beer; according to the priest, eight or ten of them consumed more than 114 pints of beer in an hour! The village administrator and several council members, according to several eyewitnesses, incited the men by telling them that it was their duty to go against the Jews.

The mob first chased away the hired guards. "Money or death!" "Everyone must die!" "The black devil must die!" and "Money, or your blood and life!" they shouted. The men threw heavy stones that smashed the doors and then broke the shutters of most of the Jewish houses with clubs, axes, and cleavers. Some troublemakers even invaded the home of one of the watchmen, Marc Weil, destroying many objects in the house. When his wife and daughter tried to flee, they caught his daughter, striking and seriously wounding her. The rallying cries could be heard in the streets. The men went on to throw stones and break windows of the house belonging to the "wealthy" Wolf Kiefe. Wolf dropped some coins (18 gulden) out of his window. The rioters were not satisfied and shouted, "Throw more money, it's not enough!" Wolf threw down even more money (50 gulden) in a leather pouch. They were still not satisfied and yelled, "That was not the right bag; we want 'the big bag'!" His wife threw down a large linen bag with even more money (300 gulden). When she leaned out, someone threw a stone at her, and she fell back, bleeding, into the room. The mob smashed the windows of the nearby synagogue and threw stones and clubs inside the building. They next attacked the home of Salomon Kiefe, the community officer. Fearing for his life, Salomon escaped out the back door with his wife and three children; his Jewish and Christian maids fled to another village.

During the tumult in front of his house, Wolf Kiefe sent his Jewish maid out the back door to the village administrator asking for help. The official sent some villagers to Wolf's house, and the troublemakers fled. No one pursued the perpetrators. Before daybreak three Jewish delegates went to the village administrator to ask him to report the events of that night to the county court. He agreed and sent the community officer and cantor-teacher to the court. They urgently asked the officials to take the necessary measures to ensure their safety. Meanwhile, Wolf and Lehmann Kiefe and Lehmann's wife went by carriage to stay in Stuttgart until peace was established. They also planned to inform important government officials about the problem.

The county court promised to protect the Jews and sent three policemen at once; other policemen followed later. The county chief official visited Wolf Kiefe's wife, who was too seriously injured to travel with her husband. He asked, as a Christian, for her forgiveness, saying he was shocked that something like this could happen to her and that such injuries could be inflicted by a Christian. Contrast this apology with the attitude of some village councilors who said that she was lucky to have gotten off so easily!

Legal inquiries began the day after the riots, and two of the suspects were taken to prison in Horb. Some villagers made menacing remarks that, according to one of the Jews, "made their hair stand on end." Again some Jews fled to neighboring villages. The men held a secret meeting in Hirsch Kiefe's house and equipped themselves with stones, iron crowbars, and other weapons to protect themselves, if necessary, against the enemy. The next morning sixty-two Christian citizens signed a petition demanding that the Jews sign a document stating they would renounce the citizenship and public benefits for themselves and their descendants forever. The Christians also demanded that the Jews request the court to release the two people in detention and terminate the investigation. The Jews had been warned confidentially that if they did not comply, their lives might be in danger. When they heard that report, the Jews sent two men with a letter to Rabbi Moses Wassermann in Mühringen, urging him to go immediately to Horb to ask the county officials to provide sufficient protection as soon as possible.

Rabbi Wassermann rushed to Baisingen to tell them that he had had no success with the officials in Horb, and they would have to sign the unjust document. As the Jews walked to the village hall, people in the streets threatened them with violence and murder. Just then a messenger arrived with a decree from the Ministry of Internal Affairs. It gave strict orders to the village officials: they should not tolerate any violence against the Jews; the entire Christian community would be responsible for the protection of the Jews and their property; and in case anyone did not heed these orders, military forces would be called up. When the Christians realized the determination of the government, they all agreed to give in, and the legal inquiry continued without interruption.

The village administrator, a council member, and the priest subsequently went to Stuttgart to ask the minister of internal affairs to pardon the suspects. Despite these efforts, the accused came to trial three years later. The local newspaper reported the trial proceedings and background information in a light that was favorable to the Jews. Of the thirty-one suspects, nine men between the ages of twenty and thirty stood trial for robbery and for threatening the lives of their victims. During the trial many Christian witnesses testified they had heard and seen nothing that night, but the presiding court officer chastised them and warned them to tell the truth. Others testified against their Christian neighbors. Rabbi Wassermann laid the blame squarely on the village leaders. At the conclusion of the process, the court sentenced Karl Teufel, a saddler, and Martin Raible, a stone builder, to five years in prison; and Georg Teufel, another stone builder, to four and a half years in a labor prison.

A member of the community memorialized the events immediately after they occurred. Its author wrote: "We designate this *Megillot Baisingen* with the seemingly kabbalistic title, 'Every Generation They Set Out to Annihilate Us, and the Almighty Saves Us from Their Hand.'" To support the seriousness of the events, he wrote that that the persecutions took place during the Passover and Easter holidays, when the emotional fervor and accusations of ritual murder and Christ killing were always at their highest. He added, at the end, that he could not omit that public opinion was entirely on the side of the Jews, and their Catholic and Protestant neighbors reprimanded the Baisingen Christians. His final thanks were to "the good God who had rescued them and would always be their Defender, Savior, and Redeemer."[4]

Subsequently the Jews returned to Baisingen and remained there for many decades. The Baisingen megillah, the story of the 1848 persecutions, was read aloud every year thereafter in the Baisingen synagogue at the Yom Kippur Eve service.

The reporting by the Württemberg correspondent for the *Allgemeine Zeitung des Judenthums* was quite interesting, as he seemed to downplay the events and gave credit to the authorities. He noted that an erroneous impression had been given in prior issues that the hostility against the Jews in the region had been widespread in terms of the number of villages and incidents involved. He stated that in only one village, Baisingen in the Black Forest, certain "admittedly distressing excesses of brutality and savagery" had occurred, but he added that these actions were caused by "certain existing circumstances." He also refuted the report that actions had been planned or taken against the Jews in Mergenheim. The correct information was that the local authorities had protected the Jews who had fled there from a nearby village in Baden, where the Jews "had evil havoc wracked upon them." The correspondent used the phrase "stormy times" to describe those months.

At the same time some Jews were experiencing persecution, others were joining Christians in shared support of the ideals of the Revolution of 1848. For instance, most of the Jews in Rottweil joined the local March Association. Seven Jewish wives and daughters banded together with 166 Christian women in their efforts to raise money to buy arms and supplies so the "poor men could arm themselves" to defend their citizen rights. They donated their jewelry and handmade crafts to sell at a fair and in a lottery. Their patriotic manifesto declared that like their mothers who shared the sacrifices with their husbands when the Fatherland was in danger, they too placed their jewelry and extra possessions on "the altar of the German Fatherland."[5] Dr. Maier Rothschild served as a respected member of the leadership of Rottweil's March Association, and Jacob Kaz worked on its committees.

In Mühringen, as in many other villages, an association was organized to support the efforts of the Frankfurt National Assembly. On Easter Monday, the day of the riots in nearby Baisingen, a Jew, Moses Perlen, dedicated the black, red, and gold flag of the new March Association. By custom, the priest would have performed such dedication ceremonies. However, the priest, who reported the event in another of his infrequent reports, most likely did not support, or was not allowed to support, the liberal group.

The negotiations and emotions of the National Assembly did bring real reforms to the Jews in Württemberg. Just as in other German states, Württemberg's Parliament accepted the idea of full emancipation rights for all men (including Jewish men) when it ratified the constitution of the Frankfurt Assembly on December 27, 1848. A few weeks later the Ministry of Internal Affairs ruled that discrimination in public and private laws against those who were not members of the three main Christian denominations was no longer permissible.

In the spirit of change, Parliament also replaced the previous lifetime tenure of community officials with six-year terms on two-year rotations. The election law of July 1849 set out the new election procedures for local elections. All inhabitants who were taxpayers were entitled to vote and to be elected to the community councils. If a partial citizen were elected, he could pay a fee to become a citizen. Jews could now vote and be elected in all local elections.

This law immediately affected the composition of the local governments. In Mühringen, where the Jews made up almost half of the village population, the elections for the village council were held the following month, and three Jewish members were elected to the council for the first time. The three newly elected council members were some of the leading members of the Jewish community. Moses Perlen, a leader of the local March Association, received the most votes of any of the Jewish candidates, only a few votes less than several of the Christians. After his father had declared bankruptcy, Moses had studied at the Esslingen Teachers' Seminary and then taught in several villages. He had returned to Mühringen only two years earlier to make his living as a merchant. The other two Jews elected were Hirsch Feigenheimer, a leather dealer, and Samuel Grünwald, a butcher and merchant. The villagers also elected members of the citizen committee, which was a lesser office than village council member. Jews had occasionally held these positions even before the recent electoral changes. Samuel Grünwald had served on the committee from 1845 to 1847. In the

1849 election two Jews, Leopold Löwenthal and Jakob Abraham Rosenfeld, and two Catholics were elected. These indeed were strange times: a year after overt anti-Jewish actions, Jews finally had representation in the village government.

Jews also became part of the electoral process for the first time in Michelbach, where the Jewish population was almost a quarter of the 723 people in the village. David Gundelfinger, a saddler and innkeeper, was elected a member of the community council alongside the five Christian members. The next year he was reelected, and Samuel Stern was also elected.

Similar inroads were made in places with smaller Jewish communities as well. Salomon Gundelfinger became a citizen of Kirchberg in 1851, only six years after he finally had obtained permission to live there. Salomon's children attended its public schools. The town also granted citizenship rights to his brother Jonathan, who worked with Salomon and lived in Kirchberg as well.

In Rottweil, Dr. Maier Rothschild tried once again to receive citizenship rights. Even after he had completed the ten years of work required by the Law of the Israelites, the citizen committee still blocked his acceptance. However, after a few months of debate, he and his family were finally accepted as citizens in 1849, a half-century after Moises Kaz saved the imperial town of Rottweil from Napoleon's army. A few months later, another local March Association was established with 161 members. Dr. Rothschild was one of the founding members listed in the local newspaper.

The turbulent times ended. Economic and political turmoil had turned the Christians against the Jews. Just as in the Hep! Hep! riots of 1819, the Jews had turned to the state for assistance. The central government responded, but for its own reasons. It intervened not to save the Jews but to quell the threats to public order and any challenges to the authority of the state. At the same time, the new basic rights extended to everyone gave renewed spirit and encouragement to the Jews' aspirations for the future.

Shifting Winds

By June 1849 the National Assembly had disintegrated, after the Prussian king refused the crown of the new German Reich. The reactionary autocratic governments of the various states prevailed. The revolutionary period in Württemberg ended on October 5, 1851, when the government unilaterally rescinded the basic civil rights laws it had adopted in late 1848. The reactionary conservative government curtailed further development of democracy, liberalism, and nationalism.

Despite these events the issue of the emancipation of the Jews was not entirely buried. King Wilhelm ordered that the legal situation of Jews be considered immediately. The king specifically asked if the German basic rights could be available provisionally to the Jews. Both chambers of Parliament subsequently requested that the government prepare a report to propose new rules regarding the Jews.

Not surprisingly, the Württemberg Jews were very upset that the law of 1828 once again controlled their status. Members of the Jewish Board, together with one of the Kaulla court factors, sent a petition in the name of all the Jews of Württemberg to Parliament in 1852. They wrote that "a great pain burns in the hearts of all Jews," who were now afraid that they would be suppressed again. The writers hoped that the parliamentary representatives would not put the Jews "back into prisoners' manacles."[1] The Jewish communities joined their leaders in supporting the petition. In Michelbach, Cantor Salomon Haarburger and the community officers (including a Gundelfinger) signed a short appeal letter to Parliament in support of the kingdomwide petition, requesting that Parliament pass a law giving all Jews the basic rights of Germans.

When a new draft of a law regarding Jewish citizenship rights came to the floor of the lower chamber of Parliament the next year, the representatives viewed the very positive trade survey statistics as a reflection of the progress the Jews had made since 1828. Some representatives acknowledged that the Jews could have made even more progress if they had not been restricted to certain trades and communities, and if they had been given citizenship rights. Another representative brought up two measures that he thought would open up society and make life better for everyone: the possibility of Jews working in public service, and intermarriage between Christians and Jews. These hard facts and forward-thinking plans did not convince those representatives who again expressed the anti-Jewish feelings of their constituents. These representatives said that they were pleased that the Jews had moved away from the "despicable" Talmudic teachings and that Jews were now teaching all subjects using German, the acceptable language. A supporter of emancipation, Representative Sigmund Schott, articulated the ambivalence of the more liberal faction in his speech to Parliament:

> A large measure of the aversion toward the Jews is based on our inferiority in comparison to them, that the Jews are far more industrious, speculative, and sharp-sighted than we are. . . . I would not deny that one might find many a Jew repulsive, yet I declare emphatically that personal repulsiveness should not determine legislation.[2]

Many representatives still spoke about the dishonest and immoral nature of the Jews' character. They felt that the new draft did not protect the Christian farmers, who continued to complain about being cheated by the Jews, and were also concerned that the draft did not prevent the Jews from reverting back to the *schacher* trade. These representatives wanted to move backward rather than forward. Once again, the merchant guild in Tübingen sent a petition warning of the dangers that emancipation posed for the well-being of the people. It used phrases like "Teutonic race" in reference to the real Germans—the Christians—and emphasized the "national feelings" of the Jews for the Land of Israel. The Tübingen merchants were also concerned about the potential influx of Bavarian Jews if immigration were freely allowed.[3]

One of the articles in the new draft, however, raised an uproar among the Jews. The new law, based on a ministerial regulation, shockingly included cattle dealing as part of the *schacher* trade. The Jewish Board vehemently opposed this article, claiming that it would be the deathblow to the cattle dealers and would diminish the rights of all Jews. Several Jewish community leaders complained that the new law would revive all the hate and prejudice against the Jews. In this instance, eighty-eight villages sent petitions supporting the Jewish cattle and horse dealers as an economic necessity and acknowledging their social usefulness. The petitions made points similar to this one from a village near Ludwigsburg:

> Rather than being detrimental to the farmers, the Jewish cattle dealers who go house-to-house are indispensable. They come to their houses and sell their cattle and even let the farmers pay in installments. If they want, the farmers can even have the cattle checked first. At the markets, on the other hand, where the farmer has to go, he loses the time to do the important chores on the farm. He has to deal with not well-known salespeople who cheat him, has to pay cash, and has no guarantee [of the animal's condition].... The complaint that the Israelite cattle dealers cheat the buyers is not heard here. The great majority are respectable and reliable men, popular with their customers, and complaints about cheating and deceit are seldom heard.[4]

Even Representative Mohl—who had voiced the anti-Jewish sentiments in the 1848 National Assembly—spoke in favor of the cattle dealers during the parliamentary debate.[5]

The progressive Stuttgart newspaper, *Der Beobachter*, urged Parliament to give the Jews equal citizenship and voting rights with the Christians. These efforts, and the precedent set by some European countries like France, Belgium, and the Netherlands that had granted full emancipation to their Jewish populations, pushed the lower chamber to approve the draft and send it to the upper chamber. But no further action was taken; all the restrictions of the law of 1828 were still in force throughout the 1850s.

Although no changes were occurring at the highest levels of government, Jews were entering into a time of transition. Some men, who had done their apprenticeships in the 1830s and had completed the necessary ten years' work in their craft in the 1850s, were now allowed to move to other cities in Württemberg. Jews continued to be elected to the village councils and to become citizens of the villages.

In Mühringen three Jewish members served on the village council throughout the 1850s. Beginning in 1854, Moses Perlen served in the prestigious position of village recorder. His education at the Esslingen Teachers' Seminary and his years as a teacher most likely made him the most qualified to record the decisions in the official minute books. The village also awarded him citizenship rights (which meant he did not have to pay the usual citizen's fees) and paid a small sum for his service as recorder. Twelve other partial citizens, most of whom were middle-aged tradesmen, were granted citizenship rights. The council (with the Jewish members abstaining) did deny an innkeeper's initial petition because he did *schacher* trade on the side, but the county overruled that decision.

Towns like Rottweil offered growing economic opportunities. Given the difficult time the Jews had experienced in Rottweil during the first half of the nineteenth century, it was surprising how well most Jews and their community developed. The involvement of the Jews in the March Associations helped bring down some of the economic and social barriers that had been so strong in the earlier decades. As individuals and as a group, they became more established and financially secure. The number of Jews in Rottweil increased from thirty-five in 1843 to ninety-four in 1859. The larger number reflected the fact that the sons of the original Jewish families were now raising their own families, and also that some of the sons-in-law had decided to build their economic futures in the town rather than having their brides move to the grooms' home villages.

As early as the first decade of the nineteenth century, the community had expressed its desire to build its own cemetery, but was unable to do so due to lack of funds. Its members continued to be buried in the cemeteries in Mühringen and Hechingen. Then, in 1850, the Rottweil town council gave the community permission to establish a cemetery in the Nicolausfeld, a block from the Catholic cemetery. The community drew up a document in 1855 that included the customary rules for internment and listed the various fees due from members, from nonmembers living in the town, and from those nonmembers living outside the town. The document required a nontraditional uniform design for all the headstones in a style that was not found in any other Jewish cemetery.[6]

The community remained an affiliate of Mühringen. It moved its synagogue to the Crown Inn, still owned by the Degginger family. In 1843 the Jewish Board assigned Maier Levi to serve as cantor-teacher for the nine schoolchildren. Maier represented the strides taken in only one generation. His father, Hirsch Levi, was a poor peddler who had repeatedly been denied protection by the Rottweil government. Maier was only an infant when his father died in 1814. Hirsch must have worked incredibly hard in his last years as he left his son some assets (400 gulden) that were held by Maier's guardian, Josef Hirsch Rothschild. Maier left Rottweil when his

ROTTWEIL JEWISH CEMETERY   According to its founding document, the headstones would have the same style and measurements, and would be placed at the same 30° inclined angle from the ground. The use of adornments and poetry was forbidden. (In Paul Rieger, *Jüdische Gotteshäuser und Friedhöfe in Württemberg* [Stuttgart: Oberrat der Israelitischen Religionsgemeinschaft Württemberg, 1932], 120.)

mother remarried, and then studied at the Esslingen Teachers' Seminary, where he received some financial support. In earlier times young men in situations like Maier's would have had no alternative but to follow their fathers into the *schacher* trade, but after 1820 becoming a teacher was a viable path to an acceptable occupation.

Maier taught in several villages before he was assigned to his birthplace. His sojourn in Rottweil, however, was not successful. After only a few months, he sent a letter to his superiors noting that with the small number of Jews in Rottweil, it was very seldom that a public service (with the necessary prayer quorum) could be held. Maier explained that he had believed that effort and unrelenting perseverance could change these bad conditions. Despite his best intentions, he said, the number of community members could not be increased, and the present members only rarely gathered for services on the Sabbath. Two months later, the Jewish Board transferred him to Esslingen, a larger and growing community. Despite repeated requests, it took five years for the board to assign another teacher and cantor to Rottweil, but that teacher did remain for twelve years until he immigrated to America to join his brother.

Members of the community did not change their professions, but their economic situation improved gradually. Benjamin Bernheim continued to run his father's inn, sold ship passages to America, and exchanged money for the journeys. He served as the community adviser, replacing Jacob Kaz, who had served for many years. Natan Degginger's son-in-law took over the inn, and his son Adolf took over a bookstore and ran a lending library. Moritz Esslinger continued his clothing business from a warehouse and a market stall. His sons joined him in the business under the name M. Esslinger & Son. Jacob Kaz and his children retained possession of the house bought by his father, Moises Kaz. Jacob's son Hugo apprenticed in trade and remained in Rottweil, and his daughter Emilie married Moses Hess and remained in the town.

Dr. Maier Rothschild's life took a most unusual turn. In 1851 he became the editor and manager of the local newspaper, the *Rottweiler Anzeiger*, and the manager of its printing company. The Uhl Company had bought the newspaper in 1845 for a considerable sum (35,000 gulden), but six years later its owner went bankrupt. The count of Mandelsloh from Ulm bought the newspaper, the building, and the printing business at a bargain price (only 8,000 gulden) and immediately announced the appointment of its new editor on the front page. Dr. Rothschild published an advertisement notifying his patients that he was still practicing medicine and would dedicate only his free time to the newspaper. The newspaper offices occupied the ground floor and basement of a four-story building.

Most likely politics were involved in these transactions. An article in the *Frankfurter Journal* pointed out that the liberal leaders were trying to extend their influence to the provincial press. The reporter observed that the appointment of the "Israelite believer" Dr. Rothschild gave credence to this idea and predicted that many articles supporting the democratic party line would be published.[7]

ROTHSCHILD HOUSE The newspaper offices and plant, the printing business, and the home of the Rothschilds (1855–1934). The presses were located on the ground floor, and the paper stock was stored in the attic. The building, in the central market area, previously had been a cloister. (Private collection, Louise Rothschild Kopulsky.)

The process surrounding the appointment of a medical doctor as the newspaper editor could have been the basis for the correspondent's theories. The count's lawyer, Sigmund Schott of Stuttgart, was the liberal representative who had claimed during the parliamentary debate that he would not let his personal antipathy toward the Jews impede their emancipation. Although he declared twice that the owner had no political agenda, Dr. Rothschild's leadership in the local March Association could have led to his appointment as editor, and the town's support of the Frankfurt Assembly could have made it a strong contender for a democratic-leaning newspaper. Dr. Rothschild announced that the newspaper would "report candidly and dispassionately the present economic and political circumstances, without fear and without hate."[8]

After only four years the count decided to sell the businesses. Dr. Rothschild bought the assets for a little more than the count had paid for them (10,000 gulden). The paper had eight hundred subscribers and was published three times a week. Dr. Rothschild received permission from the government to bring out a monthly supplement, the *Haus-Freund*, that focused on trade, agriculture, and the home.

Dr. Rothschild told his children that he had bought the business because he could not make sufficient money as a doctor. Clearly it was an investment for the future. His oldest son, Anton, apprenticed as a book printer and joined his father in business. Another son, Moriz, soon joined them as well. The newspaper gained a reputation for providing good local, national, and international information in a fair and open manner. Needless to say, no anti-Jewish articles were published in Rottweil while the Rothschild family owned the newspaper. During this period other Jews owned Jewish newspapers, but Dr. Rothschild was one of the first Jewish owners of a nonreligious newspaper, with a local or regional circulation, in the German states.

The turbulent times that had begun with the economic problems in the 1840s continued into the 1850s, affecting the village-based Jewish communities more than those in the towns. The Jewish population of the village communities was at its highest in these years, but it was clearly the beginning of the decline. The political events—going from the highs in 1848, to the depths in 1851, to the ongoing efforts to gain full civil rights in 1853 and 1854—were not, however, the controlling factors in the lives of the rural Jews. Many historical sources and personal memoirs have claimed that the dashed political ideals of those years, anti-Jewish feelings, and the desire to avoid military service were the catalysts for all immigration to America. The experience of the Württemberg Jews reveals a very different story.

The economic situation improved in 1848 and 1849, but from 1850 through 1853 the farmers once again experienced poor harvests, especially in the southern German areas. The problems of the previous decade had not been resolved, and the small business and crafts sectors suffered alongside the farming sector. One in seventy-six Württemberg families was forced to hold a foreclosure auction. In Mühringen, as in many small villages, the economic situation was very difficult. The village officials repeatedly had to pressure the residents to pay their local taxes; if nothing else worked, the quota of citizen's wood was withheld. The villagers were also in arrears on their Württemberg taxes, so a tax collector from the county seat of Horb remained in the village until the required payments were made.

The poor economic conditions and outlook in the 1850s caused immigration to America to soar. The figures can only be estimated because many people left without completing any official documents. In 1849 the population of Württemberg was 1,744,000. From 1848 to 1862 it is estimated that more than 60,000 people emigrated from the kingdom. Christians and Jews alike were pushed by the same forces to start again in a new country. Most Christians, like the seventeen who immigrated to America from Mühringen, were seeking better economic opportunities. Some young men wanted to avoid military service, while single women with limited dowries were looking for husbands.

Jewish emigration increased dramatically in the 1850s. The Jewish population in the kingdom was about 12,000. Between 1848 and 1855, about 640 Jews emigrated (99 percent went to America), and from 1856 to 1862 about 540 left (71 percent went to America; the rest to England, South America, and Australia). The Jews accounted for 2 percent of the total number of emigrants, a figure much higher than their actual percentage of the population, which was less than 1 percent. Many different reasons led to this unbalanced emigration. On a basic level, it was easier for the Jews to leave because their assets, and their emotions, were not tied to family farms. While the Christians would need money to buy a farm in America, the Jews knew they would require only a little or no capital to start out as peddlers. In addition, these young men had neither loyalty to, nor pecuniary investment in, their recently learned trades, so they were ready to abandon them for

+ Modern dispersions are contributing to assimilation through inter-marriage, employment, loss of community etc.

Portraits of Our Past

commercial opportunities elsewhere. Avoidance of military service did not seem to be an articulated reason for emigration, and since no wars were imminent, that most likely was the case. The *Allgemeine Zeitung des Judenthums* expressed righteous indignation at the articles in the German press that accused the Jews of emigrating just to avoid serving their fatherland.[9]

Other factors contributed to this increase in emigration, but the importance of these intangible elements is difficult to calculate. Young men had already loosened their ties to their families and their communities during their three-year apprenticeships and the several years they traveled as journeymen. Away from their relatives and fellow Jews, their ritual observance often became less strict. With the comings and goings of the young men, the cohesiveness of the family and the community also diminished. The religious reforms that had started in the 1830s were continuing to rattle the foundations of religious observance. How the Jews led their religious lives in the New World was well known. Through letters and newspaper articles in the Jewish press, everyone knew that no ordained rabbis served in America and that it was difficult for the men to keep kosher, observe the Sabbath, or form a prayer quorum while traveling as peddlers. All these factors made the almost inevitable break with traditions during the voyage and new life in America a viable course for potential emigrants.

The Jews in Württemberg were certainly aware of the earlier, greater emigration from neighboring Bavaria. The marriage restrictions on any increase in the number of Jewish families in Bavarian communities (the *Matrikeledikt* of 1813) and poor economic conditions had forced more poor young men and single women to emigrate. Religious and political concerns, including the dashed hopes of the Revolution of 1848, were of secondary importance. Bavaria lost more than ten thousand Jews to emigration from 1830 to 1840, and its peak population of sixty thousand Jews in 1848 decreased by more than six thousand before 1857.

Christians and Jews followed very different emigration patterns. Christians could sell their assets, including their land and livestock, to raise enough money to emigrate as family units and start farming again in America. Jewish boys, on the other hand, completed their apprenticeship and journeyman years in a craft, only to find the trade was overcrowded. Many of their fathers were no longer living or were quite poor. The bottom line seemed to be that they had nothing to lose by seeking a new life in America. The men usually emigrated first, with just a small amount of cash that they had saved or that their parents had raised by selling some assets. Months or

20% of Bavarian emigrants were Jews around 1850

even years later, their siblings and cousins emigrated, often joining their relatives. Single women occasionally traveled with male relatives. Only rarely, usually when the family was very poor or was headed by a widow, did an entire household leave together.

Technically each emigrant had to go through a formal emigration process. Unlike some other German states—Prussia, for example—Württemberg did not assess a tax on its emigrants. In the passport application and the formal renunciation of Württemberg subject rights, everyone had to state his or her reason for emigrating. The standard answers were simply "settling" or "better existence." Applicants had to provide official birth records, permission from their parents or a guardian for minors, and the signature of their guarantor for any outstanding debts or claims. Sometimes a poor emigrant did not have a guarantor, so the municipal government would place a notice in the newspaper, asking any creditors to come forward within a certain period of time. Many people did not fill out the official papers in order to elude their claimants, avoid extra expenses, or circumvent the authorities. Even if emigrants did not pass through the official county channels, their emigration was often noted in Jewish family registers or village emigration registers.

Occasionally when someone did not have any assets or property to pay for the trip, the village government would pay his travel expenses; such an action was viewed as less costly than continuing to support the person from the poor fund. Although this treatment was more common for Christians, villages in Württemberg did pay the passages for at least five Jewish emigrants.

The cost of the ship passage almost doubled (to between 90 and 95 gulden) after 1847 due to increased demand. The emigrants had to first travel by boat, wagon, or train to the ports. From Mühringen, Hamburg was 500 miles to the north, and Bremen was a little closer; Le Havre was 450 miles west. Then the ocean voyage took between twenty-four and fifty days. The ships were specifically designed to carry lumber, cotton, and tobacco from North America to Europe, and they were hastily converted for passengers for the westward voyage. The steerage quarters were cramped and poorly ventilated, the sanitary arrangements were basic at best, and the cooking facilities were inadequate. Passage on the new steamships cost a third more (120 gulden), but the journey took only about two weeks.

During the 1840s and 1850s, more than seventy Jews left Mühringen for America. Compared with the Mühringen figures, only about fifteen Jews left

Mühringen.

Auswanderung.

Ich bringe hiemit zur öffentlichen Kenntniß, daß ich von den Herren **Frank & Schäffer** in Stuttgart als Agent für ihr Auswander ungs= Unternehmen nach **Nord=** und **Süd= amerika** aufgestellt und von dem Königlichen Ministerium des Innern bestättigt wurde.

Von der vorzüglichen Einrichtung dieses Unternehmens habe ich mich überzeugt und kann es daher Auswanderungsluftigen mit bestem Gewiſſen empfehlen. Zu Auskunft=Ertheilung bin ich mit Vergnügen bereit und empfehle mich zu Abschlüſſen von Verträgen über die Seehäfen:

Antwerpen, Bremen, Havre, Liverpool und Rotterdam
beſtens.

Michael Hirsch,
isr. Schullehrer.

TRAVEL ADVERTISEMENT   These large display advertisements offered passage on ships going to North and South America. The schoolteacher, Michael Hirsch, was a shipping agent in Mühringen. (Stadtarchiv Horb, *Horber Chronik,* 25 November 1853, 540, photo: Marek Leszczyński.)

Michelbach during that period. No Gundelfingers emigrated from the village. Several young craftsmen (a rope maker, two soap boilers, and a cattle dealer and his sister), a master shoemaker with his wife and six children, and a widow with her son left for America. One of the first to leave was the son of former Rabbi-Cantor Katz, who had died a poor man a few years before his son's departure.

The only member of the Gundelfinger family to emigrate during these years was the sixteen-year-old son of the deceased tradesman, Bernhard. David had grown up with his mother and maternal grandparents in Schwäbisch Hall and had studied business in Mannheim.

Poignant articles in the *Allgemeine Zeitung des Judenthums*, along with letters, described the feelings of those who remained behind: "Not an eye

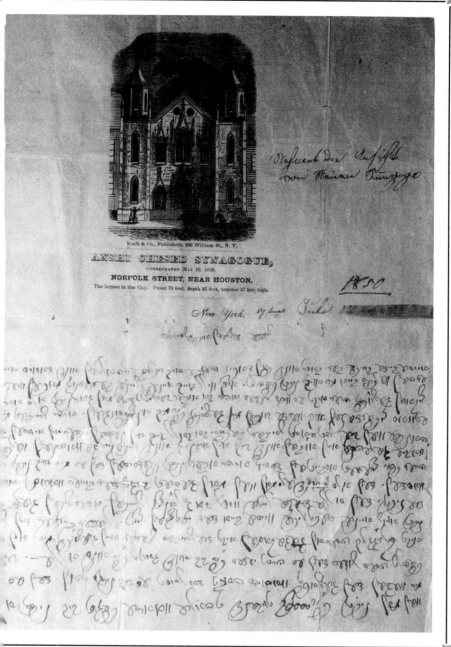

LETTER FROM AMERICA   On stationery with a drawing of his American synagogue, a recent immigrant wrote in German with Hebrew characters to his parents and siblings about his business opportunities. He wrote "the view of my synagogue" in German next to the drawing. (GArchiv Wallhausen-Michelbach, Contract #448, 1850; photo: Marion Reuter, Schwäbisch Hall.)

remained dry nor a soul unmoved when the bitter hour of parting came."[10] And from a father to his son:

> Indeed I accompanied you about five hours,...which was easy for me to do, but an hour later things weren't as easy for me. At that time, my heart was very heavy, which I didn't show. I couldn't even speak much to you although I wanted to talk a great deal with you. It was impossible for me. [When] I had to leave you,...neither could I speak or do anything, save for sending with you my blessings and my best wishes that the Lord may accompany you...in all your undertakings and may He give you good health for many years to come in America.[11]

The story of the Berlizheimer family illustrated many of these forces that came to bear on lives of the Jews in the 1850s. Joseph David's daughter's divorce proceedings, which had begun in 1847 when her husband fled to America, continued three years later in Kleinerdlingen, Bavaria. Despite the earlier legal briefs that claimed fraud and deception as the grounds for the divorce, these documents simply alleged abandonment. Although Bernhard Laudenbacher's whereabouts in America were unknown, he was ordered to appear before the court or else to appoint a representative. The court in Nördlingen published a divorce notice in newspapers in Nördlingen, in the emigration port of Bremen, and in a national newspaper. Only Hanna Laudenbacher's lawyer appeared at the court proceedings. The court official declared Bernhard Laudenbacher a missing person. A month later the court issued the divorce decree. It ruled that since Bernhard was guilty, he also had to pay the court costs, and Hanna herself was entitled to any money that might remain from her dowry. The divorce was finally issued as a public document in June 1851. Most likely no costs or dowry assets were ever recovered. The divorce issued in Bavaria was only a civil divorce. Under Jewish law the husband personally had to hand the divorce decree-letter (*get*) to his wife. Since this was impossible, Hanna was never divorced under Jewish law and could never remarry. She remained "Frau Bernhard Laudenbacher." A divorce was such an unusual occurrence among Jews that it surely was an emotional strain on her family and perhaps on the entire community.

Economic times and family events led to great changes for the family of David and Mina Berlizheimer. David's son Simson completed his apprenticeship as a weaver and his journeyman travels in 1846. Shortly afterward he immigrated to America. In the late 1840s the family's troubles began to mount. David was ill with lung problems, and he began to incur debts. He borrowed a considerable amount of money (500 gulden) from a credit institution in Horb. His brother Marx could not help him financially; Marx could not even repay the sum (300 gulden) he had borrowed from David in the 1840s. David and Mina's last child, Sigmund, born in August 1848, died seven months later. At that time David had to borrow money with interest from his brothers-in-law. Jonathan Gundelfinger lent him a sizable sum (408 gulden), and Salomon Gundelfinger lent him double that amount. In August 1849 David entered the hospital in Rottenburg am Neckar, several hours away from Mühringen. He died of lung disease on October 5, 1849, at age fifty-one.

Samuel Grünwald, David's deceased first wife's brother, served as guardian of the children of David's first marriage, and Cantor Löwenthal was named guardian of the five children from the second marriage. Salomon Gundelfinger served as Mina's official adviser and was present at the proceedings, and Rabbi Wassermann assisted the widow as well. David's possessions were inventoried in a detailed written list. The final agreement for his estate disposition was reached a month after his death.

The division of David's complex estate provided that the four adult children of his first marriage would divide the amount of their mother's original dowry (2,240 gulden). Simson, who was in America, would receive his equal share. The children also received half the house. Mina would continue the weaving factory in her own name, and her stepchildren were obligated to help her with their labor and knowledge. Mina, in return, was obliged to give them food, clothes, and housing, and to care for them in health or illness. If the factory were to cease to exist, then her stepchildren's duties would end and they would receive all their property. The young children of David's second marriage would receive a lesser amount of assets (1,200 gulden). All the children would divide up his clothes. Mina would get the most assets (3,057 gulden), half of the house, plus possessions that included the store and factory inventories (about 8,000 gulden).

Two years later Mina's widowed mother, Reizka, died in Michelbach. The community there had just established its own cemetery, so Reizka was buried in Michelbach rather than in Schopfloch, where her husband and sons had been laid to rest. The inscription on her tall unadorned sandstone headstone was carved in shallow German print letters, and read in part:

Reizka born [daughter of] Isaak from Marktbreit
Married to Jakob David Gundelfinger
Merchant in Kirchberg
1779–1851

DAVID BERLIZHEIMER'S HEADSTONE, MÜHRINGEN JEWISH CEMETERY The headstone, of carved red sandstone, was five feet high. The upper section was a carved frieze of poppy petals and seed capsules, a symbol of eternal sleep. Below the frieze a Hebrew inscription described David as "one of the leaders of our community, the respected man," and his date of death was "on Sukkot." On the lower section, his name and dates of birth and death were chiseled in German. (Mühringen Jewish Cemetery Grave #659, Stadtarchiv Horb; photo Marek Leszczyński.)

Eight months after Reizka's death, Mina went to Michelbach for the reading of her mother's will, which was linked to the 1839 will of Mina's deceased father, Jakob David. Those children who had not yet married were each to receive assets equal to the sum each of the other children had already received (1,500 gulden). Mina claimed that she was still owed a fourth of her dowry (400 gulden) because sixteen years earlier she had contributed that sum, but everyone had purposely kept the fact quiet. Her brothers and sisters rejected her claim, saying she had not actually earned that much money. Mina also represented her sister, Sophie Ottenheimer, who claimed that Reizka had pledged a nice sum to her daughter (100 gulden). Although the debt had been inscribed in the Mühringen register, Sophie's other siblings rejected the claim. After a few days Mina returned to Mühringen, but the family members negotiated these and other claims for months. In the end, Salomon assumed all the assets and obligations and compensated the other heirs. Mina received a few assets (108 gulden), her mother's gold necklace (worth 50 gulden), and a third of her mother's clothes.

At the same time, Mina had taken over her deceased husband's business dealings. The outward signs gave the impression that the prospects of the factory were favorable. The trade taxes in 1853 were higher than before David fell ill. The factory, still called D. Berlizheimer, even needed thirty to forty weavers to work in the factory; an advertisement in the *Horber Chronik* called for good workers to come to the factory with their reference letters.

The family, however, was not immune to the problems plaguing the region. The precipitous decline in the handloom linen industry and in cottage textile production affected the Black Forest region more than any other region of Württemberg in the 1840s and 1850s. The Industrial Revolution destroyed that cottage industry. Since everyone in the family was working in weaving-related businesses, the downturn in the economy most likely caused several of them to emigrate. In 1854 Mina's sixteen-year-old son Bernhard, a trained dyer, immigrated to America. Mina gave him his inheritance from his father's estate (250 gulden), and this money served as his travel money. Hanna, Mina's stepdaughter, and Hanna's new husband, Abraham Rosenfeld, left for America at the same time. Abraham, a master weaver, was thirty-five when they emigrated. David, Marx Berlizheimer's son, also departed for America; he was seventeen and had trained as a cloth maker.

The collapse of the handloom sector certainly contributed to the sudden failure of the Berlizheimer cotton-weaving factory. In July 1854 the county court in Horb declared Mina Berlizheimer bankrupt. It published the customary notices in the *Horber Chronik*. One notice advised any creditors to make their claims against "Maria [sic] born Gundelfinger, widow of the Israelite businessman, David Berlizheimer, owner of a cotton-weaving factory."[12] Another notice announced the public auction of the land and property owned by the widow of David Berlizheimer, to be held at the town hall. The third notice advertised the sale of all the possessions of the widow of David Berlizheimer, including gold and silver, ladies' clothes, paintings, kitchen dishes, handmade furniture, household goods, and various threads from the cotton-weaving factory.

Mina's father-in-law, Joseph David, died on June 2, 1855, at age ninety-four. Even when he was in his nineties, he was doing a little business and lending money to a few local residents. Members of the community and the village officials still referred to him as the former president (*parnas*). In the death register, the official registered his death incorrectly under the name Jacob and his age as ninety-seven; the cause of death was old age.

By Joseph David's will, Hanna Laudenbacher received all of his property except the synagogue seats. Hanna then owed Joseph David's other heirs (his sons Marx and Leopold, and the heirs of his deceased son, David) the value of his house (900 gulden). His widow, Gustel, did not receive any property and also ceded her entire property (1,200 gulden), including her jewelry, clothes, linens, and household goods, to Hanna. In return Hanna had the responsibility of taking care of her mother who was seventy-five years old and blind. If Gustel asked for her weekly allowance, Hanna had to give the tiny sum (15 kreuzer) to her. If the relations between them were not good, Gustel could reclaim her property (two beds, a sofa, a chair, the white sheets, and household goods). After all parties signed the document, they officially told Gustel, and she agreed to the arrangements.

JOSEPH DAVID BERLIZHEIMER'S HEADSTONE, MÜHRINGEN JEWISH CEMETERY
About three feet high, it had an unusual design for a Jewish grave: a pointed roof with J.D. Berlizheimer in German letters chiseled into the lintel. The Hebrew inscription read:

> The honorable learned Yehuda, son of David of blessed memory
> Worked hard with his hands all the days of his life
> Throughout his life he worshiped God.
> 1761–1855

(Mühringen Jewish Cemetery, Grave #521, Stadtarchiv Horb; photo: Marek Leszczyński.)

David's children did receive their share of the value of the house from Hanna in 1857, but that small sum (300 gulden), divided in so many parts, did not give them any financial relief. Meanwhile their match factory, under the management of David's second son, Nehemia, was not paying any trade taxes, and Nehemia was embroiled in several disputes with his suppliers. Mina had to consider the prospects for the children, and she must have seen no other alternative but to leave for America. Mina and her stepchildren's trustee, Samuel Grünwald, sold the house and stable to Israel Levi of Mühringen for a sum (1,800 gulden) equal to only about a third of its most recent valuation. According to the contract, the buyer had to allow her to rent the house for two months after the sale date. On September 24, 1857, the family no longer owned the house, which had originally been bought by Moises Kaz in 1796.

At the same time, Mina and her children applied for official permission to emigrate. The administrator and the community council approved the application and passport, which included Mina Berlizheimer, the widow of David; her stepson Isaak; and three of her children, Karoline, Lazarus, and Mayer. Although her daughter Sara was traveling as well, for some reason her name was not included in the application. The family took the same amount of money (700 gulden for six people) as the poorer emigrants of the time. Mina's departure was noted in the trusteeship registers because she still owed some money to her stepchildren. The family sailed from Hamburg on the *Harmonia*, arriving at the Castle Garden landing station in New York City on November 17, 1857. The family's emigration was included in the November 29, 1857, emigrant list published in the *Horber Chronik*: "David Berlizheimer, widow, Mina. With four children from Mühringen."

This event was not the result of anti-Jewish persecution or dashed democratic ideals. Rather, difficult economic times and the death of the family provider forced Mina and her children to leave their home. Would they have emigrated if there had been no one on the other side of the ocean to greet them? Fortunately, several of Mina's children and stepchildren had already settled in the American Midwest.

Jewish Emigration from Mühringen 1848–1863[13]

Year	Name, Age	Parent or Deceased Spouse	Trade and Civil Status
1848	Berlizheimer, Simson, 21	David, merchant and owner of weaving factory; partial citizen	Journeyman; apprenticeship with his father
1848	Löwenthal, Baruch, 19	Joseph, confectionery baker; a few assets; deceased	Confectionery baker; apprenticeship with his father; journeyman
1848	Bloch, Maier, 16	Samuel Bloch, deceased; poor	Foster child; trained as knife maker
1848	Rosenthal, Jette, 18 Rosenthal, Edel, 21	Marx, poor butcher	
1849	Steinharter (mother), 40 With out-of-wedlock son, Susmann, 13	Susmann	
1852	Neuhauser, Julius, 43 With wife, mother, & 4 children	Maier	Partial citizen
1852	Bloch, Mina, widow, 56 With 4 adult children	Daughter of Moses Seligmann Elsässer, innkeeper Widow of Samuel Bloch (d. 1838)	Partial citizen
1852	Marx, Jakob Marx, Marie		
1852	Rosenfeld, Maier 18 Marie (sister)	Abraham, poor peddler	Tanner and leather dealer; partial citizen
1852	Rosenthal, Jakob, 18 (2 sisters had emigrated in 1848)	Marx, poor butcher	Butcher; apprenticeship with father

(continued)

Jewish Emigration from Mühringen 1848–1863

Year	Name, Age	Parent or Deceased Spouse	Trade and Civil Status
1852	Rosenthal, Marie, 24 With brother Jakob	Marx, poor butcher	Emigrated 3 months after giving birth to an out-of-wedlock son, Heinrich, who later emigrated in 1869
1852	Rothschild (widow) With 2 adult daughters	Widow of Jakob	Very poor; no debt guarantor
1853	Levisohn, Louis, 17	Isaak	Partial citizen
1853	Polak, Maier With wife and 4 children		Poor tailor; one child had trained as a tailor
1854	Berlizheimer, David, 17	Marx, merchant; citizen	Apprentice weaver
1854	Berlizheimer, Bernhard, 16	David, deceased merchant and owner of weaving factory; partial citizen	Apprentice dyer
1854	Rosenfeld, Abraham, 35 With wife Hanna, 24	Jakob, tradesman with assets David Berlizheimer and Fany, both deceased	Master weaver
1854	Levisohn, Babette, 19 Levisohn, Hirsch, 15	Isaac, schoolteacher	
1854	Herzfelder, Gabriel, 15	Maria, unwed mother	Finished grade school
1854	Eppstein, Jakob, 18	Joseph, tradesman with assets	Butcher
1856	Reinauer, Marx, 18	Simon, few assets; deceased a few years earlier	Shoemaker
Before 1857	Rosenfeld, Josef	Abraham, poor peddler	Kaulla Yeshivah in Hechingen, 1838; scientific profession, journeyman

Year	Emigrant	Background	Notes
1857	Rosenfeld, Moriz (Directly to Rock Is., Ill., to join Maier and Josef Rosenfeld, his uncles)	Jakob Abraham, well off	Rottweil trade school, half year; training in business
1857	**Berlizheimer, Mina** Born Gundelfinger Widow, 52 Isaak, 25 Sara, 18 Karoline, 15 Lazarus (Eleazer), 14 **Maier (Mayer)**, 12 (listed as "Maria" on ship manifest) (3 children already in America)	Widow of David (d. 1849), merchant and owner of weaving factory; partial citizen	Master cotton weaver
1857	Ottenheimer, Jacob, 17 (On ship with Mina Berlizheimer)	Salomon Ottenheimer and Sophie (born Gundelfinger), very poor tradesman	Business; incomplete apprenticeships
1857	Grünwald, (2 females) (Cousins of David Berlizheimer's first wife; on ship with Mina Berlizheimer)	Isaak, poor tradesman	
1858	Rosenthal, Maier (Moses), 20 (Sister and brother had emigrated in 1852)	Marx, poor butcher	Butcher; shoemaker
1858	Rosenthal, Ernestine, 18		
1859	Rosenthal, Moritz, 18		
1859	Reinauer, Isaak, 17 (One brother already in America)	Simon, died a few years earlier; no assets; mother also deceased	Shoemaker

(continued)

Jewish Emigration from Mühringen 1848–1863

Year	Name, Age	Parent or Deceased Spouse	Trade and Civil Status
1859	Eppstein, Isaak, 18	Cattle dealer, well off	Butcher in nearby Rexingen
Before 1861	Esslinger, Isidor	Joseph, jeweler; well off	Gymnasium in Rottweil; technical school in Stuttgart; University of Tübingen; School of Law, University of Heidelberg, 1856. He was the only person from Mühringen to attend that university up to that time.
Before 1862	Grünwald, Samson	Rabbi Seligmann Grünwald, deceased	
Before 1863	Grünwald, (male)	Samuel, butcher; well off	Gold engraver in Stuttgart
Before 1863	Grünwald, Fanni (b. 1825) Schweitzer, Sara (b. 1830) Schweitzer, Fanni Levi, Fanni Rosenthal, Rebekka Rosenthal, Jakob Rosenthal, Moses	Elias, poor	

A German Village in Chicago

From a letter written in German by Henriette Chambrey, maternal aunt of Bernhard Berlizheimer's future wife:

Chicago, August 26, 1849

Dear Sister and Brother-in-Law,

I have finally reached the long-desired goal of my wishes and am in Chicago with my own family. After a sea voyage of 49 days (from the 16th of May to the 5th of July), we arrived happily in New York. The joy of seeing land again for the first time after a seven-week-long sea journey one can only feel and not describe; just as no one can imagine what it is really like living in a cabin on such a sea journey unless he has experienced it himself. The beds are fastened to the walls and always two on top of each other so that four can sleep in each cabin. Lorchen, Simmchens and I slept together, and we also became seasick together. The seasickness comes from the motion of the boat, and it causes dizziness and nausea. For three whole days I was quite unconscious and unable to eat or drink. It took three weeks until I got totally accustomed to life on the ship, but then I was very well. We spent all day on deck until ten o'clock at night, because the air in the lower cabins isn't too healthy. To see only water and sky for such a long period isn't as bad as one imagines, at least it wasn't for me. When the sea is calm, it is a beautiful sight. There were 189 passengers on board, all Germans, and mostly young people. Quite often there was dancing on deck until ten because there were several guitarists and flutists on the boat. The captain and the sailors spoke English. The cook and one of the sailors knew some German. I got on very well with my cooking, because the crew had to do its own cooking. Dried fruit and eggs were good on board the ship. Potatoes and Zwieback crackers were fair and plentiful; one could get as many as one wanted. Water one got more than enough to wash with. It tasted bad at the beginning, but less so as time went on. One night we had a storm, but although all the boxes were thrown from one side to the other and even one of

PARTIAL MAP OF THE UNITED STATES, 1850s   A geographical guide to the story of the Berlizheimers in the United States. In 1850, 1 gulden was equal to U.S. $.40.

the sails was ripped, the sailors said it was not a storm, but only a strong wind. Our journey, although it became somewhat boring, can still be called a fortuitous one since no one died or became seriously ill, except for one great misfortune which befell the bricklayer, Hitzel, because his eldest son, who, while pulling up a bucket of water, was pulled down by the force of the rope. Rescue was impossible even to think of.

On arrival in New York I went to Koblenz Inn, and I got a friendly reception. Ismael Kohn from Villingen, who boards at the Koblenzer, told the Arnsteins and Jettchen Herzog that I had arrived, and they came to visit me the next day. They went with me to the brother of Rosa, where I delivered the letter. On Friday afternoon, I had to leave New York by steamboat and arrived in Albany on Saturday morning at four o'clock. At one o'clock, I had to leave Albany by train and arrived in Buffalo on Sunday at one in the afternoon. From Buffalo on, I met a lot of people who traveled with me to Chicago. On Monday night, I left Buffalo by steamboat again and got to Detroit at noon on Tuesday. From there I took a train right away and got to Chicago on Wednesday. The train is very good from Buffalo this year because it takes only two days to get here this way, while it takes six days if one goes by boat. You can't imagine my sister and brother-in-law's joy at my arrival because I arrived unexpectedly and earlier than the letter that I had sent from New York. When I got off the boat and couldn't find my sister (since she hadn't received my letter), I was for a moment in a state of embarrassment. But I was soon helped out of that because some men who were standing nearby asked me where I wanted to go. I told them, and since they were Israelites and knew my brother-in-law, it was a great pleasure for them to be able to take me to my sister. My sister asked immediately how our father was, but I didn't tell her. I didn't want to spoil the joy of the reunion. A few days later she found it out accidentally since she noticed the mourning symbol on my dress. She had had no inkling.[1]

Simson, the first Berlizheimer to arrive in America, immigrated by 1848. The population of the United States was almost 23 million including about 50 thousand Jews. Most of them had settled on the East Coast in the large cities, but the more recent immigrants headed to the new frontier (Ohio, Illinois, and Iowa), and Simson joined them. They were looking not for cheap land or large farms or wide-open spaces like the Christians, but rather sought untapped markets for engaging in trade.

As explained by a Jewish correspondent for a south German newspaper:

Naturally, there is never any talk about purchases in the North American woods, of agriculture, landed estates, etc. One becomes a merchant, i.e., carries on trade in the ever-roaming wagons and steamboats, until one gets a house and establishes a store, or one carries on one, two, three trades, according to what he has derived from others, in addition to what he has in passing learned here. A German is gladly accepted as a workingman in America; the German Jew is preferred to any other.[2]

Of course, most of the new Jewish immigrants had neither the money to invest in land nor the skills to work in agriculture, so they progressed in a different manner than the Christian immigrants. An American rabbi recalled an explanation of Jewish life he heard in the 1840s:

Our people in this country may be divided into the following classes: (1) The basket peddler—he is as yet altogether dumb and homeless; (2) the trunk-carrier, who stammers some little English, and hopes for better times; (3) the pack-carrier, who carries from 100 to 150 pounds on his back, and indulges the thought that he will become a businessman some day. In addition to these, there is the aristocracy, which may be divided into three classes: (1) The wagon-baron, who peddles through the country with a one or two horse team; (2) the jewelry-count, who carries a stock of watchers and jewelry in a small trunk, and is considered a rich man even now; (3) the

AN EMIGRANT'S PRAYER BOOK, FÜRTH, 1842   Reproduced at slightly larger than its actual size. The title page reads "Prayers for the Entire Year: A Small Offering for the Traveler Who Walks on the Way and Who Crosses the Seas to the Country of America." Below in German with Hebrew letters was the line "A Miniature Edition with Good Lettering." (Courtesy of the Library of the Jewish Theological Seminary, New York.)

store-prince, who has a shop and sells goods in it. At first one is the slave of the basket or pack; then the lackey of the horse, in order to become finally the servant of the shop.[3]

Simson and the other German-speaking peddlers had one advantage over both the Yankee peddler and the Jewish peddlers from Russia. The German immigrant farmers generally preferred to deal in their native language and to hear news and gossip from home. However, the new German arrivals—Jews and Christians alike—would certainly have been shocked by the

JEWISH PEDDLER IN AMERICA, 1850 (By C. G. Bush. Library of Congress LC-USZ62_10082, Washington, D.C.)

great distances and the weather. In the German countryside, every mile or two brought another village or hamlet offering potential customers or a place to sleep, and the weather was more temperate. In America, farmhouses were often twenty or even fifty miles apart; the distances between potential customers and a warm refuge were barely manageable. The extreme winter cold and the deadly summer heat made travel tedious and dangerous.

It was also difficult for the peddlers to fulfill the religious rituals they had once so effortlessly followed. The distances alone could have led some travelers to break the religious law prohibiting travel on the Sabbath. Perhaps it was only on the High Holy Days and Passover that they could find it feasible to join other Jews in the established cities. Inevitably at times many of the new arrivals felt lonely and homesick. Nevertheless they persevered and improved their economic situation until they could settle in a little town. There they would join other Jewish peddlers in forming a fledgling community. On the positive side, life on the road taught the Jewish immigrants about America and forced them to learn English.

The power structure of the new American-Jewish community emerged quickly. The Sephardic Jews who had immigrated in the eighteenth and early nineteenth centuries had already established Jewish communities along the Atlantic Coast. Many of them were fully assimilated, and intermarriage was not uncommon. They considered themselves the Jewish upper crust and maintained their distance from the new arrivals. The Bavarian Jews, who had begun arriving earlier, in the 1830s and 1840s, and in greater numbers than the Württemberg Jews, stood atop the social and economic strata of the central and eastern European Jews. During the peak period of 1854 to 1857, more than 1,500 Bavarian Jews immigrated, compared with just a few hundred from Württemberg. The Bavarians assumed leadership roles in the four new synagogues built in New York City and organized new fraternal organizations. While eastern European Jews and Christians lumped the Jews from Baden and Württemberg with those from Bavaria as "German Jews," the Bavarians differentiated themselves as a special category of elite American Jews.

In the New World the Jews were still considered a distinct group. Many officers and employees of the Christian-run banks and credit-rating organizations viewed Jews through the prism of stereotypes, prejudices, and unfamiliarity—all imported from Europe. The economic situation of some Jewish immigrants gave credence to some of their practical concerns. Certainly peddlers, with only their goods and no fixed residence, were not good credit risks compared with the Christians, who could put up their farms as collateral. Even after Jews had opened shops in the urban areas, they still had no fixed residence since they rented, rather than bought, their houses and stores in an effort to improve their business location as often as possible. Because Jews usually paid with cash, they revealed as little financial information as necessary. Some reports by the representatives of the R. G. Dun & Co., the national credit-rating firm, reflected these common attitudes toward Jews.

Not surprisingly, Jews continued many of the business practices they had used in Europe. Jewish shopkeepers bought from Jewish middlemen and wholesalers. These merchants formed an informal Jewish banking organization that worked parallel to the official institutions. The merchants would extend credit, supply goods on commission, and lend money for new business ventures. Just as they were in the German lands, these transactions were treated strictly as business, not charity, even when relatives were involved.

Shortly after his arrival, Simson married Nanette Loewenthal, who had also emigrated from Württemberg. Just as many other immigrants did, Simson changed the spelling of his name to the more American Samson. He settled in Davenport, Iowa, by 1854. Iowa, then a territory, had a population of approximately 192,000. In 1846 only 16 Jews lived there. Ten years later the number had grown to 175. Davenport, with a total population of 500, had attracted a small core of German Jews. Russian and Polish peddlers had settled in the other Iowa towns, Keokuk and Burlington. At the eastern bend of the Mississippi River, Jews established three separate communities: in Davenport on the north bank in Iowa and at Moline and Rock Island on the south bank in Illinois.

As early as 1855, a small group of Jews in Davenport bought and improved a section of the Pine Hill Cemetery in the town. The headstone inscriptions, written mostly in German and poor Hebrew, often included references to the deceased's native village. B. Eiseman described his community in 1857 in an article that appeared in the English-language Jewish newspaper (published in Philadelphia), *The Occident*:

> Truly may it be said that onward and forward is the watchword of Israel. Where immigration finds its way, a part of Israel's children always follows; the reason is that our sacred cause is expounded everywhere and has its followers on the whole globe....
>
> Thinking it necessary for the advancement of our long-cherished religion, we, the young men of this city and Rock Island, Illinois, started a

society known as the "Young Men's Hebrew Literary Association" for the promotion of our sacred cause, for the benefit of ourselves and mankind at large. We number at present twelve members; the right spirit and harmony prevail, and we know no such word as fail, with the guidance from an All-Wise Providence....

There is till now no congregation formed in either place. There are enough Israelites in both places for three times a minyan, but I am at a loss to state why nothing has yet been done. The young men have indeed tried to start a congregation, but the married men keeping aloof, induced us to take the step we did in starting a literary society of young men only.[4]

Samson opened a clothing store, Berlizheimer & Fleishman, on Front Street. Fleishman, his wife's relative, was reported to have money and furnished the goods for the store. It was not a growing concern, according to the R.G. Dun & Co. reports in the 1850s:

1855: Keep a one-horse clothing store. Are German Israelites and as all Israelites do keep their own matters so close that their circumstances cannot be ascertained with any degree of certainty. They have no real estate and but a small capital. Israelites that have no real estate to bind them to a certain locality, we would not trust.

1856: Being Jews we do not think them entitled to credit.

1858: Jews, don't know anything of them.[5]

The Jewish merchants and shopkeepers became a visible if not significant group. The *Davenport Gazette* published its first piece of Jewish news in 1858:

A Holy Day—Last Saturday was a Holy Day or Thanksgiving Day [Day of Atonement] with the Israelites here and elsewhere. All the stores of these citizens were closed during the day and till evening there was a strict fast. Week before last was the commencement of the new year in the Jewish calendar.[6]

In the years following Samson's arrival in Iowa, other Jews from Mühringen settled nearby. His sister, Hanna, and her husband, Abraham Rosenfeld, might have lived there. Abraham's three cousins settled in Rock Island, where they opened a leather, saddle, and harness store. Baruch Loewenthal, who emigrated in 1848 after being trained as a confectionery baker by his father, also settled in Rock Island. He opened the Railroad Clothing Store with Aaron Block and advertised in the local newspaper in 1852. Loewenthal became embroiled in the politics of the day. He and a few other German-Jewish immigrants joined German immigrants to fight the growing anti-immigration and antiforeigner movement during the election campaign of 1856. As one of the officers of the group, whose efforts contributed to the election of a Democratic president, he made a name for himself. Shortly afterward he was elected Democratic alderman to the city council.

Samson Berlizheimer's half-brother Bernhard joined him in the Iowa-Illinois region. While Samson settled in Davenport, Bernhard settled in the young city of Chicago, Illinois, just as it was growing at a dramatic rate. Prior to 1838 no Jews had lived in Illinois. In 1837 Chicago, with five thousand inhabitants, was incorporated as a city, and by 1844 about twenty Jews had settled there.

The first High Holy Day services were held the next year. A group organized the Jewish Burial Ground Society and bought an acre of land for $46. In 1847 the burial society constituted itself as the first Jewish congregation in Chicago, Kehillath Anshe Maarav (Congregation of the Men of the West), known as K.A.M. Its twenty members held services in a room above a clothing store and followed the *minhag* Ashkenazi, the religious rituals and customs of the German-speaking Jews in Europe. When one member's elderly mother suffered from malnutrition caused by a lack of kosher meat, the congregation hired Reverend Ignatz Kunreuther from New York City to serve as its reader (*ḥazzan*) and ritual slaughterer. After six years, however, he felt that the congregation was leaning toward what he considered Reform ideas and retired to private life.

A strong wave of emigration from the East Coast began in 1849 after the completion of the Illinois–Michigan Canal and the Galena–Chicago Railroad to Elgin. By 1850, the total population of Chicago had grown to thirty thousand, including about two hundred Jews. The community needed a larger cemetery. The Hebrew Benevolent Society, a charitable organization, purchased a larger cemetery plot in the center of the North Side. It bought three acres of land just south of the Graceland Cemetery for $600. But Chicago Jewry was still a fledgling community. It did not have the facilities, for example, to prepare the matzos for Passover, so the established community in Cincinnati provided matzos for them, just as it did for the other small communities in Indiana, Illinois, Tennessee, Kentucky, and Missouri.

One of the basic contrasts all the new immigrants encountered was a completely different organization of religious denominations. In Württemberg, as in the other German and European states, each person was automatically a member of the religious community in his village, and he had to pay taxes to that community and abide by its rules. The government had

REVEREND IGNATZ KUNREUTHER Rabbi Kunreuther, born in Gelnhausen near Frankfurt am Main into a family of important rabbis, was very traditional, a good talmudic scholar, and well versed in Hebrew literature. He immigrated in the 1840s to join his brother, who was serving as a rabbi in New York City. Since Kunreuther was not an ordained rabbi, he was referred to as "Reverend" (a title already in use in England). He served as the rabbi of Congregation K.A.M. from 1847–53—the first rabbi of Chicago. (Private collection, Janet Iltis.)

to approve any new religious organization, so there was usually only one serving each denomination. In America, on the other hand, each person could voluntarily decide to join a congregation and to pay its fees, and any little group could start up a new church or synagogue. The new system encouraged small groups to join together based on a shared, transferred, or desired level of religious orthodoxy. The lack of a Jewish Board or of even a chief rabbi encouraged freedom and, consequently, some disarray. Congregations could hire and fire rabbis without getting approval from higher authorities. The rabbi's religious background and tendencies had a strong influence over the congregation, so its choice of a rabbi was very important.

In the 1850s in the German states, Reform innovations, like the use of an organ in the synagogue, were just beginning to take hold in the new urban communities but had not yet been accepted by the rural communities. The lack of traditions, the influence of the new freedoms, and the urge to become American created a fertile new arena for the Reform movement. Rabbi Isaac Mayer Wise, a participant at the 1845 Frankfurt am Main rabbinical conference, emerged as the leader of the Reform movement in America. In 1858 some members of K.A.M. formed the Juedischer Reformverein, or Jewish Reform Association, and two years later twenty-six members seceded from K.A.M. to form the Sinai Congregation under Rabbi Bernard Felsenthal. Reform congregations in America went further than those in the German cities by allowing men and women to sit together. Even in those synagogues, however, the sermons were still given in German.

The social, cultural, and even religious differences that separated the south German Jews and those from the eastern parts of the German-speaking lands (Prussia and Bohemia) traveled across the ocean as well. The early congregants themselves were divided: the south German Jews did not make the Jews from Prussian Posen feel welcome. The chasm between the German-speaking Jews and the Jews from farther east (from Poland and Lithuania) was wider still. In some cases German-Jewish relief organizations would not give aid to the eastern European Jews.

Mina Berlizheimer and her children most likely decided before their departure from Mühringen in 1857 that they would settle in the larger city of Chicago with her son, rather than in Davenport with her stepson. Their first reaction to Chicago probably mirrored Henriette Chambrey's:

> I like it here very much. Everything exceeds all my expectations. For more than a week, our house was full with all the Chicago Jews who wanted to

welcome me and congratulate my sister and brother-in-law on my arrival. I haven't finished yet with all the visits that I have to make in return because people are very friendly. Great finery is the prevailing fashion here without difference between workday or Sunday. Crossing the street without a hat and a shawl would create quite a stir here. My clothes, which I wore on Sundays at home, are here just good enough for weekdays. You don't wear some old jacket when you get up; you get dressed right away. My sister had a silk stole made for me even for the very first Sunday. It cost seven dollars. The following week, she bought me some muslin with a black and white floral design for a dress, which cost three dollars, a parasol for two dollars, and a couple more items for two to three dollars. One lives here better to a large extent than in Germany. More meat gets thrown out here every day by us than [we] bought at home. There are no poor people to whom one could give it. Every morning the baker delivers fresh bread, and milk is delivered both mornings and evenings. The cakes that we make every Sunday, even on a weekday sometimes, aren't put into the baker's oven, but into our own oven at home. No one grows anything here, one buys it all in shops to which the farmers bring their produce. Here no one lifts his hat to anyone, as there's no hierarchy, but everything's equal. One is as the other is. Women are respected much more than at home. It's not required of any woman, even a maid, to fetch a bucket of water or to carry a full basket across the street; but this is the man's responsibility. It struck me as very peculiar to see a gentleman in his best clothes carrying a basket on his arm. But people at home are under a great misconception if they believe that the blacks are rich and well respected here. On the contrary, they are the lowest class and the servants of the white people. In the South, they are even slaves.

We have a beautiful apartment and from our windows we can see the boats come and go. On the other side is the market building, which is three times larger than the Palais. On the bottom floor there are butcher shops; on the upper floor, there are concert and ballrooms. On Sundays one goes out for a ride. We did that also on the two Sundays that I have been here, and it was a particular pleasure for our Jettchen. She is a lovely little girl and gives us a lot of pleasure. Several times already I was invited to go to the theater, but I didn't accept because it is still a time of mourning for me. Also I cannot interest myself in the plays because they are given in English, which I don't understand yet, but hope to do very soon. Beginning this week I have been going to English school.

And now, how are you all at home? I wouldn't like to think that war or revolution would create trouble for you.

Give my regards to the whole neighborhood. I can't tell anything that my sister hasn't already said in her letter, namely that the prospects for a Jewish maid aren't good, because all Jews and Christians have only one maid, and one doesn't need a second one because there isn't so much to clean since all the floors are covered with small carpets.

My sincerest greetings. In the hope of hearing from you soon, I remain your loving sister.

Henriette Chambrey[7]

When Mina Berlizheimer and her children arrived in Chicago, they lived together. Bernhard was working first as a salesman and then as a clerk at Klein & Mandel. After only four years in America, Mina died at age fifty-four.

At the time of the 1860 United States census, Chicago was a growing city with 112,000 people, including 1,500 Jews. Early immigrants, like Bernhard and Samson, were moving on and becoming shopkeepers and jobbers, but new immigrants, mostly from Prussia and eastern Europe, took their place as peddlers. In 1860, 16,000 Jewish peddlers still plied that trade.

In Chicago, Bernhard and a partner opened a store called Moss & Berlizheimer. R.G. Dun & Co. stated that it was a small retail business in which he "bought for cash and seems to be doing pretty well."[8] Since Bernhard was already established, his younger brothers did not have to first peddle in the countryside before going into business in the city. The experience of the Berlizheimer brothers was typical of other Jewish family businesses: brothers working as partners, or one brother employing the younger brothers. Most small-scale businessmen adopted their family name as the name of the company, and the painted signs above the shops in towns and cities reflected the German-Jewish origins of their owners. In the 1850s and 1860s, Jews predominated in men's clothing and fabric stores, a natural progression from the centuries of the textile trade in Europe and then the years of peddling clothes in America.

Bernhard then went out on his own, opening B. Berlizheimer Dry Goods and Clothing. Two of his brothers worked in his new store. According to R.G. Dun & Co., he had bonds and cash outside the store and did a "small safe business." Their store and homes were on the Near North Side, which was a popular neighborhood with many German-Jewish immigrants.

The family in Chicago kept up with Samson in Davenport, Iowa. The R.G. Dun & Co. reported that he had no real estate, and in 1859 his business was declared "worthless" and was closed out. Samson became an agent, but again the credit-rating company stated that it was "a small concern and was not considered reliable."[9]

At the end of 1861, eighteen men approved the constitution of Davenport's first congregation, Congregation Bnai Israel. According to the

Fany Grünwald — ∞ — **David Berlizheimer** — ∞ — **Mina Gundelfinger**
1799–1834   1826   1798–1849   1835   1806–1861
                                                    1857 to America

Isaak <Isaac>
1832–[after 1864]
1857 to America

Hanna
1830–[after 1863]
∞ 1854 Abraham
Rosenfeld <Rosenfield>
1854 to America

Nehemia <Nathan>
1828–[after 1873]
1862 to America

Simson <Samson>
1827–1896
1848 to America
∞ before 1850
Nanette Loewenthal
(Württemberg)

Bernhard
1838–1915
1854 to America
∞ 1869 Henriette
Kunreuther
(Chicago, Illinois)

Sara
1839– [after 1920]
1857 to America
∞ Marx Reinauer
<Max Rinow>

Karoline <Carrie>
1842–1903
1857 to America
∞ 1866 Bernhard Moos
(Buchau)

Eleazar (Lazarus)
<Louis>
1844–1937
1857 to America
∞ 1874 Ida Bach
(Binswangen)
∞ 1877 (Lena Kunreuther)
Chicago, Illinois

Maier <**Richard M.**>
1845–1920
1857 to America
∞ 1873 **Fannie Weil**
(Ann Arbor,
Michigan)

[ ] Unconfirmed information
( ) Birthplace
If not otherwise indicated, birthplace was Mühringen.
< > Name in America

BERLIZHEIMER FAMILY IN AMERICA   Descendants of David Berlizheimer in America.

CLARK STREET, CHICAGO, 1857 Jewish owners placed their family names on their store signs—such as the store or tavern of J. Finkelstain [*sic*] and the clothing store of Abraham. (*View on Clark Street 1857—Raising the Grade*. Courtesy of the Chicago Historical Society.)

German-language minutes, the men held elections for officers, and Samson was chosen secretary. In that position Samson placed advertisements in *The Occident* and *The Israelite* (published in Cincinnati):

> WANTED: The congregation Bene Israel desires to engage the services of a married man, competent to fill the situation of Chazan and Shochet, and able to give religious instruction, and teach the German language. Salary $350 per annum, and if the candidate possessed the qualifications of a Mohel, further income of $150 may be counted upon. Applications, accompanied by certificates of competency, are to be made to the undersigned, and personal applications can only be made at the expense of the candidates.
>
> S. Berolzheimer [*sic*], Sec'y.
> Davenport, Iowa, January 1, 1862.[10]

241

The *Davenport Gazette* reported the next step the fledgling congregation undertook:

> **Jewish Synagogue**—The Jews of this city have rented a room in the third story of Forest's Block, on Perry Street, which they are fitting up for a synagogue. They were negotiating for the use of Wesley Chapel, at the time it was burned down, but that unfortunate occurrence has caused them to select more humble quarters. We understand there are quite a number of that persuasion in our city.[11]

By March the new congregation had hired Reverend Dr. H. Loewenthal as its cantor. He gave religious instruction six hours a day for four days a week and taught German to the children. He served as ritual slaughterer three times a week during the summer and twice a week during the winter. The congregation paid him $350 a year, plus $5 for each circumcision. Rev. Kunreuther performed the first recorded Jewish marriage ceremony in Iowa in Davenport in 1864; the retired rabbi wrote "State Iowa" on the second line of the Hebrew marriage contract.

Samson's brother, Nehemia, the last of David's children to emigrate, joined him in Davenport in 1862. It was clearly time for Nehemia, at age thirty-four, to try his luck in America. After his stepmother and brothers and sisters had emigrated, Nehemia had been rejected for citizen's rights in the town of Oberndorf, where several Mühringen Jews had recently settled. He had stated falsely that he possessed sufficient assets (1,500 gulden) when he actually had none. He then ran a match factory in Ebingen, in another county, although its town council had originally refused his petition. Only months later the county court ordered an investigation because Nehemia had not overseen his business properly but had gambled, had gone into debt, and had no assets to cover his debts. The next year the town council reported to the county court that he also was a "liar and untrustworthy man who tended to live off the expenses of others."[12] Nehemia returned to Mühringen from Ebingen, and was involved in some unsuccessful business transactions for his poor widowed stepaunt, Sophie Ottenheimer, and her brother, Salomon Gundelfinger. It was hardly surprising that he did not fill out the official emigration applications before he sailed from Southampton, England, to New York.

Meanwhile, the prospects for business opportunities were expanding in Chicago. After ten years in Davenport, Samson joined his family there. He lived with or near his brother Bernhard and worked as a dry goods merchant and agent. Nehemia, who changed his given name to Nathan, also moved there. Berthold Loewenthal, who changed his name from Baruch, left Rock Island for Chicago, where he eventually became an important bank officer, the president of a large Reform congregation and of many Jewish charitable organizations, and the president and a director of the Chicago Public Library. The impact of these and other departures for the larger urban areas curtailed most of the organized religious activities in the immigrants' former small-town Jewish communities for several decades.

Two years after opening his store Bernhard married Henriette, the daughter of Rev. Ignatz Kunreuther, the former rabbi of K.A.M. synagogue. The Berlizheimers' traditional rural religious background must have been acceptable to the very traditional Rev. Kunreuther. Henriette had been born in Chicago and was twenty-one when she married Bernhard. Most of his brothers and sisters lived together near the store. By this time, Lazarus had changed his given name to Louis to make it sound more American, and Maier had changed the spelling of his name to Meyer.

The immigrants' ties with their German roots remained strong. Children living in America would send money or presents home to their parents and relatives, and some recent immigrants returned to the German lands on business trips or to visit their relatives in their home villages. These trips were occasionally reported in the local newspapers. The Rock Island newspaper, for example, reported in 1858 that Berthold Loewenthal and Joseph Rosenfield (formerly Rosenfeld) were embarking on a summer tour of Europe. The distribution of inheritances was another reason to maintain contact. In 1862 a Berlizheimer uncle passed away, leaving his assets to his nieces and nephews. Their notarized papers disclaiming their inheritance were duly filed in the curator archives in Mühringen.

In 1864 and 1865 Bernhard spent several months in the southwest German region. He took a sixteen-hour fencing course (costing 7 gulden) at the University in Heidelberg. Six months later he took care of business in Mühringen. His half-brother, Isaac (formerly Isaak), sent him a full power of attorney in German to take care of his business and legal affairs. Bernhard most likely arranged for Isaac's inheritance (1,032 gulden) from his mother, which Isaac received the next year. In the same power of attorney, Isaac revoked his allegiance to the king and citizenship rights in Württemberg. Although he had been an adult when he had left, his name had merely been included in his stepmother's emigration application.

On the same trip, Bernhard attended to some family affairs for his three Ottenheimer cousins, who were living in New York City. Their parents had recently passed away, and Jacob Ottenheimer authorized Cantor Salomon Löwenthal to erect headstones on their graves, establish a charitable foundation, and give any remaining inheritance money to Bernhard, who would then distribute it to Jacob and his sisters. Bernhard signed an official receipt for the small sum (37 gulden 7 kreuzer). The matching headstones erected were not costly: the stone was very poor quality and the inscriptions were carved in very shallow German script.

In Chicago, the younger sisters and brothers were getting married, and the family was growing. Karoline Berlizheimer, who went by the name Carrie, married Bernhard Moos. Carrie's husband came from a similar background, having lived his first twenty-five years in Buchau, a town in south Württemberg, where he trained as a bookkeeper. Buchau with 625 Jews in 1843 was a larger, more cosmopolitan community than Mühringen. Most of the Jews in Buchau were shopkeepers and tradesmen and were part of one or more large extended families: Moos, Wallersteiner, Rieser, and Einstein. The Buchau synagogue was famous for its unique church bell in the Protestant-style steeple. The bell, which called the Jews to prayer, was a gift from the king of Württemberg in 1839. The story was told that when the Jews had to decide whether to accept the king's gift, they concluded that the king would not understand their refusal, but God would understand their acceptance.

As a new immigrant in 1860, Bernhard worked as a bookkeeper for the banking house of Lazarus Silverman in Chicago and then followed the path of many immigrants with limited financial resources. He and his brother opened a small cigar, tobacco, and snuff shop in the basement of Metropolitan Hall. Even during the brothers' first years in business, R.G. Dun & Co. representatives reported that they had a very good stand, paid promptly, and were "good for small amounts."[13] Bernhard considered himself quite cultured and literary minded; he served as the part-time librarian at the Young Men's Association.

Another Berlizheimer sister, Sara, remained close to the family and certainly close to her background. She married Marx Reinauer, a native of Mühringen. In the 1850s he had been training as a shoemaker when his father died; the family was split up, with several children going into foster homes or

---

BERNHARD BERLIZHEIMER'S DRY GOODS & GENTLEMEN'S CLOTHING STORE
Bernhard opened the store in 1864. The painted sign above the store at 130–132 North Clark said: "B. Berlizheimer. Dry Goods & Clothing." The signs in two display windows read: "Gents Furnishing Goods" and "Fashionable Clothing." (Private collection, Janet Iltis.)

**BERNHARD MOOS (B. 1843, BUCHAU) AND CARRIE MOOS (B. KAROLIN|
BERLIZHEIMER)**   Their photographs were taken in Chicago, probably around 186€
during their engagement. (Private collection, William Rieser.)

the Esslingen orphanage. Marx clearly had had no other viable option whe㎗
he emigrated in 1856 at eighteen; one of his brothers left shortly afterward
They changed the spelling of their surname to Rinow, and Marx adopted th㎗
name Max. Max and Sara settled 150 miles west of Davenport in Waterloa
Iowa, where Max had a store and bought some real estate.

Less than fifteen years after arriving in America, the extended Ber㎗
lizheimer family was very well established. Samson Berlizheimer, Bernhar€
Moos, and Max Rinow became United States citizens before 1870, and, al
though the documents have not come down to us, most likely the other㎗
did so as well. Most of the family members rented their own houses. Bern
hard and Carrie Moos employed a young German immigrant girl as a live-i㎗
maid. The siblings' financial situations were improving as well. Max Rino㎗
returned to Chicago and owned a flour and feed store. He eventually opene€
a notions and fancy goods store. Nathan also opened a store, under th㎗
name N. Berlizheimer. Meyer, having already changed his name once
changed it again to the more American Richard. He and Louis took ove㎗

SARA RINOW (B. SARA BERLIZHEIMER) AND MAX RINOW (B. MARX REINAUER, 1838, MÜHRINGEN) The photo was taken in Chicago between the years 1857–70. (Private collection, Janet Iltis.)

Bernhard's dry goods store and renamed it L. & R. Berlizheimer. Bernhard left the family retail business, becoming the owner of first the Mozart Billiards Hall and then a saloon. He later became a partner in a window, lock, and sash business with Henry Cahn.

Although the Jews who had settled in Chicago were still only a fraction of the 150,000 American Jews, they were involved in national causes. A local lodge of the first Jewish fraternal society, B'nai B'rith (Sons of the Covenant) was organized in Chicago in 1857, fourteen years after it had been founded by a small group of south German Jews in New York.

The Jews were part of American society, as evident from the approximately 6,500 Jewish soldiers who fought with the Union forces, and the 2,000 who joined the Confederacy in the Civil War. While most Jews in both the North and the South resisted forming specifically Jewish military regiments and hospitals, in 1862 Chicago's Jews recruited a Jewish company of a hundred volunteers to join the 82nd Regiment of Illinois Volunteers and raised $10,000 to support it. German-born Jews as well as those born in eastern Europe fought in the company. The *Chicago Tribune* commended their largesse and the rapidity of these efforts, offering its "best wishes for their future and our hopes that victory may always crown their arms."[14] No members of the Berlizheimer, Gundelfinger, or Kaz families fought in the war, but other emigrants from their native villages did. Isaak Esslinger, the well-educated son of a well-off jeweler in Mühringen, joined the Union Army under General Ulysses S. Grant and advanced to captain in the infantry in the Indiana militia. After the war, he returned to Mühringen to bring his bride back to Indiana. President Grant appointed him as a customs appraiser for the river port of Evansville, Indiana, and subsequently he returned to his father's trade, opening a jewelry store.[15]

Religious life in Chicago became more diverse. Some Jews set up new congregations based on religious leanings, while other congregations evolved for more practical issues. In 1867 a group of thirty-two Jews living on the Near North Side, finding the distance to travel to the other synagogues too far, organized the North Chicago Hebrew Congregation. Some Berlizheimer family members joined and became leaders. The congregation was founded on traditional principles but soon adopted moderate reforms. Its members paid an initiation fee and also paid for seats in the synagogue, just as they had done in their German communities. The new congregation leased a piece of property and built a modest frame synagogue for $6,000. In 1867 the German Jews founded a nonsectarian hospital. By 1870 eleven congregations served the community; seven of them owned their own buildings. Life was looking very good.

Then, on October 8, 1871, tragedy struck Chicago: on the eve of Simhat Torah, the Great Chicago Fire devastated the lives of all Chicagoans. The German Jews, who lived predominantly in the Near North Side, experienced the great blaze very personally. Bernhard Moos wrote in German to his family in Buchau—opening with a quote from a famous German poet:

Chicago, October 24, 1871.

Beloved Mother and Dear Sister and Brother:
Schiller in his Song of the Bell tells us

"Alas, with the might of Providence
We can make no pacts,
For calamity rushes on."

Were I, dear ones, to report correctly our present position I would advise you to read the song of Schiller, especially that part where he treats of fire; then indeed you would understand. He counted the heads of his dear ones and sees not a precious one is missing. First of all, I can today assure you that his last line thoroughly fits our case. Thank God not one is missing and, considering conditions, all are in good health.

It is now the first quiet moment permitted me to write you since that terrible October 9th, and at the same time to take a fresh breath and ease this burden of care and worry.

To begin, I must remark that here in this western country since the end of July a terrible drought prevailed of such severity that since the end of September, the forest and prairies hereabouts, especially in Michigan, Wisconsin, and Minnesota, for thousands of miles have been devastated by fire, everything in its path destroyed, men, cattle, farms, mills, villages, even towns.

On the 5th of October at noon, a general fire alarm was sounded, and soon the news spread that one of the largest warehouses on the South Side was afire; nevertheless the fire was brought under control by 5:00 P.M. Quiet prevailed until Saturday night at 9:00 when again the general alarm sounded. This time there was a large fire on the West Side that raged until morning.

On this Sunday evening, the 8th of October, Julius [Bernhard's brother] and my wife's brothers and sisters were at my home. We were discussing the fire and many other things. There were jokes and laughter until they left about 9:00, when my wife and I went to bed. My wife's brother awakened us shortly after 1:00 A.M. Monday, and we found heaven and earth afire. Owing to the prevailing dryness and southwest hurricane, the fire had an easy victory over all efforts of firemen and others. Like an army column in close formation, it marched forward with almost electrical rapidity. When we were aroused three hours after it started, the fire had already destroyed about thirty acres of buildings on the West Side. Driven by the high wind, it left that side, crossed the river, and was now raging in the greater part of the beautiful South Side, mocking all efforts of man and water.

Leaving my house with my brother-in-law, we rushed over to the South Side where my business was located to see whether anything could be saved. Arriving, we found all adjoining buildings in flames. I could do nothing but take what little money there was in my safe and hurry with all speed to save my life.

When I returned to my house, I found that my dear wife had had the presence of mind to pack and send the children and the maid to her sister who lived farther north and then had packed our most important possessions. The fire was now raging behind us, having crossed the river at 3:00 P.M., burning the bridges between the North and the South Sides. By this time the fire had already destroyed the water works, thus increasing the horrors. With great effort I found and hired a wagon team to move our possessions to my sister-in-law's house.

We turned our backs to the flames that rushed after us. With the wind, a hurricane of dust and smoke, almost blinding us, we left Chicago with a hundred thousand others, fleeing far out to the open prairie. At about 4:00 P.M., broken in spirit and soul, we arrived at a farmer's barn to set up our camp, mindful of the words of Moses,

> "Who is man that your thoughts are of him?
> Earth's son that you look upon him."

The conflagration raged for twenty-nine hours. An estimated 300 people perished, and a third of the population, 100,000 people, were left homeless. More than 17,000 buildings in a four-square-mile area—both businesses and homes—were destroyed. Five hundred Jewish families were left homeless, and 300 families were left destitute. Five of the seven synagogues burned down. The Jewish hospital burned, and thirteen patients perished. Countless stories of individual bravery and sacrifice were reported. Richard Berlizheimer, for example, saved an infant from the inferno and brought his charge to safety outside the city.

B'nai B'rith lodges throughout the country sent immediate relief aid. Supplies and more than $25,000 helped the recovery efforts. Even in those catastrophic circumstances, the Jews did not turn to the government or the Christian organizations but helped one another. The *Chicago Times* praised the Jews because "not one Jew has been sent to ask for the aid of the general or special relief committee of the Gentiles."[16]

In this same letter, Bernhard Moos went on to describe his very quick recovery from the fire:

Now my loved ones, about myself as briefly as possible. What I had possessed has been destroyed, and my hopes blasted. My loss was not less than from $12,000 to $15,000. Though I carried $10,000 in insurance, nearly all companies are bankrupt so that I can expect little, or more correctly, nothing from that source.

Julius, as well as myself, has each found a place to start a business. The great pains we had always taken to keep our credit good have now borne good fruit. In New York and elsewhere, we are offered as much, and even more, goods than we can use.

Chicago will arise again out of her ashes, and though the marble is still hot, building is going on in every quarter. Stronger, more beautiful than before, Chicago will grow greater than ever.

> With hearty greetings and kisses,
> your affectionate son and brother,
> Bernhard

My dear Ones,

Agreeing with every word of the above, I further wish to assure you that the children and I are well.

> Your loving,
> Carrie[17]

The leaders of Chicago shared Bernhard's optimism. Slightly less than half of the property loss, calculated at $196 million, was covered by the settlement of insurance claims. Nevertheless, the business and civic leaders immediately decided to rebuild the city and make it bigger and better than the one destroyed. More costly buildings were rapidly constructed; the value of the real estate increased greatly. Only four years later, few traces of the Great Chicago Fire could be found.

The recovery of the Jewish community was slower than for the city as a whole. The North Chicago Hebrew Congregation's synagogue was destroyed in the fire, and its rabbi had returned to Europe. He returned to serve the congregation a few years later; during that time its members held religious services in several churches. Only after a fund-raising fair eleven years following the fire did the congregation have sufficient money to start building a new synagogue. It was in the style of the other new synagogues of the day—large, dramatic structures that resembled those being constructed by the urban Jews in both Germany and America.

After the fire the Berlizheimer family members were still young enough to rebuild what they had lost and to expand into new opportunities such as real estate. Just as Bernhard had written in his letter, his strong credit rating and reputation (confirmed by the R.G. Dun & Co. reports) enabled him to open a cigar stand in Sherman House, near City Hall. The business was very successful, and the family increased its assets by buying real estate in the city.

The fire had also destroyed the Berlizheimers' notions and dry goods stores. Nathan moved his store to another location and opened it under the name Nathan Berlizheimer & Sons. Louis and Richard reopened their store as well in another location. When Richard left the business in 1875, Louis brought in Paul Stensland as a partner and renamed the store Berlizheimer & Stensland. Louis, at thirty, married Ida Bach, who died two years later. He then married Bernhard's sister-in-law, Lena Kunreuther, and their family lived near the other families. The Rinows' notions store suffered great losses in the fire. Although the R.G. Dun & Co. reported that Max was a "straight businessman" and "considered very good risk for small amounts,"[18] he sold out and moved to the town of Carthage, Illinois (240 miles west of Chicago), but a few years later he returned to Chicago. His wife bought a building where he opened another notions and fancy goods store. The Rinow family lived in the building, and for some years Samson lived there as well.

Richard, the youngest Berlizheimer brother, took over one of Bernhard Moos's cigar and tobacco stands. In 1873 he married Fannie Weil. While the couple shared a common culture of German-speaking rural Jews, they had had experienced very different paths in America. The match joined a recent immigrant of modest means with an American-born girl whose family had lived the American Dream.

Fannie's ancestors had lived in Bohumelitz (now Bohumilice), a tiny village in Bohemia surrounded by rolling hills with farms; nearby was the town of Skene (now Čkyně), with a sizable Jewish community. The community worshiped in a two-story synagogue with summer and winter sanctuaries. On the walls of the synagogue were colorful paintings with the lion of Judah painted over the Holy Ark. The Holy Ark was painted sky-blue dotted with golden stars, a style also seen in the other German-speaking lands. The old Jewish cemetery, on a hill overlooking the town, had beautifully carved Hebrew inscriptions on the headstones.

In the 1840s the Weil brothers emigrated with young members of other families. Some of the men brought their wives with them, while the others sent for their wives or fiancées after settling in America. Fannie's father, Solomon, came first in 1843 and peddled dry goods in Michigan; his four brothers followed. Three brothers were notions peddlers and then shopkeepers. Two brothers tried farming, but gave it up after a year because the "familiarity of the savage beast of the forest, added to the utter wildness of the locality, were just too much for them."[19] Jacob, the last to arrive, had studied to be a rabbi and had graduated with honors from a university in Hungary. He was fluent in French and served as an interpreter with the Canadian traders; his shop became known as the French Shop.

After sixteen years in America, two brothers bought a tannery in Ann Arbor that all the brothers joined, forming the partnership of J. Weil & Bros. The numerous R.G. Dun & Co. reports, while noting occasionally that they were Jews or Israelites, applauded their business acumen: they were "respectable men," "hard-working," "money-making men," possessing "good business capacity, good habits, and character."[20] They prospered in a region that had a large Indian population and important wool and hide trades. Just three years after they bought the tannery, R.G. Dun & Co. reported the brothers' worth as $50,000 and their business as "one of the most successful firms in the West." By 1871 their assets (including three tanneries, several stores, and real estate) were worth at least $300,000.

The Weil family members maintained their strong ties to their religion. In 1845 the first Sabbath service in the state of Michigan was held in their home. One brother served as cantor and ritual slaughterer, and in 1848 a *mohel* was brought from Cleveland, 150 miles away, to perform a circumcision. The brothers established a Jewish cemetery, where they erected a memorial headstone in honor of their mother, who had died in Bohemia. When their father, Joseph, and stepmother came to America in 1850, Joseph carried a Torah scroll in his arms all the way to Ann Arbor.

The Weils adapted rapidly to their new home. The university-educated Jacob was offered the position as chair of the Department of Languages at the University of Michigan, but he refused, citing his commitment to the family business. He was elected alderman of his ward and was nominated for mayor of Ann Arbor before his departure for Newark, New Jersey, to open a branch of the tannery. By 1870 the business's headquarters was moved to Chicago, where four brothers (including Fannie's father with his family) resided. The family suffered in the Great Chicago Fire: the tannery was destroyed, and one brother was severely injured.

Richard and Fannie lived at first with the Moos family; after six years they rented their own home. Richard's cigar stand prospered, and he became a jobber as well. None of the Berlizheimers joined the Weil family business, but the families remained very close. Richard also stayed in contact in Chicago with a Gundelfinger cousin who anglicized his surname to Gundelson.

FANNIE BERLIZHEIMER (B. WEIL, 1856) The photographs on these facing pages were taken in Chicago in 1873, most likely during the couple's engagement. (Private collection, Fannie Berliss Rosenbaum.)

RICHARD BERLIZHEIMER (B. MAIER, 1845) (Private collection, Fannie Berliss Rosenbaum.)

JOSEPH WEIL IN ANN ARBOR, MICHIGAN (B. 1777, BOHEMIA/D. 1863, ANN ARBOR) In 1861, at age eighty-four, Fannie's grandfather led the parade to commemorate Washington's birthday. The local newspaper described him as the tallest and most spry participant. (Rabbi Leo M. Franklin Archives, Temple Beth El, Bloomfield Hills, Mich.)

A German Village in Chicago

All the families joined many organizations and participated in the growing Jewish community in Chicago's North Side. The women were members and leaders in the United Order of True Sisters, a Jewish women's organization founded in 1846. The group established its Chicago lodge, Jochannah No. 9, in 1874; the records were kept in German. All the families were registered Republicans. While Bernhard Moos did not affiliate with a synagogue, he was very active in civic and cultural affairs in Chicago. Selected as a director of the new Chicago Public Library, he devoted much of his time and efforts to supervising the construction of its magnificent structure. When Bernhard passed away, the Democratic mayor, the library board of directors, and the many cigar associations honored him. The libraries were closed the day of his funeral. The city later named a public school after him; the Moos Elementary School is still located on North California Avenue.

As well as the new immigrants adjusted, anti-Jewish sentiment brought from Europe did not die in America. Christians and Jews interacted in business and civic matters, but each group still remained separate socially. German Jews were very cognizant of not doing anything to upset the Christians. The importance of proper decorum in the synagogues, the establishment of social service institutions, and the construction of substantial synagogue buildings were all efforts to be part of Christian society without making demands upon it. Nevertheless, overt and hidden anti-Jewish incidents occurred. These German Jews were very aware that they were Americans, but they also realized that they still made up a very tiny minority of a rapidly growing population.

The crisis times of the Civil War brought anti-Jewish feelings to the forefront of the news. Jews were not allowed to serve as army chaplains until President Lincoln changed the policy. Newspaper articles criticized the Jews as speculators. The most public incident of discrimination was General Ulysses S. Grant's accusations of misdealings by the "Jews as a class" and his order barring Jews from the Union-occupied areas under his command in the South. As a result of his order, Jewish families were forced to flee their homes in Kentucky and Mississippi. When President Lincoln became aware of the order a few weeks later, he immediately rescinded it. General Grant went on to promote many Jewish officers, but his order stood as a blot on the Jews' war efforts.

More than a decade later, in 1877, an important banker was refused a hotel room in the prestigious Grand Union Hotel in Saratoga Springs, New York, because he was a Jew. The clerk stated that Judge Henry Hilton, at that

POSTCARD FROM ARTHUR AND HENRY BERLIZHEIMER, 1885 The postcard reads "Dear Father: I hope you feel better, and that you stay that way. I feel very fine. My cousin feels a little better. I think we will have a hot day. We are all doing good, and Mabel is doing very good. Best wishes from all of us. Arthur." Mabel also sent her greetings in German. (Private collection, Emily C. Rose.)

ime the executor of the hotel, had "given instructions that no Israelites hall be permitted in the future to stop at this hotel." This policy was publicly supported by the developer of the resort of Coney Island, New York: We do not like Jews as a class...they make themselves offensive to the kind of people who principally patronize our...hotel and I am satisfied we should be better off without them than with their custom."[21] News of this anti-Jewish event spread across America and even to Germany. Berthold Auerbach, he German author, published a letter in a German-language newspaper, the Illinois Staats-Zeitung (the Illinois state newspaper), advising American Jews o "oppose with all energy the first germs of a dirty plague."[22]

The sons of David Berlizheimer's brother, Leopold, also immigrated to America. Leopold served as the cantor-teacher in the small Jewish community of Markelsheim from the late 1850s until his death in 1865. He was buried in the Jewish cemetery near Markelsheim; the headstone inscription was written in Hebrew. His widow did not return to Mühringen but remained in Markelsheim. She had no assets with which to support her three children. When his widow asked the Jewish Board for a pension, it refused her request, giving her instead a small one-time donation (30 gulden). The next year Widow Berlizheimer again asked the board for financial support. She reported that she earned money by doing handwork in the town of Mergentheim. Although a rabbi supported her petition, the board gave her an even smaller sum. She did receive Leopold's share of his deceased father's house in Mühringen (225 gulden) but still did not have the ability to support her children.

Leopold's eldest son, Isaac, enrolled in the Esslingen Teachers' Seminary for the class of 1864 to 1866, but in 1865 he presented his emigration application, under the jurisdiction of Mühringen, with a Jewish merchant from Markelsheim as his guarantor. At age eighteen Isaac sailed from Hamburg to New York. He settled in Cincinnati, and in 1871 moved to Philadelphia with his wife, Minna, and his young son, David. He eventually started a hosiery manufacturing business, and most certainly remained involved in the Jewish community and retained his ties to his family in Mühringen.

Leopold's younger son, David, trained as a watchmaker. Widow Berlizheimer received a stipend (in three installments of 60 gulden each) from the Jewish Board to pay for David's apprenticeship from 1866 to 1868 with a watchmaker in Mergentheim. Two years later, when he was eighteen, David sailed from Bremen to New York. He did not join his brother in Cincinnati;

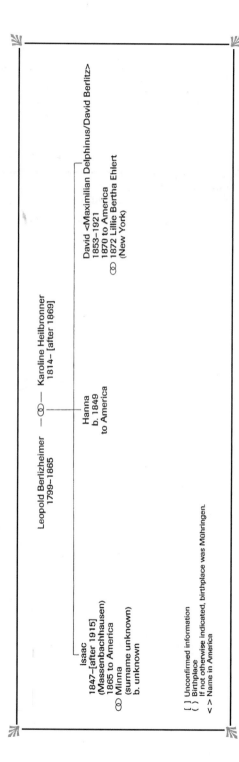

Leopold Berlizheimer — ⊘ — Karoline Heilbronner
1799–1865   1814– [after 1869]

Isaac
1847–[after 1915]
(Massenbachhausen)
1865 to America
⊘ Minna
(surname unknown)
b. unknown

Hanna
b. 1849
to America

David <Maximillian Delphinus/David Berlitz>
1853–1921
1870 to America
⊘ 1872 Lillie Bertha Ehlert
(New York)

[ ] Unconfirmed information
( ) Birthplace
     If not otherwise indicated, birthplace was Mühringen.
< > Name in America

BERLIZHEIMER FAMILY IN AMERICA   Descendants of Leopold Berlizheimer in America.

instead he settled in the town of Westerly, Rhode Island, where fewer than six Jewish families were living.

After only two years in America, David married Lillie Bertha Ehlert. Lillie, born in New York in 1854 to German immigrants, was living in Massachusetts. David's wife was Christian. By 1874 David had shortened his surname to Berlitz (sometimes spelled Burlets or Burlitz) and changed his given name to Maximilian D.—not an unusual name for a Christian of German descent. When the birth of the couple's daughter was registered in 1874, the father was listed as Max D. Berlitz, machinist

Maximilian worked days as a watchmaker in a clock repair shop. He was said to have given private Greek and Latin lessons in the evenings, and by 1875 he supposedly gave language instruction at the local high school. Maximilian claimed to have been a language teacher in France before emigrating. Although there are no documents to support that claim, he might have had some language training in Europe and certainly had an amazing ability to learn languages. In 1876, he moved his family to Providence, Rhode Island, where he was a language teacher and in charge of all language instruction at a business college. "M. D. Berlitz, Instructor in Ancient and Modern Languages," collaborated with the college's principal on a book, *The Logic of Language: An Introduction into the Science of Language*. He taught according to the traditional method of instructing in the student's native language with emphasis on grammar.

In 1877, Maximilian hired a Frenchman (who had a degree from France in literature) based on his excellent written application. Not until the new assistant arrived in Providence did Maximilian realize that the recent immigrant's English vocabulary consisted of only the few words he had used in his job as an elevator operator. How could this teacher use the traditional teaching methods with his English-speaking students? Casting about for a solution to this teaching dilemma, Maximilian told the Frenchman just to point to objects, to demonstrate verbs, and to use repetition as well as questions and answers. Under stress from overwork, Maximilian took to his bed for several weeks, tormented by visions of dissatisfied students and the ruin of his career. When he dragged himself back to school, however, he found the students fully engaged and making unbelievable progress. Although a few other teachers were using the novel communicative methods of language instruction, Maximilian took advantage of the situation and opened his own language school in the same building as the business college.

Providence Daily Journal, July 1, 1878. Classified Advertisement

Instruction—Languages

Prof. Berlitz, a native German and former resident of France, of late a teacher of English branches in this country, will receive pupils in Ancient and Modern Languages, especially in French, German and Latin; THREE MONTH'S DAILY INSTRUCTION FOR $10.

Rooms light and pleasant; method original and easy; very little memorizing required; rapid progress guaranteed; individual instruction to every student; a few days trial free; students not confined to any one hour.

Special attention to Conversation and Correspondence in French and German. Highest references, foreign and America. Apply, between 8:30 and 5 o'clock, at Room 26, Hoppin Homestead Building, 283 Westminster Street. Use the elevator.

In the 1880s he expanded The Berlitz School of Languages to Boston, Brooklyn, and Newark. The success of the Berlitz Method, combined with his entrepreneurial acumen, led to his subsequent achievements.

Young David Berlizheimer from his early years in America conscientiously sought a destiny different from his past and from that of his family. He took on a new name, Maximilian D. Berlitz, and married a Christian. It is not certain that he converted to Christianity, but his children were brought up as Christians. Whether Max cut off his ties from his Jewish siblings and cousins in America, or they from him, the families seemingly never communicated again. Among the Jewish German immigrants in the mid-nineteenth century, his story was not unique, but it was certainly unusual according to anecdotal information. Accurate statistical records do not exist of those who intermarried and left the Jewish community, since often the goal of these Jews was to hide their Judaism. In any case, it was perhaps more surprising that it was the son of a cantor and Jewish teacher who was the only Berlizheimer who chose to live as a Christian in America.

The story of the Berlizheimers was typical of first-generation immigrants who recreated their little German village in America. They lived, worked, and socialized with their family, moving together from one house to another seemingly every year. After a few years, the young people got married, but the marriages were not arranged, nor did anyone have to bring assets or dowries to their marriages. Family members served as informal character references. Given that the social circle of German Jews was limited, it was inevitable that the new members of the family would have similar backgrounds. They spoke German, saw themselves as German, and did

MAXIMILIAN DELPHINUS BERLITZ (B. DAVID BERLIZHEIMER, 1852) Founder of the Berlitz School of Languages in Providence, Rhode Island, in 1878. (Berlitz Language School brochure, Florence, Italy. Courtesy of Berlitz International, Inc.)

BERLIZHEIMER FAMILY Seated: Sara Rinow (b. 1839), Bernhard (b. 1838). Standing left: Louis (b. Lazarus, 1844). Standing right: Richard (b. Maier, 1845). This formal family photograph was taken in Chicago between 1906 and 1910. (Private collection, Janet Iltis.)

not weaken their ties with their homeland until the second generation became firmly established in its new country. By 1880 the first generation was giving way to the children who were born in America. Ties to Germany and the German language weakened but did not disappear. The Illinois German-language newspaper, the *Staats-Zeitung*, for example, was still an integral part of their lives.

The Berlizheimers did not progress from peddler to merchant prince; only a select few German Jews accomplished that meteoric rise. Rather, they were among the thousands of German Jews who flourished and joined America's growing middle class. The Berlizheimer family was still German, still Jewish—but now American.

German Jews

Meanwhile, in the 1860s several German states, including Baden, Bavaria, Hesse, and Württemberg, revisited the issue of Jewish emancipation. The Württemberg government began the process by presenting to Parliament a draft of a law revising the 1828 Law of the Israelites. The Jews were concerned that the government would only revise, and not repeal, the earlier law. Three hundred leaders met in 1861 in the Jewish Orphanage in Esslingen, and from that session emerged a special fifteen-member Jewish Emancipation Committee.

The composition of the Emancipation Committee reflected the fusion of the past supporters of the struggle with the emerging liberal leaders. Several members of the Jewish Board, one of whom was a scholar, served on the committee. The Kaulla family, still very wealthy and well connected, continued its support of Jewish civil rights. Isaak Hess, the book dealer, also had served on the Jewish Committees since 1821. Several lawyers, including Max Kaulla, provided their legal expertise. They represented the professionally trained people who continued to be restricted in their career opportunities. The political power and influence once held by Jewish communities like Mühringen in the 1820s, however, was now transferred to the places that maintained substantial communities. Members from these communities included Dr. M. Einstein from Buchau, S. Steiner, a hops wholesaler from Laupheim, and delegates from Esslingen, Schwäbisch Hall, and Ulm. Rabbi Moses Wassermann of Mühringen was a first-time member of the committee; his participation represented the growing involvement in political issues of some members of the rabbinate.

The Emancipation Committee first sent a memorandum to the king asking him to grant the Jews full equality of rights with the Christians. Another petition to the upper chamber addressed several other issues: eliminating the humiliating special Jewish oath, permitting unrestricted immigration of foreign Jews, and allowing the Jews to participate in the Christian funds for the poor. The committee's final point dealt with the restrictions stating that Jews could not be state employees. It wrote that this limitation directly hurt the Jews' self-esteem.[1] The *Allgemeine Zeitung des Judenthums* covered the emancipation efforts throughout the German states, and the Württemberg Jews knew they were part of a larger movement.

The government conducted another survey of its 12,000 Jews.[2] The number of *schacher* traders had decreased by half to 459 since 1846. Although some cattle dealers were probably *schacher* traders, the number of cattle dealers had increased slightly, indicating that young men saw it as a less speculative, and more organized, respectable, and growing, business.

Jewish Men Involved in the *Schacher* Trade and Cattle Dealing*

Trade	1828	1845	1861
Schacher traders	2,600	860	459
Cattle dealers	Included in the figure for the *schacher* trade	445 (some cattle dealers might have been in the *schacher* trade)	488
Butchers (many were cattle dealers as well)	150	412	240
Total	2,750	1,717	1,187

*1828 survey included 3,041 men over age 14; 1845 survey included 3,930 men over age 14; 1861 survey included 2,985 men over age 14.

When the Ministry of Internal Affairs asked the county governments to comment on the draft, several counties presented reports that supported revising the law, based on the improved situation of the Jews.[3] The counties felt that their officials and the police could monitor the few Jewish *schacher* traders in their district. Everyone agreed that the Jews who did *schacher* trade were equal to everyone else. Remarkably, a county official stated what the Jews had argued for decades: many Christians worked as *schacher* traders, and a general law should regulate *all* such dealers. The

Rottweil county official also had no objections to the law since the Jews did very well in all positions. He concurred that the number of Jews in the *schacher* trade was decreasing while the number of Christians involved was increasing. He acknowledged that since the Jews seldom asked for charitable support, they would not be a drain on the municipal funds for the poor.

A petition from Schwäbisch Hall presented the liberal view that it was the role of the government to bring its law in line with modern thinking. Its official admitted that the lot of the Israelites would still be one of utter wretchedness if they had depended on the moods of the public. Both chambers agreed that Jews should be given equal rights and asked the government to draft an amendment to the 1819 constitution.

On December 31, 1861, the 1819 constitution was amended. The sentence "State citizenship rights are independent of religious beliefs" was added, and the reference to "belonging to one of the three Christian faiths" was deleted.

Although the Jews were now equal to Christians under the Württemberg constitution, the Law of the Israelites of 1828 had not been repealed or revised, leaving in place some restrictions and limitations on the Jews. Five months after the constitutional amendment, the lower chamber set up a commission to draft a new law. The Ministry of Internal Affairs wrote in its report that the Jews were good citizens, paid attention to the laws, and were careful and thrifty, adding that their family life merited the highest respect. In October 1862 the parliamentary commission presented a long report that once again reviewed in detail the history of the Jews and the processes of emancipation that had taken place in the other German states. Fourteen months later Parliament discussed the draft legislation.[4] The speeches were reported in detail in the *Schwäbische Chronik*.

The representatives' speeches reflected the feelings of their constituents. The concerns of the Christian public could no longer focus on the more politically acceptable issue of the *schacher* Jews since that problem had been basically resolved. Rather, it brought out into the open the real issues that had earlier been couched in other terms and hidden just below the surface. It raised the invisible bar and simultaneously introduced into public debate "new" threats and dangers posed by the Jews. The anti-Jewish sentiments were now aimed at the emerging urban, middle-class Jews whom the representatives meticulously differentiated from the poor Orthodox Jews remaining in the countryside. Some representatives introduced subtle and

+ utterly absurd.

polite forms of anti-Jewish expressions. A Catholic priest in the lower chamber, for instance, referred to the Jewish lawyers as "Salomo" and to the Jewish women as "Rachel."

Several representatives quoted the phrase "Stuttgart as their New Jerusalem." This was the sardonic twisting of one of the resolutions adopted by the rabbinical conferences in the 1840s. That resolution had stated that the messianic idea should receive prominent mention in the Jews' prayers, but all petitions for their return to the Land of Israel and for the restoration of a Jewish state should be eliminated from them. Some representatives reacted to that concept with concern; to them it meant that the Jews would never leave the German lands to return to Israel.

Even a liberal-democratic representative, Friedrich Rödinger, a lawyer in Stuttgart, issued a dire warning concerning the future: "The future will belong to the Jews...Even now almost the whole capital in the world is in their hands; in education, *Bildung* [cultivated cultural upbringing], and intelligence, they are the fortunate rivals of the Christians; and in the not too distant time, external power will be theirs as well." Representative Rödinger also interjected the theory of the Jews as a race in his speech even as he seemingly was sympathetic to their plight. He blamed his fellow Christians for their contribution over the centuries to the isolation of the Jews so that they were without rights and a homeland. He added that it was the Christian rejection of the Jews' integration that brought about the present situation: "Now they stand after a thousand years still without a homeland and without rights in the midst of life. As a nation? No, as a race. You have cultivated the curse of a race in them whom you now condemn as standoffish and hostile."[5]

The intermarriage debate was even more heated and anti-Jewish. Up to that time, the number of intermarriages and conversions in Württemberg had been negligible. Most representatives, nevertheless, were very strongly opposed to the threat intermarriage posed to Christian society. Some representatives referred to the anti-Jewish pamphlets written by Moser and Fries in the 1820s. One representative asked what would happen if a Jew married a Christian, given that Jews hated the Christian religion and saw Christ as a blasphemer and cheater. Some representatives supported intermarriage as a means to further the Jews' assimilation into Christian society: as a result Jews would disappear as Jews. Many Christians were frustrated that only a few Jews had taken advantage, as they perceived it, of conversion as a road to assimilation. Another representative warned that

emancipation without assimilation would be the greatest error the legis-
ature could make."[6]

When in 1862 the government abolished the guilds, the centuries-old
voice of the masses, the Protestant Church, stepped forward to replace that
organization in its opposition to the Jews. Local church councils from about
thirty villages and towns (in which no Jews lived) sent strong letters, and
one county organized a letter-writing campaign for several small Protestant
villages. Broader political issues supplanted villagers' earlier concerns about
local emancipation (communal rights and acceptance of the Jews in their
municipalities). These petitions expressed the peoples' fear of intermarriage
and their concerns about the disturbance of Sunday observance by Jewish
traders, the abolition of the special Jewish oath, and the installation of Jewish teachers, county officials, and judges—all threats to the Christian character of the state.[7] The villages and small towns registered their complaints
about the revisions, but just as in earlier decades, they did not have much
political influence. The power resided in the larger towns and cities that
were generally supportive of the changes.

Nevertheless, again alarmed at the tone and strength of the public
outcry, the members of twelve Jewish communities in towns and cities, in
a coordinated effort, sent petitions supporting the legislation. The Jews
explained that although they thought that intermarriages would seldom
occur, they viewed the option as the removal of the last barrier for full
equality. The Rottweil Jewish community presented a pro-emancipation
petition that also included a long list of signatures of prominent Christian
townspeople, the local Catholic Church leadership, and the citizens
committee.

In the end, the representatives concluded that Württemberg would survive as a Christian state even if the law of 1828 were repealed. All but one
member of the lower chamber voted to take that action, and the upper
chamber concurred. The upper chamber, however, did not include the elimination of the intermarriage restrictions, reflecting the consensus that this
issue should best be left to the people, the churches, and the laws governing marriages.

Since the Jews were already in the process of moving on and moving
up, the final law came somewhat as an anticlimax and a nonevent. It was
the end of a long process, as emancipation had not just been handed to
them as a gift. For decades Jews had joined together to fight for their
rights. They had changed parts of their culture and even some religious

rituals in an effort to be more acceptable. While the Jews most likely would have adopted some of these changes as the inevitable and necessary steps to becoming part of the modern world, these transformations showed their commitment to attaining equal rights and the possibility to live and work on an equal plane with their Christian neighbors. It was a fight well fought.

King Wilhelm I died in 1864, before the final law was issued. During his forty-eight-year reign, he and his government had pushed, and had been pushed, on the emancipation process. Their ambivalence and reluctance caused the process to take decades instead of years and prevented the Jewish Question from being resolved in a timely and emphatic manner. Compared to the church, the nobility, the guilds, and the lower levels of government, however, the king and his ministers did articulate and support the Jews' struggle for civil rights. Often their motivation had to do more with the efforts to diminish the power of other interest groups, such as the territorial rulers and the guilds, or with political pressure from the other German states, but overall their goals did coincide, and they championed the Jews' efforts. Finally the time was right; Bavaria and Baden enacted their emancipation legislation in these years as well.

However, some Christians viewed the king's support as preferential treatment of the moneyed Jews that worked to the detriment of the poor Christians. They believed that the government had forced them to share their limited communal property with the Jews and had threatened their livelihoods by pushing the Jews into the guilds. Now they felt that the government was handing over their government and their schools to the Jews. They resented that their traditional society was being sacrificed for the benefit of modern bourgeois liberals. Each time the government had enacted a new law, the legislation was forced upon some people who were resistant and resentful.

On August 13, 1864, King Karl (Wilhelm's son) issued the *Gesetz betreffend die bürgerlichen Verhältnisse der israelitischen Glaubens-Genossen* (Law regarding the citizenship conditions of the members of the Israelite faith). Jews were henceforth to be governed by the same laws, rights, and obligations as Christians. A Jew, when swearing an oath, was required only to raise his hand and say the words, "I swear, so help me God." The articles of the Law of the Israelites of 1828 (except for those articles regarding marriages and "church" affairs) were rescinded and replaced by the general laws of Württemberg. The Jews in Württemberg were now legally equal to the Christians.

The Jewish Board ordered that thanks be given for the new law in all the synagogues of the kingdom.

It was significant that the enactment of the law did not immediately stem the flow of immigrants to America. But then, neither did the anti-Jewish fervor of the emancipation debate increase America's attraction. Just as in the prior decade, it was the poor economic situation of their families that forced most emigrants to seek new lives in foreign countries. Christians were also emigrating, but not in the massive numbers of the previous decade. About sixty thousand people emigrated from Württemberg in the 1860s, especially after 1865 and the conclusion of the American Civil War.

The children of the Berlizheimer brothers continued to leave. One of Marx's sons who had emigrated in the 1850s died after only three years in America. Another son, Adolph, emigrated in 1865, after completing a tailor apprenticeship with financial stipends from the board. Compared with the large number of Jewish emigrants from Mühringen in earlier decades, only sixteen Jewish young men and four women emigrated in the 1860s. Most of their fathers were alive, and they seemed to have more assets than the parents of the earlier emigrants, but a few poor Jews also left.

Always a bit behind Mühringen, emigration from Michelbach picked up its momentum in the 1860s, and it was the Gundelfingers who contributed to this increase. Family circumstances pushed eight young Gundelfingers to leave for America. These eight boys, in three separate families, had been left fatherless when they were young. They all had some assets, and most had done apprenticeships in trade in the cities. Two sons of teachers left as well. At least ten other young men immigrated to America and England. Just like the emigrants from Mühringen, most of them took twice as much travel money (350 to 500 gulden) as the earlier generation of emigrants had.

Most young people in Rottweil, however, did not view emigration as a necessity. Two of the innkeeper Degginger's sons did leave, and Dr. Rothschild's youngest son, Otto, left in 1871 at age nineteen to try his luck in California. After 1870, Jewish (and Christian) emigration dropped off almost entirely from Württemberg. Germany was now the place to be.

The emancipation laws did have a direct effect on the rural Jewish communities. Now the Jews were able to join the land flight from the countryside to the urban areas. It was an inevitable situation. Most of the

Moises Kaz ⊗ — **Sara (daug. of) Mayer Samuel**
1750–1829   1765–[after 1831]

Gustel — ⊗ — **Joseph David**
1779–1861   **Berlizheimer**
                   1761–1855

Hefel — ⊗ —Josef Hirsch
1787–[1830]   Rothschild
                 1782–1860

Maier — ⊗ — Henriette Bernheim
1813–1884   1812–1875
1 son to America
2 sons newspaper owners
in Rottweil

Viktoria
1803–1872
⊗ 1829 Aaron Fränkl
5 children to America
1 son in Illereichen

Jacob
1793–1878
⊗ 1817 Babette Maier
⊗ 1837 Esther Maier
2 sons in Rottweil
2 daughters in Rottweil
1 daughter in Stuttgart

David
1798–1849
⊗ 1826 Fany Grünwald
⊗ 1835 **Mina Gundelfinger**
1806–1861
(Michelbach)
to America
6 sons to America
3 daughters to America

Löw (Leopold)
1799–1865
⊗ 1841 Karoline Heilbronner
1814–[after 1869]
2 sons to America
1 daughter to America

Marx
1802–1884
⊗ 1835 Rosa Auerbacher
⊗ 1844 Viktoria Degginger
2 sons to America
1 son to Mainz
1 son to Hanau
1 son to Rottenburg/Neckar
1 son and 1 daughter in Mühringen

Hanna
1805–1890
⊗ 1846 Bernhard Laudenbacher
1847 Bernhard to America
⊗ 1851 civil divorce

[ ] Unconfirmed information
( ) Birthplace

KAZ AND BERLIZHEIMER FAMILIES   The Kaz and Berlizheimer families after 1848.

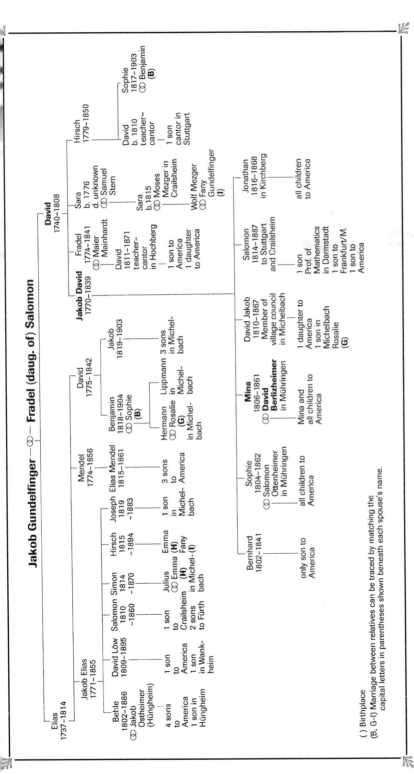

GUNDELFINGER FAMILY The Gundelfinger family after 1857.

( ) Birthplace

(B, G–I) Marriage between relatives can be traced by matching the capital letters in parentheses shown beneath each spouse's name.

villages were dominated by their former feudal rulers and had not devel
oped industry or trade, as the more dynamic, growing cities had done. In
the 1850s the effects of emigration compounded the situation. Financially
the exodus of both Christian and Jewish emigrants shrank the number o
potential taxpayers, and the assets the emigrants took with them decreased
the total assets of the villages. The population had not grown to compen-
sate for those losses, so the villages could not support better educational
and cultural facilities.

The industrial revolution was changing the economic landscape. Just
when the need for farmers and skilled craftsmen was declining, the Jews
were poised to move into the growing sectors of small industry, banking,
and wholesaling. More than half of them had already left the trades they
had just learned. Jews were no longer tied to shops in the village, but rather,
they were evolving into merchants and wholesalers. The 1861 survey of Jewish men showed an increase in the number of merchants and manufacturers
since 1845 and the comparable decrease in the number of shopkeepers and
craftsmen (especially in the cloth sector).

Many Jews had done business in the markets of the larger towns and
cities over the years and had connections and clients in place. These Jews

Occupations of Jewish Men*

Trade	1828	1845	1861
Professionals	7	201	181
Farmers	32	68 (as their only occupation) 83 (as their main occupation)	170
Merchants	106	349	823
Shopkeepers	33	557	150
Manufacturers	—	21	47
Craftsmen			
Cloth-producing	8	266	64
Butchers	150	412	240
Other	124	729	363
Subtotal of craftsmen	282	1,407	667

*1828 survey included 3,041 men over age 14; 1845 survey included 3,930 men over
age 14; 1861 survey included 2,985men over age 14.

had more liquid assets and the financial bases to start up new businesses. If they needed more capital, they looked just as they had done before to their families, fellow Jews, and Jewish lending associations, who would lend money to them often without surety.

During these years the railroad lines expanded and industrialization brought new energy and potential to the urban areas. With freedom of movement permitted, more Jews relocated to the cities to find opportunities for themselves in business. Others moved for the sake of their children's education. Once the restrictions of the Law of the Israelites were lifted in 1864, the Jews could—and did—move away from their villages.

Several of Marx Berlizheimer's sons started businesses in the cities. Marx and Viktoria's son, Nathan, had been an apprentice with the book trader Adolf Degginger (Viktoria's brother) in Rottweil in 1863 and was supported by a stipend. He became an important wine dealer in Mainz. Max Louis, Marx's son by his first wife, studied at the trade high school in Rottweil. He moved to Hanau, near Frankfurt am Main, as an apprentice to learn trade with K. T. Cahn for five years. After working in the city, he joined his fellow apprentice Moritz Mendel to open a fabric and clothes store. Later Max Louis opened a similar store that became an important department store in Hanau, Haus Berlizheimer.

Some men used their apprenticeship training to develop their businesses in the cities. A son of a poor peddler trained as a gold craftsman in Esslingen and then started a jewelry factory there. The son of a well-off cloth trader joined that jewelry business. The son of a well-off butcher trained as a cotton weaver and opened a cloth factory in Esslingen. His partner, his cousin by marriage from Mühringen, studied in the trade high school in Hechingen. Unlike Marx's sons who moved far away, many men went to Stuttgart and to neighboring Esslingen. With the growing railroad system, the trip to Stuttgart was no longer difficult: it was just a one-hour walk to the Horb train station and then a two-hour train trip.

The railroad system offered professional opportunities for Naphtali Esslinger, son of a well-off jewelry dealer, who used his technical education to rise to the position of inspector in the Württemberg railroad company. Naphtali's family moved with him to cities along the railroad lines.[8] Moreover, the railroads opened new opportunities for smaller businesses. Many cattle dealers moved to towns and cities along the railroad lines to be able to transport larger number of livestock to markets. Horb, on the main line, attracted merchants and large-scale cattle dealers from Mühringen and the other local communities. They had always attended Horb's markets and had a strong client base in the town. Esslinger's two other sons also joined the movement to Horb; one became a banker and the other owned a clothes store. By 1872 twenty-seven Jews lived in the town that had been closed to Jewish residents for centuries.

The movement from rural Michelbach to the cities was slower to develop. Most of the poorer men were involved in village-to-village cattle dealing and could not easily relocate to a city. Many Gundelfingers, however, did go to the urban areas. The son of a teacher in Baden became the cantor and teacher in Stuttgart. Another family moved to Crailsheim.

Salomon Gundelfinger, who had lived in Kirchberg since the 1840s closed his store and moved to Stuttgart when his son Sigmund was ready for higher education. Sigmund attended the academic high school in the city and went on to study law, physics, and mathematics at the University of Tübingen. After transferring to the University of Heidelberg, he studied philosophy, and graduated as a doctor of philosophy (in theoretical mathematics) in 1867; he was only twenty-one when he graduated summa cum laude.

In one instance, maternal relatives, the Holzingers, brought the eldest sons of a deceased Gundelfinger into their expanding cut goods business in the Bavarian city of Fürth. After Hirsch and Elias Salomon apprenticed in business in Fürth, they completed their emigration forms in order to immigrate to England "for luck and to find business." Although their emigration is noted in the Michelbach emigration register in 1869 and 1867, respectively, it is not clear whether they ever did emigrate to England since Hirsch was registered as working in Fürth for the Holzingers in 1869, and Elias Salomon had begun working for the company by 1878 at the latest. Elias Salomon married his Holzinger first cousin, and the next generations maintained ownership of the large wholesale and manufacturing fabric business.

Rottweil gradually became an urban center that not only retained its Jewish population, but also attracted a small number of other Jews to move there. Only one Jewish family relocated to a larger city. Moritz Esslinger moved to Stuttgart, where he and his sons opened a bank—Esslinger & Company, Bank & Money Exchange—that became quite successful.

The Rottweil Jewish community grew to 122 people. The core of the community, however, remained the original families. In the 1860s, the community finally bought a house on a lane just off the main street and remodeled the building for its synagogue. The community remained an affiliate of Mühringen. The descendants of peddlers and innkeepers Abraham Bernheim and Natan Degginger continued to run the Golden Goblet Inn and the Crown Inn, respectively. Bernheim's inn served as a meeting place for civic associations and singing clubs. Over the years the Golden Goblet became a banking house as well.

The descendants of Moises Kaz remained in the town. When Jacob Kaz died at age eighty-five, his children continued to live in the house that Moises Kaz had bought seven decades earlier. Dr. Maier Rothschild and his sons expanded the scope of their newspaper, changing its name from the *Rottweiler Anzeiger* to the *Schwarzwälder Bürgerzeitung* (Black forest citizen newspaper). Their publishing company, M. Rothschild, brought out a number of history books covering a wide range of subjects. In 1870, after almost twenty years at the helm, Dr. Rothschild sold his newspaper and other assets to his sons.

Two events in 1868 exemplified the positive and supportive relationship existing between Christians and Jews in Rottweil. A massive fire badly damaged Dr. Rothschild's house and printing business. Despite that catastrophe, his newspaper missed only one issue. A childhood friend, Wilhelm Brandecker, printed the newspaper the day after the fire on his own printing presses in Oberndorf. Another book publisher, Riecker of Tübingen, also helped out. In a large notice in the newspaper, Dr. Rothschild thanked his friends and the firefighters for their support in his time of need.

On July 23, 1868, cannon salvos marked the start of a long-awaited event in the town. The fire department led a parade of gymnasts, musicians, singing clubs, and townspeople down the steep hill to the railway station. Everyone cheered as the first train pulled into the station: Rottweil was finally on the railroad line. The celebration continued with a banquet where many dignitaries gave speeches commemorating the day. Anton Rothschild spoke and thanked Dr. Carl Rheinwald, who had worked so tirelessly to bring the railroad to the Black Forest region. The audience reacted with great support and loud cheers. Moises Kaz's great-grandchild had certainly come a long way.

Despite the increased migration to the urban areas, Württemberg remained basically rural in character. In 1870 only 14.3 percent of its inhabitants lived in cities of more than five thousand people; this was an increase of merely 3 percent since 1815. Of the German states, only Bavaria had a larger percentage of rural inhabitants and showed an even smaller percentage increase of urbanization.

Württemberg became part of the North German Confederacy in 1869. One law of the confederacy stated that "all existing restrictions of civic and political rights imposed on the grounds of differences of religious persuasion were abolished."[9] This law removed the final legal barrier for the Jews in Württemberg—the restriction against intermarriage. After 1871 the newly formed Second German Reich had a Jewish population of more than half a million. Although Jews remained only 1.25 percent of the total population of more than 41 million people, this newly enlarged population was viewed as a threat by those Christians who were accustomed to having only a few thousand Jews in their smaller individual states.

As part of a newly united country, Jews from Württemberg were among the 7,000 Jews who fought alongside the 314,000 Christians in the Franco-Prussian War from 1870 to 1871. The names of Josef Grünwald and Emanuel Feigenheimer were inscribed in the official military honor roll along with those of thirteen Christians from Mühringen. Two Michelbach Jews served as well, and many joined the war effort by supplying requisitioned horses.

Most probably for the first time during a military conflict, Jews were allowed to publicly observe a religious holiday. Acting Sergeant I. Hirschberg described this experience in the *Allgemeine Zeitung des Judenthums* a few weeks after the event in October 1870:

Yom Kippur Behind the Front Lines

After Rosh Hashanah had passed without taking any consideration for its celebration by the Jewish soldiers, we were pleasantly surprised that [as a result of requests by Jewish soldiers and the Mannheim rabbinate] two days before Yom Kippur, through an armywide order issued by his Excellency General von Manteuffel, the regiments and battalions were instructed to release from duty the soldiers of the Mosaic faith for the afternoon of October 5 and the following day to celebrate the Day of Atonement and to send them on leave to St. Barbe, the current headquarters of the army, provided that the troops were not put on battle alert.

Fortunately, this did not happen, and so we [150] Jewish soldiers of the First Army Corps were granted our deeply desired wish! Our hearts were overjoyed that we could observe Yom Kippur in communal devotion with services conducted by a rabbinical candidate in the manner of our fathers [but without benefit of a Torah scroll]. Not one of us ever prayed with such ardent devotion in the most magnificent temple back home as in this small, humble room with its broken-down door, knocked-out windows, and walls riddled by shells. From time to time, a short distance from us, our cannon thundered toward Metz, and we felt the impermanence of our existence, and the need to reconcile ourselves with our God, since soon it might be too late. For many of us, for whom the meaning of Yom Kippur until this moment had been inwardly quite strange, it had now become unforgettably clear in the deepest depth of our hearts in a way never before suspected.[10]

This heartfelt description communicated the Jews' newfound confidence in the compatibility of Judaism with the demands and obligations of citizenship.

With freedom of movement, Jews from all parts of the Reich could come and go for business and were even more visible in the cities and in the countryside. The population shift to the cities also made the Jews more conspicuous as a group. The number of Jews living in Stuttgart increased from 265 in the 1850s to more than 1,800 in 1872. The total population of the city had more than doubled since the 1840s to 60,000, but the number of Jews had increased sevenfold during that period. In 1861 the Stuttgart community had built its synagogue in the center of the city. With its enormous, dramatically designed Moorish exterior, it was similar in style to the other new synagogues that were being built in Leipzig, Vienna, and Berlin. The new synagogue bore no resemblance to the small village synagogues where the Jews had spent so many Sabbaths and holidays in prior years. This synagogue announced that the Jews in the capital of Württemberg had arrived.

The period from 1866 through 1872 was a period of economic prosperity for Germany, and certainly Jews were part of its rapidly growing industrial revolution. After the Franco-Prussian War, Germany profited from reparations from France, and rampant speculation struck the immature German economy. Tension in the cities began building. Once again some Christians turned against the Jews, this time in Stuttgart. The events there were reported in detail in the Stuttgart newspaper, *Schwäbische Chronik*. On Tuesday, March 25, 1873, at 4:00 P.M., a soldier got into an argument with a widow, Helene Baruch, who was working in her clothes store in the city center. The soldier thought that he had been cheated, and when the police were called in they mistreated him while trying to remove him from the premises. Since it was a lovely Easter-week holiday evening, many people were in the streets. The police quieted down the observers and thought the incident was over. Despite their efforts, almost immediately a mob, including soldiers on leave, gathered outside the store and yelled, "The Jew must come out!" and "The Jew must go away!" A number of people broke store and house windows,

Yom Kippur-Feier vor Metz 1870.

YOM KIPPUR FESTIVAL IN METZ, 1870 "Not one of us ever prayed with such ardent devotion in the most magnificent temple back home as in this small, humble room with its broken-down door, knocked-out windows, and walls riddled by shells." —Sergeant I. Hirschberg (Oberrat der Israeliten Badens, Karlsruhe, ed., *Juden in Baden, 1809–1984* [Karlsruhe: Oberrat der Israeliten Badens, 1984], 177.)

including those of a clothes dealer, a Mr. Süsskind. The police took some people into custody, but the mob forcibly secured their release.

The unfounded rumor circulated that the soldier who had been mistreated had died or was gravely wounded. At 8:00 P.M., the military closed off the streets. A larger mob gathered in the Marktplatz and broke windows with heavy stones and clubs, looting the Jewish stores. The mob tried to seize another Jew, a Mr. Blum. More military and the cavalry were called in, but the mob threw stones at the soldiers and police. After taking more than forty people into custody, the military and police were able to get everything under control by midnight.

The next day the officials carefully monitored the situation, and a smaller group of mostly curiosity seekers gathered in front of the City Hall. On Thursday another group came together in front of the City Hall. This time the mob broke into and plundered Süsskind's clothes store. They threw stones at Helene Baruch and yelled, "The Jew must go!" As the cavalry protected the Marktplatz, the mob moved to other unprotected areas of Stuttgart and broke the windows of other Jewish houses. Later the police and soldiers took some of the perpetrators into custody, but the mob again tried to seize the prisoners. The unrest continued for two more days, even though the streets were being patrolled.

The *Schwäbische Chronik* questioned what was happening to its usually tranquil city. The reporters thought the anger was aimed against the police and was a problem of law and order. The newspaper saw the prompt sentencing of one of the accused to four months in prison as a good course of action. It observed that other cities were experiencing unrest among factory workers.[11] The *Allgemeine Zeitung des Judenthums* also published an article on the riots. Its correspondents viewed the events as anti-Jewish rather than as a protest against the police, the military, and the government. The paper's writers emphatically blamed the disturbances on the people's always-agitated feelings against the Jews.[12] None of the articles, however, mentioned what the Christians and Jews instinctively knew: the anti-Jewish riots had occurred during Easter week and the Passover holiday, when the accusations against the Jews as Christ killers and practitioners of ritual murder customarily resurfaced and were fueled by sermons in the churches. The Jews once again were a handy scapegoat for external problems.

Just as they had looked to the central government in 1819 and in 1848, once again the Jews had turned to the government to save their lives and their businesses. Each time the higher levels of government did come to

+ A few yrs ago, Presidential appointees were often confronted during confirmation proceedings by accusations that they belong to clubs excluding negroes. This issue seems to have almost disappeared. I doubt many clubs have admitted negroes, Jews etc. In big cities the Jews still have their own city & country clubs.

their defense, even if it was just to restore order and to prevent chaos among the masses.

While no further anti-Jewish actions were reported for decades, tangible and intangible barriers still existed. Jews could enter the lower ranks of many professions, but an unwritten requirement kept them from being appointed to prestigious positions as judges, government officials, or army officers. Likewise they had difficulty entering national politics. The unwritten prerequisite was a baptismal certificate. The university system illustrated how the line between meeting qualifications and discrimination could be blurred. By the late 1870s more than three thousand Jews (more than 8 percent of the student bodies) were attending German universities, but only a handful of Jews were professors, and even fewer were full professors. The requirements to become a university professor, however, were very stringent, so it was difficult to ascertain (except in some obvious cases) whether the Jewish applicant was not qualified or was denied an appointment because he remained Jewish. After Sigmund Gundelfinger, for example, completed his impressive academic training in theoretical mathematics, he followed the usual professor track by becoming a private teacher and lecturer at the University of Tübingen. He did not receive a university appointment, but he taught for his entire career at an important technical high school in Darmstadt. Sigmund went on to make important contributions in theoretical mathematics and geometry. Based on his qualifications and achievements, it would seem that Sigmund was a victim of discrimination.

In addition, only a very few of the Jewish elite or their wives were invited to join the very important Christian social clubs, associations, and Masonic lodges. These situations, however, were not unique to the German states; most of these forms of discrimination also affected the lives of Jews living in other European countries and in the United States.

The Jewish author Berthold Auerbach expressed what many of the Jews who remained in the villages were experiencing when he wrote:

> Dead! Emigrated! is what one hears constantly, when you ask about someone or other. Now the freedom of migration within the land has joined the addiction to America, and it is just like in private society: when one stands up to leave, the others stand up as well and afterward are not tranquil. Over in Schwandorf the synagogue is deserted, and the Jewish cemetery has been abandoned. There are no Jews there anymore. I see it coming, maybe already in a decade, that the same will be true in Nordstetten.[13]

In Michelbach the remaining descendants of Elias Gundelfinger's line took over their fathers' businesses or started new small trades. Those who were cattle dealers could not or did not want to move their businesses to the cities. One descendent owned a fabric and haberdashery shop and went door-to-door selling. A master shoemaker who listed his trades as shoemaker and wool dealer went on to become a cattle dealer.

Several Gundelfingers continued the practice of marrying their cousins. Rosalie married her distant cousin, Hermann, and thus became the only descendant of David's line to remain in the village. She inherited her father's saddle shop and inn. Her husband, the son of a poor cattle dealer, went on to become a respected land dealer, community officer, and village council member. Cementing an even closer blood relationship was the marriage of the children of two brothers. Julius, a tradesman with considerable assets (equivalent to 4,624 gulden) married his first cousin, Emma, who brought a sizable dowry (equivalent to 11,463 gulden). Both of these unions produced several children.

Other families stayed in Michelbach but with fewer young members. The men worked in the trades of their fathers—a wool dealer, a glassmaker who also dealt in hops and leather, many cattle dealers—and continued to play a significant role in the rural economy. Just like the Gundelfingers, they lived in the houses their fathers or grandfathers had bought. Most of them owned a few small fields and meadows. The Jewish community reported that many families were poor, and some of them were just schmoozers.

These rural Jews remained very religious and loyal to their traditional way of life. Several Gundelfingers, who were butchers and cattle dealers, served as the ritual circumcisers, and others were community officers. Planning for a sustained or increased population (from the 255 Jews in 1858), in the 1850s and 1860s the community had expanded its cemetery, renovated the school, enlarged the synagogue, and built a new women's ritual bath at the end of the Jews' Lane. Not only did the projected growth not materialize to support the new infrastructure or to pay the debts incurred, but the community's population decreased until it could count fewer than 200 Jews living there after 1870.

Although Mühringen had been a more thriving and important Jewish community than Michelbach, its fate was much the same. The older generation passed away, and a very small group of the younger generation remained in the village. Its Jewish population had begun to decrease in the 1850s, when

DR. SIGMUND GUNDELFINGER The professor and mathematician was born in 1846. (Hanna de Mieses collection, Courtesy of Leo Baeck Institute, New York.)

AMALIE GUNZ Born in 1857, she was the wife of Dr. Sigmund Gundelfinger. (Hanna de Mieses collection, Courtesy of Leo Baeck Institute,
New York.)

the five hundred Jews living there had accounted for almost half of the village population. By the 1870s the Jewish population numbered only about two hundred.

The changes in the Berlizheimer family mirrored those evident in the rest of the community. Joseph David's widow, Gustel, died in 1861 at age eighty-two. His remaining children, who were now quite elderly, were not in strong financial situations. Marx died in 1884 at eighty-two. The stone and style of his headstone was a replica of that of his brother David, who had passed away in 1849. The divorced Hanna Laudenbacher was poor and lived off donations from her nieces and nephews and the village fund for the poor. She passed away in 1890 at eighty-five. The inexpensive quality of the stone and the shallow inscription—compared with other Berlizheimer headstones—attest to Hanna's impoverished and most likely lonely last years.

Only two of Marx's children, Berthold and Auguste, remained in the village. Marx's other sons had moved away for business reasons, and his other daughters had married and moved to other Jewish communities. Auguste owned a hat and fashion business. She never married and had her own apartment. She kept in touch with her relatives who had left the village for America or the cities.

Berthold's initial apprenticeship as a gold and silver craftsman had been too expensive, so he trained to be a weaver. In 1864 he married Babette Feigenheimer, whose father was a leather dealer in the village; both brought considerable assets to the marriage (about 2,500 gulden each). Berthold became a clothes dealer and received local citizen's rights based on his being the son of a citizen. Berthold bought his grandfather's house from his aunt, Hanna Laudenbacher, and his store and clothing trade business thrived.

In most of the other families in Mühringen, one son took over the family's business, which had not changed much over the generations. They were butchers and cattle traders; innkeepers; bakers; leather and hides dealers; cloth, clothing, and trousseau salesmen; and cigar, glass, and porcelain dealers. Even if they had a shop or a small cottage industry in the village, the men left each Monday to visit their customers and the markets and returned for the Sabbath on Friday afternoon. Many continued to travel by foot. They attended the seasonal markets, but perhaps their presence was not as necessary as earlier in the century, when the dates of the markets were carefully coordinated with the Jewish holidays. In 1873 the Horb market conflicted with one of the High Holy Days. A month before the holiday Jewish representatives requested, especially on behalf of the cattle dealers, that

BARON KARL VON MÜNCH, 1834–1882   The portrait of the baron still hangs in the castle overlooking the village of Mühringen. (Private collection, Freiherr v. Podewils, Schloss Hohenmühringen; photo: Weber-Horb.)

the town council postpone the market until the following day. The Horb Council refused their request due to the costs and logistics involved; it did not apologize for the error.

Nevertheless, the Jews' influence continued to be felt in the villages. The Mühringen village council did change the date of its cattle and goods market when it fell on the Sabbath. According to the survey of Horb County compiled by the central government's statistical and topographical office in 1865, the large number of stucco buildings gave the village the appearance of a town. The report stated that the lifestyle there was half like that of city dwellers and half like that of rural people; this influence was attributed to the Israelites who lived there. Now, with so many relatives and friends in the cities, the Jews brought even more urban culture to the village. A tradesman's wife was the president of a women's literary club. She had many shelves of books in her attic: classical and popular books in German, and even some books in French. The men formed a social smoking club that met weekly at a local inn.

The legal status of the Jews in Mühringen was not yet equal to that of the Christians. Even in the 1870s the village did not extend communal rights for the pasture and wooded areas to many of its Jewish partial citizens. Other facets of village life, however, showed a growing connection between Christians and Jews. They joined together to celebrate organized events. Each year the celebration of the king's birthday began with morning commemorations at the Catholic church and the synagogue. Afterward a large number of Christians and Jews, the village administrator, the priest, the rabbi, and the Jewish teacher gathered in the Zum Lamm (the Lamb Inn) to celebrate the festive day.

From time to time the entire village would honor a Jewish member of the community. The village honored Moses Perlen for his thirty-five years of service as the village council recorder and substitute village administrator. Another time, Salomon Löwenthal celebrated his fiftieth year as cantor. The community decorated his house with banners. Rabbi Wassermann led a procession to the synagogue, where the king's representative presented the cantor with a silver medal to honor his commitment to duty. Moses Perlen, speaking for the municipal government, praised him for his friendliness and warmth, and granted him the status of honorary citizen. That evening the villagers continued the festivities and set off fireworks. Afterward they gathered at the Zum Bären (the Bear Inn) to celebrate late into the night with both serious and humorous speeches.

[handwritten notes:] ...ere some villages friendlier to the Jews? Had times changed? ...ly No villages were without anti-Semites. How much were ...ch events governed by a few leading organizers?

German Jews

The village organized and enjoyed an even larger celebration in 1873, when the king selected Rabbi Moses Wassermann, who had served in the Black Forest District since 1834, as the highest-ranking Jewish official on the Jewish Board and as the rabbi of Stuttgart. The event committee was composed of Cantor Stern, the Catholic priest, and Moses Perlen. Among the guests at the farewell party held at the Bear Inn were Baron Karl von Münch, the royal administrative judge from Horb, the county head official, a representative of the important Baron von Ow from nearby Bad Imnau, many Christian clergymen from the surrounding areas, officers and teachers of the district, friends, and other well-wishers. The priest from Bad Imnau presented a long, flowery toast that was printed in its entirety in the newspaper. He wished Dr. Wassermann well in his new position and concluded with a shared toast: "Mr. Church Leader, Dr. Wassermann, a man of universal education, Bildung, and knowledge, live long, live happy, and live well!"[14]

Everyone shared a much smaller event when the Jewish school children presented a Purim play (Purimspiel) for the townspeople. According to a newspaper report, the teacher received many compliments for his excellent direction, and the applause and shouts of approval seemed to continue forever.

These glimpses of life testify to the validity of communal experiences in the villages. Christian and Jewish families had lived as neighbors for two centuries. Together they had shared economic hardships and personal tragedies; they had watched the village fragment as people left for America and the cities. Together those that remained still lived in their little village tucked in the hillside below the baron's castle. *and apart.*

Fifty-four Jewish communities and thirty-two religious elementary schools functioned in 1871 in Württemberg. Those who remained in the villages continued to observe their traditional Jewish way of life, but it was becoming more difficult for them to support the upkeep of the buildings, the salaries of the cantors and teachers, and the needs of the poor. This reality exacerbated the inevitable tension between the new city Jews who wanted to move forward and the village Jews who represented their past. This conflict was the basis of a pamphlet published in the 1860s in which the traditional village Jews pointedly reminded their Reform city cousins that they were just rural Jews recently transplanted to the cities.[15] The author also chastised those who might consider Stuttgart their Jerusalem. The rural communities' resentment of the Jewish Board's power over and interference in their lives, which had existed since its establishment in 1831, had not abated. The selection of Rabbi Wassermann, a rural and traditional rabbi rather than a nonclerical official, to head the Jewish Board could have been an effort to bridge the chasm that Dr. Maier had widened during his years of reforms.

The roots of the new Jewish Americans were now in American soil, with the new immigrants retaining only a tenuous attachment to their rural German past. The new generation of German city-dwellers, as much as they might try to ignore it, on the other hand, were still very much part of rural Jewish history, and their roots went deep into the German countryside. Their ancestors were buried under the broad branches of the towering trees in the old cemeteries. By the 1870s, however, some of these communities had disappeared completely, and those like Michelbach and Mühringen were becoming mere shadows of their earlier vibrant communities. Still, their roots were deeply intertwined in the winding village lanes and wooded hills.

The time frame of the changes was incredibly fast when viewed in the continuum of the thousands of years of Jewish history. In four generations, spanning less than a century, the Jews had overcome political, legal, and economic obstacles to improve their lives and to give opportunities to their children. They were not rich by any means, but they were beginning to live comfortably. Their religious, cultural, and social life had been transformed by outside forces, and they, in turn, had transformed themselves from their isolated, premodern situation of Jews merely living in the German states, to Jews who identified themselves as Germans. These thirteen thousand people did not choose to leave for America or England but chose to stay in Württemberg as a tiny minority of the population. They felt secure in a united fatherland. They remained—as Jewish Germans, German Jews, and German citizens of the Jewish faith. *In 60 years the processes of degradation, ruin and annihilation rooted in 1500 years of Christian anti-Semitism would wipe away nearly every trace of Jewish life not only in Germany, but wherever the inhibitions of civil society were overtaken by its hatreds.*

And the Story Continues: Portraits of My Past

 Two portraits hung above the fireplace mantel in my grandparents' living room in New York City. I now know these were paintings of Joseph David Berlizheimer and his wife, Gustel Kaz. Their son David married Mina Gundelfinger from Michelbach an der Lücke. Their grandson Maier (Richard in America) was my great-grandfather. His son, Arthur David, was my grandfather.

The history of the portraits is intertwined with the tragic end of the German Jews. In the late nineteenth and early twentieth centuries, the descendants of Joseph David Berlizheimer, Jakob Gundelfinger, and Moises Kaz lived in cities throughout Germany and worked in many professions. Among them were doctors, lawyers, department store owners, factory proprietors, salesmen, and middlemen. Friedrich Gundolf, son of the mathematics teacher Sigmund Gundelfinger, became a renowned professor of German literature, authored important books on Goethe and Shakespeare, and served as dean of the philosophy faculty at the University of Heidelberg. Some of the women also worked in the cities. Other families continued the businesses started by their fathers and grandfathers in the rural towns and villages: they were cattle dealers, shop owners, small textile factory owners, and newspaper and book publishers.

Members of all the families were among the 100,000 Jewish men who fought for their country during World War I. Some were severely wounded, others became prisoners of war, and several received the Iron Cross and other military honors. Among the twelve thousand Jewish men who fell "on the field of honor" were Private Theodor Berlizheimer, Infantryman Nathan Gundelfinger, and Lieutenant Siegfried Rothschild (an Iron Cross recipient). They felt they were German, and they gave their lives as Germans.

With the rise of Hitler, times changed. Jewish businesses were confiscated and restricted, and the Jews were forced to flee their fatherland. A few descendants of the Kaz, Berlizheimer, and Gundelfinger families fled to England, Switzerland, and Palestine, but the United States was the destiny for most of the refugees. For each immigrant to the United States, a financial guarantor was a necessity. Some Jews had maintained contacts with their relatives who had immigrated to America more than eight decades before, and these relatives usually sponsored the would-be immigrants. Others, however, had to search out relatives from whom they had not heard in years. After being forced to close their newspaper in Rottweil, some Rothschild descendants of Moises Kaz were sponsored by their maternal relatives. Other Rothschilds turned to the descendants of Otto Rothschild, who had settled in Oregon. Some Gundelfingers were sponsored by descendents of their maternal lines as well. Until her death in 1936 Auguste Berlizheimer had kept up with the descendants of Isaac Berlizheimer who had settled in Philadelphia, and that family sponsored two of their distant cousins.

The pogroms of Kristallnacht, November 9, 1938 (the anniversary of Martin Luther's birth), unleashed rampages in the villages. This sounded the alarm to the older generation that even they were not safe in the place their ancestors had lived for centuries. Berthold Berlizheimer Levi, great-grandson of Marx Berlizheimer, fled Germany in 1936 and in 1939 was desperate to find sponsors for his parents, Sigmund and Marie, and his uncle, Julius Berlizheimer. Sigmund, a war veteran and Iron Cross recipient, had just been released from the Dachau concentration camp, where he had been imprisoned since Kristallnacht. Neither Auguste nor the family in Philadelphia knew of my grandfather, who had moved from Chicago to New York City and shortened his name. Berthold's mother was frantic; she told him to search the telephone books for any Berlizheimer. In the New York City telephone book, he found two names with not exact but similar spellings. He went to the first apartment to find a recent refugee who could not help him. Berthold had no choice but to try the other name. The doorman of the building announced a relative from Mühringen. To his great surprise and relief, my grandfather warmly welcomed him. He introduced his wife, Marie, and explained that it was her birthday. Berthold replied softly that it was his mother's birthday that day, and her name was also Marie. A special bond was forged, and my grandfather sponsored the immigration applications.

Berthold's parents reached America safely. When Julius Berlizheimer fled Mühringen in May 1941, he carried with him the portraits of his great-

amazing!

292

grandparents. He gave the portraits—the symbol of the family's history—to my grandfather.

Some Berlizheimers and many Gundelfingers were not so fortunate. They died in the Holocaust.

I belong to the Jews who put down their roots in rural Germany. Before I began this journey, I did not know them. I did not know their brothers and sisters, their cousins, and the others who shared their experiences as Jews in the German countryside. Now I do, and I will never forget their story. The portraits remain a symbol of our past—and our survival—for future generations.

The innermost point that determined the personality of the *Land-jude* [rural Jew] was a simple, deep-seated and genuine feeling of both awe and love of God.… [T]he word "religiosity" does not fully convey the exact meaning. The Jew in the villages did not even attempt to define his attitude towards religion, let alone verbalize the indescribable feelings of wonderment about the enigma of life when one blesses God in the morning, but he had such feelings and they were anchored in unswerving faith in Jewish tradition.… He would not have started the day without praying in the manner of his forefathers. He knew instinctively that only…the Minyan could imbue him with the sense of having publicly worshipped God, for in public service we are citizens of the Kingdom of God, just as we are citizens of our country whether or not we confess to it or verbalize it.

This … emotional-religious attitude of the village Jew [was] something, which made him strong and resistant.…

One has to stress this religious attitude so fundamental to the village Jew because without doing so it would be impossible to describe adequately his character or personality.…

—Rabbi Emil Schorsch

"The Rural Jew: Observations on the Paper of Werner Cahnman"
Year Book Leo Baeck Institute

"faith in Jewish tradition" means??? It is not easy, it is probably IMPOSSIBLE, for a secular person to imagine the role of these traditions in the emotional life and world-view of its practitioners. But they have largely disappeared. Once all Jews (except isolated souls far from communities) were Observant. Now it seems less than 10% are, and an unknown but large percentage are not even remotely affiliated with any religion. Query: what does it take to permit (or, even, encourage) the abandonment of tradition? And what accounts for the occasional RETURN to it??

Traditional Jewish Life in the Villages and Small Towns

How did my ancestors worship, celebrate, and live their lives as Jews? The documents I found shed some light on the more practical facets of religious life—salaries, fees, duties, problems—but I had to turn to other sources to learn about their daily lives. What follows is not a definitive, encompassing essay on Jewish life; rather, I have tried to summarize what I learned, and found especially interesting, about rural religious life, particularly in southern Germany. Memoirs, fiction, and interviews with people who had spent their childhoods in rural villages emphasized the importance of traditional values and religiosity. When seen against the realities of the times, perhaps these memories are idealized, but I can not, and do not, attempt to judge them. While customs and rituals varied from place to place, I have tried to depict a general view of life in southwest Germany. I have also tried to show Jewish life from the perspectives of the Jews' Christian neighbors and of those Christians who had little or no contact with Jews.

RITUALS, CUSTOMS, AND CEREMONIES

The Jewish profession of faith—the *Shema*—proclaimed belief in only one God. Jews believed that the Messiah had not yet come, and when he came, he would return his people to the Land of Israel. The Prophet Elijah, who would announce the coming of the Messiah, figured prominently in several rituals. The circumcision ceremony centered on a special two-seated bench, with one seat being for the prophet. During the Passover seder, the door was opened for Elijah, and a cup of wine was set on the table in expectation of his arrival.

The synagogue served as a place of study as well as prayer. While in some eastern European countries the fear of non-Jews being disturbed or affronted by the sound of the Jews praying caused the Jews to build windowless structures, the synagogues built in the German-speaking rural areas included numerous windows of all sizes. In the sanctuary the same families sat next to each other for generations. Each family owned seats in both the men's section and the women's gallery (*Weiberschul* or *Frauenschul*) Marriage inventories, promissory notes, and inheritance inventories listed the seats as tangible assets with a monetary value. Not surprisingly, conflicts within families as to the ownership of the seats occasionally arose.

The cantor (*hazzan*) or learned men led the communal worship services in the synagogue. Prior to the early nineteenth century, the rabbi did not perform any communal duties except for presenting the Great Sermons twice a year. The community and individuals paid for services performed by the rabbi and cantor. (Details regarding the early-nineteenth-century services and the fees may be found on pages 55, 56, and 126.)

The Torah and Jewish Learning

Jewish men studied Torah—the laws handed down by God to Moses at Mount Sinai. Jews believed that the entire Torah (known also as the Pentateuch or Five Books of Moses), not just the Ten Commandments, came from God. God had commanded the Jewish people to uphold the Law. Thus the Torah, together with the Talmud, was the guiding force behind Jewish daily life. The Torah scroll (*Sefer Torah*), written on sheepskin parchment by a specially trained scribe (*sofer*), played an important role in a number of Jewish rituals and holy days.

After the destruction of the Second Temple in 70 C.E., it fell to the rabbis and sages to interpret the Torah. Over the centuries, these oral interpretations were recorded and gathered together. The result was the Talmud, a multivolume compilation of oral law (the Mishnah) and further commentary (the Gemarah). It was codified by the sixth century C.E. Rabbis and scholars further interpreted these texts as historical developments and conditions warranted. The rabbis were the arbiters, the judges, who decided all issues of Jewish law and ritual based on the Talmud; Jews looked to these men for guidance. The Talmud was studied in a special school of higher learning called a yeshivah.

The level of Jewish learning was not high in the countryside. Men would have studied only the weekly Torah portion. The Hebrew, written from right to left, did not include any vowels, which made it quite difficult to read without extensive study. Only the rabbis, and some cantors and teachers, would have had some knowledge of the Talmud.

The sacred texts stored for centuries in Michelbach reveal, however, that indeed some of the rural Jews studied religious and ethical tracts. They consulted an explanatory Hebrew Bible glossary that was used in the Ashkenazic area. The glossary was written in German with Hebrew characters and in Hebrew in 1597. It was originally published in 1699, and later was published in Fürth about 1780. Among the religious and ethical texts the Jews read was a tract printed in Homburg in 1747 by Jacob son of Moses, from Janow, Poland. The author lived in Merchingen, which was at that time the seat of a rabbinical district and also a center of religious study. Books written in High German with Hebrew characters usually contained glossaries for readers who had limited German vocabularies.

The market for daily and holiday prayer books was large enough that several printing houses were established. A prayer book for the services for the special night vigils (*Tikkunim*) for Shavuot and Sukkot has come down to us. It was the property of Josef Hirsch Rothschild, who wrote his name, the date (1810), and his town (Rottweil) in the front of the prayer book. The title page explained that the Hebrew prayers were according to Lurianic Kabbalah. Josef Hirsch's prayer book was published in 1805 in Vienna by Anton Schmid, a very enterprising Christian who received around 1800 the exclusive permission from the Austrian emperor to print Hebrew books. Schmid reedited nearly all the Hebrew literature, including the Torah and Talmud, with the aid of the most competent Jewish collaborators. For this enormous achievement the emperor bestowed upon the publisher the title of nobility, Anton von Schmid.

In the German states Jewish publishers brought out prayer books to appeal to the many economic levels of purchasers. To serve the market of the Jewish women who were only able to, or later preferred to, read German texts written in Hebrew characters, publishers produced books of devotional prayers (*tekhines*), which were written in a heartrending style, most often by women. Publishers also printed Jewish and German fables and novels in this style. This genre most likely appealed to the rural men as well. Rural community schools also purchased school instruction books printed in Fürth to teach children to write German in both cursive and traditional Hebrew characters.

So sacred were the religious texts that no damaged parchment could be used for a Torah scroll, nor could any book or paper with the name of God on it be thrown away. Centuries of old sacred papers, prayer books, and ritual objects were either buried in the Jewish cemetery or stored in a special storeroom (*genizah*) in the synagogue attic. Only men could go up to the storeroom. Berthold Auerbach, a nineteenth-century German author, recalled his mother's interpretation of the *genizah*'s special meaning:

> Beneath the synagogue's roof is an attic, and in that attic are all the centuries-old prayer books. The breath of the living floats up to the printed pages upon which the dead have breathed their prayers and dropped their tears, and the words of the dead and the words of the living join together, and together rise toward God.[1]

The Community and Its Language

To support their religious customs and for social purposes, Jews formed a local Jewish community (*kehillah*) within the Christian villages. These communities were not the separate, segregated ghettos of medieval Europe. Rather, the Jews openly practiced their religion, and the Christian villagers would see, hear, and feel the rhythms of Jewish life.

The Jewish-German dialects (*Jüdischdeutsch* or *Judendeutsch*) were another strong connection that both brought the members of the community together in the Diaspora. These dialects are also referred to as Judeo-German or Hebrew-German. In Swabia and Franconia, for instance, all the people spoke distinct German dialects. Hebrew words and expressions were mixed with the local dialects to produce a jargon used in daily transactions and communication. All the Jews, and especially the cattle dealers and schmoozers, in the region of Franconia used the trade dialect called *Lachoudisch*. The name of the jargon was a corruption of the Hebrew words for sacred language (*lashon ha-kodesh*). Christians felt comfortable speaking *Lachoudisch* in the marketplace as well because it was quite close to their local dialect. Stories in memoirs tell of the Christian dealers who pretended not to understand what the Jews were saying among themselves in order to strike better business deals. These dialects were often referred to in the vernacular as Yiddish-German (*Jiddisch* or *Jiddischdeutsch*).

Jiddischdeutsch differed from the language spoken by the Jews living in eastern Europe. When the Jews immigrated to Poland and Lithuania in the late Middle Ages, they brought with them the High German language and the Jewish-German dialect they had spoken for centuries. Once cut off from their German roots, these Jews adopted and adapted the Slavic vocabulary of the new lands to form the basis of their Yiddish dialect. It is not surprising that the dialects developed in different ways, so much so that modern scholars refer to them as Western Yiddish and Eastern Yiddish. With the more insular lives of the Jews in eastern Europe, their Yiddish became a language of their culture within their world. Jews in the German-speaking lands, on the other hand, mostly used the dialect for casual communication or personal written communication, and by the mid- to late-nineteenth century its use had declined considerably, although some Yiddish expressions continued to be part of the German vocabulary.

The Jewish Calendar

Traditional Jewish life has always been regulated by the Jewish calendar that is based on the lunar cycle. The Christian Gregorian calendar is calculated from the birth of Christ, which Jewish writers indicate by the designations B.C.E. and C.E.—before the Common Era and in the Common Era, respectively. The Jewish calendar, on the other hand, is reckoned from the year of Creation. Some personal family documents and official papers in the nineteenth century included only the Jewish year and month; others listed both the Christian and Jewish dates. For example, David Berlizheimer and Fany Grünwald married on the thirteenth day of Av in the year 5586, which corresponded to August 16, 1826. The sighting of the crescent of the new moon in Jerusalem indicated the start of the lunar month, and this information then had to be communicated to Jews living outside the Land of Israel. Thus, in the Diaspora, Jews celebrated the important biblical festivals for two days to ensure that at least one day would be correct.

The history and rituals of many holidays went back to life in the desert in biblical times. Most of the holidays, and especially the three pilgrimage festivals, had an agricultural and seasonal component. The Christians might not understand the religious ceremonies, but the importance of the seasons and the harvests was a concern shared by all the villagers. Each holiday (*yom tov*) was celebrated in both the synagogue and the home. The youngest children to the oldest adults felt the importance and significance of these nights and days. The joy or sadness of each holiday gave a special feeling to the village and gave a structure to its year.

Dietary Laws and Customs

The Christians knew the Jews had special dietary and slaughtering rules but did not understand the meaning behind these regulations. Everyone knew that the Jewish butcher got the front half of the cow and the Christian butcher the rear half. Christians often bought their meat from the Jewish butchers, and some Jewish butchers would open their shops on Saturday night for their Christian customers. Since neither Jewish butchers nor cattle dealers dealt in swine, the Christian butchers would handle that business for the other villagers.

Jews complied with the religious laws of kashrut concerning permitted and forbidden foods. Religious sanctification and holiness were the motivating factors in the dietary laws. The Hebrew Bible listed only certain kosher animals: those that have cloven hooves and chew their cud (thus excluding pigs), familiar poultry, and fish with fins and scales. The biblical rules also prohibited boiling a kid (baby goat) in its mother's milk. From this injunction came the rule that meat and dairy had to be separated: they could not be eaten at the same meal, and Jewish families used distinct dishes and utensils for each product group. Wine touched by non-Jews was also forbidden. Prohibited foods were designated as *treif* or nonkosher.

Each Jewish community had a ritual slaughterer (*shoḥet*) who fulfilled the religious laws of ritual slaughtering of nonprohibited animals (*sheḥitah*). These laws, which were very detailed and exact, were based on the biblical verse that prohibited eating an animal torn by beasts. Usually the person who served as the teacher and cantor also served as the *shoḥet*, but often the Jewish butcher also received the proper certification from the rabbi. Once the *shoḥet* was certified, he was fully responsible for examining the animal but remained accountable to the rabbi or cantor. After saying a benediction, the *shoḥet* had to swiftly and smoothly cut the animal's throat using a very sharp, smooth knife; then, the animal's feet were bound and it was hung upside down so the blood—held to contain the life force that should not be consumed—would drain immediately.

Berthold Auerbach recalled the communal feeling that surrounded the occasion of the ritual slaughtering. On an occasional Saturday evening, the ritual slaughterer killed a cow and skinned the animal. Then the rabbi inspected the knife to check for nicks, and the innards and lungs of the animal for adhesions or diseases. If the rabbi found any problems, the Jews could not eat the meat, and the nonkosher meat had to be sold door-to-door as quickly as possible. According to tradition, nonkosher meat was bad luck for the entire community. If the animal were kosher, everyone would be happy since the Jews could then buy the meat. On those occasions, Berthold's grandfather and his friends would play cards until late at night.[2]

Although the Jews kept kosher, they ate many of the same traditional south German foods as their Christian neighbors. They would just prepare the dishes according to kosher recipes. Common village fare the Jews enjoyed included noodles (*Spätzle*), sweet-and-sour red cabbage with meat, boiled meat with white horseradish sauce, sweetbreads, jellied calves' feet, fried goose rinds, and bread with goose-fat spread. The south German desserts—jellyrolls, cakes topped with sliced seasonal fruits (baked in the bakery's oven), and wine creams—were an integral part of the German afternoon coffee hour.

Daily and Weekly Rituals

While Jewish life centered around the home, communal life revolved around the synagogue. In German-speaking areas, the synagogue was called a *schul*; it was a place of learning—a school—as well as a house of worship. Every morning a designated synagogue employee would "knock for synagogue" (*schulklopfen*), using a special mallet, on the wooden shutter of each Jewish house. All males age thirteen or older walked to the synagogue for morning prayers. If a man were at home, he would always attend the service. Sometimes during the markets when the men were away, it might be more difficult to form the prayer quorum of ten males (minyan) necessary for communal prayer. On Mondays and Thursdays mornings, Torah portions were read. The Jews who did business near the village left after morning prayers and returned just before evening prayers, when the men again went to the synagogue.

Men would carry their phylacteries (tefillin) and prayer shawl (tallis) to the synagogue for morning services in small embroidered bags. The wearing of the tallis was specifically enjoined in the *Shema*; the Israelites were commanded to "make for themselves fringes on the corners of their garments...to remind them to observe all My commandments." The tefillin—two small, cubical leather boxes containing parchment scrolls with texts written by a Torah scribe—were strapped to the left arm and forehead. They symbolized the observance of the commandment in the *Shema* to "bind them as a sign upon your hand and upon the frontlets between your eyes." The

Hebrew letter *shin*, representing the word *Shaddai* (Almighty, another name for God), was hammered in relief on the outside of the boxes, and parchment with verses from the *Shema* and other Torah verses were enclosed within. A few months before a boy became a Bar Mitzvah, the cantor or teacher would teach him how to "lay" the tefillin.

Another Jewish ritual was performed many times a day as Jews entered or left their homes: the touching of the small box (mezuzah, originally meaning "doorpost") nailed on the right doorpost of each door (except for the entrances to any sanitary facilities). Some families chiseled a shallow base for their mezuzah in the stone front doorpost. Within the carved box was a parchment inscribed with the first verses of the *Shema* commanding Jews to write the laws "upon the doorposts of your house and upon your gates." The Christians attributed magical qualities to the box and the ritual.

The *Mikveh*

In all communities married women regularly visited the ritual bath (*mikveh*). Immersion in the ritual bath symbolically cleansed a person who had come in contact with the dead or with an unclean flux from the body (for instance, a woman's menstrual flow). In some communities, especially those where a yeshivah was located, men would visit the *mikveh* before attending Sabbath and festival worship services. New cooking utensils were also immersed to sanctify them before they were used for the first time.

Most communities built a *mikveh* in a room under the synagogue or in the basement of its school or its community house; in some places, individual families built ritual baths in their houses or in separate buildings. The construction had to be done according to exacting regulations: the predominant source of water had to be at least twenty-five gallons of natural spring water or rainwater. A bathing room for cleansing was built in an area adjacent to the immersion bath.

The ritual immersion cleansing was a ceremony of consecration, which meant that it was subject to many religious regulations. The women recited special prayers or supplications (*tekhines*). A woman's first visit to the *mikveh* was the evening before her wedding. She would then go each month before resuming sexual relations with her husband (seven clean days after the end of her menstrual flow). A woman was also required to go to the *mikveh* before her first visit to the synagogue after giving birth. An adult woman, usually the cantor's wife, observed the immersions and the benedictions. After

RITUAL BATH This *mikveh,* built around 1735 in the Bavarian village of Schnaittach near Fürth, was in use until the 1830s. The size of the immersion bath was roughly three cubic feet. (Jüdisches Museum Franken in Schnaittach.)

leaving the ritual bath, the woman's friends and acquaintances would pub
licly wish her good health and fertility. Again, Christians would see th
women's comings and goings—often with several young children in tow.

Childhood Rituals

With the ritual circumcision ceremony (*berit milah*) the male Jewish baby er
tered the Covenant with God. All male members of the community attende
the ceremony, which was performed in the synagogue by the circumcise
(*mohel*) when the infant was eight days old. It was a great honor to serve a
the community *mohel*. According to the birth registers, several Gundelfinger
in Michelbach (who were most likely butchers as well) acted in that capacit
for decades. A special two-seated bench was placed in the sanctuary. Th
infant's godfather (usually the paternal grandfather or the most senior mal
member of the family) sat on one side holding the baby, and the other sid
was left as a place of honor for the prophet Elijah. In addition, the canto
chanted prayers at the ceremony.

An additional ritual, based on biblical verses, was performed thirty day
after the birth of a firstborn son to redeem him from obligatory service t
the Temple and God. In the ceremony of redemption of the firstborn son
(*pidyon ha-ben*), the father paid a *Kohen* (a descendant of the high priests i
the ancient Temple, who themselves were descended from Aaron) fiv
shekels (silver coins) so that the boy would be released.

The boy's connection with his religion, learning, and the communit
was strengthened further by another ceremony when he turned three. Whe
a child reached this milestone, his father would bring him to the synagogu
for the first time. The little boy would present a special linen scroll (*wimpel*)
and it was wrapped around the Torah scroll as a binder. The father guide
his son in touching the "trees of life," the wooden finials of the Torah scroll
while the boy's mother watched proudly from the women's gallery.

The importance of the transmission of Jewish law from father to son, th
importance of both the home and synagogue as educational institutions, an
the importance of learning Hebrew to understand the Torah greatly increase
the level and interest in education among Jews. When a boy reached his thir
teenth year, he became a full member of the community and took on th
obligation to observe all the commandments. The term "Bar Mitzvah" (sor
of the commandments) applies to both the boy and the ceremony. Althougl
the concept was established from about the second century C.E., the forma
ceremony was not recorded before the fifteenth century. The entire commu

WIMPEL MOTIFS A piece of linen, placed under the baby during the circumcision, was stored until the boy was about two and half years old. Then it was cut into four long strips and sewn together. The boy's name, date of birth, and good wishes were written or stenciled in Hebrew, and often the mother embroidered over the inscriptions. "May the Lord raise him up to the study of Torah, to the nuptial canopy, and to good deeds" was the traditional inscription adorning the *wimpel*. (Baisingen, Gedenkstätte Baisingen.)

nity witnessed when the boy was called to the Torah for the first time on the Sabbath after his thirteenth birthday. The decorated *wimpel*, saved since his third birthday, would be used as a binding for the Torah scroll on that day and until the next Bar Mitzvah. With these rituals the Jewish male became part of the community and was counted as eligible for a minyan. Voting membership in the community, however, went only to married men.

The *Holegrasch* ritual was a special ceremony celebrated in the southwest lands to mark the naming of a baby girl. After the mother attended Sabbath services for the first time following childbirth, the infant's parents would invite all the Jewish children to their home. When everyone had assembled, they placed their baby in her cradle. The children would raise the cradle as high as they could and shout loudly, "What will be the name of the child?" and then call out the baby's name. After the children repeated the ritual three times, the teacher offered a prayer. The parents gave treats to the children to commemorate the joyous event, and the children carefully carried the sweets home to share with their own families.

Marriage

When a girl or boy reached a marriageable age, usually between the ages of twenty and twenty-seven in the nineteenth century, the parents naturally tried to make the best possible match for their child. Matches for Christian marriages were made within the village or neighboring villages, while matches for Jews were made using personal contacts and even an official matchmaker (*shadkhan*) over a wider geographical area (now referred to as marriage networks or marriage circles). The parents of both the man and woman would undertake a search based on the financial situation of the potential partner and the parents. The size of the woman's dowry was usually comparable to the assets given by the man's parents to their son or his financial prospects. Important factors included family status and character. These marriages became the basis for commercial and social networks for the entire family. Most matches and engagements were made during the holidays, particularly Shavuot in the spring and Sukkot in the fall, when relatives and friends visited one another.

The dowry and trousseau given by the bride's parents, and the assets and possessions brought by groom, were carefully detailed in the formal document of engagement arrangements and in the written marriage contract

HOLEGRASCH (BABY-NAMING) CEREMONY   This special ceremony in southwestern Germany celebated the naming of a baby girl. The ritual might have had its roots in a pagan rite. In a few places, it was also performed to give a boy his vernacular name. The Sabbath lamp hangs in the center of the room. ("Hoolegrasch, Lengnau: aus meiner Kindheit," painting by Alis Guggenheim, c. 1950. Original in Israel Museum, Jerusalem. Courtesy of Ruth Guggenheim, Zurich.)

(*ketubbah*). These documents specified the obligations of the husband to-ward his wife, including the statement that the bride's full dowry would be returned if the marriage ended in divorce. Before the wedding the groom would be invited to the bride's village and would be called to the Torah in the synagogue. As stipulated in the engagement arrangements, the costs for the wedding would be paid by one or the other family; in some cases, the families split the costs.

The bride visited the ritual bath for the first time on the evening before the wedding. Before the wedding ceremony, the women of the community would ceremoniously comb, braid, and twist the bride's long hair until it fit under a small bonnet. From that moment on, she would wear a bonnet in front of strangers or outdoors as a voluntary surrender of all coquetry and as a sign of modesty. Talmudic injunctions against exposing a woman's hair because to do so was considered immodest led this custom to be strictly observed. In the latter part of the nineteenth century, some married women did cut their hair and wear wigs. The mother-in-law of Moriz Rothschild, the newspaper owner in Rottweil, continued to wear a *shaytl* (as such a wig was called) when she and her husband moved to the more modern town of Rott-weil in the 1870s. Luise Lea Bloch had been born in the very traditional community of Randegg on the Swiss border and had married in the tradi-tional community of Rexingen:

The bride and groom fasted the day of the wedding to remind them in this time of joy to be humble and repentant and to remember the destruc-tion of the Temple. The bride and groom and their families then walked to the synagogue in a procession led by musicians. During the wedding cere-mony in the synagogue courtyard, four boys held poles supporting a wed-ding canopy or a prayer shawl over the bride and groom. The canopy (*ḥuppah*) symbolized the Jewish home the couple would build together. Be-fore the nineteenth century, for the ring ceremony, the couple used a large engraved wedding ring owned by the Jewish community. At the conclusion, the groom, or the synagogue caretaker (*shammes*), threw a glass against the wedding stone, which was carved as a frieze into the outer wall of the syna-gogue and was usually in the shape of a six-pointed star. The Shield of David (*Magen David*) was thought to ward off demons and evil spirits. The broken glass symbolized both the destruction of the Second Temple and the fragility of life. The couple then retired to a special room to share their first meal. In some villages everyone, Jews and Christians, attended the wedding. Berthold Auerbach, in one of his *Schwarzwälder Dorfgeschichten* (Black Forest

THE MATCHMAKER   Alphonse Lévy humorously depicted the role of the matchmaker in this scene of rural life. (In Daniel Stauben, *Scenes of Jewish Life in Alsace,* trans. and ed. Rose Choron [1860, Reprint, London: Joseph Simon, 1991], 132. Courtesy of NightinGale Resources, Cold Spring, New York.)

stories), wrote that the occasion of a Jewish wedding brought the spirit of fun and frolic to the village, and the farmers, always glad of an excuse to be idle, gathered around to watch.

Like the Christian bride, the Jewish bride brought her household trousseau in an open wagon so that her new neighbors would know exactly what she contributed to the marriage. Friends and relatives gave presents to the couple. A Michelbach couple's 1837 register of "Presents for the House" included decorative gifts (pottery, porcelain bowls and plates, a silver coffee set and serving spoons, etched glasses, a sugar canister, brass candle holders, a teapot) and small amounts of money (from 35 kreuzer to several gulden) from relatives and friends, including the Gundelfingers. The bride also received a small prayer book.[3] Berthold Auerbach wrote in his stories that both Christians and Jews, some bearing presents, came to the wedding dance after dark. Auerbach warmly described how friends danced and shared the wedding cake, but his descriptions and stories were later criticized as being idealized.

Only after marriage did a woman take on the responsibility of transmitting Judaism to the next generation. In terms of procreation, Jewish law stated that a baby was Jewish only if his or her mother were Jewish. In the eighteenth and nineteenth centuries, childbirth was a very dangerous time for both mother and baby. To ward off evil spirits, the family hung kabbalistic (mystical) drawings and amulets in the birthing room. The cantor would recite prayers in an outer room and then would pray for the mother in the synagogue. About a month after giving birth (when the "impure" postnatal bleeding had stopped) and when it was felt that no more evil spirits could threaten the mother or child, the mother would go to the *mikveh* and resume attending Sabbath services. Even on that *Shabbos* day she was guarded by women friends. There the cantor would recite special prayers mentioning the mother's name, and she was reintegrated into the community as she was safe as any "pure" woman.

Charity and Death

The Jews in the community shared the difficult times. The practice of visiting and caring for the sick and poor was both an ancient duty (mitzvah) and a necessity. The Jewish communities formed their own charitable organizations. Justice or righteousness (*tzedekah*) meant that charity was not a patronizing act, but simply justice a Jew owed his fellow man. From ancient times charity boxes had been placed in homes and in the synagogues to provide for the poor and those in mourning. The donor was always anonymous, and, as much as possible, the recipient was as well. Another system provided meal tickets (*billeten*; popularly pronounced *pletten*) to transient and beggar Jews. Usually the village authorities and the Jewish community allowed a stranger to stay only three days.

Each community also established groups to care for the sick and deceased. A village would have, at best, one nurse who was affiliated with the parish to care for all the patients in the village and its environs. The society for visiting the sick (*hevra bikkur holim*) organized financial aid and other help to care for the ill person and his family. Members of the community would ake shifts day and night to watch over the patient. Women cared for an ailing woman, and men cared for a sick man. When the end approached, the lying person tried to recite the *Shema* so that he or she would die with the name of God on his or her lips. The synagogue caretaker would be with the person at the end and would close the deceased's eyes. Jews believed that he spirit continued in some way known only to God. They also believed that after the Messiah came, God would do away with death and restore the souls into their bodies. Just as a birth was announced in the community, he caretaker announced a death. The Holy Brotherhood (*hevra kadishah*) made arrangements so that the deceased would not be left unattended. Everyone who came in contact with the dead was considered ritually impure so they had to ritually cleanse themselves. Therefore, a pail of water with a ladle was left outside the door of the deceased's home, so that as visitors left the house, they could wash their hands.

According to Jewish law the deceased had to be buried as soon as possible. This responsibility fell to the Holy Brotherhood. Election to this group of men required a good reputation, and it was an honor to be selected and to serve. In Mühringen in the 1840s, for example, there were forty members. The members made a simple pine coffin because of the almudic requirement that rich and poor be treated equally in death. At he entry to the cemetery, a small ritual washing house was used for the itual cleansing of the body (*taharah*) on a special stone bench. If the deceased was a woman, the members' wives would wash and dress the body. A man would be buried in his funeral shirt (*kitel*; called *sarjenes* in this area) and his prayer shawl. As a substitute for burial in the Holy Land, the *hevra kadishah* placed in the coffin a small bag of earth brought from Palestine by traders. On the day of the funeral, all the friends and relatives of the departed would stand at the foot of the coffin and ask the deceased for forgiveness for any wrongdoings they might have done to him or her during that person's lifetime. Six Jewish men carried the coffin to the cemetery. Behind the coffin the rabbi and the cantor led the funeral procession, followed first by the male family mourners and then by the female mourners. In the late nineteenth century, the Christian villagers sometimes joined the procession.

The Jewish cemetery was called the Good Place or the House of Everlasting Life. The grave for the deceased was placed a small distance from the grave of the most recent burial. Each coffin was placed so that the deceased's head faced east toward Jerusalem. Children were often buried in a special section. In the cemetery, the cantor said the Hebrew prayers, and often the rabbi delivered a special sermon. The cantor tore the shirts of the closest blood relatives as a sign of grief (*keri'ah*). The deceased's son had the obligation of reciting the ancient Aramaic *Heiligung* prayer (*Kaddish*). While the prayer was referred to as the Mourner's *Kaddish*, it actually contained no references to death; rather, it extolled God's greatness. The mourners stood on both sides of the grave as each relative placed three shovelsful of dirt on the coffin.

In the house of mourning, preparations were already made for sitting *shivah* (from the Hebrew *sheva*, or "seven") which lasted seven days. A box with a cushion was the usual seat for the mourners. As people returned to the house after the funeral, everyone ate a hard-boiled egg without salt, a symbol of the cyclical, eternal, and continuous nature of life. Members of the congregation brought in the meals for the first three days after the funeral because it was not proper to cook in the house of mourning. In the morning and at night, a minyan would pray in the house. After the services the teacher or a learned man would lead a study session. From the day of the funeral to the end of the *shivah* period, an oil lamp burned. Lesser signs of mourning continued for eleven months. *Kaddish* was recited every day. No funerals or visits to the cemetery could take place on the Sabbath or on holidays as these were days of joy and celebration.

The local Christian stonecutter made the headstone, usually out of sandstone. The Jewish teacher wrote out the inscription in Hebrew letters, and the stonecutter copied it exactly. Above the inscription, certain symbols identified the deceased: blessing hands symbolized a *Kohen*, and a pitcher indicated a descendent of the tribe of *Levi* (because in ancient times the Levites washed the hands of the *Kohanim*). The headstone was placed on the grave at the time of the first anniversary of the death, according to the Jewish calendar (*Jahrzeit*).

It was the obligation of a son to say *Kaddish* for his parents. In some cases, the deceased did not have a son, or the son was not yet thirteen. For example, Bernhard Gundelfinger in Michelbach died when his son was very young. In his will he set up a small charitable fund to ensure that *Kaddish* would be recited for him. Bernhard wrote: "If my son is old enough at my death, he should say the usual *Kaddish* for me in the synagogue. If my son is not old enough or is deceased, part of the interest from my charitable foundation should be given to a religiously qualified man who will recite *Kaddish* and will learn a religious passage. The remainder of the interest will pay for

314

he man to read a portion of the Bible. The community officer should choose only a man with knowledge who needs the money."[4]

Each year on the *Jahrzeit* of a parent's death, the children would light a lamp or candle, fast, give charity, be called to the Torah, and go to the cemetery and recite *Kaddish*. At the cemetery, they would place one or several stones on the grave to show they had not forgotten the deceased.

JEWISH HOLY DAYS AND FESTIVALS

The Sabbath

The Ten Commandments enjoined Jews to keep the Sabbath, and the Book of Exodus instructed Jews to rest on the seventh day, "that your ox and your ass may have rest, and the son of your handmaid, and the stranger, may be refreshed." The Sabbath (*Shabbos*, or *Shabbes*) had two purposes: it imposed a day of rest for all and it sanctified a day holy unto God and His chosen people. Although work was forbidden on the Sabbath, any act involving the saving of life was permitted.

Everyone would have been aware of the different feeling in the village when *Shabbos* was approaching. Preparations for the Sabbath began on Wednesday, when the wife went to the market to buy a live chicken that she took to the ritual slaughterer. Sometimes the housewife bought kosher meat from the Jewish butcher. After cleaning the entire house on Thursday, the woman prepared the dough for the Sabbath bread by mixing together flour, grated cold potatoes, water, and yeast. Friday morning she shaped the dough into two loaves, placed a little braided piece on top of each loaf, and then sprinkled them with poppy seeds. To distinguish her loaves, she affixed her personal tiny dough symbol on the side of each one. She carried the loaves on a wooden board through the streets to the bakery. The baker, regardless of whether he was a Christian or a Jew, was careful not to bake anything else with the Sabbath bread.

The housewives also prepared Saturday's midday dinner, making a thick rice, barley, or pea soup with meat or chicken—"a setting" (*gesetzt*) soup. (In other parts of Europe, this was called a *cholent* from the French *chaud et lent*, hot and slow.) They also cooked a noodle casserole with eggs, raisins, and flour that sometimes contained apples. (In this area, this dish was called a *schalet*, adopted from the word but not the ingredients of the *cholent*, while in other southern regions it was called a *kugel*.) After the baker removed the Sabbath loaves from his oven, he placed all the heavy iron kettles with the Sabbath meals there, leaving them to simmer or bake slowly for twenty hours.

Excitement mounted in the village as the men returned by foot or wagon. Male voices were again heard in the streets as the returnees greeted their families. Ritual law did not allow a man to use a razor on his beard, so he cut it with scissors. In some villages the Jewish barber was very busy Friday afternoons trimming beards and sharing village news. Meanwhile, the housewives would pull the chain or rope to lower from the ceiling the six-branched Sabbath oil lamp, which was called a Jewish Star (*Judenstern*). A popular Sabbath saying expressed the special spirit that as Sabbath approached, the cares of the week must be pushed away:

> Sabbath lamp down.
> Want and worry up.

To honor the day, everyone put on clean clothes—preferably clothes that were not worn on weekdays. Even the poorest men would do something to honor the event; sometimes they could only turn their single shirt inside out. The men and children walked to the synagogue before sunset; the women remained at home and lit the Sabbath lamp.

The village took on a special atmosphere, and all was quiet except in the synagogue, where the Sabbath, personified as the Sabbath Bride or Sabbath Queen, was welcomed. The cantor, singing the familiar melodies, led all the prayers. At certain points he would raise his voice so everyone would chant in unison; passersby would hear the sounds of many voices reciting the Hebrew prayers. For the sake of the poor people who could not afford wine in their homes, the prayer of sanctification (*Kiddush*) was recited in the synagogue.

When the services ended, the Jews wished one another "*gut Shabbos*." Often students at the yeshivah, Jews passing through the village, or beggars, would be invited to share in the Sabbath meal. Each Jewish home was already alight with the flickering Sabbath lamp. Fathers stopped briefly at their parents' homes so that the grandmothers could give their blessings to the children.

The husband and wife greeted each other in a respectful and loving tone: the husband blessed his wife, and then together, mother and father blessed each child. Next the blessings over the wine and bread were recited.

hen, using a special Sabbath bread knife inscribed with "God's Blessing En-
iches," the Hebrew proverb that gave the Sabbath loaf (generally called
allah) its name, *berches*, in southern Germany, the father cut one of the two
oaves. The two loaves represented the two portions of manna that the Is-
aelites wandering in the desert had gathered. Since no work, and therefore
io gathering of manna, could be done on the Sabbath, God sent a double
ortion of manna the day prior to the Sabbath. The two loaves also symbol-
zed the abundance of the Sabbath, compared to the single loaf that was on
he weekday table.

Friday night dinner was always special. The meal would start with noodle
oup or a special south German smoky-flavored soup made with roasted
reen wheat. Whitefish fillet covered with a sweet raisin sauce was served be-
ause when God created the world, He told man to be fertile and multiply as
lo the fish. Then came potted meat with sauce, or crispy baked stuffed
pleen, or chicken. Even the poorest family would include a little meat and
ish in the meal. A baked pudding or pie would conclude the festive meal.

In the wintertime everyone sang Sabbath table hymns (*z'mirot*) after the
neal. The whole family enjoyed the peace and festiveness of the Friday
evening. It seemed as if they were in a different world; business and the sor-
ows of everyday life were forgotten. Later during the cold nights the family
layed board games, retiring to bed early when the fire died down. In the
ummertime everyone visited in the streets until the night watchman's horn
sent them to bed.

The religious rules governing the Sabbath included the prohibition
against walking more than about half a mile outside the walls of a town. For
:hat reason, Jews who were visiting from other places would remain in the
iost village from Friday evening to Saturday evening. Rabbi Adler in Mührin-
3en, for example, assured ministerial officials in 1821 that the Jews knew
iow far they could travel ("less than a half an hour") because a rabbi had
measured the permitted distances.[5]

Saturday morning, the person who called the worshipers came to each
iouse. He did not knock with the special mallet he used on other days
because that was considered work. On the Sabbath he rapped with his fist or
called out. In winter a Christian helper or Sabbath woman (*Schabbesfrau*,
called in some homes a *Schabbesgoy*) would light the stove since ritual law
did not allow the Jews to do any work on the Sabbath. The family walked together to the synagogue, but once inside the women went upstairs to the
women's gallery. The women attended the morning service because

although women were exempt from the reading and studying of religious texts, they did have the obligation to hear the Torah read.

At each Sabbath morning service, eight men received the honor of being called up (*aufgerufen* or *aliyah*) to say the blessing before and after each section of the weekly Torah portion was read. By custom, the first person to be called up was a *Kohen*; the second person was from the tribe of Levi, traditionally the lesser priests and servants of the high priests; and the others would be members of the other tribes, collectively known as the Israelites. These honors and that of carrying the Torah would be auctioned to the highest bidder; the money collected went to the community treasury. The at times noisy transactions were held inside the synagogue. Although the government tried to restrict this procedure in the 1840s, the Jews continued this and many other customs. Since no one was allowed to write on the Sabbath, a wooden board, in which little prewritten papers were placed in holes, recorded the winning bids. The most honored person each week, the one who was celebrating a special personal event, was called upon last.

During the service the Torah was removed from the Holy Ark and carried ceremoniously around the sanctuary; each man would touch the Torah mantle reverently with his prayer shawl and then kiss that place on the shawl. So as not to embarrass the men being called to the Torah, who might not know the blessings by heart, the cantor would always recite the words as well; or, in some synagogues, the honorees could read them off a wooden board. Each person called up to the Torah also paid the cantor a small "contribution" after the Sabbath; these sums were set in his employment contract.

After the morning service all the women gathered outside the bakery while the baker used a long-handled bar to remove each family's Sabbath meal from the depths of the oven. The Sabbath helper then carried it home. After the meal the family members took the traditional Sabbath nap (a luxury not enjoyed on weekdays) or gathered in study groups to hear the teacher speak about the weekly Torah portion. The men visited the inn for chicory coffee to discuss the politics and news of the day. Then the family took a Sabbath promenade and greeted friends and relatives. In summertime following the afternoon service in the synagogue, family and friends would have a picnic in a tavern garden; again, the Christian helper would do the work of carrying the baskets. Herring salad made with sour cream and apples or potatoes in clotted cheese would be served. Everyone would enjoy drinks from the establishment. Since no one was allowed to carry anything, including money, on the Sabbath, all the accounts would be paid up on Sunday.

As darkness approached, the men and boys gathered in the courtyard of the synagogue to await the first three stars in the sky before going inside for the evening service. The *Havdalah* ceremony, which marked the end of the Sabbath by separating it from the weekdays, was celebrated with wine, braided candles, and aromatic spices in decorative containers. As people left the synagogue, they wished one another, "A good week!" The new week had begun.

Rosh Ḥodesh

The Jews' lunar calendar gave special religious significance to the new moon, which marked the start of the new month (Rosh Ḥodesh); special blessings were recited. Women prayed and refrained from sewing and other housework on that day. On the evening of the first Sabbath after the new moon, the men would gather in the courtyard of the synagogue and, holding burning candles, recite prayers as the new moon became visible in the clear evening sky.

Rosh Hashanah and Yom Kippur

At the onset of autumn the first preparations for the High Holy Days began. Everyone tried to have new clothes for the New Year, and so it was the time to order a new suit or dress. No markets or trips were scheduled for these weeks; it was a time for solemn devotion. The holidays fell in September or early October. For the month before the High Holy Day season, the ram's horn (shofar) was blown each day.

Commencing the Sunday before Rosh Hashanah, the New Year, penitential prayers (*Selichos*) of great beauty and poignancy would be said each day in the synagogue before sunrise. The person who called the worshipers would knock on the house shutters at 3 A.M.; on the first morning, the women also attended the services.

The colored curtain for the Holy Ark and the mantles covering the Torah scrolls were replaced with ones made of white, the color of forgiveness. For the High Holy Day services, women wore white dresses with white scarves and small white bonnets, and the men put on their white funeral shrouds. They brought their festival book of prayer (*mahzor*); on the inside pages of these special prayer books, their ancestors had inscribed their family his-

tory—births, deaths, and marriages. The prayers of thankfulness and rever
ence recited the first evening of Rosh Hashanah were felt deeply. After the
service, everyone greeted each other with, "May you be inscribed for a happy
year." At home, each person dipped an apple in honey, saying, "May it be a
sweet and good year."

The next day, following the afternoon service, the adults walked to the
village stream to perform the *Tashlikh* ceremony. At the water's edge, they
prayed to God to cast away their sins as they shook out their pockets into
the running water. The Jews asked God to treat them with kindness and com-
passion and to protect them. The Christian villagers, seeing the ritual, would
comment: "The Jews are throwing their sins and vows into the water." During
the two days of Rosh Hashanah, families and neighbors tried to visit one
another, and friends and relatives came from other villages. Rosh Hashanah
was a joyful, but at the same time solemn, occasion.

During the next seven days each person spent time reflecting on the
past year. The rabbi gave a Great Sermon on the Sabbath before the Day of
Atonement (Yom Kippur). Also referred to as the Day of Forgiveness or the
Day of Reconciliation, Yom Kippur was the holiest day of the year. The
morning of Yom Kippur Eve, men and women performed the ritual of
atonement (*kappores*). An uncovered table was set up in the main room of
the house where the holiday prayer book was opened to a special passage.
On the floor would be a rooster (for the boys and the men) and a hen or
chicken (for the women), each with its legs bound. While reciting a special
prayer, each person would untie the legs of the appropriate fowl and swing
it around his or her head three times, praying: "Be my redemption for what-
ever comes over me; to forgive my sins, this rooster [or hen] must be put to
death." The bird was the atonement; the animal would go to its death, and
the person would proceed to a good, long life. As soon as the ceremony
was finished, the ritual slaughterer killed the animals; the meat was given
to the poor.

After a special dinner on Yom Kippur Eve, the fast would begin; both
men and women fasted the whole day, but children fasted only half a day.
The women dressed in white again. Immediately after entering the synagogue, the men removed their shoes and put on felt shoes and their funeral
shirts. Only married males wore the shroud. Anyone who had had some dis-
agreement over the past year would shake hands in the spirit of good friend-
ship and forgiveness. In that way problems within the community would not
continue into the new year.

The custom on Yom Kippur was to burn candles for family members who had passed away. These long candles were placed on a stone near the cantor's lectern, and each candle had a little piece of paper attached to it with a name of the person who had passed away. The men would light these candles, which would burn until the following evening.

The whole village was still as the sound of the cantor's voice filled the quiet void. The melody of *Kol Nidrei* (all vows) filled the night. A few men would stay to pray the entire night, or at least until midnight; some men remained standing the whole night and all the next day. The caretaker remained all night both to symbolically guard the synagogue and to ensure that the memorial candles did not start a fire.

The entire day of Yom Kippur was spent in the synagogue. In the afternoon, the *Kohanim* would cover their heads with their prayer shawls, and with outstretched arms, they would pronounce the traditional priestly benediction: "May the Lord bless you and keep you. May the Lord cause His Countenance to shine upon you and may He be gracious unto you. May the Lord lift up His Face unto you and grant you peace." The shofar was blown to signal the end of Yom Kippur. The fast was then broken in the home with light dairy foods.

Sukkot

Immediately after the Days of Awe ended, the atmosphere and feelings in the family and in the community changed to those of joyous thanksgiving, as preparations began for Sukkot, the Festival of Tabernacles. After the meal at the conclusion of Yom Kippur, the father might remove several shingles of the roof above a room in the upper story of the house. Or, he might build an enclosure—a booth (*sukkah*) in the courtyard or in front of the house. The family would spend the next four days feverishly decorating their *sukkah*. Christian farmers, knowing the Jewish calendar, would go house to house selling the Jews tree branches from the nearby woods.

For the eight nights of the holiday, the family and guests ate and recited prayers in the *sukkah*, just as their ancestors did in their tents in the desert, when God led them out of Egypt, and also to recall the third major pilgrimage festival in the Land of Israel (in ancient Israel, the agricultural year began with Passover). Cakes topped with luscious sliced plums were baked in the baker's large ovens and later shared with guests visiting the *sukkah*. Everyone in the village knew which families had the most elaborate and beautiful decorations. In the synagogue the Sukkot services were

DECORATING THE *SUKKAH* Leaves and branches were woven onto grids to form the walls and roof, and these were decorated with chains of chestnuts and colorful berries and fruits, and with garlands of ivy and evergreen. Biblical motifs and Jewish symbols served as themes for paper cutouts and painted decorations. A parchment with the Hebrew word *mizraḥ* (east) hung on the eastern wall so occupants would know which direction to face while praying. Chains also decorated the Sabbath lamp. (By Alphonse Lévy. In Daniel Stauben, *Scenes of Jewish Life in Alsace,* trans. and ed. Rose Choron [1860, Reprint, London: Joseph Simon, 1991], 98. Courtesy of NightinGale Resources, Cold Spring, New York.)

even more special as the congregation formed a procession led by the cantor or rabbi carrying the Torah. As they walked they waved the *lulav*—the palm branch bound together with willow and myrtle branches—and held aloft the citron fruit (*esrog*). The rustling sounds and foreign scents gave an exotic feel to the procession. Some poorer families or even entire communities sometimes shared a single fruit since it was an imported, and consequently expensive, fruit. As part of the religious service, the prayer for rain was recited. On the seventh night of Sukkot, a special learning session (Hoshana Rabbah) was held, and the next day was the solemn last day Shemini Atzeret.

Simḥat Torah

Joyousness returned again with the arrival of Simḥat Torah, the Festival of Rejoicing in the Torah, on the ninth day of Sukkot. On this day one member read the last portion of Deuteronomy, and, immediately following, another read the first portion of Genesis. The highlight was the procession at the morning service with the Torah scrolls. Every adult male had the opportunity to carry the Torah, or one of the household Torah scrolls, during the seven circuits around the sanctuary. The children excitedly marched behind the procession waving small flags and were rewarded with sweets and cakes.

Ḥanukkah

For all the villagers, the end of Simḥat Torah really proclaimed the advent of winter. The weather began to turn cold and raw. Winter, with its damp, gray days, made the synagogue uncomfortable. It was impractical to heat such a large hall, so each person just kept on his coat and used little wooden footrests. To further accommodate the worshipers at that time of year, several prayers that were usually recited aloud and responsively with the cantor were recited rapidly to oneself.

Ḥanukkah, the Festival of Lights, was a welcome diversion as snow was beginning to fall and the nights were very long. It commemorated the rededication of the Temple in Jerusalem in 165 B.C.E., when Judah the Maccabee led the Jews to victory over the powerful Syrian army that had captured the Temple. Finding only sufficient oil to burn for one day, the Jews filled the seven-branched Ḥanukkah-lamp (called a menorah in other areas) anyway, and it miraculously lasted for eight days. Centuries later the event was celebrated as a very minor holiday. The festivities began when the men went to the synagogue for the lighting of the holiday lights in the synagogue Hanukkah-lamp (*Chanukkaleuchter*). Everyone then rushed home because, as darkness fell, the whole family would gather in the living room to celebrate. A Hanukkah lamp was hung on the wall or set up on a windowsill facing the street. The small brass or pewter Hanukkah-lamp, with its eight small oil receptacles with wicks and a separate receptacle for the lighting wick (*shammes*), was often handed down within the family. After the Hanukkah lights were kindled, the family sang special songs, including some about the ancient victories, while marching up and down in the room. As long as the lights were burning, no one did anything in the house but enjoy their soft glow.

In some villages, each child received a small coin the first night of Hanukkah. No special foods were prepared for this holiday. There was always a lot of visiting: the young people socialized while the adults played cards and board games. The children played with a top (*Trendel*; called a dreidel elsewhere). The four-sided top, made out of ivory or wood, displayed a Hebrew letter on each side. The letters stood for the four Hebrew words that translated as "a great miracle happened there." Competition with fresh nuts as the prizes was intense, and the skill to spin the top for a long time on the uneven wooden floor was greatly appreciated. For each of the next seven evenings, an additional wick was lit until the windows in all the Jewish homes gleamed with light. Hanukkah fell at different times in late November and December, but it never competed with the importance and holiness of Christmas in the village.

Purim

In February or early March, the cold, snowy days led to the first signs of spring. Christians celebrated the days before the commencement of Lent with major carnivals. For three days, especially in Catholic areas like Mühringen, and on a very grand scale in Rottweil, everyone donned costumes and masks and paraded through the streets. The minor holiday of Purim happened to coincide with the beginning of the carnival season and took on some of its customs.

On Purim evening the synagogue was festively lit. The Purim legend had Queen Esther, the Jewish wife of Ahasuerus, king of Persia, interceding with him to save her people from the evil chief minister, Haman, who had planned to kill all the Jews. It was commanded that everyone hear the story read aloud, so all the women were present. The entire biblical story unfolded while the cantor pulled the old parchment from its single-post scroll (megillah). Some families followed along with their own elaborately decorated scrolls. The telling of this story produced a special response by the young boys who had brought with them specially crafted wooden hammers. Every time the evil Haman's name was read, the boys beat symbolically on Haman's back for about five minutes by pounding their hammers on the synagogue floor. Other boys vigorously shook handmade wooden rattles to make as much noise as possible.

The housewives baked a special cookie—Haman—as a gift for the children. It was shaped like Haman in the story, with raisins for his eyes and a dough noose around his neck. In some places, they "hanged" the Haman cookie from curtain cords. In other locales, the Haman figure would be stuffed with a mixture of finely chopped raisins, prunes, and nuts to create a Haman-pocket (*Hamantasch*). Adults and children dressed in costumes: typical local German dress or the fantasy royal characters in the ancient story. Everyone visited from house to house, presented a special play (*Purimspiel*), or attended a party at the inn.

Passover

After the long winter, everyone in the village was eager for the warm weather. The Christian holidays of Palm Sunday and Easter, and the Jewish holiday of Passover (Pesaḥ), celebrated rebirth and spring. The Christians would see all the Jews' preparations and know the important holiday of Pesaḥ was approaching. No markets were scheduled during the eight days of Passover or even on the few days before the holiday. Since it occurred around Easter, most Christians, and even some Jews, referred to Pesaḥ as the "Easter Festival."

In the Ten Commandments, God said: "I am the Lord your God, who brought you out of the land of Egypt and the house of slavery." On the eve of their departure, the Jews sacrificed a lamb and daubed its blood on the lintel and doorposts of their homes to secure divine protection so that the angel of death would pass over their households, claiming only the eldest sons of the Egyptians. This reference to blood gave rise to the false accusations of ritual murder of Christian children.

When the Jews fled Egypt, the bread for the next day did not have time to rise, so it remained unleavened. The Book of Exodus stated the commandments for celebrating Passover: holding a feast, eating matzos (unleavened bread), and clearing the house of all leaven or fermented grains (*hometz*). Therefore, to remind themselves of the Exodus, Jews were required to eat matzos and to clean their homes of any food or drink containing leaven. The foods eaten during the festival also commemorated the great Spring pilgrimage festival in ancient Israel.

Beginning right after Hanukkah in December, and continuing with even greater intensity after Purim in late February, the official Passover cleaning occupied the days of all the housewives. Everyone worked to spruce up the home. Most important, every room in the house, from the attic to the basement, was thoroughly cleaned to remove any trace of leaven. Each family ordered matzos from the matzo baker in the village or placed their order with the baker in a nearby village. The matzo baker was usually the Jewish innkeeper or a baker, or in some places, the community owned the special matzo-baking utensils and even the oven. Everyone helped draw the water for the dough and watched the baking process. The baker could not take longer than eighteen minutes to mix the water and special flour to ensure that no leavening occurred. His helpers rolled out the dough and cut the matzos with little iron wheels. They used a simple comblike tool to make the perforations. These handmade matzos were not uniform in shape or size. After the matzos baked quickly in the very hot oven, the helpers delivered them in the villages.

At religious school, the teacher taught the children the customs and prayers, and the special melodies, for Passover. Students reviewed the haggadah, the special book used to conduct the seder, and memorized the Four Questions in Hebrew.

The families took seriously the prohibition regarding the eating or possessing of leaven. The housewives bought special ingredients for Passover recipes in the shop selling dry goods. Because all the foods for Passover had to be separate from all other foods and utensils, the shopkeeper used special bags, serving spoons, and even scales. About a week before Passover, the housewife brought all the Passover dishes, stored in straw baskets, down from the attic to the kitchen. Everyday silverware and metal pots and pans were made kosher for Passover by thoroughly cleaning them, dipping them in boiling water, and rinsing them with cold water. The stove and oven were thoroughly cleaned and heated to a high temperature.

There were, of course, many kitchen staples that could be obtained only at the time of the harvest. So that the family might have a clear conscience on Passover, all these products were "sold," and thus they were "removed" from the house. The Christian synagogue helper went to each house and "bought" all the products. After a "discussion," a "compromise price" would be agreed upon, and the helper made a small down payment for the goods.

On the Great Sabbath (Shabbat ha-Gadol) before Passover the rabbi preached in the synagogue. By custom, the rabbi lectured at length on the laws of the holiday; the Sabbath service was longer than usual by several hours.

The evening before the first night of Passover, the entire family gathered for a ritual called the disposal of the leaven (*hometz battel*). One of the children, holding a lantern with a small burning candle, led a cheerful but silent procession to each room in the house from the attic to the cellar. The father would say a blessing, and then the mother would place a few pieces of bread on the table that the father would sweep into a paper bag with a feather duster. In each room, everyone looked for any leaven, and, if any were found (an unlikely occurrence), the mother was chided in a joking manner to be even more careful. Before ten in the morning the day of Passover Eve, the older boys set a small bonfire in the courtyard of the synagogue, and all the leaven was burned. The cantor declared that all the leavening in the house, seen or unseen, was annulled and regarded as "the dust of the earth." Everyone, adults and children, came to watch the burning, sharing the joyous feelings of anticipation.

On the first night of Passover, during the service at the synagogue, the *Kiddush* was not sung because it was assumed that everyone would have his own Passover seder at home or would be an invited guest at one. Many communities provided matzos and wine for every poor family. Others welcomed the poor to their tables.

The seder, a ritually ordered feast, was accompanied by the reading of the haggadah. The haggadah was decorated with drawings of the seasons, symbols, and scenes depicting the story and songs. A very popular haggadah was published in Offenbach by Zvi Hirsch Siegel. On the title page the publisher placed his large seal depicting a jumping deer, representing his name, which meant "deer" in both Hebrew and German. Each page of the haggadah included a German translation and explanation printed in Hebrew characters. One such haggadah was the possession of Josef Hirsch Rothschild of Rottweil in 1818. Still today we find stains from wine droplets, small bits of matzo, and a sprig of parsley in the binding attesting to its decades, if not centuries, of use.

Family and friends shared in the ceremonial meal as the story of the Exodus was told through questions and answers, songs, and symbolic foods. The seder concluded with everyone joining in the refrain, "Next year in Jerusalem!" The following day everyone broke off a small piece of matzo and kept it in his pocket as a talisman that "no bad dog would bite." The complete seder was repeated that evening. During the eight days of Passover, no leavened food was eaten, and no one went to the inn. The children ceremoniously delivered matzos to the Christians in the village. Popular belief held that the matzos provided magical protection against lightning strikes.

Pesaḥ was the holiday that inspired the creativity of the housewives. Each housewife baked and cooked using special Passover recipes. Since flour and leaven were forbidden, she used homemade ground matzo meal to prepare nut cakes and other delicacies. Each morning everyone would enjoy *Mazzokaffee*—pieces of matzo broken up into hot coffee with plenty of milk and sugar. At other meals, matzo dumplings (*Mazzoklösse*) were served.

The last two days were full holidays on which work was forbidden. On the eighth day of Pesaḥ, the housewives started to gather the special dishes together. After the service in the synagogue ended the holy day, they, with the assistance of the washerwomen and other helpers, started the event called rumble night (*Rumpelnacht*). All the dishes were washed, dried, packed in the straw baskets, and brought back up to the attic, and the regular dishes were brought down to the kitchen. After the holiday the Christian synagogue employee returned to each house. He ceremoniously offered to return the leaven he had bought right before Passover because he "had no use for it": the father refunded the "down payment" and usually added a small tip.

Counting the Omer

Linking Passover to Shavuot were the days of the Omer. In ancient times the people waited and watched with hope and faith for rain to ensure a plentiful second harvest. Each day ceremonies at the Temple included offerings of barley sheaves. The forty-nine days of the Omer were figured on special calendars in the form of tablets, rolls, or wall calendars hung in both the home and the synagogue. At nightfall prayers were recited in the synagogue, and the number of days of Omer that had already passed was counted. Nobody scheduled marriages or parties during those days. The thirty-third day—Lag ba-Omer—was the exception; it commemorated the day on which the lives of some students of the great Rabbi Akiva were spared from the plague in 135 C.E. The counting culminated with Shavuot.

Shavuot

Seven weeks after Passover, Shavuot, the Festival of Weeks, was celebrated. Passover had signaled the beginning of the spring planting in ancient times, and this second pilgrimage festival commemorated the bringing of the first fruits of harvested grains to the Temple in Jerusalem. In the German lands, the farmers were busy with spring planting and early harvests, and the apple and pear trees were forming their tiny fruits.

The villagers knew the Jews were celebrating the early summer harvest festival because their front doors and the fronts of their houses were decorated with small birch tree branches and flowers in wreaths. The holiday was religiously significant because it commemorated the giving of the Torah on Mount Sinai, and the greenery recalled the offerings brought on that day in the Land of Israel. On Shavuot individuals would donate religious objects to the community in gratitude for some wish that had been granted or for some good fortune. Members gave Torah mantles that were made of silk or satin and decorated with symbols embroidered in silver or gold thread; silver Torah adornments were also given. Donating a Torah scroll would be a very high honor; some wealthy communities had more than one in the synagogue ark. If a Torah was being donated, it was cause for a special celebration. The rabbi carried the new scroll through the streets, followed by the members of the community in festive dress.

In the evening the men, wearing their holiday clothes, gathered for a formal study-session. If a family was in mourning, it was held in that house; otherwise it took place in the home that won the honor by making the highest monetary donation to the community treasury. All the tables were piled high with cookies and cakes—especially cheesecake—to be enjoyed during a study break. The teacher was in charge. He read prayers and led discussions, and everyone participated by reading a verse of the Torah. The session lasted all night or at least very late into the night, and the men would take home samples of the sweets for their wives. The months of holiday preparations and rituals finally ended, and the men could now give their full attention to their trade.

Tisha be-Av

In late summer, the mood of the village changed. Tisha be-Av, which commemorated the destruction of the First and Second Temples in ancient times and other tragic events in the Jews' history, was approaching.

Beginning three weeks before the date, everybody refrained from eating meat and drinking wine, except on the Sabbath or unless a circumcision was celebrated. It was a time of mourning: there were no celebrations or festivities during these three weeks, and no one attended any official meetings or social functions. The fast on the ninth day of the Hebrew month of Av began shortly before darkness fell. In the synagogue the curtain in front of the Holy Ark and the covers of the reading platform had been removed, the carpets had been rolled up, and only a few candles shone in the sanctuary. At the beginning of the service, the men removed their shoes and put on house slippers, and they sat on low wooden stools. The wailing chant of the cantor echoing in the darkened, stark synagogue set the tone for the solemn service. The next day everyone could eat meat only after noon because supposedly the Temple burned until that time. Tisha be-Av marked the end of the formal calendar; as the month of Elul approached, everyone looked inward because the yearly cycle would soon begin again.

These religious traditions, the Hebrew language, the Torah and Talmud, and a shared history were forms of expression of a national culture. The Jews were a minority, a subgroup of German society. This separation and differentiation, whether actively endorsed by Jews or placed upon them by Christian society, continued to play a salient role in history.

An idealized view of the depth of religious feeling was expressed in many of the memoirs, and the reality could have approached this ideal for some or most of the rural Jews. Every Jew from childhood felt the purity of the Jewish ideal, the deep relation to God during prayer. Even if he did not understand each prayer, his singing and praying were heartfelt. If he could not read Hebrew well, or even at all, he would recite the prayers from memory. The rituals repeated each day—the morning and evening prayers, the benedictions before meals and the grace afterward, and the many blessings that sanctified everyday activities—made the Jew's life holy and connected to God.

A Blueprint for Researchers

T he research for this book took years to accomplish. While looking for documents, I learned how German archives were organized, and how someone who does not read or speak German could track down information. Although I generally thrived on the challenge of uncovering documents, more precise research techniques would have saved me hours of frustration. In most instances, the information presented here reflects my experiences doing research in Baden-Württemberg, but it may be used as a guideline to undertaking research in the archives in the other German states. I hope that this section will serve as a blueprint for future researchers.

GENERAL GUIDELINES

1. Call ahead to check when the archives are open as the local archives often have very limited hours. Frequently there is no archivist in a given location, so the researcher must coordinate with the village hall staff. Ask if there is a photocopy machine available.

2. Be prepared to undertake all research without the assistance of the archivist or staff.

3. Bring a research packet that includes the following: long strips of paper (to mark what you need to photocopy, to locate indexes, and to indicate from where you removed a document or volume in the village archives), a stapler (clips are not secure enough for photocopies), bracket clips (for documents from the same source), pencils, a sweater (often the archives are in damp or cool locations), and comfortable

walking shoes (for the cemetery). Use legal and larger-size manila envelopes and sturdy plastic bags to organize your documents.

4. Ask to see *Jüdische Friedhofsdokumentation*, the Jewish cemetery documentation information, first. These are usually typed, making it easier for the non-German reader to locate names.

5. Ask for the *Findbuch* or *Repertorium*, the archive organization register, to find the location of the documents or volumes.

6. When you locate a volume, look first for the index. The indexes are usually at the beginning or end, but sometimes they are located in the middle. In most volumes, the pages are numbered 1 followed by 1b; then 2, 2b; and so forth. In the index, look under last and first names, "*Juden*," "*Jud*," and "*Israeliten*"; sometimes the index is incomplete. Photocopy the front page of the volume or any identifying number.

7. After you photocopy a document, write the archive, name of volume, page number, and location of the volume in the archive on the back of the document. Be sure the document date is on the page you photocopied or search for a date in the preceding pages.

8. When in doubt, photocopy. You never know what additional information you will find when you have time to study a document. The cost of photocopying in the state and some town archives can be quite high, while some local archives do not charge a fee.

9. Often transactions or proceedings begin at the local or county government level, proceed to the regional and state levels of government, and then return to the local or county level. The researcher needs to check in the archives at all levels of government.

10. Always print, and write the numbers "1" and "7" in the European style, and spell out the month.

11. Ask the local village or town which state archives pertain to your locale.

Symbols Used in A Blueprint for Researchers

(G) indicates that information on the Jews was grouped together in a specific section in the files or in the volume.

(A)   indicates that the information can be located in two or more archives.

(USA)   indicates that the information is available on microfilm in America through the Church of Jesus Christ of Latter-day Saints. It is worth checking to see if other information is available through its Family History Centers or online.

Information about family members and historical events can be found in the following archives and documents:

- *Jüdisches Familienregister, Ortssippenbuch*: Jewish family registers for each locale. Also birth, marriage, and death registers. Each film/book is identified with RSA (Reichssippenamt) and a number. Up until the late 1930s, the registers were maintained in the local communities. Under National Socialism the registers were sent by all civil governments to Berlin, where the Nazis microfilmed them in 1944 and 1945 so that they could be used in the future to hunt down anyone who might have hidden Jewish ancestry. The microfilms survived the war, but the registers themselves did not. The volumes for Württemberg and Baden, reconstructed from microfilm, are located in the Hauptstaatsarchiv Stuttgart (Central State Archive in Stuttgart). Ask to see the Register Index for J 386 and order the volumes you need. When you place your order, note on your own paper the place, corresponding volume number, RSA J number, and type of register. This will save you considerable time because the old script is often very difficult to decipher. The volumes, reconstructed from microfilm, are also located in the offices of the Israelitische Religionsgemeinschaft in Stuttgart, and some original films are in the Central Archives for the History of the Jewish People, Givat Ram Campus, Hebrew University, Jerusalem.

- *Kirchenbücher*: church registers. In some places, church registers include Jewish births, deaths, and marriages. (A) (USA)

- *Familiennamensannahmelisten*: surname adoption lists. *Matrikel*: matriculation and residency lists. (A) (USA); and lists in *Amtsblätter*, official gazettes.

- *Jüdische Friedhofsdokumentation*: cemetery documentation. Published or unpublished lists and photographs of headstones. These are located in the village, town, or county archives.

- *Gemeindearchiv, Stadtarchiv*: village or town/city archives. The following materials can be found in these archives:

○ *Gemeinderatsprotokolle /Stadtratsprotokolle*: community and town council minute books. Chronological; usually with an index. All deliberations of community or town councils: transactions, certificates, citizen status, trade status, relations with the town, complaints, etc.

○ *Kaufbücher*: contract registers. Chronological: house, field, and sometimes other sales and purchases. Usually there is an index, but often lists the buyer only.

○ *Güterbücher*: property registers. Property number, owner, previous and subsequent owners, value of property. Organized by name or property number. Sometimes a single index serves several volumes. (G)

○ *Gewerbesteuerkataster*: trade tax registers. Lists of individuals with the trade category and amount of tax paid. Several years of payments are listed in each register. (G)

○ *Verträge*: contracts. Listed and numbered in chronological order by the date of the end of the process.

    A. *Eheverträge*: engagement documents and wedding contracts. Information on parents, birth village, trade of fathers, trade of individual, dowry, possession inventories of bride and groom, and *halitzah* letter. Engagement documents and wedding contracts are sometimes included in wills or divisions of property.

    B. *Testamente* and *Erbschaftsunterlagen*: wills and divisions of property. Names, parents, children, children's birth dates, children's spouses and domiciles, assets and debts, house ownership, special requests, business relations with other Jews and Christians, emigration.

○ *Totenregister, Leichenschauregister*: death or corpse registers. Chronological. Name, spouse, death date, burial date, age or birth date, cause of death, doctor.

○ *Brandversicherungskataster*: fire insurance registers. Organized by house number. Name, house number, value of house, house description, additions to house.

○ *Bürgerlisten* and *Beisitzerlisten*: lists of citizens and partial citizens. Chronological. Includes trade, status, and reason for status.

○ *Hypothekenregister, Schuldenregister*: mortgage and debt registers. Chronological. Creditor and debtor, amount, and dates of payments.

- *Verzeichnis der Gemeinderatsmitglieder*: community council members. Chronological.

- *Verzeichnis der Gemeindediener*: community employees. Chronological.

- *Justizprotokolle, Gerichtsprotokolle*: court protocols. Located in local and county archives. Legal and financial transactions. (A)

- *Pflegerlisten* and *Pflegertabellen*: guardian registers. Chronological. Parents, children, birth dates, curator, assets to distribute, amount paid, emigration.

- *Zunftmitgliederlisten*: guild member list. (A)

- *Auswanderungsliste* and *Akten*: emigration registers and applications. Local, county, and state archives. Chronological. Name, destination, trade, assets taken, parents, guarantor, reason for emigration. (USA) (A)

- *Adressbücher*: address books. Late nineteenth and twentieth century. Name, address, business or profession.

- *Karten*: maps. Property numbers, location of synagogue, school, and cemetery.

- *Alte Fotos*: old photographs. Synagogue, school, ritual bath, cemetery.

- *Zeitungen*: local newspapers. Advertisements, announcements. These sometimes have an index.

- *Schicksallisten*: lists of last Jewish residents and their fate. Usually a typed list. Name, death or emigration.

- Other sources: Historical books on individual villages and towns are located in local libraries, archives, and town halls. Some are also in the state libraries. The author usually includes a section or sections on the local Jewish community and mentions specific people's roles in the locale. In the course of his research, he will usually include information from the parish reports; these reports are very difficult to access for the non-German reader.

- *Kreisarchiv*: county archive. A variety of materials can be found in these archives.

  - *Auswanderungslisten* and *Anträge; Tabellen der Auswanderungslisten*: emigration registers or documents. Chronological. Name, destination, trade, assets taken, parents, guarantor, reason. (USA) (A)

335

- ○ *Justizprotokolle, Gerichtsprotokolle:* court protocols. Legal and financial. (A

- ○ *Familienregister:* family registers. After 1873. Usually these may not be photocopied unless the researcher can prove that he is a direct descendent. (G) (A)

- ○ *Zeitungen:* local newspapers. Advertisements, announcements. Sometimes the bound newspaper volumes have an index. (A)

- ○ Literature on state and county history. Law compilations.

- *Staatsarchiv:* state archives. These archives are the repository of materials relating to the regional or central governments. Many local matters did reach the higher levels of government or were collected there, so it is worth checking these archives. The scope and the usefulness of the inventory and indexes vary considerably. As an accommodation for other researchers, I have included in the endnotes file locations that contain documents about many Jewish communities. (For links to the specific German archives, see *www.lad-bw.de.*)

  The following state archives are the most useful for researching the region of southern Württemberg:

  HStASt   Hauptstaatsarchiv Stuttgart, Central State Archive in Stuttgart.

  StAL   Staatsarchiv Ludwigsburg, State Archive in Ludwigsburg. Certain political regions, and archives of Königlich Israelitische Oberkirchenbehörde, Jewish Superior Church Authority (referred to as the Jewish Board in the text).

  StAS   Staatsarchiv Sigmaringen. State Archive in Sigmaringen. Region including Mühringen and Rottweil.

  Materials in these state archives are more difficult for the non-German reader to locate. The following are general guidelines for using these archives:

1. Call to find out the archive hours and at what times you may request materials. After a request is submitted, it can take up to a half an hour to receive materials.

2. Bring as many citations as you can find. Many of the endnotes in this book are aimed at giving researchers a place to start searching.

3. Ask to see as many registers or indexes as possible to search for names or places.

4. Do not remove documents from the files. Ask the staff to show you how to place markers for photocopying.

5. Only staff members are permitted to make photocopies. Usually it takes several days or weeks to get the photocopies, which will be sent overseas if necessary.

6. The documents are organized in basically the same way in each of the state archives, but the designations differ from archive to archive. Ask a staff member to check your order form to be sure you have written the required information correctly. I have included examples from the endnotes to illustrate the system with the pertinent information in bold letters:

- Name of archive. **HStASt** E146/2 Bü 1193 I; or **StAS** Wü 125/23 Bd. 1 Nr. 28.

- Documents are organized into broad subject matter sections based on governmental sectors and departments, *Bestände*, a "file cabinet." HStASt **E146/2** Bü 1193 I; or StAS **Wü 125/23 Bd. 1** Nr. 28.

- Within that "file cabinet" the documents are organized into *Büschel*, "file drawers." These "drawers" can contain only a few files or a stack two feet high. HStASt E146/2 **Bü 1193 I;** or StAS Wü 125/23 Bd. 1 **Nr. 28**.

- Within the "drawer," the files are usually organized chronologically, but it is best to check all the files. In some cases, the files are numbered or the pages with a file are numbered and you should use that number for your photocopying list. Identifying the document by date, however, is the most consistent method for your own records.

- *Staatsbibliothek*: state libraries. Sources for:

  ○ *Regierungsblatt*: annual Württemberg law registers. Some indexes are located in the middle of the volumes.

  ○ Volumes of parliamentary proceedings.

  ○ Compilation of the laws regarding the Jews: see Friedrich Mayer, ed., *Sammlung der württembergischen Gesetze in betreff der Israeliten* bound in

Sammlung der württembergischen Gesetze in betreff des Post-und Landboten-Wesens (Tübingen: Fues, 1847).

○ *Württembergisches Hof- und Staatshandbuch*: statistical handbooks. Population figures for villages, towns, and counties; often divided by religious affiliation.

○ *Beschreibung des Oberamts*: county descriptions, by Königlich statistisch-topographisches Bureau in the nineteenth century.

○ Württemberg teacher information: see Dr. Joachim Hahn, *Jüdisches Leben in Esslingen* (Sigmaringen: Thorbecke, 1994).

Notes

In the endnotes I have incorporated the source of specific citations and documents that may be useful to researchers undertaking family, historical, or sociological research regarding the rural Jews in Germany in the eighteenth and nineteenth centuries. Unless otherwise indicated, all documents are free translations by native German-speakers. Information about abbreviations can be found in "A Blueprint for Researchers" on pages 331–338.

THE STORY BEGINS: SETTING DOWN ROOTS

[1] Martin Luther, *On the Jews and their Lies* (1543) in Helmut Lehman, gen. ed., and Franklin Sherman, ed., *Luther's Works*, vol. 47, bk. 4, *The Christian in Society* IV (Philadelphia: Fortress, 1971), 268–70, 285, 292; *Vom Schem Hamphoras und vom Geschlecht Christi* (1543), in Gerhard Falk, *The Jew in Christian Theology* (Jefferson, N.C.: 1992), 225–27.

[2] Hans Peter Müller, 1200 *Jahre Mühringen* (Mühringen: Ortsverwaltung Horb-Mühringen, 1986), 135–38.

[3] Adapted from Berthold Auerbach, "Lederherz," in Friedrich Thieberger, ed., *Jüdisches Fest, Jüdischer Brauch* (Königstein/Ts.: Jüdischer Verlag, 1979), 463–66.

[4] Glückel Hameln, *The Memoirs of Glückel of Hameln*, trans. Marvin Lowenthal (New York: Harper, 1932), xx.

[5] Stadtarchiv Rottweil, *Stadtprotokollbuch* 1799 (10 May 1799).

[6] HStASt B352 Bü 82 (28 Nov. 1800) (Loe); (24 Dec. 1800) (Kaz).

NEW TIMES

[1] HStASt E143 Bü 3226 (1804, 1806).

[2] HStASt E143 Bü 3226 (1806, 1807, 1812).

[3] HStASt E143 Bü 3226 (1812).

[4] HStASt E143 Bü 3232, Bü 3226; HStASt E10 Bü 1, Bü 10, Bü 32 (1811–16).

[5] StAL E212 Bü 129 (1816; trans. Rabbi Adler 1832–34).

[6] StAL E212 Bü 41 (1828).

7 HStASt E143 Bü 3226 (31 Oct. 1807); HStASt E31 Bü 997 (June–Oct. 1807); Paul Tänzer, *Die Rechtsgeschichte der Juden in Württemberg*: 1806–28 (Stuttgart: Kohlhammer, 1922), 50.

HEP! HEP! RIOTS

1 Guild petitions: StAS Wü 65/30 Bd. 3 Nr. 1278 (1818); HStASt E146/2 Bü 1193 II (1817); HStASt E143 Bü 3227 (1819).
2 Stadtarchiv Horb a. N. A1386, 16 June 1815.
3 HStASt E146/2 Bü 1193 II (15 Mar. 1818).
4 Trade surveys: HStASt E146/2 Bü 1193 II (1818).
5 Friedrich Rühs, "Ueber die Ansprüche der Juden an das deutsche Bürgerrecht," in Werner Keller, *Und wurden zerstreut unter alle Völker: Die nachbiblische Geschichte des jüdischen Volkes* (Munich: Knaur, 1966), 440.
6 Jakob Friedrich Fries, "Ueber die Gefährdung des Wohstandes und Charakters der Deutschen durch die Juden" (1816), 11, in Rainer Erb and Werner Bergmann, *Die Nachtseite der Judenemanzipation: der Widerstand gegen die Integration der Juden in Deutschland 1780–1860* (Berlin: Metropol, 1989), 114.
7 *Gemeinnütziger Anzeiger*, Rottweil, 12 Nov. 1818, 853–55; 19 Nov. 1818, 865–74.
8 Stadtarchiv Rottweil, *Stadtratsprotokolle* (1819): 73b.
9 HStASt E143 Bü 3227 (Sep.–Oct. 1819).
10 Berta Rau, "Die Geschichte der israelitischen Gemeinde Braunsbach" (Braunsbach, 1970), 6.
11 *Schwäbische Chronik*, 31 Aug. 1819, 599–600; 2 Sep. 1819, 605.
12 HStASt E143 Bü 3227, Sep.–Oct. 1819.
13 Hartwig von Hundt-Radowsky, *Judenspiegel: Ein Auszug* (Würzburg: Daniel Wagner, 1819), 15, 143–44.

TRANSITIONS

1 Robert Klein, *Beiträge zur Geschichte der Juden in Rottweil a. N.* (Rottweil: M. Rothschild, 1924), 59–61. Specific conditions are discussed in subsequent paragraphs.
2 HStASt E146/2 Bü 1193 II, (15 Mar. 1818).
3 HStASt E146/2 Bü 1193 II no. 43 (1821).
4 HStASt E146/2 Bü 1193 II, (15 Mar. 1818).
5 Memoirs of Berthold Auerbach in Anton Bettelheim, *Berthold Auerbach: Der Mann, sein Werk, sein Nachlass*, (Stuttgart: J. G. Cotta, 1907), 29–31.
6 Ibid., 37.

MOVING BACKWARD

1 *Verhandlungen der Kammer der Abgeordneten* "Abtheilung," Beylage 92 (1820): 630–631.
2 HStASt E33 Bü 663 (1820): 1, 11–13b.
3 *Verhandlungen der Kammer der Abgeordneten des Königreichs Württemberg auf dem ausserordentlichen Landtag von 1828 Heft 3* (deliberations from 1823–24): 67–168 (exact citation, 97).
4 Ibid., 98.

Notes

[5] Trade surveys: HStASt E146/2 Bü 1193 (1828).

[6] HStASt E146/2 Bü 1193 I no. 74 (18 Oct. 1827); [Jewish Committee], *Bitten und Wünsche der Israeliten des Königreichs* (Stuttgart, 1828), 1–32 (exact citation, 5).

[7] HStASt L15 F36 1(a), Rottweil, Ulm, Tübingen, Stuttgart, Schwäbisch Hall (1828).

[8] HStASt E146/2 Bü 1193 I no. 86 (10–12 Feb. 1828).

[9] Rudolph Moser, *Die Juden und ihre Wünsche* (Stuttgart: Hoffmann, 1828), 46.

[10] *Verhandlungen der Kammer der Abgeordneten des Königreichs Württemberg auf dem ausserordentlichen Landtag von 1828*, Heft 3 (21 Feb.–1 Mar. 1828), 669–1067 (exact citation, 677, 686); *Schwäbischer Merkur*, 21 Feb.–5 Mar. 1828, various articles.

[11] C. J. Zahn, *Bemerkungen über den König. Gesetzes Entwurf: über die offentlichen Verhältnisse der Israeliten*; HStASt L15 F36 1(a) (1828), 1–24.

[12] *Staats und Regierungs Blatt* (Württemberg), 8 May 1828, 307.

[13] *Verhandlungen der Kammer der Abgeordneten des Königreichs Württemberg auf dem ausserordentlichen Landtag von 1828*, Heft 3 (21 Feb.–1 Mar. 1828): 669–1067 (exact citation, 670–86); *Schwäbischer Merkur* (21 Feb.–5 Mar. 1828).

[14] [Friedrich Lindner], "Gesetzesvorschlag, die offentlichen Verhältnisse der Israeliten betreffend," *Verhandlungen der Kammer der Abgeordneten. Allgem. polit.* Annalen 27. Bd. 2tes Heft besonders abegebrucht. (after Apr. 1828): 1–108.

[15] *Staats und Regierungs Blatt* (Württemberg), 8 May 1828, 301–20.

CHANGES IN THE FAMILIES

[1] Friedrich Carl Zink, *Protokolle des Kirchenkonvents Reubach* (1831), in Otto Ströbel, *Michelbach a. d. Lücke, Geschichte einer Dorfgemeinschaft zwischen Christen und Juden* (Crailsheim: Hohenloher, 1993), 216–17.

[2] StAL E212 Bü 219 (1810/1835), trans. Prof. Steven Lowenstein, University of Judaism, Los Angeles, California.

THE NEW JEWISH COMMUNITY

[1] HStASt E11 Bü 84 (1828); StAL E212 Bü 18 (1849–50).

[2] StAL E212 Bü 159 (1834).

[3] StAL F382 Bü 200 (1829–32).

LEAVING THE SCHACHER JEW BEHIND

[1] HStASt E146/2 Bü 1193 I no. 86 (10–12 Feb. 1828).

[2] Ibid.

[3] HStASt E146/2 Bü 1194 (1836).

[4] *Verhandlungen der Kammer der Abgeordneten des Landtags*, Heft 2, 1833 (24 July 1833): 888–948; *Verhandlungen der Kammer der Abgeordneten des Landtags*, 1836, Band 8, Beilagenheft 1 & 2 (26 Apr. 1836): 119–143; *Verhandlungen der Kammer der Abgeordneten des Landtags*, 1836, Band 4 (4 May 1836): 33–80.

[5] HStASt E143 Bü 3234 (1835); Bü 3229 (1835).

[6] Simon Kramer, *Memoirs of Simon Kramer*, ed. and trans. Emma Schemel (1882; reprint, Chicago: Aetna Stationers, 1942), 19.

[7] Trade surveys: HStASt E146/2 Bü 1193 (1828); HStASt L15 F36, 1(b) (1833); HStASt E146/2 Bü 1194 (1846). Some figures for this and subsequent tables varied from survey to survey and some people were included in more than one category.

[8] HStASt E146/2 Bü 1194 (1836).

[9] HStASt E146/2 Bü 1194 (26 Jan. 1846).

[10] HStASt L15 F36, 1(b) (1833).

[11] Verhandlungen der Kammer der Abgeordneten des Königreichs Württemberg auf dem ausserordentlichen Landtag von 1828, Heft 3 (21 Feb.–1 Mar. 1828): 929–30.

[12] Verhandlungen der Kammer der Abgeordneten des Landtags, Band 4, 1845, (9 June 1845): 1–3; Verhandlungen der Kammer der Abgeordneten des Landtags, Band 9, Beilagenheft 2, 1845 (14 June 1845): 888–948; Verhandlungen der Kammer der Standesherrn, 1845, Heft 4 (10 July 1845): 1375–1414 (exact citation, 1383).

[13] Trade surveys: HStASt E146/2 Bü 1193 (1828); HStASt L15 F36 1(b) (1833); HStASt E146/2 Bü 1194 (1846).

FIGHTING FOR CIVIL RIGHTS

[1] Landeskirchliches Archiv Stuttgart A 29/2847, in Gerhard Taddey, Kein kleines Jerusalem: Geschichte der Juden im Landkreis Schwäbisch Hall (Sigmaringen: Thorbecke, 1992), 287.

[2] Conversations-Lexikon der neuesten Zeit und Literatur [Brockhaus], vol. 1 (Leipzig: Brockhaus, 1832), 769–75 (exact citation, 769).

[3] Johann Ludwig Beck, Protokolle über Visitationen der christlichen und jüdischen Schulen in Michelbach (1831), in Otto Ströbel, Michelbach a. d . Lücke, Geschichte einer Dorfgemeinschaft zwischen Christen und Juden (Crailsheim: Hohenloher, 1993), 39, 258–59 (exact citation, 258).

[4] Gemeinnütziger Anzeiger, Rottweil, 2 June 1831, 395.

[5] HStASt L15 F36 1(b) (17 June 1833).

[6] Verhandlungen der Kammer der Abgeordneten des Landtags, Heft 2, 1833 (24 July 1833): 888–948.

[7] HStASt L15 F36 1(b) (2 Feb. 1836).

[8] Verhandlungen der Kammer der Abgeordneten des Landtags, 1836, Band 8, Beilagenheft 1 & 2 (26 Apr. 1836): 119–43; Verhandlungen der Kammer der Abgeordneten des Landtags, 1836, Band 4 (4 May 1836): 33–80.

[9] "Emancipation," Allgemeine Zeitung des Judenthums (various, 1845).

[10] Verhandlungen der Kammer der Abgeordneten des Landtags, Band 4, 1845 (9 June 1845): 1–3; Verhandlungen der Kammer der Abgeordneten des Landtags, Band 9, Beilagenheft 2, 1845 (14 June 1845): 888–948 (exact citation 932–33); Schwäbische Chronik, 8 June 1845.

YEARS OF TURMOIL

[1] Korrespondent, "Politische Rundschau, Vom oberen Neckar," 1 Feb 1848, Rottweiler Anzeiger, 4 Feb. 1848, 68.

[2] Diözese Rottenburg-Stuttgart, DAR, Bestand M 30, Pfarrarchiv Mühringen, Band 19 (1848).

[3] GArchiv Mühringen, Gemeinderatsprotokolle 1848–57 (30 July 1848).

[4] Abraham Gilam, "German Village Jewry and the Revolution of 1848: The Evidence of the Scroll of Baisingen," East European Quarterly 13 (2 Nov. 1979): 129–43; Abraham Gilam, "Die historische Bedutung der Megillat Baisingen," Bulletin Leo Baeck Institute 52 (1976): 78–95. See also Schwarzwälder Bote Oberndorf, 13 Apr. 1851, 271–72; 15 Apr. 1851,

Notes

275–76; and 17 Apr. 1851, 281–83; *Pfarrer Chronik* in Karlheinz Geppert, "Vom Schutzjuden zum Bürger," *Der Sülchgau*, Band 32, (1988): 134–36, 150–167; and *Gemeindezeitung für die israelitischen Gemeinden Württembergs*, Jg 4, Nr. 21 (1 Feb. 1928): 638–43.
⁵ "Aufruf und Unterschriftenliste der Frauen und Jungfrauen von Rottweil vom Juni 1848," Stadtmuseum Rottweil.

SHIFTING WINDS

¹ HStASt L15 F36 2(a) (11 Mar. 1852).
² *Verhandlungen der Kammer der Abgeordneten des Landtags* (29 Nov. 1854): 131.
³ HStASt L11/36 2 (1855).
⁴ Stammheim (Ludwigsburg County), HStASt L15 F36 2(a) (1 Dec. 1853).
⁵ *Verhandlungen der Kammer der Abgeordneten des Landtags* (1 Dec. 1854): 147.
⁶ StAS Wü 65/30 Bd. 1 Nr. 1292 (1855).
⁷ Korrespondent, *Frankfurter Journal*, 31 May 1851, in Heribert Dom, *Das Pressewesen in Rottweil* (diss., Munich, 1956).
⁸ *Rottweiler Anzeiger*, 14 May 1851, 249.
⁹ Glanz, Rudolf. "The Immigration of German Jews up to 1880," *Yivo Annual of Jewish Social Science* 2–3 (1947–48): 89.
¹⁰ *Allgemeine Zeitung des Judenthums*, 20 July 1839, 347.
¹ Wolf Fischer to Salomon Fischer, 27 Oct. 1847, Fischer-Hecht family correspondence (trans. from German), American Jewish Archives, Hebrew Union College, Cincinnati.
² *Horber Chronik*, 1 Aug. 1854, 348.
³ StAS Wü 65/13 Bd. 1 Nr. 60 and Bd. 2 Nr. 242, Mühringen Liste der israelitischen Söhne (1837–63); Ira Glazier and P. William Filby, eds., *Germans to America: Lists of Passengers Arriving in U.S. Ports* (Wilmington, Del.: Scholarly Resources); Trudy Schenk, Ruth Froelke, and Inge Bork, *The Wuerttemberg Emigration Index*, 7 vols. (Salt Lake City: Ancestry,1986); Herman Dicker, *Creativity, Holocaust, Reconstruction: Jewish Life in Wuerttemberg, Past and Present* (New York: Sepher-Hermon, 1984).

A GERMAN VILLAGE IN CHICAGO

¹ Private collections, Janet Iltis and Steven Kunreuther. Adapted from Dr. Dorothee Krahn's translation.
² [3 Sep 1839], in Rudolph Glanz, *Studies in Judaica Americana* (New York: Ktav, 1970), 21.
³ Isaac Mayer Wise, *Reminiscences*, trans. and ed. David Philipson (Cincinnati: L. Wise, 1901; reprint, New York: Arno, 1973), 38.
⁴ *The Occident* 14 (Feb.1857) 550–51.
⁵ Iowa, vol. 47, 217, R.G. Dun & Co. Collection, Baker Library, Harvard University Graduate School of Business Administration [HBS].
⁶ *Davenport Gazette*, 20 Sep. 1858, 1.
⁷ Private collections, Janet Iltis and Steven Kunreuther. Adapted from Dr. Dorothee Krahn's translation.
⁸ Illinois, vol. 38, 176, Dun, Baker Library, HBS.
⁹ Iowa, vol. 47, 217, 224, Dun, Baker Library, HBS.
⁰ *The Occident* 19 (Feb. 1862), 522; *The Israelite* 8 (21 Feb. 1862), 267.
¹ *Davenport Gazette*, 17 Feb. 1862, 1.
² StadtA Ebingen, *Gemeinderatsprotokolle* (22 Oct. 1860).

[13] Illinois, vol. 33, 61; vol. 38, 176, 177, Dun, Baker Library, HBS.

[14] *Chicago Tribune*, 16 Aug 1862, 4.

[15] Otto Leib, "Esslinger Family Tree," Memoirs collection, Leo Baeck Institute, New York.

[16] Ron Grossman, "Touring Chicago's Older Jewish Neighborhoods," *Jewish Chicago* 1 (Sept. 1982), 45.

[17] Bernhard Moos to Willhelmine Moos (b. Mändle); English translation (only extant) by Joseph Moos from the German original. Private collection, William Rieser.

[18] Illinois, vol. 38, 41, 448, Dun, Baker Library, HBS.

[19] Jacob Weil in David Heineman, "Jewish Beginnings in Michigan before 1850," *The American Jewish Historical Society Publication* 13 (1905), 67 fn53.

[20] Michigan, vol.77, 79, 216; Illinois, vol. 29, 130, 137,141, Dun, Baker Library, HBS.

[21] Nathan Belth, A *Promise to Keep: A Narrative of the American Encounter with Anti-Semitism* (New York: Times Books, 1979), 24–25.

[22] *Illinois Staats-Zeitung*, 19 July 1877, in Anton Bettelheim, *Berthold Auerbach: Der Mann, sein Werk, sein Nachlass.* (Stuttgart: J. G. Cotta, 1907), 375.

GERMAN JEWS

[1] HStASt E146/2 Bü 1195 (1 Mar. 1861).

[2] Trade and community surveys: HStASt E146/2 Bü 1193 (1828); HStASt L15 F36 1(b) (1833); HStASt E146/2 Bü 1194 (1846); HStASt E146/2 Bü 1195 (1860–63) and no. 103; *Verhandlungen der Kammer der Abgeordneten des Landtags* (1862–64), Protokoll Band 1 (22 Oct 1862), 1167–1285.

[3] Various petitions in HStASt E146/2 Bü 1195 (1860–61).

[4] *Verhandlungen der Kammer der Abgeordneten des Landtags* (1862–64), Protokoll Band 1 (2 Dec. 1863–4 Dec. 1863), 238–322.

[5] Ibid., Protokoll Band 1 (3 Dec. 1863), 281; *Allgemeine Zeitung des Judenthums*, 26 Jan. 1864, 65–68.

[6] Ibid.

[7] Various petitions, HStASt L15 F36 2(b) (Dec. 1863–Jan. 1864).

[8] Otto Leib, "Esslinger Family Tree," Memoirs collection, Leo Baeck Institute, New York.

[9] Article 1, "Gesetz betreffend die Gleichberechtigung der Konfessionen in bürgerlicher und staatsbürgerlicher Beziehung" (The law of the equality of religions as regards common and state civic rights), 3 July 1869, *Bundesgesetzblatt* 1869, 292.

[10] I. Hirschberg, "Ein Jom Kippur im Kriegslager" (7 Oct. 1870), *Allgemeine Zeitung des Judenthums*, 18 Oct. 1870, 823–25.

[11] *Schwäbische Chronik*, 27 Mar.–7 Apr. 1873 (6 articles).

[12] *Allgemeine Zeitung des Judenthums*, 8 Apr. 1873.

[13] Berthold Auerbach: "Letter 484, Nordstetten, 5 Aug 1873," in Berthold Auerbach, *Briefe an seinen Freund Jacob Auerbach*, vol. 2 (Frankfurt a. M.: Rütten and Lönig, 1884), 165–66.

[14] *Horber Chronik*, 26 Oct. 1873, 510–11.

[15] Sabiah ben Psisa, *Wohin kommen wir? Ein Wort an die gesetzestreuen Israeliten Württembergs* (Mainz: Le Roux, 1863–64), 8, 19.

Notes

TRADITIONAL JEWISH LIFE IN THE VILLAGES AND SMALL TOWNS

[1] Memoirs of Berthold Auerbach, in Anton Bettelheim, *Berthold Auerbach: Der Mann, sein Werk, sein Nachlass* (Stuttgart: J.G. Cotta, 1907), 24–25.

[2] Ibid., 11–12.

[3] Private collection, Henry Landauer.

[4] [Bernhard] Jacob Gundelfinger, Last Testament, Jan. 1840, Contract #302, 1843. GArchiv Wallhausen-Michelbach.

[5] OHStASt E146/2 Bü 1193 II (1821).

Selected Bibliography

The following sources complement the archival documents described in "A Blueprint for Researchers" and the endnotes. These books and articles give useful information and further reader suggestions regarding the history and daily life of the rural German Jews in the eighteenth and nineteenth centuries.

Altmann, Alexander, ed. *Studies in Nineteenth Century Jewish Intellectual History.* Cambridge, Mass.: Harvard Univ. Press, 1964.

Auerbach, Berthold. *Black Forest Village Stories.* Trans. Charles Goepp. New York: Henry Holt, 1874. Reprint, Freeport, N.Y.: Books for Libraries Press, 1969.

————*Briefe an seinen Freund Jacob Auerbach,* 2 vols. Frankfurt a. M.: Rütten & Lönig, 1884.

————*Schwarzwälder Dorfgeschichten.* Stuttgart: Staufen, 1982.

Ballmann, Bernd. *150 Jahre: Schwarzwälder Dorfgeschichten von Berthold Auerbach, 1843–1993.* Horb: Kultur- und Museumsvervein, Herbst, 1994.

Bauer, Alex. "The Roots of Alex Bauer." Unpublished memoir, 1991. Leo Baeck Institute, New York.

Berlinger, Simon. *Synagoge und Herrschaft: Vierhundert Jahre jüdische Landgemeinde Berlichingen.* Sigmaringendorf: Glock und Lutz, 1991.

Bettelheim, Anton. *Berthold Auerbach: Der Mann, sein Werk, sein Nachlass.* Stuttgart: J. G. Cotta, 1907.

Birnbaum, Pierre, and Ira Katznelson, eds. *Paths of Emancipation: Jews, States, and Citizenship.* Princeton, N.J.: Princeton Univ. Press, 1995.

Brenner, Michael, Stefi Jersch-Wenzel, and Michael A. Meyer. *Emancipation and Acculturation*: 1780–1871. Vol. 2 of *German-Jewish History in Modern Times*, ed. Michael A. Meyer. New York: Columbia Univ. Press, 1997.

Breuer, Mordechai, and Michael Graetz. *Tradition and Enlightenment* 1600–1780. Vol. 1 of *German-Jewish History in Modern Times*, ed. Michael A. Meyer. New York: Columbia Univ. Press, 1996.

Cahnman, Werner. *German Jewry: Its History and Sociology: Selected Essays*. Ed Joseph B. Maier, Judith Marcus, and Zoltán Tarr. New Brunswick, N.J. Transaction Books, 1989.

Daxelmüller, Christoph. *Jüdische Kultur in Franken*. Würzburg: Echter, 1988.

Dicker, Herman. *Creativity, Holocaust, Reconstruction: Jewish Life in Wuerttemberg Past and Present*. New York: Sepher-Hermon, 1984.

Erb, Rainer, and Werner Bergmann. *Die Nachtseite der Judenemanzipation: de Widerstand gegen die Integration der Juden in Deutschland* 1780-1860. Berlin Metropol, 1989.

Frankel, Jonathan, and Steven Zipperstein. *Assimilation and Community: The Jews in Nineteenth-Century Europe*. Cambridge: Cambridge Univ. Press, 1992.

Gay, Ruth. *The Jews of Germany: A Historical Portrait*. New Haven: Yale Univ Press, 1992.

Gidal, Nachum. *Jews in Germany from Roman Times to the Weimar Republic* Cologne: Könemann, 1998.

Glanz, Rudolf. *The German Jew in America: An Annotated Bibliography*. Cincinnati Hebrew Union College Press, 1969.

Grab, Walter. *Der deutsche Weg der Judenemanzipation*: 1789–1938. Munich: Piper 1991.

Groiss-Lau, Eva. *Jüdisches Kulturgut auf dem Land: Synagogen, Realien und Tauch-bäder in Oberfranken*. Munich: Deutscher Kunstverlag, 1995.

Guth, Klaus, ed. *Jüdische Landgemeinden in Oberfranken 1800–1942: ein historisch-topographisches Handbuch*. Bamberg: Bayerische Verlagsanstalt, 1988.

Hahn, Joachim. *Erinnerungen und Zeugnisse jüdischer Geschichte in Baden-Württemberg*. Stuttgart: Theiss, 1988.

———*Synagogen in Baden-Württemberg*. Stuttgart: Theiss, 1987.

Harris, James. *The People Speak! Anti-Semitism and Emancipation in Nineteenth Century Bavaria*. Ann Arbor: Univ. of Michigan Press, 1994.

Hirschler, Gertrude, ed. *Ashkenaz: The German Jewish Heritage*. New York: Yeshiva Univ. Museum, 1988.

Hirshler, Eric, ed. *Jews from Germany in the United States*. New York: Farrar, Straus, & Cudahy, 1955.

Selected Bibliography

Hyman, Paula. *The Emancipation of the Jews of Alsace.* New Haven: Yale Univ. Press, 1991.

Jeggle, Utz. *Judendörfer in Württemberg.* Tübingen: Tübinger Vereinigung für Volkskunde, 1969.

Katz, Jacob. *Exclusiveness and Tolerance: Studies in Jewish-Gentile Relations in Medieval and Modern Times.* New York: Schocken Books, 1973, 1961.

———*From Prejudice to Destruction: Anti-Semitism: 1700–1933.* Cambridge, Mass.: Harvard Univ. Press, 1997, 1980.

———*Jewish Emancipation and Self-Emancipation.* Philadelphia: Jewish Publication Society, 1986.

———*Out of the Ghetto: The Social Background of Jewish Emancipation 1770–1870.* Syracuse, N.Y.: Syracuse Univ. Press, 1998, 1973.

Katz, Jacob, ed. *Emancipation and Assimilation.* Farnborough, England: Gregg International, 1972.

———*Toward Modernity: The European-Jewish Model.* New Brunswick, N.J.: Transaction Books, 1987.

Kober, Adolf. "Jewish Emigration from Württemberg to the U.S. of A., 1848–1855." *Publications of the American Jewish Historical Society* 41 (1952): 242–68.

Kohler, Max. "The German-Jewish Migration to America." *Publications of the American Jewish Historical Society* 9 (1901): 87–105.

Liebeschütz, Hans and A. Paucker, eds. *Das Judentum in der deutschen Umwelt 1800–1850: Studien zur Frühgeschichte der Emanzipation.* Tübingen: Mohr, 1977.

Lowenstein, Steven. *Frankfurt on the Hudson: The German Jewish Community of Washington Heights 1933–1983.* Detroit: Wayne State Univ. Press, 1989.

———"The Pace of Modernization of German Jewry in the Nineteenth Century." *Year Book Leo Baeck Institute* 21 (1976): 41–56.

———"The Rural Community and the Urbanization of German Jewry." *Central European History* 13, no. 3 (1980): 218–36.

Lowenstein, Steven, Paul Mendes-Flohr, Peter Pulzer, and Monika Richarz. *Integration in Dispute: 1871–1918.* Vol. 3 of *German-Jewish History in Modern Times,* ed. Michael A. Meyer. New York: Columbia Univ. Press, 1998.

Mandelbaum, Hugo. *Jewish Life in the Village Communities of Southern Germany.* New York: Feldheim, 1985.

Meyer, Michael. *The Origins of the Modern Jew: Jewish Identity and European Culture in Germany 1749–1824.* Detroit: Wayne State Univ. Press, 1979, 1967.

Mosse, Werner, Arnold Paucker, and Reinhard Rürup, eds. *Revolution and Evolution: 1848 in German-Jewish History.* Tübingen: Mohr, 1981.

Mostov, Stephen. A *"Jerusalem"* on the Ohio: The Social and Economic History o Cincinnati's Jewish Community: 1840–1875. (Ph.D. diss., Brandeis Univ. 1981). Ann Arbor, Mich.: University Microfilms, 1983.

Picard, Jacob. "Childhood in the Village." *Year Book Leo Baeck Institute* 4 (1959) 273–93.

Richarz, Monika. "Jewish Social Mobility in Germany during the Time o Emancipation, 1790–1871." *Year Book Leo Baeck Institute* 20 (1975) 69–77.

———"Viehhandel und Landjuden im 19. Jahrhundert. Eine symbiotische Wirtschaftsbeziehung in Südwestdeutschland." *Menora (Jahrbuch fü deutsch-jüdische Geschichte)* 1 (1990): 66–88.

Richarz, Monika, ed. *Jewish Life in Germany: Memoirs from Three Centuries*. Bloom ington: Indiana Univ. Press, 1991.

Richarz, Monika, and Reinhard Rürup, eds. *Jüdisches Leben auf dem Lande: Stu dien zur deutsch-jüdischen Geschichte*. Tübingen: Mohr Siebeck, 1997.

Ritterband, Paul, ed. *Modern Jewish Fertility*. Leiden, The Netherlands: E. J. Brill 1981.

Rohrbacher, Stefan. *Gewalt im Biedermeier. Antijüdische Ausschreitung in Vormär und Revolution: 1815–1848/9*. Frankfurt: Campus, 1993.

———"From Württemberg to America." *American Jewish Archives* 41 (fall/win ter 1989): 144–71.

Rürup, Reinhard. *Antisemitismus und Judentum*. Göttingen: Vandenhoeck, 1979

———"An Appraisal of German-Jewish Historiography." *Year Book Leo Baeck Institute* 35 (1990): xv–xxiv.

———"Emancipation and Crisis—The 'Jewish Question' in Germany 1850– 1890." *Year Book Leo Baeck Institute* 20 (1975): 13–25.

———*Emanzipation und Antisemitismus: Studien zur Judenfrage der bürgerlichen Gesellschaft*. Göttingen: Vandenhoeck & Ruprecht, 1975.

———"Jewish Emancipation and Bourgeois Society." *Year Book Leo Baeck In stitute* 14 (1969): 67–91.

———"Die Judenemanzipation in Baden." *Zeitschrift für die Geschichte des Ober rheins* 75 (1966): 241–300.

———"The Tortuous and Thorny Path to Legal Equality." *Year Book Leo Baeck Institute* 31 (1986): 3–33.

Rürup, Reinhard, ed. *Juden in Deutschland zwischen Assimilation und Verfolgung*. Göttingen: Vandenhoeck & Ruprecht, 1983.

Sauer, Paul. *Die jüdischen Gemeinden in Württemberg und Hohenzollern*. Stuttgart: Kohlhammer, 1966.

Selected Bibliography

Schorsch, Emil. "Judische Frömmigkeit in der deutschen Landgemeinde," *Der Morgen*, 6 Berlin (April 1930), 44–54.

———"The Rural Jew: Observations on the Paper of Werner Cahnman." *Year Book Leo Baeck Institute* 19 (1974): 131–33.

Schwab, Hermann. *Jewish Rural Communities in Germany*. London: Cooper, 1956.

Sorkin, David. "Emancipation and Assimilation: Two Concepts and their Application to German-Jewish History." *Year Book Leo Baeck Institute* 35 (1990): 17–33.

———*The Transformation of German Jewry*. Detroit: Wayne State Univ. Press, 1999, 1987.

Stauben, Daniel. *Scenes of Jewish Life in Alsace*. Trans. and ed. Rose Choron. 1860. Reprint, London: Joseph Simon, 1991.

Stern, Bruno. *Meine Jugenderinnerungen an eine württembergische Kleinstadt und ihre jüdische Gemeinde*. Stuttgart: Kohlhammer, 1968.

———*So war es*. Sigmaringen: Thorbecke, 1985.

Stern, Theodore. Memoir. 1982. Private collection, Henry Landauer.

Strauss, Herbert and Hanns Reissner, eds. *Jubilee Volume: Dedicated to Curt C. Silberman*. New York: American Federation of Jews from Central Europe, 1969.

Taddey, Gerhard. *Kein kleines Jerusalem: Geschichte der Juden im Landkreis Schwäbisch Hall*. Sigmaringen: Thorbecke, 1992.

Tänzer, Aron. *Die Geschichte der Juden in Jebenhausen und Göppingen*.1927. Reprint, with Appendix 1927–1945 and ed. Karl-Heinz Ruess, Weissenhorn: Konrad, 1988.

———*Die Geschichte der Juden in Württemberg*. Frankfurt am Main: Kauffmann, 1937. Reprint, Frankfurt am Main: Weidlich, 1983.

Tänzer, Paul. *Die Rechtsgeschichte der Juden in Württemberg: 1806–1828*. Stuttgart: Kohlhammer, 1922.

Toury, Jacob. *Der Eintritt der Juden ins deutsche Bürgertum: eine Dokumentation*. Tel Aviv: Diaspora Research Institute, 1972.

———*Soziale und politische Geschichte der Juden in Deutschland 1847–1871: zwischen Revolution, Reaktion und Emanzipation*. Düsseldorf: Droste, 1977.

Treml, Manfred, and Wolf Weigand. *Geschichte und Kultur der Juden in Bayern: Lebensläufe*. Munich: Saur, 1988.

Voralberger Landesarchiv and Jüdisches Museum Hohenems, eds. *Landjudentum im Süddeutschen-und Bodenseeraum*. Dornbirn: Vorarlberger Verlagsanstalt, 1992.

Walker, Mack. *German Home Towns: Community, State, and General Estate 1648–1871*. Ithaca, N.Y.: Cornell Univ. Press, 1971. Reprint, with a new foreword, 1998.

Weill, Alexandre. *Ma Jeunesse*, vol. 1. Paris: Libraire de la Société des Gens de Lettres, 1870.

Wiesemann, Falk. *Genizah—Hidden Legacies of the German Village Jews*. Vienna: Bertelsmann, 1994.

Acknowledgments

M y gratitude and appreciation go to many people in Germany, America, and Israel who supported my efforts in so many different ways: historical research, translations, editorial critiques, financial underwriting of publication costs, and enthusiasm.

Special thanks are due to my relatives and friends who shared their personal knowledge of rural Jewish life with me: Johanna Levi Friedlein, Berthold Levi, and Gustel Elsaesser for Mühringen; Manfred Neuman, Henry Landauer, Hans Gundel, and Bertyl Gross (Niederstetten) for Michelbach; and Louise Rothschild Kopulsky for Rottweil.

Georg Abröll, Landratsamt Augsburg; Dr. Renate Adler, Director, Stadtarchiv Horb; Hollis Alpert; Helen Aminoff; Dr. Dorothy Ciner Armstrong; Irmela Bauer-Klöden, Archivist, Eberhard-Karls-Universität, Tübingen; Hartwig Behr; Simon Berlinger; Arthur Berliss; Rite Book; Karina Böttiger; Maria Bräutigam; Wilhelmina Breuker; Karl Brueker; Clementine Carsen; Ruth Berliss Ciner; Robert Caplan; Gisela Dehlinger; Werner Dienel, Archivist, Kirchberg; Peter Dietz, Village Officer, Wallhausen; Ruth Dröse; Cynthia Edelman; Mr. and Mrs. John Elder; Hans Elsaesser (deceased); Nils-Christian Engel; Hedy Epstein; Irmgard Erikson; Kenne and Janine Fant; Pastor Anton Feil; Arno Fern, Director, Israelitisches Religionsgemeinschaft, Stuttgart; Jiří Fiedler, Jüdisches Museum, Prague; Ursula and Sy Finkelstein; Harriet Finn; Josef Fischer, Mayor, Markt Fischach; Anne Frankel; Hans Gabriel; Karlheinz Geppert, Director, Stadtarchiv Rottenburg am Neckar; Prof. Alice Goldstein; Eugene Greener; Walter Gundel; Werner Gundelfinger; Katia Guth-Dreyfus, Director, Jüdisches Museum der Schweiz; Dr. Joachim Hahn; Prof. Dr. Helmut Hanisch; Dr. Winfried Hecht, Director, Stadtarchiv Rottweil; Maria Heitland; Dr. Paul Hemreich, Wheaton College, Massachusetts; Dr. Hans G. Hirsch;

Dr. F. Gil, Hüttenmeister; Janet Iltis; Prof. Dr. Utz Jeggle, Ludwig-Uhland Institut, Tübingen; Marian Berliss Katzenstein; Dr. Uri Kaufmann; Monika Kessl; Werner Kessl; Dieter Kleinhanss, Village Officer, Michelbach; Carsten Kohlmann; Lydia Kolbe; Karl Lambrecht; Ruth Landauer; Helga LeBong; Otto Leib; Michael Lenarz, Jüdisches Museum, Frankfurt; Dr. and Mrs. Bruce Levi Kaete Lindauer; Dr. Steven Lowenstein, University of Judaism, Los Angeles Erich Maier, Stadtarchiv Schramberg; Lorie Mayer; Veronika Messmer; Markus Meyer; Dr. Michael Meyer; Karl and Anita Miesel; Susan Elsaesser Millé; Dr. Franz Moegle-Hofacker; Dr. Hans Peter Müller, Director, Kreisarchiv Schwäbisch Hall; Hans Peter Müller, historian, Black Forest District; Karl Müller, former mayor, Michelbach; Dr. Elaine Newton; Olaf Paeschke; Rabbi James Perman; Wolfgang Porschmann; Hubert and Nora Prem; Bernhard Purin, Director, Jüdisches Museum Fürth und Schnaittach; Eberhard Pütter Monika Rademacher, Stadtarchiv Hanau; William Rieser; Edeltraud Riester Village Administrator, Mühringen; Fannie Berliss Rosenbaum (deceased) Michael Rosenheimer; Susanne Sacksetter, M.A., Director Franken Hohen lohesches Heimatmuseum, Crailsheim; Dr. Paul Sauer; Lyn Scanlon; Dr Aldolf Schmid; Elke Schmid; Christian Schmitt; Dr. Stefan Schultes, Mayor Reutlingen; Dr. Reinhard Seitz, Director, Staatsarchiv Augsburg; Ingrid Severin; General and Mrs. Stanley Sheridan; Knut Siewert; Diane Spielmann Public Services Coordinator, Leo Baeck Institute, New York; Charles Stanton Manfred Steck; Lore Rothschild Stone; Dr. Stihler, Stadt- und Hospitalarchiv Schwäbisch Hall; Karlheinz Streich; Otto and Ruth Ströbel; Dr. Gerhard Taddey, Director Stadtarchiv Ludwigsburg; Erwin Taenzer; Temple Shalom of Naples, Florida; Sigrid Tschöke; Ilse Vogel; Dietrich Weiss; Prof. Dr. Lothar Weisser; Werner Wittman; Dr. Georg Wochner; Roland Wohlfart; Hugo Wyler; Joyce Yohai; Charlotte Zarm (deceased); Dr. Andreas Zekorn, Kreisarchiv Balingen; and Lilli Zekorn.

My thanks to the staffs of these organizations who helped me in my research: Generallandesarchiv Baden, Karlsruhe; Staatsarchiv Ludwigsburg; Hauptstaatsarchiv Stuttgart; Staatsarchiv Sigmaringen; Town Hall Wallhausen; Germania Judaica, Hamburg; Interlibrary Loan Department, Collier County Library, Naples, Florida; Interlibrary Loan Department, Bonita Springs Library, Bonita Springs, Florida; Chicago Historical Society; Library, Spertus College of Judaica, Chicago; Davenport, Iowa, Public Library; and Plotkin Judaica Museum, Phoenix, Arizona.

My gratitude to the publishers of the German edition of this book: Dr. Andreas Auth, Director; Jürgen Beckedorf, Production Manager; Hans

Acknowledgments

Schleuning, former director, and the entire staff at Konrad Theiss Verlag, Stuttgart, publisher of *Als Moises Kaz seine Stadt vor Napoleon rettete: meiner jüdischen Geschichte auf der Spur* (When Moises Kaz Saved His Town from Napoléon: On the Trail of My Jewish History), 1999; and to Matthias Steffen Laier, translator. My thanks also go to The Jewish Publication Society: Dr. Ellen Frankel, Editor-in-Chief and CEO; Carol Hupping and Sydelle Zove in the editorial department; and copyeditor Bryna Fischer.

And finally, my greatest thanks and deepest gratitude to my husband Stanley. He has been with me every step of this long journey.

Index

Notations
t= table, i = illustration, *italics* = title or non-English term

Index

Index

Index

Index

Index